The Human Puzzle

Other Wadsworth titles of related interest in sociology

James Spates/John Macionis, *The Sociology of Cities*, 2d

Martin Marger, *Elites and Masses*, 2d

Martin Marger, *Race and Ethnic Relations: American and Global Perspectives*

Arnold Sherman/Aliza Kolker, *The Social Bases of Politics*

Robert Atchley, *Social Forces in Aging*, 5th

Robert Atchley, *Aging: Continuity and Change*, 2d

Donald Cowgill, *Aging Around the World*

Judith Perrolle, *Computers and Social Change: Information, Property, and Power*

John Weeks, *Population*, 3d

David Miller, *Introduction to Collective Behavior*

Fredric Wolinsky, *The Sociology of Health*, 2d

THE HUMAN PUZZLE

AN INTRODUCTION TO SOCIAL PSYCHOLOGY

JACK LEVIN
Northeastern University

WILLIAM C. LEVIN
Bridgewater State College

Wadsworth Publishing Company
Belmont, California   A Division of Wadsworth, Inc.

Sociology Editor: Sheryl Fullerton
Editorial Associate: Cynthia Haus
Production Editor: Harold Humphrey
Designer: Andrew H. Ogus
Print Buyer: Karen Hunt
Copy Editor: Hinda Farber
Cover Photographer: Garry Gay
Compositor: Harrison Typesetting, Inc.
Signing Representative: John Moroney

The cover art shows details of *L'être solitude et l'autre rencontre*, a combination of pastel and silkscreen by Danièle Desplan. Copyright ©1987 by Danièle Desplan.

The puzzles facing each chapter are composed of tangrams, an ancient Chinese game in which seven pieces are arranged to represent objects, flowers, animals, and people. All seven must be used to create each figure. The tangrams reproduced in this book are from Ronald Read's *Tangrams*, copyright ©1965 by Dover Publications, Inc., New York. Used by permission of the publisher. Our thanks to Susan Breitbard for her help in finding and rendering the tangram designs.

Copyright ©1988 by Wadsworth, Inc. All rights reserved. No part of this book may be reproduced, stored in a retrieval system, or transcribed, in any form or by any means, electronic, mechanical, photocopying, recording, or otherwise, without prior written permission of the publisher, Wadsworth Publishing Company, Belmont, California 94002, a division of Wadsworth, Inc.

Printed in the United States of America   50

1 2 3 4 5 6 7 8 9 10——92 91 90 89 88

Library of Congress Cataloging-in-Publication Data
Levin, Jack, 1941-
   The human puzzle: an introduction to social psychology / Jack Levin, William C. Levin.
      p. cm.
   Bibliography: p.
   Includes index.
   ISBN 0-534-08924-0
   1. Social psychology.   I. Levin, William C.   II. Title.
HM251.S2887   1988
302—dc19   87-21172
                                CIP

To teachers who have inspired us

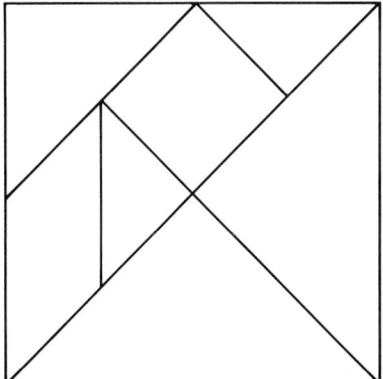

Contents

PREFACE xii

CHAPTER 1 THE HUMAN PUZZLE 1

The Social Psychological View 2

Common Sense and Social Psychology 5

Three Perspectives in Social Psychology 7

CHAPTER 2 THE SELF 27

Looking Ahead 28

The Self in Social Interaction 28

PERSPECTIVE: *The Effect of Social Definition: Self-Concept across the Ages* 35

The Development of the Self 39

PERSPECTIVE: *The Effect of Social and Cultural Forces: Cultural Images of Race* 42

The Self in Adult Life 54

PERSPECTIVE: *The Effect of the Immediate Situation:
Is a Divided Self Unhealthy?* 61

Presentation of Self in Everyday Life 64

Looking Back 70

CHAPTER 3 OTHERS 73

Looking Ahead 74

The Influence of Others Who Are Present: Conformity 75

PERSPECTIVE: *The Effect of the Immediate Situation:
Conformity Outside the Lab* 81

The Influence of Others Who Are Absent: "Different Drummers" 88

The Functions of Reference Others 90

PERSPECTIVE: *The Effect of Social Definition:
Second-Hand Experience* 97

PERSPECTIVE: *The Effect of Social and Cultural Forces:
American Competition for Morality* 111

Looking Back 112

CHAPTER 4 COMMUNICATION AND LANGUAGE 115

Looking Ahead 116

Communication and Social Order 116

Meaning, Symbols, and Language 119

Meaning and Symbols 121

PERSPECTIVE: *The Effect of the Immediate Situation:
Criticism and Praise to Fit the Situation* 127

Acquiring Language 131

PERSPECTIVE: *The Effect of Social and Cultural Forces:
Male and Female Voices* 137

Language in Everyday Use   138

Universals and Variables in Nonverbal Communication   146

PERSPECTIVE: *The Effect of Social Definition: Communication and Gender Identity*   150

Looking Back   156

CHAPTER 5 ROLES   159

Looking Ahead   160

Social Behavior by "Script"   161

The Qualities of Roles   161

Role Taking   167

PERSPECTIVE: *The Effect of the Immediate Situation: An Experiment in Cruelty*   170

Role Strain   172

PERSPECTIVE: *The Influence of Social and Cultural Forces: Sex-Role Expectations*   177

PERSPECTIVE: *The Effect of Social Definition: The Emergence of Roles for Extraordinary Circumstances*   185

Role Making   189

Roles and the Self   191

Looking Back   191

CHAPTER 6 AGGRESSION AND VIOLENCE   195

Looking Ahead   195

What Is Aggression?   196

PERSPECTIVE: *The Effect of Social Definition: How Do We Define an Aggressive Situation?*   198

The Causes of Aggression   202

PERSPECTIVE: *The Effect of the Immediate Situation:
Can a Situation Release Aggression?*   210

The Catharsis Hypothesis   213

PERSPECTIVE: *The Effect of Social and Cultural Forces:
Family Roles and Family Violence*   217

Social Learning and Aggression   218

Looking Back   220

CHAPTER 7   PREJUDICE AND DISCRIMINATION   223

Looking Ahead   224

The Elements of Prejudice and Discrimination   224

The Functions of Prejudice and Discrimination   235

PERSPECTIVE: *The Effect of Social and Cultural Forces:
Racism as Colonialism*   242

PERSPECTIVE: *The Effect of Social Definition:
Attributing the Causes of Success*   244

PERSPECTIVE: *The Effect of the Immediate Situation:
Racial Composition of Desegregated Classrooms*   248

The Reduction of Prejudice   249

Looking Back   259

CHAPTER 8   PROSOCIAL BEHAVIOR   261

Looking Ahead   262

Why Do People Like One Another?   262

When Will People Help One Another?   271

PERSPECTIVE: *The Effect of Social and Cultural Forces:
Are There Norms of Helpfulness?*   273

PERSPECTIVE: *The Effect of the Immediate Situation:
              Reducing the Bystander Effect* 279

The Roots of Altruism 282

PERSPECTIVE: *The Effect of Social Definition:
              The Influence of Role Taking* 284

Looking Back 288

REFERENCES 289

INDEX 316

Preface

WE ONCE BELIEVED that writing an effective social psychology text for a broad audience of sociologists and psychologists was an exercise in futility. The major obstacle, especially among sociologists, was that the field seemed to lack widely accepted standards of method and substance. This may explain why so few introductory social psychology texts have been written by sociologists and why those that exist have tended to be dominated by only one of several possible theoretical positions. How could one text satisfy so many different approaches and such diverse needs?

Recent changes in our own thinking and in the field of social psychology have changed our minds and have guided our efforts in producing *The Human Puzzle*. We now recognize that this apparent theoretical disorganization can be eliminated by organizing the ideas of social psychology in terms of three major perspectives. We introduce these three perspectives in Chapter 1 and then highlight them in special "Perspective" sections within each chapter. Briefly, they are 1) the effect of the immediate social situation, 2) the effect of social and cultural forces, and 3) the effect of social definition. If we have done our job as we intended, instructors should be able to identify examples of their own perspective throughout the text. More importantly, perhaps, it should also be possible to compare and contrast different approaches in the field, so that students become familiar with the strengths and weaknesses of each.

In the last few years, some important differences dividing social psychologists have diminished. Many more of them now accept the concept of an *active self in society* as a core or beginning principle. So do we. Indeed, we begin our discussion of the substance of social psychology in Chapter 2 with a major discussion of the self in society. In Chapter 3, we then turn our attention to "the other side of the coin"—the place of others in the development of the self. The relationship between self and others is highlighted in Chapter 4 in the topic of communication and language; and the product of that relationship is examined in Chapter 5 in the concept of role. Chapters 6, 7, and 8 explore important issues and problems—aggression, prejudice, and prosocial behavior—investigated by means of social psychological research. Other issues could have been chosen, but none would likely have been so important as these to the future of the human race.

We never intended to produce a comprehensive and imposing hardcover text; and we didn't. Instead, we wrote the kind of book that we personally prefer to use with our own students: a brief, flexible, and selective introduction to the field, one which can be used alone or in conjunction with more specialized readings. In line with our goal, we attempted to produce a series of essays, rather than all-inclusive summaries, which selectively draw upon a balanced mix of classic as well as up-to-date research. Most importantly, we sought to write a book that was oriented toward students' needs and interests without sacrificing either rigor or credibility. We hoped to impart information about the field of social psychology and, at the same time, to convey the excitement that we feel about it.

We are grateful to the following social psychologists who reviewed the manuscript in various stages of its completion:

Vern L. Bengtson, University of Southern California; Dean J. Champion, University of Tennessee; Bess Cleveland, Jefferson Community College; Pauline E. Ginsberg, Utica College; Ethan Gologor, Medgar Evers College; Ernest B. Gurman, University of Southern Mississippi; Bruce Hill, Triton College; Michael C. Kearl, Trinity College; Sherryl Kleinman, University of North Carolina, Chapel Hill; William Lacy, University of Kentucky; Bernard H. Levin, Blue Ridge Community College; Ruth H. Munroe; Pitzer College; Jerome Rabow, University of California, Los Angeles; Ira E. Robinson, University of Georgia; Ralph J. Shirley, Bay Path

Junior College; Nancy N. Thalhofer, Eastern Michigan University; and Nathan Weinberg, California State University, Northridge.

We acknowledge the generous support by Bridgewater State College toward completion of this project in the form of course release and research assistance to William Levin.

We also wish to thank our colleagues Arnold Arluke, Walter Carroll, Herbert Greenwald, Ruth Hannon, Stephen Harkins, Howard London, Bruce MacMurray, Wesley Perkins, and David Richards for permitting us to borrow their ideas (and sometimes their books). We gratefully acknowledge the generosity and competence of our editor, Sheryl Fullerton, who once again managed to improve our project while moving it toward completion and still remain a friend. Finally, we owe special thanks to Flea, Michael, Bonnie, and Andrea for tolerating the many disruptions created by Jack's work on the project, and to an even larger number of people (you know who you are) inconvenienced by Bill's.

JACK LEVIN AND WILLIAM C. LEVIN

The Human Puzzle

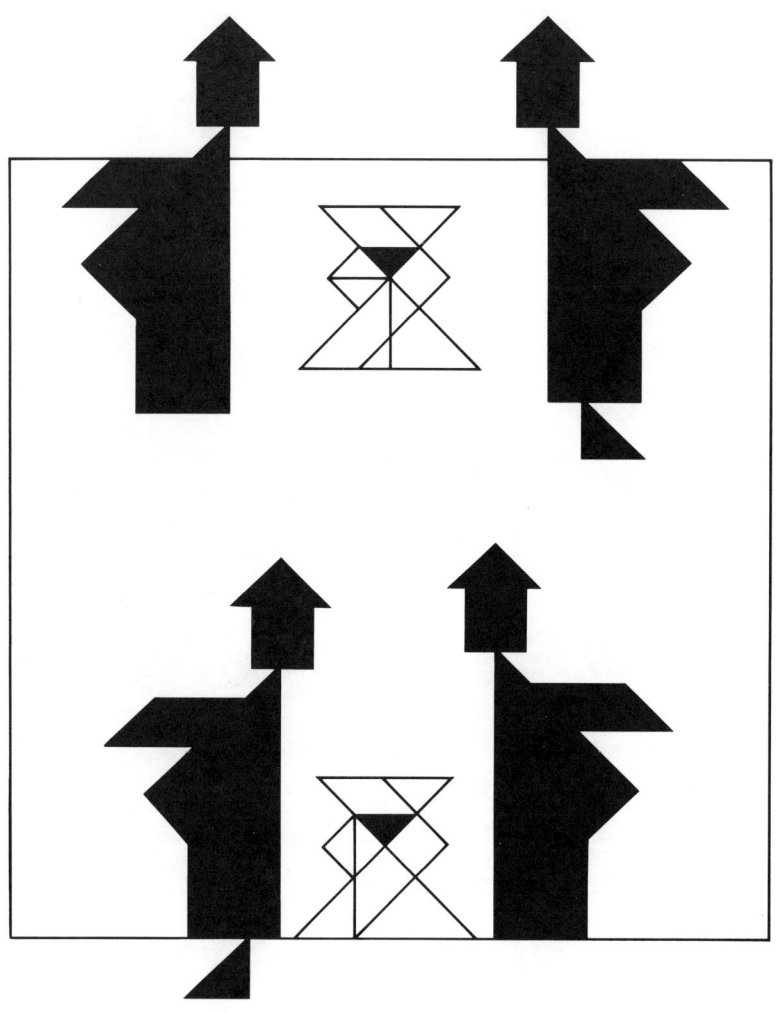

CHAPTER 1

The Human Puzzle

WHILE WE CAN'T PROVE IT, we strongly suspect that the most popular all-time subject for discussion is human behavior. In novels, magazines, poems, songs, television programs, and plays and over the phone, coffee, and the back fence, we exchange information about what people have done, and speculations about why. The range of such information is spectacularly wide, drawing our attention whether it is about the behavior of a neighbor or an entire generation or culture. Some behavior, like the man who has been married six times, seems only mildly interesting compared with those varieties that stretch our ability to believe that people could behave in such ways. How are we to understand a man who kills ten people and apparently feels no guilt? The more we try to make sense of the varieties of human behavior, the more we are impressed by the complexity of the task.

At the very least, human behavior presents us with something of a puzzle. But, unlike the kinds of puzzles with which most people are familiar, the human puzzle is composed of countless pieces which may not be the same shape tomorrow as they are today, simply because people and circumstances change. In addition, unlike normal puzzles, the human puzzle may have many, or even no, satisfactory solutions.

Attempts to understand why we act as we do have come from a variety of fields. Biologists, for example, have suggested that just as genetic instructions determine characteristics for hair color or height, so we are born with behavioral tendencies. As an extreme example, consider the recent report of twins who were separated immediately after birth and had no contact for 40 years. When reunited in 1979, they were found to drive the same model and color of car, smoke the same brand of cigarettes, and both own dogs named "Toy" (Leo, 1987). Or consider the studies that have suggested that criminal behavior is associated with the appearance of an extra Y chromosome in a person's genetic structure for gender (Witkin et al. 1976).

Theological explanations of human behavior predate the Bible and include a range of ideas such as the belief that madness in people is caused by direct possession of individuals by devils and the current fundamentalist and spiritualist beliefs in divine influence in daily human affairs. Philosophers also have an ancient tradition of concern with human behavior, focusing on issues such as the level at which humans can know and experience the world and the extent to which human understandings of good and evil shape behavior. And psychologists have tried to understand how the mental and emotional characteristics of individuals, such as their personalities or emotional well-being, influence how they act.

The Social Psychological View

Among the many ways of looking at human behavior, we are specifically interested in the fact that human behavior is *social*. That is, the way people behave is profoundly influenced by the fact that they live in society. *Social psychology* is the study of the individual in his or her social context.

As its name suggests, social psychology is related to both sociology and psychology, but the three disciplines differ in terms of (1) what they wish to explain about human life (their *dependent variables*) and (2) the types of factors they think might be important causes (their *independent variables*). For sociology, the critical dependent variable is the relationship between people, not individual behavior. Sociologists use a range of independent variables to help examine social bonding, including economic, political, and biological forces. For the psychologist, the critical dependent variable is the behavior of the individual and the independent variables are the characteristics of individuals.

For social psychology, the behavior of individuals is the critical dependent variable, while the independent variables have to do with the social contexts of that behavior. In other words, social psychology examines how people's behavior is influenced by the fact that they live among other people. Social psychology, then, is not the combination of all of sociology and psychology. It is a unique field with a specific focus. However, the range of human behaviors with which social psychology is concerned is still quite broad.

As a starting point in examining human behavior from the social psychological perspective, consider the following, each of which is an illustration of behavior discussed in a chapter of this book.

1) Two children from the same family, males who are only one year apart in age, seem to their parents to have been raised in very much the same way. Neither has suffered a traumatic experience nor been given unusual advantages over the other. However, at age seventeen, they could not be less like one another. One is conservative, hard-working, community-minded, and personally ambitious, with specific plans to become a wealthy corporate lawyer or real estate broker. His brother lives exclusively in the present, will only admit to liking loud rock music and sleeping, and refuses to discuss career, college, or any future plans on the grounds that no one can count on there being a future.

2) A woman who has spent most of her adult life fulfilling the traditional female domestic role by caring for her children, husband, and home now finds that her part-time job in a local company is becoming more appealing. She is highly valued as a worker and is offered a full-time position with a raise and promises of more to come. She decides that she wishes to pursue the professional career without giving up any of her domestic involvements, but realizes this course will create conflicts. How can she minimize or eliminate them?

3) After World War II it was discovered that the rumors of Nazi atrocities were not only true, but that the realities of the death camps were many times more horrible than anyone could have believed of the German people. After all, German society had produced some of the most "civilized" expressions of human talent in Western history, including the music of Mozart and Beethoven and the psychoanalytic theories of Freud. The

world was shocked when, in defense of their actions, most Germans who had taken active part in the mass exterminations claimed that they were merely "following orders," while countless others displayed an exceptional lack of awareness that anything immoral was taking place in the country.

4) A committee formed at a college consisting of students and faculty members conducts an election of officers. The recording secretary of the committee sends all the members the minutes of the first meeting, in which the female head of the committee is referred to as the "chairman." The entire next meeting is taken up by a debate as to whether the head of the committee should be called the "chairman," "chairwoman," "chairperson," or "chair." A vote is eventually taken in which the term "chairman" is chosen (in line with the argument that the word "chairman" should be understood to refer to women as well as men), resulting in the resignation from the committee of three of its female members.

5) In New York City some years ago, 38 people watched from their apartment windows as a young woman was stabbed to death by a male attacker. Not a single individual came to her assistance; in fact, no one even bothered to call the police, though the attack lasted approximately 30 minutes.

6) It is common in our culture to define prejudice as, literally, prejudgment; that is, judgment of others without adequate knowledge of them as individuals. It is therefore expected that the level of prejudice towards blacks within a segregated school will decline when the school is integrated. Learning that black people are individuals, not an undifferentiated mass, should teach white children that their stereotypes are unfounded. However, the result of increased interracial contact turns out to be increased levels of prejudice.

7) A woman has accused a man she had been dating of rape. She testifies that during a date she told the man "no" when he began to get too intimate, but he forced himself on her. The defendant argues that the woman had said no, but had not struggled physically against him, suggesting that she really did not mean what she said. The jury finds the defendant not guilty on the grounds that unless a woman reinforces what she says by

physical actions to prevent the sexual contact, her saying "no" may be interpreted by a man to mean "yes."

We chose these examples of human behavior because they are particularly interesting. Though some of them are clearly extraordinary, such as the behavior of Germans under the Nazi regime, many of the others are far from unusual. Everyone has wondered at the relationship between adult personality and childhood experiences, or has personally witnessed the failure of bystanders to help someone in need. But to describe an instance of such behavior without attempting to explain why it occurred is not adequate. It fails to raise the discussion of human behavior beyond the level of entertainment. How can we make sense of behaviors like these?

Common Sense and Social Psychology

Most explanations of human behavior are based on *common sense*, that is, what anyone "knows to be true" because it is obvious from personal experience. For example, you don't have to go into a great deal of fancy reasoning to know that if you drive too fast, you are more likely to have an accident and to be injured in it. Why? Well, personal experience probably has shown any driver that the faster you go, the less time there is to react to others on the road and the less traction there is between the tires and the road surface. It seems unnecessary to collect data and calculate formulas for the relationship between speed and accidents. Most of the time we have no trouble depending upon our common sense. It is often either right or, because everyone shares common-sense explanations, good enough. However, when we try to explain human behavior, common sense can be misleading.

Compare the experiences of two people we know. Both were raised in racially integrated neighborhoods, but one was a wealthy place with a long history of programs to diminish the importance of race in social relations. In the other, integration was resisted for generations; then, when it was forced on the neighborhood by a court-ordered desegregation plan, opposition was violent and prolonged. Our acquaintance from the first neighborhood says that people can get along if they just try, because it is obvious (common sense, that is) that people are basically the same under the skin.

By contrast, our friend from the second neighborhood is as powerfully convinced that people of different races should not mix, and that one only has to use common sense to see that terrible things happen when people try to integrate the races.

The inability of these people to discuss school desegregation without fighting is due to their contrasting notions of what is "apparently true" about human interaction. Because they have had such different experiences on which to base their common-sense notions, there is no common ground for discussion.

We are not trying to suggest that all our common-sense assumptions about human behavior are wrong. But it is clear that common sense is fallible to the extent that it is based upon the *limited* range of an individual's experiences. For another example, we have found that in the Boston area where we work, residents typically overestimate the percentage of Americans who are Catholic. Though the actual figure for the country is around 20 percent, the average guess our students make is near 40 percent, and sometimes as high as 75 percent. This happens because people tend to generalize from their experiences to those of others. The more narrow and specific a person's experience, the less likely that he or she can imagine a range of possible explanations for some event. An extreme case is the woman we know who once was made extremely ill by some bad fish she ate. Ever since, whenever she hears that someone is sick, no matter what the illness, she launches into a lecture about the dangers of eating fish.

A second difficulty with common sense is that it is *subjective*. That is, the process by which an individual comes to believe that something is true cannot be explained to anyone else. If you ask someone how they know something to be true and they answer that "it's just common sense," they have explained nothing more than if they had said "I just know." Common sense is commonly not testable. For example, if you ask the person who opposes racial integration why that is the case, he or she is likely to say that the groups can't get along. If you ask how that person knows, the best you can get by way of explanation is that he or she has "seen it." There is no way to recreate the circumstances in which this individual has gained the information on which the common sense is based. This knowledge, then, is subjective.

By contrast, *objective knowledge* is gained by methods of investigation which are matters of public record. This allows the results of objective investigations to be subjected to reexamination. If any individual tells me exactly what techniques he or she used to discover that one group of people is superior to another or incapable of getting along, I can reproduce their study to see if I get the same results. If I am not given the information to do this, the original assertion suffers the same flaw as common-sense notions, that they are beyond examination and testing.

Social psychology, like any discipline that calls itself a science, tries to avoid subjective, common-sense explanations of human behavior, preferring to conduct studies by objective methods ranging from controlled forms of observation to the experiment. The specific research method chosen by a social psychologist depends upon the type of behavior being studied and on the particular perspective the researcher uses in explaining human behavior.

Three Perspectives in Social Psychology

Recall that we defined social psychology as the study of the individual in his or her social context. However, there are a number of ways in which we can look at social context. Adapting the model provided by Ritzer (1975), we have focused on three major perspectives: (1) the effect of the immediate situation, (2) the effect of social and cultural forces, and (3) the effect of social definition. These perspectives differ not only in terms of how they define social context, but also in terms of the theories that fall within each and the research methods most appropriate to each. Because these views of social context differ in relatively abstract ways, we will use a familiar example of social behavior, namely interaction in a college class, to help us illustrate these differences.

Social context 1: The effect of the immediate situation

The first view of social context which we shall discuss treats *social situations* as powerful and direct influences on the behavior of individual participants. Thus, the behavior of an individual can be attributed to the effects of the presence of other people, and all individuals present in that situation can be expected to be influenced in a similar way. From this point of view, then, the social situation is an independent variable (assumed cause) and the behavior of individuals is the dependent variable (assumed effect).

To apply this perspective to the college classroom, think of the special characteristics of class meetings to which all students are subjected. For example, the authority of the professor might be an important independent variable, the effect of which is to create compliant behavior in students. Another characteristic of some courses is the existence of competition among students for high grades (an independent variable), which creates a lack of cooperation and cohesion among students and an unwillingness to help one another (dependent variables). In classes where no such competitiveness exists, students are likely to be more cooperative.

Notice that according to this view of social context, no matter what the participants are like as individuals, the character of the situation is expected to apply a uniform pressure on the behavior of everyone. Thus, whether a person is by nature compliant or not, he or she will be more likely to be compliant in a social situation in which there is an authority figure (like a professor) than in one in which no authority figure is present. And whether a person is competitive or not, being enrolled in a course in which grade competition is built into the situation (for example, a limited percent of the students will be allowed to earn A's for the course) is going to increase the likelihood of competitiveness among all students because the situation demands it.

In discussing this perspective, we often use the shorthand of "the effect of the immediate situation." The character of the situation is treated in the way psychologists talk of a *stimulus* (a condition which elicits a response), while the behavior of participants in the social situation is taken to be the *response* (a reaction to a stimulus). As in much of psychology where the characteristics of the situation are the focus of attention, the preferred method of research is the experiment, and people studied are called "subjects" because they are regarded as passive recipients of the stimuli.

An *experiment* is a method of research which is designed to maximize control. That is, if a researcher wishes to establish that a specific quality of a social situation (the independent variable) influences how people behave (the dependent variable), it is necessary to show that nothing but the specific independent variable of interest to the researcher likely influenced the dependent variable. In order to accomplish this kind of control, the researcher actually "manipulates" the independent variable; that is, she or he exposes some subjects to it (called the *experimental group*) and withholds it from others (called the *control group*). The decision as to which subjects are assigned to the experimental or control group is made by the researcher on a random basis (for example, by the flip of a coin), so that the characteristics of the subjects in the two groups do not differ except by chance.

Here is an example of such an experimental study. Suppose a social psychologist is interested in studying the effect of the presence of other people on an individual's willingness to help in an emergency. It is hypothesized that the presence of others reduces willingness to help a stranger. (See Chapter 8 for an explanation.) In a simple experiment, the researcher might ask a number of college students to sit in a waiting room, supposedly for the purpose of eventually being interviewed by an instructor in the next room. To manipulate the independent variable (the presence of others), half of the subjects wait with four other students (the experimental group), while the other half wait alone (the control group). While they wait, members of both groups hear a scream from the next room which sounds as though the instructor has fallen and hurt himself. Of course, the entire "accident" has been concocted by the researcher to create the condition in which help would be called for. If the presence of others really reduces the likelihood of helping, then the members of the experimental group should be more reluctant to go to the aid of the stranger than those in the control group, that is, those who waited alone.

Given its ability to manipulate characteristics of the immediate situation, it is not surprising that the experiment is the method of choice among those who use the situational perspective. The experimental method is also useful in testing the various theories of human behavior which have developed out of the situational perspective. All these explanations focus on characteristics of the immediate situation, but they conceptualize issues in different ways. Among the best-known explanations in this tradition are (1) behaviorism, (2) exchange theory, and (3) social learning theory.

Behaviorism. Though we have not specifically identified it as such, much of the approach we have so far been discussing with terms like stimulus and response is actually called behaviorism. In fact, it is sometimes called stimulus-response theory. The term behaviorism indicates its emphasis on studying only those variables in the environment that can actually be observed. For example, strict behaviorists might be interested in the effect of a concrete reward (such as giving extra credit) on class participation. They would not, however be interested in the thoughts and feelings of students (sometimes called "internal states"), because you can actually see and measure extra credit and participation, whereas you must infer the reality of thoughts and feelings.

The most famous modern behaviorist is B. F. Skinner (1971), whose work is based on the principle that all behavior is created, maintained, and extinguished because of environmental rewards and punishments. It had long been known that animals of various kinds can be *conditioned*, that is, that rewarding a given behavior tends to cause that behavior to be repeated. What is of interest to social psychologists is the assumption of behaviorism that the stimulus-response model applies equally well to the conditioning of a pigeon to peck at a bar for a reward of food as to students working for grades in a classroom.

A classic example of the use of reinforcement to control human behavior was conducted by Verplanck (1955). In this study he trained his students to determine the course of conversation with friends through the careful use of reward and punishment. In dormitories, in restaurants, and over the phone, each of his students spoke with a friend for 30 minutes. During the first 10 minutes, they neither supported nor rejected anything that was said. During the second 10-minute period, however, the student would respond with a reinforcing comment or gesture such as nodding the head or agreeing each time the friend voiced an opinion. During the last 10-minute period, each student resumed the nonresponsive style of interaction. Verplanck's results indicated that his students were indeed able to control the rate at which their friends expressed opinions. In all 24 cases, reinforcement produced an increased rate of opinion expression. Moreover, in 21 of the cases, the rate of opinion expression decreased in the third 10-minute period, during which reinforcing responses were removed.

Exchange theory. Behaviorism is an important element in other social psychological theories focusing on the effect of the immediate situation. Exchange theory, for example, is based upon both behavioristic psychology and elementary economics. It is most closely associated with the work of George Homans (1961), in which he attempts to explain the elementary face-to-face interaction that occurs between two individuals. That is, at the psychological level people exchange both rewards (positive reinforcements such as praise, gratitude, recognition, and affection) and costs (negative reinforcements such as criticism, punishment, anxiety, and blame). Borrowing from economics, Homans believes that *profit*, the degree to which rewards are greater than costs, can operate at the psychic level between individuals just as it does in the marketplace of other currencies. Therefore, a person can be expected to seek out and maintain relationships which provide the greatest profit from the individual's point of view.

For example, the extent to which two people like one another and decide to continue their friendship can be explained in exchange terms. That is, each perceives benefits or rewards derived from the interaction which outweigh any costs. Exchange theory, then, can help explain why a relatively unattractive male might put up with a great deal of abuse and mistreatment from a very attractive female partner. From an exchange point of view, the prestige that he gains from being seen with her may greatly outweigh the costs of her nasty behavior toward him.

One of the most important ideas in Homans' exchange theory is the concept of *distributive justice*, which he describes as the equitable or fair exchange of rewards and costs between individuals. For Homans, individuals in an exchange relation will expect their rewards to be roughly proportional to their costs. When the rule of distributive justice is violated (an imbalance between costs and rewards), the individual whose costs outweigh his or her rewards will feel anger; the individual whose rewards outweigh his or her costs will feel guilt. A number of studies have confirmed the importance of distributive justice or equity in understanding the stability of relationships ranging from casual interaction to marriage (see, for example, Walster, Walster, and Traupmann 1978).

Social learning theory. Much of what we know about the way humans learn stresses the importance of directly rewarding or punishing them to increase the probability of desirable behaviors. Think, for example, of a young child who is praised by his parents for his polite behavior and scolded by them when he is rude. The intention is that the child, in order to gain rewards and avoid punishments, will learn to become more polite in the future. However, social learning theory, as represented in the work of Albert Bandura (1977), emphasizes that learning can take place in the absence of direct rewards or punishments through the observation and imitation of the behavior of others.

According to social learning theorists, we have *models* for our behavior whom we emulate and with whom we identify. They set an example for us to follow, though they may not directly provide us with rewards or threaten us with punishments. Children do not have to touch a hot stove to learn that it is dangerous. It is enough that they see someone else make the mistake.

What makes social learning so effective is that we see many of our models being rewarded or punished for their behavior. Bandura and his associates (1963) showed that children become more aggressive after watching television characters rewarded for their aggressiveness. Interestingly enough, it is the heroes on television rather than the villians who seem to gain the most from their violence. Both the criminals and the police on "Miami Vice" use their guns and fists frequently, but it is only the police who are rewarded in the end. The criminals are typically caught or killed while the stars of the show live luxurious lives, at least until the next episode.

Social context 2: The effect of social and cultural forces
The second view of social context extends its focus beyond the immediate situation in which the individual is located, to allow for the effects of social and cultural forces. *Culture* refers to a shared way of life that is learned by human beings and is taught from one generation to the next. It includes *values* and *norms* which tell people what is desirable to obtain and how they are expected to act. *Society* refers to the stable and structured relationships that express our values and norms, including such institutions as the family, education, government, and religion. Through the process of *socialization* (see Chapter 2) members of a society learn from parents, teachers, and peers the rules for behavior which allow them to successfully play their roles (see Chapter 5) within such institutions. For example, in the family the norms specify how interaction should proceed between the parent and child, the two critical roles.

To return to our illustration of the college classroom, much of the behavior expressed in the role of student reflects forces from beyond the classroom which each participant brings from a life of learning the social rules for interaction in that setting. For example, students know simple norms for behavior in a classroom such as where to sit, to arrive reasonably on time, to have notebooks and pencils, to raise their hands to ask a question, and to expect to be examined on course material. Students also bring with them cultural values for achievement, competition, and respect for authority. To the extent that these values are held, students can be expected to study hard (achievement), to be concerned with the performance of classmates (competition), and to do what the teacher asks (respect for authority).

The above behaviors can be attributed largely to cultural values and norms. The effect of society can be seen in the way particular social relationships from outside the classroom influence student and teacher behavior. For example, the student's social class membership can influence a wide range of her or his behaviors. Take the example of college students whose family background is lower class. Their class membership may help determine whether they have less time to study, since they must take a job after school; how hard they must work to make up for the quality of their high-school preparation; whether they feel free to share information about their classes with friends who have not gone to college; in fact, whether they get to go to college at all.

How do we measure the influences of society and culture? The very advantage of the experiment in controlling a situation makes it less appropriate to this task. After all, social and cultural forces, being located beyond the immediate situation and in the histories of the students' experiences, are not amenable to manipulation. Even if you could, you wouldn't. For example, consider the ethical problems which would result if we tried to assign infants at birth to different social classes by the flip of a coin merely to see what the effect would be on their later college experiences. Instead, social psychologists need a method of research which allows them to measure previous experiences in individuals. The *survey* is retrospective. That is, using self-administered questionnaires or conducting interviews, researchers can attempt to reconstruct the social and cultural influences on an individual's behavior. Survey questions have measured belief in values like individualism and competetiveness, and position in the social structure such as social class.

One of the advantages of survey research is that it allows results to be generalized to large numbers of people. In a typical survey, a small subset, or representative *sample* of individuals, is chosen from a larger population and studied. The most effective way to obtain a representative sample is *random sampling*, whereby every member of the population has an equal chance to be chosen to be in the study. We may study the values of only 1,000 college students in the hope of generalizing our results to the entire campus of 30,000.

Social structural theory. Talcott Parsons (1951) conceptualized human behavior as existing at four different levels which stand in a hierarchy of control from culture to society to personality to the biological organism. He argued that small changes in culture produce progressively larger changes at each of the other levels. Thus, a change in cultural values will have major consequences for the personalities of society's members. For example, the development of the Protestant ethic as a major value system in the Western world taught that human fate was predetermined by God and that people are on earth only to glorify the supreme being. Humans could do nothing to influence whether they would achieve eternal salvation or damnation, but they might get some clue about their standing in the hereafter by noting the extent of their good works on earth.

At the societal level, the acceptance of Protestantism as an important cultural idea stimulated the rapid and widespread growth of capitalism as a legitimate economic system. This was because good works came to be indicated by success in business and the accumulation of capital. Making money was not undertaken to enjoy life, but to reinvest in business for the glorification of God. At the personality level, Protestantism and its structural counterpart in capitalism created tremendous anxiety as to where people stood in relation to God. These cultural values became translated into a personal preoccupation with achieving economic success; hard work was regarded as a sign of election, if not an indicator of self-esteem (Weber 1905).

Parsons suggested that society and personality were immediate environments for one another, because they stood together in his hierarchy of control. The relationship between society and the individual was a reciprocal one which, in fact, defined his view of social psychology. Society was important for the psychological well-being of its members, because it gave to them patterned ways of behaving that made their lives predictable and therefore comfortable and secure. (Some might more negatively call this an "escape from freedom.") Personality also gave something back to society. It provided the mechanism through socialization whereby individuals felt motivated to *conform*; that is, to play the roles upon which society depended for its maintenance.

To illustrate this reciprocal relationship between society and personality, think once again about the social structure of the college classroom in relation to individual students. Students feel much more comfortable if the rules of the classroom are obeyed; that is, the instructor is on time for classes and the course runs according to the syllabus. Conversely, surprise often makes students unhappy. They complain a great deal about being subjected to unscheduled exams and being called on to answer questions at random. As to the effect of student personalities on the structure of the classroom, consider what would happen if students suddenly refused to play the role of student as we know it today. In fact, this is precisely what happened in the late 1960s, especially on a number of urban college campuses, when students became vitally concerned with political and social issues of the day. In many cases, college classes were suspended in favor of demonstrations, often with the consent and participation of instructors. At times, even grades were ignored. Clearly, the roles of student and teacher were dramatically different. In some cases, the social structure of the classroom disappeared entirely.

Parsons' brand of social structural theory has been criticized for its assumption that individuals in a society are generally motivated to conform with the rules and roles they are taught. A number of theorists have suggested, instead, that compliance occurs not out of choice, but out of coercion. That is, the members of society are compelled by more powerful forces such as autocratic government, schools, and parents to conform to the status quo whether they like it or not. For example, is it more likely that students agree to take tests because they believe in education or because the teacher forces them to? Perhaps there is a bit of both in a student's decision to comply.

Another point of criticism of Parsons' work concerns his view of the primacy of culture. Conflict theorists such as Karl Marx (1867) suggest that economic forces are more important than religious values in determining human behavior. Marx emphasized that capitalist economic arrangements, such as whether one owns or works for those who own the means of production, will determine an employee's feelings about work. Under socialism, he believed, there would be no alienation from labor, since each worker would control, on a small scale, the process of work.

Social context 3: The effect of social definition The third view of social context differs dramatically from the two previous perspectives we have examined. In both the situational and social forces views, the individual's behavior was regarded as determined by the external reality of his or her social context. In both views, the individual was seen as a passive recipient of influences from either the immediate social situation or the larger social structure.

From the social definition perspective, however, the social context is located in the *definition of the situation* of the actors. The concern here is to see and understand things from the individual's point of view. In other words, people do not merely walk into social situations that have ready-made meanings and influences. They interpret or "define" each others' actions instead of merely reacting to them. Because of this peculiar quality of human interaction, we actually take part in a *social construction of reality* every time we interact, because we bring to any interaction a set of ideas about the meaning to us of what is going on. From this point of view, human beings are active participants in creating their own social contexts (Ritzer 1975).

To illustrate the process, let us return to the example of the college classroom. As we showed earlier, the behavior of students and teachers in a classroom is to some extent determined by characteristics of the immediate situation (e.g., the authority of the teacher) and the social-cultural forces in the larger society (e.g., the norms for testing). From the social definition point of view, however, the character of any classroom is also shaped by the interactions between teachers and students.

To see this, we can learn from our own experiences as teachers. During the first few meetings of any college class that we have taught, there is always a period of "negotiations," sometimes very subtle, between our students and us. We bring to the class broad expectations for what the class will be like, and the students do the same. Though we hand out course outlines and describe course assignments, we are still uncertain as to specifically how the students will react. The students, for their part, are just as unclear about what will be expected of them. From our point of view: Will they accept our standards and do the assignments? Will they laugh when we try to be funny? Will they come to class on time and consistently? From the point of view of the students: Will the teacher be flexible in his or her grading? Will he or she bore us to tears? Will the exams be appropriate to the material?

In the first few classes, students and teachers are groping for clues that they share a similar understanding of the social context in which they interact. The process of negotiating a social reality begins. The teacher gives a smile or joke that sets the tone. He or she may also frown, however, if students come to class unprepared. The students give a nod of the head showing interest in a subject or willingness to do an assignment. They may also let the teacher know when they think he or she is too demanding. After a few meetings, there usually develops an unstated agreement between teacher and students, a *shared* definition of the situation which allows the class to proceed smoothly. For example, all the participants understand what the tone of the class will be, what work will be assigned, how the grading will be accomplished, and so on.

As you can well imagine, it is difficult for a social psychologist to "get into the minds" of the individuals as they take part in the defining of their social situation. Think how you would feel if someone asked you what was going on in your mind during the first few classes of a course. People are typically not conscious of this process, and the interference in it by a researcher would be destructive. However, if the way people think about their situation influences how interaction will proceed, some method for studying it must be found. This problem has generated several theoretical perspectives and associated methods of research.

Symbolic interactionism. According to one of its leading exponents, symbolic interactionism is the study of the "peculiar and distinctive character of interaction as it takes place between human beings" (Blumer 1969). Unlike other animals, humans define or interpret one anothers' behavior instead of merely reacting to it. Thus interaction is mediated by the meaning that individuals give to one anothers' actions. In this view, the process of *interpretation* is inserted between stimulus and response. That is, in direct contrast with strict behaviorists, the symbolic interactionist considers, in fact gives primacy to, the internal state of the actor.

Some of the most important ideas in the tradition of symbolic interactionism are found in the work of George Herbert Mead (1934), a social philosopher who, writing at the turn of the century, emphasized that the human being has an *active self*. That is, that the human being can act towards himself as he acts towards others. This idea was crucial in Mead's thinking because he saw human society as consisting of individuals who have selves whose behavior is an active construction rather than a passive release. The problem, then, is to understand how individuals can interact in an organized or coordinated way. How do they actually come to share a definition of the situation? (See Chapter 2.)

Mead called his brand of social psychology *social behaviorism* in order to emphasize how it departed from the strict stimulus-response behaviorists of his day. Mead rejected their view of human beings as passive recipients and instead emphasized that they select the stimuli to which they respond. His conception of human behavior was much broader than that of behaviorists, including as it did not only the observable external elements, but also the internal elements (meaning and interpretation) that can be inferred from what people do. Mead, then, saw the social behavior of individuals as inseparable from the evaluations made by their internal selves. Self and society were, for Mead, two sides of the same coin.

But methodologically, Mead's view requires that we gain access to the minds of the actors in social situations. Perhaps the most direct route the social psychologist can use to understand the process by which people define social situations is to take advantage of the fact that we have all taken part in the process. That is, even a researcher can appreciate the point of view of others if he or she intentionally participates in their social situations. In the method called *participant observation*, a social psychologist "participates in the daily life of the people under study, either openly in the role of researcher or covertly in some disguised role, observing things that happen, listening to what is said, and questioning people, over some length of time" (Becker and Geer 1957). Thus, participant observation gives the social psychologist a chance to learn the meaning of social behavior from within the group, to take the perspective of its participants without disrupting the social process. For example, in order to understand the way teachers and students come to create and share a definition of their situation, researchers have actually enrolled in classes where they have played the role of student. Participant observers have also joined Alcoholics Anonymous, played in a jazz group, volunteered for an emergency cleanup crew after a tornado, worked with surgical teams in hospitals and animal experiment research groups, joined a group of people who prophesized the end of the earth, and in one famous and controversial case, acted as a voyeur-lookout in homosexual encounters in public bathrooms.

Rather than become participant observers, symbolic interactionists sometimes also conduct interviews containing semistructured or open-ended questions to obtain the point of view of a set of respondents. In a recent study, Levin and Arluke (1987) conducted personal interviews with regional and national gossip columnists from newspapers, magazines, and tabloids around the country. These researchers wanted to determine how gossip columnists justify their use of covert and sometimes intrusive journalistic methods for obtaining information about the personal lives of celebrities. The interview schedule employed by Levin and Arluke provided enough structure to ensure that they covered the major issues relating to the work of gossip columnists, but was sufficiently flexible and open-ended to allow respondents to express their own definition of the situation. Columnists' responses revealed that many of them had indeed developed a set of justifications for violating the privacy of celebrities. Some indicated that they felt like "crusaders" breaking through the secrecy of people who control the news; others referred to their targets of gossip as "public figures" who live by the fact that they are celebrities; still others seemed convinced that any celebrity who ostensibly tries to conceal his private life is really begging for publicity.

Ethnomethodology. One of the most interesting offshoots of symbolic interactionism and participant observation is known as ethnomethodology—*ethno* meaning people and *methodology* meaning procedure. This school of thought investigates the procedures that people employ to make sense out of their everyday interactions (Garfinkel 1967). Like the interactionist tradition from which it sprang, ethnomethodology assumes that human behavior can only be understood from the point of view of individuals as they subjectively experience their social environment. Each person, it is argued, has his or her own unique view of social reality, but they all share certain assumptions or rules for interaction which generally go unnoticed until they are violated. Garfinkel argues that these taken-for-granted rules can be made apparent by finding an everyday routine in which people are involved and then disrupting that routine by deviating from it.

For example, what sorts of rules for politeness would you say are common in middle-class American households? Such rules, though they are minor enough to escape our notice, can cumulatively be very important to how comfortable we feel in our dealings with others. Garfinkel (1967) asked his students to violate the normal assumptions for level of politeness in their households by acting at home as though they were visiting guests rather than family members. For example, one student asked his mother for permission to have a small snack before bedtime. Her angry reaction indicated that he had broken an important but normally invisible social rule: family members have permission to help themselves, while strangers do not. The mother took it as an insult that she should be treated by her son the way a stranger would treat her. In other households in which this study was conducted, family members saw the students' behavior as mean, selfish, nasty, or impolite. Yet the students had been told by Garfinkel to act in a polite, if formal, way; for example, to speak only when spoken to. Ethnomethodological studies have used this technique of intentional disruption of social interaction to highlight those rules for normal interaction which might otherwise go unnoticed.

Cognitive theory. The social psychologists we have been discussing in this section have focused on how definitions of social situations emerge from the process of interaction. Now we turn to a view which still gives primacy to internal processes rather than external forces, but which stresses the role of the individual to a much greater degree. Cognitive theory bases its arguments on the human being as a creature that thinks, interprets, and finds meaning in situations (Shaw and Costanzo 1982).

To illustrate, let us return to the college classroom. A cognitive theorist might ask what sorts of beliefs the students bring with them and how they influence their behavior as students. For example, a student who has a particularly strong belief in the importance of living up to one's potential could be expected to work harder in class, and to show contempt for those who do not try to do well. A student who explains the successes of classmates as the result of "dumb luck" may use this belief to justify his or her own failures.

One of the most important ideas to come out of the cognitive tradition is known as *attribution theory*, because it is concerned with the ways in which people make inferences about the causes of events in their lives. You just read one example of attribution theory: the student who attributed the success of classmates to their luck. Attribution theorists make the assumption that individuals have a need to understand their own and others' behaviors (Harvey and Weary 1981). In fact, they have found in a number of studies that people often will take credit for their successes but refuse to take blame for their own failures. Specifically, like the student we just described, they tend to attribute other peoples' successes to external factors such as good luck, and their own successes to internal factors such as effort and ability. Naturally, they also attribute their own failures to external forces like bad luck and failures of others to internal factors such as laziness or incompetence (Arkin, Cooper, and Kolditz 1980).

Which social-psychological perspective, when? It would be convenient, we suppose, if a discipline had just one way of explaining the phenomena it studied. Research would be simplified greatly if we did not have to think about data in more than one way. In fact, the historian of science Thomas Kuhn (1970) argued that sciences like physics and chemistry do tend to settle on one *paradigm* or model which comes to dominate its discipline until it cannot explain events as well as some competing paradigm. In biology, for example, a theory that diseases are caused by bad blood is replaced by a germ theory of disease which does a better job of explaining and helping us to treat illness.

From the point of view of the behavioral sciences, Kuhn's theory has been particularly troublesome: not one of the behavioral sciences, not sociology, not psychology nor anthropology, has ever claimed to have one theoretical perspective which is shared by all its members. In sociology, for example, practitioners can be broadly divided into (1) functionalists, who emphasize the influence of patterns of social agreement in creating social order, (2) conflict theorists, who focus on the struggles among contending forces for scarce resources, and (3) symbolic interactionists, who stress the process by which people define the situations in which they interact and, by doing so, give it a shared meaning for the actors. And there are large numbers of sociologists who would resist any of these labels.

As we have shown in this introductory chapter, social psychology has also developed a number of theoretical perspectives. We have identified three broad perspectives in the field: the first focusing on the effect of the immediate situation on human behavior, the second on the effect of social and cultural forces, and the third on the effect of social definition. But if it is granted that social psychology has more than one perspective, how do we deal with that fact?

Perspectives used as alternative explanations To understand how to cope with the existence of several theoretical perspectives in social psychology, we must begin by setting aside Kuhn's notion of competition among perspectives for dominance in a discipline. Though one day a specific way of explaining human behavior may rise to a position of dominance in its discipline, the fact is that for now the various perspectives within the behavioral sciences tend to coexist relatively peacefully. That is, researchers who share different assumptions about the causes of human behavior may examine the exact same issue but never see the need to disagree with one another, though they explain the phenomenon very differently. In other words, the perspectives in social psychology provide us with alternative ways of understanding any issue we study.

For example, in this chapter we used the college classroom as an example of human social behavior and had no difficulty applying each of the three social-psychological perspectives to it. Student behavior might very well be shaped by the character of the immediate situation in the classroom. Perhaps the presence of a given number of other students or of a style of teaching adequately explains their behavior. Alternatively, the students may behave as they do because they have been taught cultural beliefs about education and teachers and everyday rules for behavior in the class. Lastly, the interactionists' view also seems to explain a good deal. Perhaps the way a class is to proceed is essentially a matter of negotiation among the participants. Clearly the understanding of what the class will be like at first differs between students and teacher; then, they manage eventually to settle into some shared pattern.

Rather than search for which of the perspectives is right or wrong, we think it is to our advantage in the study of human behavior to consider that there can be more than one helpful way of examining and explaining human behavior. Yes, social psychologists do tend to become proponents of one way of thinking. For example, there are social psychologists who describe themselves as taking the interactionist point of view. Specializing this way allows one to become expert in the ways of conducting research and thinking about issues which characterize a perspective. However, for the time being, we hope you can resist the temptation to choose which point of view is "best" for any given issue. We believe that since we do not know that human behavior is generated by some specific and concrete set of principles, and since we *do* know that it is complex and richly varying by place and time, it would be best not to limit the pool of our intellectual resources for explaining what we study.

The research methods used by the perspectives As we introduced the perspectives in social psychology, we also described the methods of research which each tends to employ. Because we thought it would only confuse things to say so earlier in the chapter, we decided to save until this point the fact that the proponents of each perspective have available a wide range of research methods beyond the one most common for that perspective. Thus, those who focus on the effect of the immediate situation are not limited to experimental research. They might, for example, conduct survey research, asking people to explain specifically what influenced them in a given social situation. Or they might conduct participant observation to experience firsthand what characteristics of an immediate situation influence behavior.

Similarly, researchers who are concerned with social and cultural forces are not limited to survey research. Many have employed experimental and participant observation techniques. For example, an experiment might be designed in which sex roles (a culturally learned characteristic) are examined in relation to behaviors such as the tendency to conform.

Lastly, those concerned with the process of defining social situations have used both survey research and experiments rather than the participant observation techniques commonly preferred within this perspective. For example, the ethnomethodologists (whom we discussed earlier in this chapter) conduct experiments with human behavior when they intentionally disrupt a social situation in order to examine its underlying assumptions. Cognitive theorists also use experiments. Those who examine the process of attribution (also discussed in this chapter) have, for example, varied the race or sex of individuals to see how their successes are explained by others.

Just as we suggested that it would be best not to be limited about which perspective is most successful in explaining human behavior, we would also like to make a plea for open-mindedness about the research methods that should be employed to examine an issue.

Perspectives used in combination As a final note concerning flexibility in social psychology, we wish to point out that researchers may find it useful, even necessary, to combine perspectives to make sense of an instance of human behavior. Consider the following study of the kinds of decisions people make when they are alone, as compared with when they are part of a group. A number of studies have reported that decisions made in a group tend to involve more risk than those made by individuals on their own. For example, asked to make a hypothetical choice between a conservative medical procedure for a heart condition (e.g., medication) and a riskier one (e.g., a bypass operation), people who make such a choice alone are more likely to choose the less risky alternative, while those who make the decision as part of a group tend to choose the riskier course.

This phenomenon, called the *risky shift*, is clearly within the tradition of those who focus on the effects of the immediate situation on human behavior. There must be something about being in a group as opposed to being alone which influences the kinds of decisions we make. However, Lawrence Hong (1978) suspected that there might also be some sociocultural factors at work in the phenomenon. He decided to reexamine the difference between solitary and group-based decision-making processes, comparing the behavior of native Americans with that of Chinese from Taiwan. As with previous studies, he presented members of each group with a questionnaire which posed a series of dilemmas about twelve issues such as buying stocks, getting married, and having a heart operation. In each group, some individuals were to make their decisions alone, while others made their choices in groups.

Hong did, indeed, find striking differences in the risky shift phenomenon between the Americans and Chinese. As in previous studies, the Americans made riskier choices when in groups than when alone. However, in direct opposition to the risky shift displayed by the Americans, the Chinese shifted to even *more cautious* choices when in the group setting. Hong suspects that this phenomenon is a result of the Asian (Confucian) cultural teachings, which emphasize moderation in all things. But whatever the origins of the differential effects of the group situation on Americans versus Chinese, it is clear that the combination of the sociocultural perspective with that of the immediate situation contributes to our understanding of a fascinating instance of human behavior. By combining perspectives we may learn more than any one perspective could explain alone.

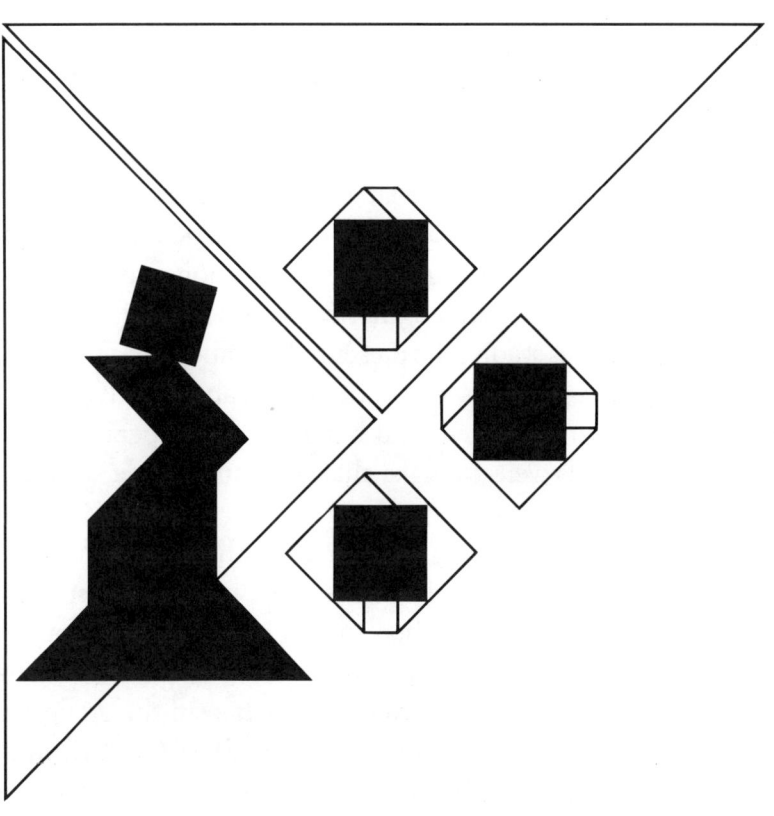

Chapter 2

The Self

If you think about it for a moment, you know you have a self, even if you haven't called it that. To begin with, you are aware of the boundaries separating "you" from "not you." Everything that's not you is called environment, and it includes other people. You can recognize your self and distinguish it from other elements of the environment. If you look in the mirror you know you are seeing yourself, and not some stranger. Infants can't do this until late in their second year; and animals, with the exception of certain higher primates, never can.

The fascination of a parakeet with its reflection in a mirror is not a fascination with self but with "another parakeet." In the same way, a baby looking in a mirror thinks he has a playmate. Neither has the ability (although the infant will soon develop it) to see its self as an object in the environment; both lack a sense of self—any personal conception of who they are.

This explains an interesting fact about language development. Did you ever notice that by far the word a baby hears most from its parents is its own name: "Hello, Benjamin... How's Benjamin feeling today?... Is Benjamin hungry? Benjamin... Benjamin... Benjamin!" Wouldn't you think that the first word out of little Benjamin's mouth would be his own name? But it never is. Instead, it is almost always Mama or Dada. The reason is that the infant is still unable to see its self as a separate object in the environment. It can clearly identify Mama and Dada, but not Benjamin.

Once we have developed a self, we can act toward it the way we act toward other objects around us. Just as we might admire the accomplishments of a friend, so we can admire what we have done. Just as we might disapprove when that person lies or cheats, we can criticize ourselves. In fact, any evaluation we make of others, or any action taken towards them, can be turned inwards. The self becomes a concrete entity, as concrete as any other.

Looking Ahead

In this chapter, we shall take a close look at the identification and development of the self. First, we examine the theories of Cooley and Mead, according to which the self originates in an individual's perceptions of the appraisals made by others. We ask: What evidence exists to support the notion of the looking-glass self? To what extent is self-concept actually a reflection of the attitudes of other people? We then turn our attention to theories of the development of the self—the process known as socialization. After looking at Mead's view that society is absolutely essential for the development of self, we then examine Freud's view that self and society are in essential conflict. Once we have established how the self develops over the course of the life cycle, we then focus on the self in adulthood—in socialization to particular careers and to total institutions. Next, we examine the operation of the self in everyday life. We ask: To what extent is the self consistent over situations and time? Just how flexible is the self in response to changes in environment? Finally, we introduce the closely related concepts of self-presentation and self-consciousness and discuss Goffman's dramaturgical model of everyday interaction, including his conception of stigma.

The Self in Social Interaction

Much of what we believe about the nature of the self comes from what Charles Horton Cooley and George Herbert Mead had to say on the subject early in the 20th century. In 1902, Cooley suggested that the *self* is a reflection of how we think others see us. In his concept of the "looking-glass self," Cooley contended that how individuals regard themselves—whether they view themselves as decent, smart, or attractive—is not necessarily related to how decent, smart, or attractive they really are. Instead, their perceptions of how others see them are used in constructing a sense of self.

Expanding on the work of Cooley, George Herbert Mead (1934) saw the self as *reflected*, arising out of experiences with other people. In his view, the self was a dynamic process within the individual—something akin to a continuing story always subject to change, which is captured on motion picture film. The two phases of the self Mead called the I and the Me.

The *I* represents the impulsive, spontaneous, and innovative dispositions of the individual, those dispositions which have their roots in biology and have not yet come under the control of what society expects. As a result, the I is responsible for both individuality and nonconformity. In this phase, the individual acts without thinking and behaves as he or she wishes, regardless of what others might desire or demand.

Of course, almost nobody is "all I." Such an individual would be incapable of living by the rules of any social group—family, school, or community. In fact, he or she would hardly be considered a human being in anything but a biological sense.

The *Me* phase of the self is the internal agent of conformity and social control. It emerges out of social interaction, out of the appraisals that others make of the individual. If a person were "all Me," he or she would be absolutely obedient, merely a "rubber stamp" of those in the immediate environment. Nothing would change in social life; innovation would be nonexistent.

As phases of the self, the I and the Me interact. Every action of an individual begins with the I and ends with the Me; the individual's initial behavior (in the I phase) eventually comes under the control of society and is evaluated by its internal representative (in the Me phase).

The presence of the I in Mead's conception of the self indicates he believed that the self is not totally determined by the appraisals of other people or by society. You might say that he saw a crack in Cooley's looking glass. In fact, if someone acts very impulsively or "abnormally" over time, the I can change the Me and therefore the self.

Of course, everybody acts impulsively now and then. It is not unusual for a conservative family man to skip out of work some afternoon to go fishing by himself or to have one too many drinks in a local pub. Occasionally giving in to the I does not, however, change his self-concept: He still thinks of himself as a stable family man. By contrast, persistent impulsive behavior can lead to significant changes in the Me. Take, for example, the now-famous concept of midlife crisis. A man who has for most of his adult life lived a relatively stable family existence with job, home, car, and so on, begins to question the meaning of his life as his 40th birthday approaches. He begins to indulge some of the impulses which previously he had thought of as selfish. He trades in his station wagon for a sports car, takes a vacation without the family, and begins wearing flamboyant clothing. If the I continues to shape his behavior this way, he might well begin to see himself differently. He might even want to change careers or get a divorce.

The presence of the self—the I and the Me—in an individual indicates, in a sense, that he or she is both subject and object at the same time. The individual with a self can reason and think, can communicate with himself as he communicates with other people, can respond to himself as an object. Even private thought is dialogue rather than monologue: in a sense, the individual is conversing with himself by alternating between the roles of speaker and audience. As Mead pointed out, when the self has arisen, "we can think of a person in solitary confinement for the rest of his life, but who still has himself as a companion..." (1934, p. 140).

Evidence for the interactionist view of self Mead's idea that an individual's self is derived from interacting with others is at the core of the interactionist perspective. However, interactionists have faced a difficult problem in testing Mead's ideas. If an individual creates a self by accumulating private perceptions of how others see him or her, how is an investigator to "get inside the individual's brain" to discover whether such a process does, in fact, occur? Interactionists have conducted many close and detailed observations of how the self develops and operates, but these studies have been criticized for being subjective. That is, no matter how insightful such observations might be, there was no way to show that the conclusions of the researchers were free of their personal views of the world. There was also no way other researchers could reproduce such a study. For years, Mead's theory of the self was understood and respected, but lacked support by objective, empirical evidence. However, such data began to accumulate in the mid-1950s.

The first of these studies was conducted by Miyamoto and Dornbusch (1956). To measure self-concept, they asked college students to rate themselves on scales for intelligence, physical attractiveness, likability, and self-confidence. In addition, each student rated all the others in the sample for the same four characteristics (to measure the actual perceptions of others). Finally, respondents indicated how they thought they would be rated by others (to measure perceived, as opposed to actual, evaluations of others).

The results of Miyamoto and Dornbusch provided clear support for Mead's theory of the self. Students who indicated a strong, positive sense of self (high self-esteem on the measures) were, in fact, more highly rated by others than were those with negative self-concepts. In other words, the self-concepts of these individuals were closely related to the way others actually saw them. Further, it was found that self-concept was more closely related to an individual's perceptions of how he or she was seen than to his or her actual evaluation by others. That is, a respondent who thought other students evaluated him or her very positively (even if they did not) was likely to have a strong, positive sense of self. Similarly, a respondent who thought others evaluated him or her negatively (even if they did not) was more likely to have a negative sense of self.

The advantage of such empirical evidence in testing theories was clearly illustrated approximately ten years later when Quarantelli and Cooper (1966) repeated Miyamoto and Dornbusch's study, adding some improvements of their own. They obtained measures of self-concept by asking dental students to rate themselves on a 10-point scale ranging from "dental student" at one end (1 on the scale) to "dentist" on the other (10 on the scale). Reasoning that in dental school the evaluations of students by faculty members carry the most weight, they obtained scale measures for each student from the school's professors.

The authors then tried to improve on Miyamoto and Dornbusch's earlier study in two ways. They measured the students' perceptions of how other students saw them (as the original research had done), but also obtained from the respondents their guesses as to how they would be judged by faculty members, parents, friends outside the school, and spouses. These additional measures were intended to provide a broader and more specific base for examining the influence of the generalized other of which Mead spoke. Lastly, they asked students to predict how they would evaluate themselves, and how they would be evaluated by others, two years in the future. The researchers added these questions in order to look at Mead's contention that the development of self occurs over time.

The results of this study support the earlier findings of Miyamoto and Dornbusch, and add further confirmation to Mead's ideas concerning the self. Students' self-perceptions were found to be related to how other people actually evaluated them. Specifically, students who thought well of themselves (had positive self-concepts) tended to be the ones who were judged favorably by faculty members. And again, it was found that self-concept was more closely related to how students thought they were evaluated by others than to how they actually were rated. In addition, the study showed that one's perception of how professors evaluate an individual is only one element in the making of a self-concept. In fact, those with high self-ratings also had more positive perceptions of how they were seen by a variety of other people (in Mead's terms, the *generalized other*), not just faculty members.

The questions about future evaluations also yielded interesting results. Students who thought a lot of themselves said they anticipated having such positive self-concepts in the future. Moreover, they also anticipated that their ratings by other people—whether by specific groups such as faculty or by the generalized other—would continue to be positive.

Since Quarantelli and Cooper, other researchers have added considerable evidence that people's self-perceptions are related to the way they think others feel about them (Shrauger and Schoeneman 1979). For example, Edwards and Klockars (1981) found that the self-concepts of husbands and wives were consistent with the perceived and, to a lesser extent, the actual evaluations of their spouses.

Such evidence in support of Mead's theory of self is impressive but incomplete: It is also important to establish the causal chain of events between what other people think of us and what we think of ourselves. For example, do the evaluations of others have a direct and independent effect on self-evaluation? Or, as Mead contended, do the actual appraisals of others operate only indirectly through an individual's perceptions of those appraisals?

Schafer and Keith (1985) attempted to answer these crucial questions about Mead's reflected self-concept by asking 333 married couples to describe themselves on a series of adjective pairs such as capable/incapable, friendly/unfriendly, and useful/useless (self-concept), to describe their spouse on the same adjective pairs (appraisal by spouse), and to indicate how they believed their spouse would describe them on the same adjective pairs (perception of their spouse's appraisal of them). As in previous studies, Schafer and Keith found that self-concept was related to both actual and perceived appraisals by spouse: the more positive a spouse's evaluation, the more positive was the self-evaluation.

Unlike earlier research, Schafer and Keith were also able to show that marriage partners' actual appraisals of one another had only an indirect effect on a spouse's self-concept—an effect that was mediated through, and therefore dependent on, their viewing the self from the point of view of a spouse. This finding emphasizes a key element in Mead's theory of the self; namely, that our *perception* of how we appear to others is the essential process whereby a self-concept is acquired.

The active self   As we shall see, the self has often been treated in the literature of social psychology as a passive recipient of social influences as well as unconscious biological urges over which the individual could exercise no control. Only the symbolic interactionists totally rejected this prevailing view of the self from the beginning.

In recent years, however, a different conception of the self has gained popularity among social psychologists, even among those outside of symbolic interactionism. In this new view, the self is an active agent in everyday life; it possesses the capacity to master the stimuli of the social environment which impinge upon it on a daily basis, the capacity to choose and organize from among the developmental possibilities. This emerging view suggests that "the self is author of its own story—an active, participating agent in the process of prospective construction" (Scheibe 1985, p. 62; see also Sarbin 1976; Boswell 1983; Mancuso and Sarbin 1983; Gergen 1982; Gergen and Gergen 1983).

Gecas and Schwalbe (1983) suggest that even this new view underestimates the active nature of the self as it operates in everyday life. They argue that the "looking-glass self" is overly passive, because it assumes that the self is a mirror-image of what an individual imagines others perceive him or her to be. Gecas and Schwalbe's alternative view is that self-conception is also based on our actions in the world, especially on how effective we are in our dealings with others, on our accomplishments and the products of our efforts. Not only does this viewpoint promote the notion of an active self, but it also connects the concept of self with theories of social and cultural forces. According to Gecas and Schwalbe, self-esteem is largely dependent on the ability of an individual's social context to (1) grant personal autonomy, (2) grant individual control, and (3) provide resources for the attainment of an individual's goals.

Felson (1985) argues, in addition, that the influence of the "looking-glass self" has been exaggerated. He indicates that the direction of cause and effect between self-appraisal and the appraisals of others can go either way: evaluations made by others influence self-evaluations, but self-evaluations also affect the evaluations made by others. In one recent study, for example, Bohrnstedt and Felson (1983) found that children with high self-esteem tended to believe that they were well-liked by their peers, but these children's perceptions of their own popularity did not affect their self-esteem. In fact, children with high self-esteem apparently projected their positive self-feelings onto their classmates. No looking-glass self could be found when it came to perceptions of popularity!

Felson suggests that there are certain factors which can interfere with the process of reflected self-appraisals. First of all, people may use objective or institutionalized indicators of their performance rather than the attitudes of others. For example, in deciding how smart they are, children rely more on their grades than on what their classmates think. The appraisals of teachers may be important, but only if they are perceived as having some decision-making role in the assignment of grades.

Felson believes that the perceived appraisals of others may have greater effect on self-concept for characteristics that are defined in terms of the reactions of others than for characteristics such as academic or physical ability, which are regarded as objective. For example, physical attractiveness is, by definition, considered to be "in the eye of the beholder" (that is, how you appear to other people). Therefore, an individual's perception of his own attractiveness may be greatly influenced by how he or she sees others perceiving him (Felson 1985).

Those who see self-concept as a result only of the evaluations of others must also assume that perfect communication exists. In reality, however, there are frequently barriers to communication which prevent individuals from securing accurate information regarding the appraisals of others. To conceal their true opinions, for example, adults will frequently gossip in the absence of the target, so that he or she may never determine what the neighbors actually think (Levin and Arluke 1987). By contrast, children are more open in expressing judgments of others. In fact, they often gossip in front of their victims (Fine 1977). As a result, reflected appraisals may tend to be more important for the self-concept of children than adults.

▶ Perspective:
The Effect of Social Definition

Self-concept across the ages The notion of self-concept was for a long time a theoretical concept: an abstract idea that sounded important but was difficult to pin down and study. Everybody seemed to agree that social behavior in everyday life depends directly on how individuals think of themselves. But such private perceptions were thought to be so subjective as to be beyond the examination of social psychologists. The task, then, was to make self-concept measurable. The work of Manford Kuhn solved this problem.

The solutions to difficult research problems are sometimes pleasingly simple. Kuhn's (1960) method of measuring self-concept required one simple question—"Who am I?"—answered with twenty different responses. For example, a person might answer that she is a female, lawyer, American, Bostonian, home owner, sister, daughter, tennis player, Catholic, violinist, and so on, until she had given twenty responses.

Kuhn administered his Twenty-Statements Test to a wide range of respondents, including children and adults. He found that children tend to define themselves in very specific, behavioral terms. For example, they might say that they are "nice to a brother" or "good at games." Adults, on the other hand, tend to define themselves in broader, more abstract categories such as "father," "teacher," "Protestant," or "home owner."

Also using Kuhn's Twenty-Statements Test, Montmayor and Eisen (1977) compared the self-concepts of children from grades 4, 6, 8, 10, and 12. As in Kuhn's study of how self-concept changes with age, Montmayor and Eisen concluded that "with increasing age, an individual self-concept becomes increasingly abstract." But these researchers also concluded that the relationship between age and abstractness of self-concept is not simple or pure. They found that some categories of response (sex, name, kinship, abstract categories of membership and tastes) were used increasingly as children aged, but only to a certain age, at which point their use declined. They suggest that this might have been due to specific events in the lives of the respondents which made for exceptions to the general rule of "the older the respondent, the more abstract the self-concept." For example, younger children who defined themselves with the very abstract term "human" may merely have been reflecting their recent addition of the concept to their vocabularies.

As you have just seen, there is good evidence that people tend to define themselves in different ways at different ages. But do styles of self-concept change across time as well? That is, do Americans today define themselves in the same ways as they did some decades ago? Some recent studies have suggested that there has been a shift in the nature of the self in America.

Much of this research began with the work of Ralph Turner (1976), a well-known symbolic interactionist who was very much influenced by G. H. Mead. Based in part on Mead's distinction between the "me" and the "I," Turner distinguished between two basic styles of self-definition which he termed institutional and impulsive selves. The *institutional self* is based on the individual's concern with group membership and officially established social goals and rules. For example, a person who expresses an institutional self might cite occupation or other group membership ("physician" or "Catholic"), responsibility and achievement ("bread winner" or "veteran"), or control ("reliable person"). The institutional self is deeply aware of and defined by the demands of his or her social situation.

By contrast, the *impulsive self* reflects concerns for personal feelings and spontaneous experience. A person with this orientation is likely to cite acts motivated by immediate desires rather than social rules ("I do what feels right at the moment"), discovery rather than responsibility ("I'm trying to find out who I am"), or chance and fallibility rather than control and performance ("I do not know what I'll eventually be like" or "Perhaps I'll do well and perhaps not").

According to Turner, over the last few decades Americans have increasingly defined themselves in impulsive terms, reflecting the growing concern in the culture with the search, through experience, for one's own values. This change over time is also reflected in some of the well-known trends of our popular culture, including all the self-help books and courses designed to make one more assertive, more confident, thin and attractive, free to express emotion or "be one's own best friend."

Turner's work has received support from studies conducted by Louis Zurcher (1972, 1977), who administered the Twenty-Statements Test to college students of the late 1960s and early 1970s and compared the results with similar data collected earlier from college students in the 1950s. He divided their responses into four categories: (1) responses based on physical characteristics (height, weight, hair color) or demographics (hometown or state), (2) responses based on membership in a social category (religion, educational level, club membership), (3) responses citing personal behaviors or attributes (liking to bowl or being funny), and (4) responses that are abstract and categorical (human being or living person).

Zurcher defined category 2 responses as characteristically institutional (using Turner's model) and category 3 responses as impulsive. His results showed that college students in the closing years of the 1960s and opening years of the 1970s tended to define themselves in impulsive terms (using category 3 responses), whereas those from the 1950s sample tended to define themselves in institutional terms (using category 2 responses).

Zurcher reasoned that the change from institutional to impulsive selves in America has been adaptive. That is, the decade of the 1960s was one of rapid social change, including such critical events as the Vietnam War and the mass protests it prompted, the height of the civil rights movement, and a crisis of confidence in American national leadership occasioned by the Watergate cover-up hearings and President Nixon's resignation. Zurcher's findings make sense if, during times of such dramatic change, individuals feel more secure if they shift their orientation toward the self and away from the larger social institutions whose stability is in question.

But what about the college students of the 1980s? Do they tend to have self-concepts that are, like their counterparts of the '50s, institutional? Or, are they impulsive, more like students of the early 1970s? Asked this question, many of our students (based perhaps on their common sense and television reports) predicted that 1980s students, with their concern about earning high salaries and working for established corporations, would be institutional. They were wrong.

David Snow and Cynthia Phillips (1982) administered the Twenty-Statements Test to a large sample of 1980s college students and found that their self-concepts were every bit as impulsive as those of Zurcher's sample. Snow and Phillips too were surprised by their results. They had reasoned that college students of the 1960s had developed impulsive orientations in reaction to the turmoil and unrest of the Civil Rights—Vietnam decade. They hypothesized that, by contrast, the 1980s emphasis on career success and materialism reflected a return to the institutional orientation of the '50s. They were faced, then, with the problem of explaining their findings.

The researchers suggested that the impulsive self-concepts of students during the 1960s and 1970s were of a different sort. The focus on self of '70s students was aimed largely at self-discovery and personal growth in order to come to terms with the larger social issues of the day—a war they saw as unjust and the struggle for civil rights by black Americans. In short, they rejected institutional membership on ethical grounds. By contrast, the impulsive self-concepts of 1980s students was seen as motivated by personal survival and achievement in the economic sphere. Snow and Phillips contended that 1980s students might be willing to take jobs in large organizations, but would do so in order to achieve personal, not organizational, goals. Thus, though 1970s and 1980s students were both shown to have impulsive self-concepts, those of the earlier time interval might be termed the "me" generation (focus on self-discovery), while those of the more recent period would better be termed the "my" generation (focus on material self-aggrandizement). ■

The Development of the Self

Now that we have some idea of what the self is, we can turn our attention to what social psychologists call *socialization*—the process whereby the self develops and an individual internalizes the norms and values of his or her social group.

G. H. Mead's (1934) conception of how the self develops focuses on how our experiences with others, especially in early life, are absorbed and adopted as elements of our selves as adults. From the moment we are born, we are immersed in a world of people who act toward us in a rich variety of ways. Humans are the premier learners of the animal world. Each time someone acts toward a child, that experience leaves some sort of imprint. A child learns something every time he or she is fed, comforted, washed, talked and read to, or taken for walks and visits with others. For Mead, the sum total of the actions of others toward the individual forms the self he or she develops. One way to understand this essential notion of the development of self is by analogy with the idea that in terms of your physical development, "You are what you eat." Mead's ideas suggest that in terms of social development, "You are who you meet."

The capacity of humans to learn develops rapidly. At first, a newborn cannot even focus his or her eyes on objects nor coordinate movements of the limbs. But as these skills develop with growth, humans increasingly learn about the physical environment. The brain collects information about the difference, for example, between hard and soft objects, between loud and soft noises, and between one person and another. Each of these bits of physical knowledge is stored in the brain of the infant as a sort of "vocabulary" of the nature of the world.

As adults, we understand such physical facts readily, because they are things we can sense by sight, touch, hearing, and so on. But at the same time that infants learn about their physical environment, they are also learning about their social world: the way people act toward one another. The social environment is sometimes more difficult to understand than the physical, because social behavior takes place at the level of symbols. That is, a human word or gesture has no intrinsic meaning. It only means what people agree it means. Thus, clapping hands may mean happiness or approval among one group of people, while among others it may symbolize fear or disapproval. The word "boot" stands for a type of footwear in America only because we agree to use it that way, while in Britain it can be used to refer to the trunk of a car. Mead recognized that social behavior takes place at the level of symbols (which Mead referred to as *gestures*), the primary medium for which is spoken language.

In order to take part in the social world, then, a child must first learn to use the symbols or gestures of its environment. Parents speak to their infant child long before he or she can respond. A father may, for his own pleasure, ask his own baby, "What do you think of peas for lunch?", expecting no response. But the question is not wasted on the child. Because he or she is spoken to repeatedly, a child learns the names of objects in his or her environment, including the names of specific objects (like peas) or individuals (like father).

The acquisition of language is, for Mead, the beginning of the development of self. He believed that the self, the unique capacity for self-awareness and self-evaluation, develops out of the actions of others toward the individual. Since human social behavior takes place at the level of symbols, a child must have symbolic, or language, skills, in order to be able to learn and absorb its own unique "vocabulary" of social behaviors. Mead described three stages in this process: imitation, play, and the game.

Imitation. While first learning a rudimentary vocabulary, we may only imitate the sounds that adults make without knowing what they mean. A parent says to the child, "Can you say apple?" and the child says the word. Of course, a 1-year-old can as easily be asked to say the word "senator" and do so with no chance of knowing its meaning. He can say "senator" nonetheless. The same capacity to imitate can be applied to the behavior of others. Parents enjoy noticing that their child takes on the mannerisms of family members, perhaps pursing lips exactly the way father does or saying to a visitor to the house "come in" in an uncanny imitation of mother.

In this stage of development, the child may display a repertoire of behaviors which often appear adult. However, at this point, the child's words and gestures lack the symbolic meanings they carry in the adult world. Pursing lips, for example, does not necessarily express concern, nor does saying "come in, come in" mean hospitality. It is not until the next stage of development that meaning is attached to social behaviors.

Play. Children practice meaningful adult behavior in the stage of development that Mead called play. The emphasis on the word meaningful in the previous statement is critical. In the imitation stage, a child may sometimes seem to be acting like an adult but lacks the knowledge of why or when such behavior is appropriate. In the play stage (about the ages of 3 or 4), children begin, by a process Mead called role taking, to attach appropriate social meanings to their behaviors. *Role taking* is the process whereby an individual not only can act like another person, but also take that person's point of view. By this time, children who act like their mother when saying "come in, come in" are actually taking the role of the mother in expressing hospitality to a visitor. Children can figuratively put themselves in "mother's shoes." More importantly, by means of role taking, they are now able to view themselves as mother or father views them.

Watch children of this age while they play alone. Often they take the role of a particular family member or other important person in their lives. Playing with a doll, a little boy may take the role of father as disciplinarian by delivering a lecture to himself through the doll. "You shouldn't have done that! You're a bad boy. No dessert for you tonight." That is what parents are expected to do in the experience of the child. In such a case, the child sees himself from the point of view of another person in a specific situation, here, his father. In another situation, the child might take the role of the mother as teacher, instructing a doll or imagined person in how to read.

The game. During the play stage, a child is only capable of taking the role of one person at a time (in Mead's terms, a particular other). During the final stage of development of self, which Mead termed the game, the child learns to take into account the expectations of a number of roles simultaneously (in Mead's terms, the generalized other, which represents "the organized community or social group which gives the individual his unity of self..."; in Mead 1956, p. 231).

Games with rules place the impersonal authority of a group above that of any single individual who is part of the game. Children who play a game like hide and seek must accept the rules of the game for the game to work. Unlike taking the role of a particular other, games have a number of different roles involved. Hide and seek only has two; a seeker and a number of hiders. By contrast, a baseball game has at least nine distinct roles, any one of which a participant is expected to understand. In order to play the game, any participant must simultaneously anticipate the reactions of all the role members. For example, in a single play, a fielder must know what a pitcher, batter, and catcher do, and what is expected if the ball goes to any player in the field. As the capacity to take the role of the generalized other develops in the child, games become more complex with greater role differentiation (compare hide and seek with baseball).

It is important to realize that taking the role of the generalized other is not merely a matter of subjecting one's self to the will of others. It actually entails internalizing what the group expects in a specific situation in the form of the game's rules. What others expect of one group member, the child expects of him or herself. Playing games with friends develops in children the capacity to take into account simultaneously the expectations of a number of others. By internalizing the expectations of the group, the child comes, over time, to internalize more than just rules for playing games. Mead contended that children's games are the prototype for living in a society; they pave the way for taking the role of the entire community and remaining as a legitimate member of it (Karp and Yoels 1979).

Thus, the socialization process, for G. H. Mead, culminates in the formation of a self possessing the capacity to make self-evaluations based on the perspective of other people in a wide variety of circumstances and settings. Going from the ability to imitate, to the ability to take the role of one person at a time, to the ability to take the role of the generalized other, we see the emergence of a fully developed, consistent, and unified self.

▶ Perspective:
The Effect of Social and Cultural Forces

Cultural images of race   Racism is an integral part of American history and culture. As such, we tend to learn it early in life through parents, peers, teachers, television, and so on.

By age 3, most children seem to be aware of racial differences. Moreover, their self-concepts have already begun to be shaped by cultural images of race and racism.

In support of the famous 1954 Supreme Court decision barring racially segregated schools, social psychologists testified about the harmful effects of segregation on the self-concepts of black children. Racial separation, it was argued, implied the inferiority of blacks to whites.

Based on their classic research, Kenneth and Mamie Clark (1947) reported a strong preference for "whiteness" on the part of both black and white preschool children. When asked to choose between a white and a brown doll identical in every other respect, black and white preschoolers, some as young as age 3, expressed a strong preference for the white doll, which they saw as being "the doll they want to play with best," "the doll that is good," and "the doll that is a nice color." By contrast, the brown doll tended to be viewed as "the doll they don't want to play with," "the doll that is bad," and "the doll that is not a nice color."

In 1970, Hraba and Grant replicated the Clark and Clark research. Unlike the Clarks, however, the more recent study found that the majority of black children, like their white counterparts, preferred the dolls of their own race. Apparently, the preference of black youngsters for white dolls had all but disappeared since the original study was conducted decades earlier.

According to Hraba and Grant, one interpretation of their results is that "interracial contact may engender black pride." If so, then, the Supreme Court may have been right and the self-concept of black children may have improved as a result. A number of studies have indeed indicated that black Americans do not presently have lower self-esteem or more negative self-concepts than do white Americans (see, for example, Clark 1986). Such findings strongly suggest that white Americans are no longer the looking glass for the self-concept of black Americans. Instead, black Americans may internalize positive self-esteem from their immediate environment, that is, members of their family and neighborhood (Barnes 1972; Clark 1986). ■

Conflict between self and society As we have seen, Mead emphasized the part played by society (i.e., the role of the generalized other) in the formation of a mature and consistent self. For him, there could be no self without society. By contrast, some psychologists recognize little if any cooperation between individual and group, between self and society. Sigmund Freud (1930) asserted instead that conflict inevitably developed between individual needs and the desires of civilized society. In his book *Civilization and Its Discontents*, Freud argued that an individual is born with certain primitive needs—sex and aggression. Rather than help the individual satisfy these needs, however, society typically thwarts them. It tells the individual that he or she must limit sexual experiences to a socially acceptable time, place, and form (for example, it imposes a dating ritual). Society also reduces the individual's opportunities for aggressive behavior to a few carefully restricted situations—situations which do not threaten to disrupt the flow of ongoing activities (for example, the individual is allowed to play football or watch a violent movie, but not to indulge in random violence). Thus, the needs of society always overrule the needs of any given individual: society compels the individual to delay the discharge of sexual and aggressive energies and then to express those energies in a less-than-satisfying manner.

Freud may have been the first psychological theorist to emphasize the early years in the life of a child as playing a decisive role in the formation of the self or personality. He believed that a young child passes through a series of *psychosexual stages* during the first five years, each of which is defined by a reaction of a particular region of the body called an erogenous zone. An *erogenous zone* is any part of the body—such as the mouth, the anal region, and the sex organs—which is extremely sensitive to irritation and can be manipulated to produce pleasurable feelings. (Clearly, Freud had a broader view than most of us as to what should be regarded as sexual.)

For the first year of life, a child passes through what Freud referred to as the *oral stage*. During this period, the mouth is the erogenous zone which becomes a focal point of psychosexual activity; sucking and biting produce oral pleasure.

While they are in the oral stage, children are totally dependent on others for sustenance and protection. At this early point in the development of the self, they are psychologically "all *id*"—an uncontrolled reservoir of sexual and aggressive urges—and cannot possibly fend for themselves. If problems arise in the oral stage (for example, if a baby is given a bottle without ever having to wait for it or if a baby is not allowed to satisfy the need for sucking), there may be long-term issues of dependence which continue to go unresolved throughout life. At the extreme, for example, heavy cigarette smoking or alcoholism may later become a permanent reminder of such unresolved issues, according to Freud.

Sometime during the second year, the initial dependency of the child on his parents begins to subside and the focal point of development shifts to the anal region. According to Freud, toilet training during the *anal stage* gives the child his or her first major experience with regulating instinctual, impulsive behavior. Through toilet training, the child is expected to postpone—until the appropriate time and place—the pleasure which comes from relieving his or her anal tensions. As he or she learns to delay satisfying bodily needs, the child gradually develops an *ego*—the capacity to deal with the social environment, with other people.

Freud contended that the manner in which the child is toilet trained determines many important adult characteristics. For example, if the child is subjected to early and extreme standards for anal self-control (by expecting a 1-year-old to perform such tasks with adult control), he or she may grow up to be obsessive compulsive about order and cleanliness. If, on the other hand, the toilet training of a child is neglected, he or she may later be comfortable with a socially inappropriate level of personal disorganization.

Freud believed that the anal stage of development lasts through the second year of life and is succeeded by the *phallic stage*, in which the sex organs become the primary erogenous zone. This is the psychosexual stage when the child might play with his or her genitalia and engage in rich sexual fantasies. This is also the stage responsible for the development of the child's *superego*—the internalized set of social rules for behavior.

Specifically, the superego emerges in all children between the ages of 3 and 5 as a result of the manner in which they experience the *Oedipus complex*. During this period, the child has a strong sexual desire for the parent of the opposite sex and a strong feeling of hostility for the parent of the same sex. Freud argued, in fact, that children going through the phallic stage feel themselves in an intensely competitive struggle with the parent of the same sex for the love of the parent of the opposite sex. Thus, boys love their mothers but hate their fathers; girls love their fathers but hate their mothers.

The Oedipus complex is resolved over time; but only when the child realizes that he or she cannot possibly win the competition and begins to fear the response of the competitive parent to his or her hostile behavior. A boy normally develops what Freud called *castration anxiety*; he comes to believe that, as a result of the rivalry between them, his father might eliminate his sex organs. For anatomical reasons, of course, girls do not fear castration. According to Freud, however, they develop during the phallic stage a condition known as *penis envy*, whereby they are painfully aware of their own lacking of a male sex organ. For females, this is a profound source of insecurity, one which can determine behavior not only during the phallic stage but throughout life. For example, Freud argued at one point that the desire of women to give birth to babies, and especially male babies, was a result of penis envy (babies, you see, are phallic symbols). Freud also believed that the female's absence of castration anxiety during the phallic stage makes it problematic for her to resolve the Oedipus complex and develop a moral self, a profound sense of what is right and wrong. (Obviously, Freud was a sexist by today's standards. Some feminists argue that he was the ultimate sexist, given his influence on popular thinking about gender.)

To end the phallic stage, there is a major shift in the attitude of the child regarding his or her parents. The child *represses* (selectively forgets) the hatred felt for the parent of the same sex and the sexual desire for the parent of the opposite sex. That is, the entire battle leaves the awareness of the child and becomes part of the unconscious. Instead, *identification* occurs: a boy seeks to become like his father in order to gain the affection of his mother; similarly, a girl tries to become like her mother in order to gain the affection of her father. Identification assures not only that the child will assume the sexual orientation of the parent of the same sex (i.e., heterosexuality), but also that he or she will internalize the parents' cultural standards. The child's psychic energy becomes invested in the superego, with its intense feelings of guilt and pride, which then guides the child's behavior. Freud argued that identification leaves a more or less permanent mark on the self.

If, during the phallic stage, something major goes wrong—if, for example, identification cannot take place because of the absence of a relationship with either parent—then, Freud predicted, sexual deviance would result. More generally, under such conditions, the child fails to develop a strong superego or sense of what is right and wrong.

With the satisfactory resolution of the Oedipus complex, the most profound aspects of the self have developed. The child moves into a stage of *latency*, a period of development during which psychosexual urges remain dormant and quiet until puberty. Of course, the child may later be influenced by other people—an admired teacher, a trusted friend or relative—but the basic makeup of the self remains unchanged. For Freud, the self is essentially a product of the experiences during the oral, anal, and phallic stages—the psychosexual stages of development which occur during the first six years of life.

Self vs. personality   Both Mead and Freud were influential in determining present-day views of social psychologists concerning the self and its development. Both recognized the importance of social interaction in the formation of the self; both traced the development of the self through a series of stages beginning in the young child.

In many important respects, however, Mead and Freud represent divergent views regarding self-development:

1) Freud proposed a structure of the self, better known as *personality*, consisting of a set of characteristics which endure over time (the id, ego, and superego). By contrast, Mead viewed the self as a process, as an always-changing set of phases which he referred to as the I and the Me.

2) Freud's theory posits that the personality is essentially developed by the age of 6, marking the completion of the phallic stage and the child's entrance into latency. By contrast, Mead set no such absolute limits on the development of the self, although he too emphasized childhood socialization.

3) Freud saw the individual's personality as a more-or-less passive recipient of external and biological influences, being shaped primarily by adults who socialize the child or by unconscious urges over which the child

has no control. Mead instead conceptualized the self as an active agent in its own development. He proposed that individuals are much more than merely passive reactors who are programmed by others. Instead, actors consciously develop plans of action "out of the bits and pieces supplied by culture and...attempt to execute these plans in social encounters" (Schlenker 1985, p. 17).

4) Freud's theory of the development of personality emphasizes pathology or mental illness, a characteristic which he perhaps acquired in his role as psychotherapist rather than theorist. He sought, for example, to explain the origins of the "neurotic behavior" which he saw in so many of his patients. By contrast, Mead focused on the development of the normal, coherent self.

5) Freud's concept of penis envy in women has been dismissed by feminists as a blatantly sexist idea which treats females as an inferior gender. There is no such comparable notion in Mead's theorizing. His view of the self seems to apply equally well to both male and female development.

6) As indicated earlier, Freud argued that personality was in basic conflict with civilized society. According to him, civilization and social order require that the individual subordinate the fulfillment of personal needs to the will of society. More specifically, Freud saw a process of *sublimation* of individual needs, whereby an individual is asked to strive toward a set of less satisfying but more socially acceptable goals such as art, music, and business competition, rather than to satisfy basic urges for sex and aggression. In sharp contrast, Mead argued that "selves can only exist in definite relations to other selves" (1934, p. 196)—that the self and society were inextricably bound together; in fact, the self could not exist at all apart from social interaction. In order to develop a consistent, coherent self, Mead believed it essential that an individual be connected with society by taking the role of the generalized other. Only through social interaction can individuals be expected to form coherent views of themselves and others.

The self throughout the life cycle A student of Freud, Erik Erikson (1950) proposed a theory of development that differed from Freud's in at least two important ways. First, Freud's theory seemed too restrictive in its assertion that the development of the self was essentially completed by about the age of 6. Erikson argued instead that the process of development continued throughout life. Second, Freud focused on the way the inborn reservoir of sexual and aggressive energies (id) drive the development process. Each stage of development is seen as an adaptation to these internal impulses. Erikson, however, contended that an individual's experiences with others present challenges and opportunities for change in the self. This "psychosocial" perspective gives great weight to the way social and cultural experiences originating outside individuals motivate formation and reformation of the self.

Erikson proposed eight stages of development, each of which is initiated by social experiences that are relatively predictable and patterned in most people's lives. With each set of experiences, the ego component of the self, and therefore its very structure, is transformed in some way. This scheme is much more flexible than Freud's, since it allows for the possibility of corrections or adjustments in the self throughout life. While not everyone experiences the world in the same way, the stages are fairly consistent, since they are generally linked to culturally shared changes in status, such as that from adolescence to young adulthood or from middle to old age.

Stage 1. An infant is, at first, totally dependent on adults for nurturance such as food, comforting, cleaning, and warmth. Out of such interactions with the environment, the child may develop a sense of either *trust* (if nurturance has been consistent and adequate) or *mistrust* (if it has not) as a character of the self.

Stage 2. From the ages of 1 to 4, as the child develops both physically and mentally, he or she learns, with instruction from adults, a variety of skills, such as walking and talking. To the extent that such skills develop, the child may emerge from this stage with feelings of *autonomy* (self-reliance and independence from parents) or *doubt* and *shame* about his or her abilities and independence.

Stage 3. Between the ages of 4 and 5, largely through interaction with peers, the child explores the boundaries of his or her social environment. He or she may range from flights of imagination to imitation of parents' behavior to establish a sense of the limits of social reality. For the child, such experiences may lead to the development of a sense of *initiative* and self-confidence, or, if adults have restricted the child's explorations with overly strict discipline, a sense of *guilt*.

Stage 4. Between the ages of 6 and 13, children are typically faced with their first concrete tasks outside the home, especially in school. They must satisfy the demands of peers and adults other than only their parents. The challenge is to achieve and satisfy duties and responsibilities which are judged by independent standards of performance. From these experiences, the child may emerge with a sense of *industry* or *inferiority*.

Stage 5. In adolescence, the task is to develop a sense of individual *identity*. If, however, roles and group membership do not provide clear and consistent models for identification of the self, the consequence is *confusion*.

Stage 6. In young adulthood, close personal relationships may be formed, developing a sense of *intimacy*. If such relationships are not successfully established, the result is a sense of *isolation*.

Stage 7. In midlife, approximately between the ages of 30 and 50, the challenges of work, raising a family, citizenship, and so on can create in the individual who successfully meets the challenges a sense of *generativity*, a concern with the next generation. The failure to master such tasks may result in a nonproductive, egocentric sense of self, Erikson's term for which is *stagnation*.

Stage 8. In the final developmental stage, the individual is faced during later life with the need to come to terms with the meaning of his or her life. A satisfactory evaluation and acceptance of life within the context of the culture's values lead to a sense of *integrity*. For the individual who is unable to find meaning in life, perhaps because of isolation from social contacts, or excessive self-absorption in the questions posed by the limitations of later life, the result can be a condition Erikson calls *despair*.

Erikson's view is that development of the self is extremely flexible. His theory allows for individuals to add elements of the self to those developed in previous stages. For example, a child who develops a sense of autonomy in the second stage maintains that sense of self when initiative is added in the next stage. In addition, the outcome of each stage is not "either or," as in a person who develops either total intimacy or complete isolation in stage 6. Rather, the typical outcome of a set of experiences for this stage is a capacity for intimacy which has limits. Normally, individuals can establish a degree of intimacy, but cannot give their whole selves over to social relationships. We all tend to keep some of our selves in what Erikson would term isolation.

Lastly, Erikson's theory gives a good deal of weight to the social experiences of individuals in the formation of the self. As a result, his views about the development of the self have proved to be of great interest not only to developmental psychologists but also to sociologists. It is fundamental to social psychologists that we understand the link between the individual and the social world in which he or she lives. Giving such importance to the social experiences we all have, Erikson's ideas make this relationship concrete and plausible.

Development of specific aspects of self While the views we have discussed so far have been concerned with the development of the self in its broadest sense, two well-known psychologists have described the development of specific aspects of the self. Piaget examined the development of the intellectual or cognitive component of the self, whereas Kohlberg studied moral development.

Piaget conceived of human beings as thinking animals. We not only experience the environment through our senses, we also store our experiences as memory, organize those experiences into categories (for example, comparing experiences in terms of duration or intensity), and use such organized information in contemplating possible lines of action. This ability to perceive and think, called *cognition*, is essential to human social development. To understand why, think about the process of role taking as described by G. H. Mead.

A child who takes the role of his or her mother by punishing a doll for "getting dirty" has already acquired the ability to perform a number of intellectual tasks, including the abilities to use symbolic language (talk to the doll), correctly classify "getting dirty" as disapproved behavior, and create an abstract reality (the doll did not really do anything and the child is not really the mother). In short, for the child to develop a self, he or she must have mastered a certain set of cognitive skills.

To learn how the cognitive skills of humans develop over time, Piaget conducted years of detailed observations of children at play. He concluded that children learn from interaction with their environments, for example by discovering the properties of the objects they manipulate in games. Each new bit of information is assimilated into a growing body of information stored in the brain in organized schemes, and each scheme is also modified or accommodated to allow for the inclusion of new or contradictory information. Take the situation of a child who has previously only played with tennis balls or small rubber balls. Given a beach ball for the first time, this child learns what its qualities are (assimilates) and also modifies his or her previous notions of what size, color, or weight a ball can be and what it means to "play with the ball" (accommodates).

Piaget concluded that cognitive skills develop in humans in four stages, each of which is a necessary condition for the next:

Stage 1. In the *sensorimotor* stage, from birth to about the age of 2, children learn through sensory experience. By touching or seeing objects, by moving about in their limited worlds, children can develop physical skills and, at the same time, an appreciation for cause-and-effect relationships. Step on clay with your bare feet and it squishes; but step on a marble that way and it hurts.

Stage 2. Between the ages of 2 and 7, children develop symbolic language skills. That is, they learn that words can be used to represent reality. It is possible, for example, to talk about a dog without that dog actually being in the room, or to talk about even a dog one has never seen.

During this stage, which Piaget called *preoperational*, children are able to play imaginative, make-believe games.

Stage 3. During the *concrete operational* stage, which lasts from ages 7 to 11, the child begins to think logically about experiences. He or she develops some ability to think in numerical terms, to classify objects in terms of qualities like volume, shape, or distance from one another (spatial relations), and to construct complex mental images for planned objects. For example, a child of 10 can visualize many of the actions necessary to combine a pile of blocks to create a house or car.

Stage 4. In the *formal operational* stage, which begins about the age of 12 and spans the remainder of the life cycle, an individual is able to employ formal logic. In this most advanced of cognitive skills, he or she is capable of hypothetical thinking in which thoughts contrary to reality can be considered ("Imagine a world without gravity"), plans made ("What will I do tomorrow?"), or one's own thoughts evaluated ("What do I really believe in?").

Piaget focused on the ways in which humans develop the capacity to make sense of the world. Clearly, our ability to deal with other people in a symbolic, social world requires such cognitive skills. But the rules we learn so that we can get along in the social world are not just intellectual; they are moral as well. They specify how others expect us to behave, and, thus, reflect a shared sense among people of right versus wrong.

Lawrence Kohlberg (1969), like Piaget, studied children to discover how their capacities developed; but his interest was in moral rather than cognitive reasoning. Kohlberg described a series of developmental levels through which increasingly complex moral thinking is achieved:

Level 1 – preconventional morality. At first, a child's sense of how he or she ought to behave is motivated by punishment and reward. In stage 1 of this level, the punishment stage, a child acts as it is expected only in order to avoid punishment. The child cannot understand the reason that his or her parents compel or prohibit certain behaviors, beyond the fact that they have the power to punish. In stage 2 (the satisfaction stage), the child fulfills parental expectations in order to get some reward. "I was good, so I get extra dessert." Once again, as in the punishment stage, there is no appreciation for the broader social reasons for rules.

Level 2–conventional morality. At this level, rules are accepted beyond mere punishments or rewards. In stage 3 (the interpersonal agreement stage), rules are obeyed because the child wants the personal approval of the adult who established the rule. A child may pick up clothes because that is the parents' rule, and children who obey such rules are acting as they should. In the 4th stage (the law-and-order stage), the developing individual understands for the first time that rules for behavior are necessary for the operation of society. At this point, the individual can appreciate the existence of an impersonal authority, that there is a group of people who need its members to follow communal rules.

Level 3–postconventional morality. At this level, individual behavior is motivated by ethics that supersede specific social rules. The 5th stage (the social contract stage) requires that individuals understand that the social rules by which a society runs are created by humans and are conditional. That is, that even though the society may teach that killing is prohibited, there are circumstances in which the rule can (and even must) be suspended. War is an example. In the final stage (the conscience stage), which Kohlberg claims few individuals reach (he has even expressed some doubts as to its validity), a person develops and is motivated by private moral principles. The nonviolence of the Indian leader Mahatma Gandhi is an appropriate example.

The Self in Adult Life

Everything we know about the process of socialization suggests that what happens to us while we are young is disproportionately influential in shaping our adult selves. The work of both Mead and Freud focused a good deal on the events of early childhood. But theorists like Erikson, Piaget, and Kohlberg have argued persuasively that while the early years are critical, development continues throughout life. Their work reflects the fact that the events of adult life, such as the responsibilities of earning a living and raising children, stimulate the development of components of the self which differ from those of childhood. Recall, for example, Erikson's assertion that in midlife, approximately between the ages of 30 and 50, the challenges of work, raising a family, citizenship, and so on can create a new aspect of the self he called generativity.

The recognition that the events of adult life can continue to shape the self has led a number of social psychologists to examine a variety of circumstances in which the selves of individuals are influenced well after childhood. Many of these circumstances involve careers.

Socialization to careers In American life, one's self-concept is often intricately tied to one's work. On first meeting someone, it is common for the introductions to include information about careers. "I'd like you to meet Ruth. She's in computer design." In fact, if you think about it, such exchanges are naturally occurring examples of Kuhn's Twenty-Statements Test. When people describe themselves to strangers, what they do for a living is usually among the first of the self-identifying statements they make.

Social psychologists, recognizing that careers are so important in our self-concepts, have paid a good deal of attention to *career socialization*, the way individuals come to adopt the practices and values of their work. The earliest and best-known of these studies examined professions like medicine and law, probably because they are among the strongest of occupational identifications in America, and because they carry clearly stated sets of standards for practice and belief. In fact, such standards are maintained and enforced by formal organizations within each profession: the American Medical Association for physicians and the American Bar Association for lawyers, each of which has the power to determine who is to be licensed to practice in the profession. How, then, is an individual socialized into a profession? That is, how is the individual's self shaped or modified by entry into a particular career?

Socialization to the medical profession. To understand how physicians are taught the profession's values and beliefs, Howard Becker and his associates (1961) attended medical school classes with regular students and carefully observed the lessons they were taught beyond the specific facts of anatomy, biochemistry, and so on. The researchers observed that first-year students were highly idealistic when they first entered medical school. Many expressed the intention to devote their lives to the "service of humanity" and believed that they would be able to master the body of medical knowledge while in school. They also believed that what they learned in classes would have some direct application to the diagnosis and treatment of disease. In fact, however, though the public statements of medical school deans and faculty supported such ideas, the reality of their medical school training taught them a very different, less apparent, set of professional lessons.

Students quickly learned that they would not "learn it all." Their basic courses were so demanding that they soon discovered that they would have to "cut corners" in order to be able to pass exams. Rather than try to memorize all the material from lectures, students became adept at figuring out what material was most likely to be on exams. They tried to find copies of old exams from which to study and made judgments about what sorts of work in the lab were most time consuming, choosing to do only time-efficient procedures. In short, they became rather less idealistic about the practice of medicine and about the ability of medical school classes to produce competent physicians.

Once in the hospital setting, medical students learned more of the same sorts of lessons. Students were now subjected to living, rather than paper and pencil, exams. Staff physicians asked them questions about the cases seen "on rounds" and expected rapid, accurate answers about any of a number of medical situations. Expected to be familiar with so many technical details about so many cases, it is no surprise that students learned they had no time to attend to the needs of patients as individual humans. The patient came to be seen as a *living exam*, a collection of symptoms on a chart about which the student might be quizzed at any time. In fact, the more complex the symptoms of a given patient, the more he or she would be seen as a threat to the peace and well-being of the student.

By the time the student left medical school for an internship in a hospital (with a degree in hand, if all had gone well), he or she had learned well the lessons of the profession. Medical school, Becker and his colleagues learned, tempered the student's idealism with a certain brand of professional realism. It taught the student that it is the goal of the physician to cure disease, and that the best tools for achieving this end are technical. The physician cannot know it all, and so must accept the limits of the knowledge of the field and his or her access to it. (Narrow specialization within medicine is a common response to these facts.) While it may be desirable for the patient's care that he or she be treated with understanding and compassion as an individual, the practical demands on a physician's time and resources are likely to prevent this.

Becker discovered, then, that career socialization may occur on two levels. The surface level, which is what the general public and beginning students learn, consists of the most idealistic goals of the profession. In medicine these include notions of competence, compassion, and service to humanity. While these are not abandoned in medical training and practice, they are, however, modified by the second level of professional lessons, which consists of the practical limits of medical knowledge and practice.

Socialization to the legal profession. In a recent study, Robert Granfield (1986) attended classes at a large and prestigious Eastern law school to discover how law students are socialized. Like Becker, Granfield found that the lessons of law school exist at two levels. The first, more popularly understood professional standards, include the fundamental principles of case law and the goal of achieving justice. Again, as in Becker's study of medical education, Granfield found that during the three years of their legal education, students' idealistic notions of devotion to the law eroded under the weight of a second set of less admirable lessons about the law.

As an integral part of their legal education, law students were taught an intellectual style called "thinking like a lawyer." This meant that, rather than arguing cases strictly on the basis of legal precedents or morally "correct" sets of principles, students were expected to learn to selectively cite those cases that would result in winning. Students were asked, even required, to abandon the notion of the law as an impartial body of findings which serves the search for justice rather than the needs of a specific client. As a result, they came to express considerable cynicism about the law.

For many students, such a view of the law was far from distasteful. In fact, Granfield reports that most of the students intended in their practices to represent large corporations and were comfortable with the idea that the best lawyer knew how to "use the law" in the client's interests. Other students, however, had to rethink their goals and beliefs in order to accommodate the view of the law they were learning. For some, it was simply a matter of recognizing the great opportunities available for money and influence if they would adopt this view of legal practice. Others engaged in a more complex process of compromise in which they told themselves (and Granfield) that if they worked at high salaries for large firms for a few years, they could make enough money to afford to do free work for people who really needed the legal help, or that they could do so while working for the big firms.

Granfield also found that some students resisted the pressure to abandon their idealism about the law. These were the students who expressed an intention to promote social change and to represent poor and powerless people. In order to maintain their views, such students formed organizations of like-minded individuals within the school.

From the studies of Becker and Granfield, it seems clear that professional schools socialize individuals into careers in ways not always understood by the general public, or even by most incoming students. The self-concept of the physician or lawyer, then, is not acquired by simply learning the words contained in an oath to cure illness or serve justice. It is shaped by professional education which prepares students to cope with the practical demands of specific professions.

Adult socialization to total institutions As adults, we can anticipate and look forward to changes in our lives. Going to college, getting married, having children, and entering a new career are typically regarded as desirable stages of a normal life. However, some of life's events are unplanned, unforeseen, and decidedly unpleasant. If a person becomes ill or is sent to jail, the normal life he or she has led may be thrown into turmoil, and the old self-concept may become completely useless. At times like these, adult socialization to dramatic changes tends to be dramatic as well. Hospitals and prisons are sometimes called *total institutions* because they have complete control over the lives of the persons who inhabit them. Beyond providing for all the needs of their residents, such places also socialize patients and inmates to their new lives, developing in them radically different self-concepts.

About the same time that Howard Becker was studying how medical students are socialized, Erving Goffman (1961) was observing the way mental patients are treated in an asylum or mental hospital. What he saw may have been one of the purest examples of adult socialization, because the hospital staff had assumed absolute power to define how patients should think and act. Thus, the institution was in total control of the terms by which its patients could define themselves.

A new inmate in the asylum would first have to learn a new way of thinking if he or she were to get along in the institution and, eventually, be released. All the old self-concepts, if any remained intact, would have to be discarded. Goffman described the new set of definitions which the staff taught to all inmates. Not surprisingly, they bore little resemblance to the normal self-concepts as used by people "on the outside."

First, the inmate must define him or herself as sick. Forced into a life that nobody would voluntarily choose, inmates were constantly reminded that they were ill and, as a result, dependent on others for help. To reinforce the acceptance of this self-concept, the staff labeled as a symptom of mental disease any claim by a patient that he or she was not psychologically sick. You may have heard it said of mental illness that the first step on the road to recovery is the admission that you are sick. Keep in mind that part of a normal self-concept is the idea that one is sane. Such a belief about the self becomes not only useless, but actually disapproved of, in an asylum.

Goffman identified a range of such aspects of self-concept that are "turned upside down" in this total institution. Boredom in the asylum was defined as depression, anger as "acting out," independence as irrationality, and the desire for privacy as withdrawal. With the urging of the staff (who had at their disposal a range of rewards and punishment, the most powerful of which was a decision that someone had been cured), inmates were compelled to redefine themselves. A patient who had accepted the role of sick person, that is, had been successfully resocialized by the institution, was rewarded by the staff for acting the part. The patient who adopted the style of life of a mentally ill person readily submitted to the routines demanded of the asylum such as taking medications and therapy sessions. All this made things easier for the staff whose higher goals of curing mental illness, Goffman suggests, were frequently subordinated to the need to predict and control the behavior of patients.

In his compelling novel about this socialization process in a psychiatric hospital, *One Flew over the Cuckoo's Nest*, Ken Kesey described a man who, though sane, was put into such a mental institution as Goffman had studied. It is testimony to the power of such a place to resocialize people that, by the end of the story, the main character, who heroically refused to define himself as sick (in fact, he tried to convince other patients that they were not sick either), had been forced by the staff to conform. He was subjected to a crude surgical procedure (prefrontal lobotomy) to make him "fit in."

If you think such a story is fanciful, that it could only occur in fiction, then consider the results of a study conducted by D. L. Rosenhan (1973). In this experiment, 8 sane individuals (5 males and 3 females of varying ages and occupations) gained secret admission to mental hospitals across the country. None had ever exhibited symptoms of mental illness, and admission was gained merely by complaining that he or she "had been hearing voices."

All but one of the "pseudopatients" were diagnosed as schizophrenic. No hospital staff members were told of the experiment, and upon entering the institutions the pseudopatients stopped displaying any symptoms. Beyond the understandable nervousness any person might feel upon entering a strange and somewhat scary place (nervousness which soon disappeared), the pseudopatients behaved and spoke normally for the duration of their stay.

Immediately after their admission, all but one of the pseudopatients expressed their desire to be discharged. Each was told that discharge depended upon the ability of a patient to convince the staff that he or she was sane. However, despite their normal behavior, the average length of hospitalization for these people was 19 days. One was unable to achieve release for 52 days. Not one of the pseudopatients was suspected by any of the hospital staff members. (Interestingly, some 25 percent of the patients on the admissions wards accused the pseudopatients of being sane, guessing they were professors or journalists in the hospital to conduct studies.) Finally, every pseudopatient was eventually discharged with a diagnosis of schizophrenia "in remission." In other words, none ever really convinced a hospital staff that he or she was sane, merely that the symptoms of their "illness" had subsided.

One might think that Rosenhan's pseudopatients were well protected against being resocialized by the mental institutions, since they went into the experiment with strong self-concepts as participants in a study. Many reported, however, having to fight severe feelings of powerlessness and depersonalization on the wards. Imagine what it must be like for a patient who has entered a mental institution with some doubts about his or her sanity, and wishes to maintain some sense of self-concept from a former life.

Thus, a number of conditions exist in mental institutions which make them uniquely able to alter the selves of their patients. First, they have total control over the lives of inmates. Second, they have institutional schedules and restrictions which require that they control the behavior of patients. And third, they have their own ways of interpreting the meaning of behaviors so that concepts of normalcy from the "outside world" (the world in which most of us live) become useless upon entering an asylum.

▶ Perspective:
The Effect of the Immediate Situation

Is a divided self unhealthy? During World War II, hundreds of Nazi doctors conducted cruel and fatal experiments on concentration camp inmates. They also supervised the slaughter, from beginning to end, of countless "enemies of the State." How could such physicians, having been trained as healers, become mass killers?

Lifton (1986) explains that the concentration camp doctors formed a second, relatively independent self in a process he calls *doubling*: "the division of the self into two functioning wholes, so that a part-self acts as an entire self" (p. 418). Doubling, according to Lifton, was the psychological vehicle for the Nazi doctors to be able to function in an environment which was so much in opposition to everything they had believed to be proper and ethical. The doctors' "Auschwitz self" performed the "dirty work" of the concentration camp, whereas their prior self permitted them to escape feeling excessively guilty and to maintain the self-concept of a humane husband, father, and physician.

At the turn of the century, psychologist William James recognized the universal potential for opposing tendencies in the self. But he called an individual "a sick soul" who possesses a divided sense of self. As we have seen, G. H. Mead similarly emphasized the importance of developing a unified, coherent self by taking the role of the generalized other.

Clearly, the assumption that an inconsistent self is unhealthy and may even encourage evil is deeply embedded in popular culture as well. Movies such as *Three Faces of Eve* and *Sybil* reflect the view, pervasively held, that a divided self is suggestive of multiple personality or manic depression, if not schizophrenia. When we meet someone, we tend to expect consistency, even if it is more apparent than real. As suggested by the concept of situated identity, we might easily confuse a particular role with the entire person playing it. For example, college students who bump into their professor in a bar might see her as "out of place." Some might not even recognize her at all!

There is no denying the presence of certain "central tendencies" or areas of consistency in self (Gergen 1972; Serpe 1987). In most situations, for example, men typically see themselves as "masculine," whereas women see themselves as "feminine." Moreover, some individuals have been so profoundly socialized that they become completely trapped in self-definitions such as "stupid," "ugly," "intelligent," or "attractive," even if these definitions no longer apply.

There is very compelling evidence to indicate that people generally prefer to have a stable, consistent image of who they are, and indeed that they tend to act to maintain that image intact in the face of the most challenging evidence (Rosenberg 1979; Elliott 1986). On the negative side, this tendency toward self-consistency may complicate efforts to overcome the harmful effects of early school failure on children's feelings of personal competence or academic potential, even if such failure can be shown to be a result of a biased teacher, a substandard school, or economic disadvantage (Lepper, Ross, and Lau 1986). On the more positive side, people with a consistently high level of self-esteem may be able to withstand important negative life events. Shamir (1986) has shown, for example, that the self-esteem of well-educated adults does not usually deteriorate under the impact of prolonged unemployment. Indeed, high self-esteem seems to protect these unemployed individuals from experiencing severe psychological distress such as depression and anxiety.

Gergen (1972; 1978) asserts, however, that we have paid too much attention to such central tendencies and too little attention to the complexities of the self. He argues that most people don't develop an entirely coherent sense of self and that those few who do probably suffer emotionally for it. Even the divided self is, in a sense, quite normal, he contends.

In a series of experiments, Gergen demonstrates that individuals seem to have many selves and that the situations an individual encounters in everyday life help determine which of these selves is evoked. He shows that subjects' self-esteem can be increased, for example, by experimentally giving them subtle signs of approval (a nod of the head, a smile, or spoken agreement), by having them read the words of a "braggart" (a peer who describes herself in writing as "cheerful, intelligent, and beautiful," as someone who "loved school, had a marvelous childhood, and was optimistic about the future" p. 263), or by competing for a job against another applicant described as Mr. Dirty (a "real slob" who wore a torn sweatshirt, was unshaven, and came unprepared for his interview).

Gergen's studies do not contradict the notion that the self has an essential consistency; but they do emphasize that the self also can be amazingly flexible, that it is "made of soft plastic and molded by social circumstances" (p. 265). Going beyond his data, Gergen suggests that our society encourages one-dimensional consistency and discourages a broad range of interests and talents. We make career alternatives which constrict our opportunities for variation and impose work routines that vary little on a daily basis. We develop long-term, intimate relationships—for example, through marriage—which typically impose predictability, stability, and rigidity at the expense of the personal growth of the self. ∎

Presentation of Self in Everyday Life

To this point, we have been concerned with the self as it develops and operates in the lives of individuals in society. We now shift our attention from the development to the presentation of self. As human beings, we have a unique ability to pay attention to ourselves and be concerned with the impression we wish to present to others. Are my clothes proper? Is my hair combed? Are my manners correct? Do I look like the kind of person who reads pornography for pleasure? Just as we pay attention to others, Mead suggested that the capacity for self-awareness is a result of role-taking, of the "back-and-forth interaction with others" (Buss 1980, p. 82).

Given the self-concept that a person has, he or she has the need and the ability to project that identity to others and, simultaneously, confirm it to him or herself. In most cases of social interaction, there is little conflict between how a person behaves and that person's self-concept. But for a variety of reasons it is often necessary to put on something of a performance, to actively shape others' definition of the situation much the way actors do on stage. Social psychologists call this *impression management*.

For example, a newly graduated medical student works in a hospital as an intern. Though he or she has the title of doctor, the experience and power to make independent diagnoses and treatments of illness are still in the future. In this situation, it is common for the intern to carefully cultivate the mannerisms and appearance of more experienced colleagues in order to be accepted by staff and patients in the role for which he or she has been trained. Another extremely common instance of impression management is the job interview. By dressing the part and preparing a few bits of knowledge and vocabulary appropriate to the job opening, applicants try to convince the interviewer that he or she is speaking to a certain kind of person, hopefully one suited to the job.

We can speak of our selves as having *situated identities*. That is, the self a person projects is chosen or tailored to the situation in which he or she is participating. The self you try to project while sitting in class may be the "interested student," while the self you project at a job interview may be the "pragmatic problem solver."

In trying to understand how people present themselves to others in everyday life it is not important whether any situated identity is "true" of a person. What is important is that people, shifting from one aspect of the self to another, or even inventing a self for the situation at hand, attempt to shape others' impressions in the playing of roles. If the impression is successfully managed, from the point of view of the participants, the self presented is the truth. If the woman you meet at a party dresses and acts the part of a drama critic, then whether or not she is employed in such a job, she succeeds in being a drama critic, at least to you.

Goffman's dramaturgical model Some awareness of the self as a social object is, of course, essential for living among other people. It informs us whether or not we are making a good impression, whether or not we are effectively managing the impression of ourselves we wish to convey to others. Successful politicians seem to have a particular talent for using self-awareness to their personal advantage. So do Hollywood actors—they base their entire professional lives on a special ability to project an image and stage a character.

Erving Goffman (1959) suggests that in this respect we are not so different from Hollywood actors giving a stage presentation to an audience. For Goffman, everyday life is like a theatrical production. In this *dramaturgical model* he sees us as a team of performers who cooperate in managing the impression we seek to project to others.

Carrying through his model, Goffman talks about what goes on *backstage* where a routine is rehearsed and prepared, versus what happens in the *front* region, where a performance is given before an audience. This distinction seems to apply to numerous everyday situations in which the self is presented to strangers. For example, anyone who has ever worked in a restaurant will recognize that the kitchen is, in Goffman's terms, backstage, whereas the dining area is the front region where the "show" is presented to customers. Waiters who seek to define the situation as one of "careful and attentive service" may go out of their way to present themselves as "deferent," "alert," and "happy" while serving their customers in the dining room. In the kitchen, however, they more likely "let it all hang out" by mocking nasty patrons, complaining about their hangovers from last night's party, or voicing their desire to go to the beach for the day rather than wait on tables.

Goffman begins his analysis of the presentation of self in everyday life with the fact that strangers who meet for the first time—at parties, over lunch, on the street—need information about one another in order to continue their interaction comfortably. Obviously, individuals *give* information about themselves by what they say; but they also *give off* information by what they do—their dress, hairstyle, gestures, and expressions. Often, an individual will judge the validity of verbal information by whether it is consistent with nonverbal information given off by the same person. For example, does a new acquaintance smile appropriately when telling you how pleased she is to meet you? While a man tells you how interested he is in what you are saying, is he looking at you or over your shoulder to see what is going on elsewhere in the room?

By the information given and given off, an individual hopes to control the image of self being projected to others, to manage the impression of self that others will accept. For this purpose, Goffman argues, the appearance of competence is actually more important than competence itself. In a first-impression situation, an individual who hopes to be viewed as competent must appear to discharge the requirements of the role being played, whether or not he or she actually discharges those requirements.

Many first encounters in everyday life do seem to depend on individuals maintaining the appearance of competence. How many parents, for example, are qualified to evaluate the talents of the new pediatrician in town? What they are qualified to judge is his or her "bedside manner"—how quickly the doctor puts their child at ease, what sort of "personality" the doctor has, how caring the doctor looks, whether the doctor reminds them of some image they have of a caring physician.

Self-consciousness   In some instances, acute social awareness can be extremely uncomfortable, as in the case of people who are forced by circumstances to behave in a manner which is out of character with their self-concept. One reaction to such a situation is to feel anxious, experience lowered self-esteem, and attempt to escape the situation. Under such conditions, an individual might put on a silly smile, laugh nervously, or blush and stutter. He or she may feel foolish and ridiculous when exposed to public view. We call this condition *embarrassment*. It can occur only when an individual has an acute feeling of being observed, when there is an awareness of the self as a social object—in a word, when someone experiences self-consciousness (Buss 1980; Gross and Stone 1970).

To effectively stage a character, individuals must be careful not to provoke a disruptive incident—an incident which might end in an embarrassing scene. Depending upon the role being played, they must guard against improper clothing, slips of the tongue, clumsiness, and displays of excessive emotion in public. This requires *defensive* moves on the part of the performing team. For example, a dental hygienist might make sure she eats breakfast before going to work in the morning so that her stomach is less likely to "growl" while working on a patient. A salesman who works closely with people might gargle with mouthwash to avoid offending customers with "bad breath," or a waiter might be especially careful not to trip while carrying a tray of hot food over the heads of diners.

But defensive moves are not enough—the performer must also have reason to receive help from those he is seeking to impress. Members of the audience must engage in what Goffman calls *protective practices*, or tact—they must be committed to assisting the performer stage the character—to helping save face in a potentially embarrassing scene or restore face when an embarrassment cannot be avoided.

Goffman's view is a cooperative model of interaction. He argues that norms exist in everyday life, unwritten rules for interaction, according to which individuals are supposed to help one another give the appearance of competence. The norm does, indeed, seem to apply to many everyday situations. For example, a waiter carelessly spills water on a customer's dress. Rather than complain, however, the customer ignores the waiter's blunder, pretending instead that it had never happened. Or, a teacher stumbles over his feet at the blackboard. His students are tempted to laugh, but instead they bite their lips and continue to take notes as though nothing has happened.

Many people become embarrassed because they are made to feel conspicuous. In a violation of the norm, this can happen when others ridicule an individual's appearance, background, or behavior. But it can also happen in a more subtle fashion, as when someone is stared at by a member of the opposite sex—indeed, whenever you receive more than your normal share of attention from others. Thus, even being praised in public can create embarrassment (Buss 1980).

The norm of helping role performers save or restore face might actually be used to their advantage. In a recent study, Levin and Arluke (1982) had a confederate posing as a "research assistant" walk into different college classes and ask the students for help in completing her research project. The students in each class could help her by volunteering to answer a series of mail questionnaires on a specific topic.

In the first condition (no embarrassment), things went off without a hitch; the research assistant explained her purpose, asking for volunteers and then collecting the names and addresses of students who volunteered to help. In the second condition (embarrassment), the assistant entered the room and began her request for help, but was interrupted when she "accidentally" dropped five hundred sheets of paper on the floor. At this point she made mention of her nervousness, gathered up the papers and, though still obviously embarrassed, completed her plea for volunteers.

If Goffman is correct about the presence of a norm for helping, then the research assistant should have received more help from the class in which she was embarrassed by dropping all the papers than in the condition in which no embarrassment occurred. Indeed, this is precisely what happened: Students in the embarrassment condition were more likely to volunteer.

What happened in a third condition was a different story. The research assistant began talking to another class, dropped the 500 sheets of paper, but apparently overcome by anxiety, was unable to continue. Instead, the instructor made reference to the extreme nervousness of the research assistant and passed out the sign-up sheets himself.

In this third condition, almost nobody volunteered to help the research assistant with her study. Despite her extreme distress (or more accurately, because of it), students were unwilling to sign up. They apparently felt that she had violated their "social contract" by failing to complete her request for help. She was no longer defined as a competent role performer. As a result, they no longer felt obligated to help her restore face by volunteering. Is it possible that people only help those who appear to be helping themselves?

Stigma There is a special case of self-presentation that Goffman (1963) refers to as *stigma*—a condition which arises when there is some gap in a first impression between our assumptions about a person we meet and the actual characteristics that person possesses. For example, unless otherwise informed, we usually expect the people we meet to have two arms, have sight, and be free of severe scars or extensive birthmarks. We probably do not expect them to be prostitutes, mental patients, or ex-convicts, or to arrive in a wheelchair. And the same is true of peoples' role performances. We do not, for example, expect physicians to be forgetful and clumsy, nor for elementary school teachers to be foul-mouthed and slovenly in their appearance. In Goffman's view, individuals can be stigmatized on grounds including some physical disability or a presumed defect of moral character. In all such cases, the problem for the stigmatized person is the management of what Goffman calls *spoiled identity*.

Goffman identifies two kinds of stigmatized individuals. First, there is the *discredited* person, who has little, if any, control over the information given off concerning his stigma because it is physically visible to everyone, and the discredited person feels its direct effects. There is only one possibility open—try to manage the tension or anxiety generated by the presence of the stigma during social interaction with nonstigmatized individuals.

By contrast, the *discreditable* individual has the ability to manage not just the tension but also the information that others have about this stigma. Thus, the discreditable person may be concerned with passing, with managing potentially discrediting facts that have not yet been disclosed. Some may avoid other people who "know too much." The ex-convict, for example, might move to another town or state; a person born with a deformed hand might wear a glove around strangers. For the discreditable person, there are always decisions to make. Great psychic energy may be expended in determining those situations in which the stigma is concealed from others and those in which the individual can be "up front."

Labeling the self According to the approach called *labeling theory*, the imposition of stigma can have serious implications for the self-concept of the stigmatized individual. Having been labeled by the public or by various agents of social control (for example, by the courts and the police), he or she may have severely limited economic and occupational opportunities and limited associations with nonstigmatized members of society (Liska 1981). For example, the stigma of being defined by others as an ex-con often makes it more difficult for a person to find legitimate employment and to make friends among people who haven't been imprisoned. In many cases, the label itself is responsible for this series of events, which leads the ex-offender to return to a life of crime. Labeling theorists call this phenomenon *secondary deviance*, because it is a consequence of applying the label to an offender rather than a consequence of what the offender did to get stigmatized in the first place (Bourne and Levin 1983).

The self-concept of the recipients of a discredited stigma can be severely damaged by labeling. If others see them as "deviant" or "morally undesirable," the discredited individuals may come, through role-taking, to accept these judgments as accurate self-definitions (Liska 1981). Even a discreditable individual—one whose stigma has not yet been discovered by others—may suffer a loss of self-esteem. He may then label himself as "deviant" because of what he knows he has done wrong and may punish himself for it (Becker 1963; Goode 1984).

Both labeling by others and self-labeling can be seen in attitudes toward aging. There is in American society pervasive negative labeling and stigmatization of the elderly—indeed, they are frequently seen by younger people in stereotyped fashion as "helpless," "passive," and "sick"—in a word, as "senile." As a result, younger people often make fewer intellectual demands on elderly people who, in turn, lose self-esteem and come to believe in their own incompetence and inability to control their lives (Rodin and Langer 1980).

Looking Back

By this point it should be clear that the concept of self is basic to social psychology. In fact, it would be impossible to exaggerate its importance for understanding human behavior or for solving the human puzzle. Indeed, it would not be too much of an exaggeration to think of the self as related to social behavior the way the human body is related to physical behavior. Clearly, if we wish to understand how people move, work, write, exercise, or engage in countless physical activities, we begin with the study of the body. In order to understand how people behave with others, a critical point of reference is the self.

In this chapter, we examined the self as a reflection of how we think others see us. Overall, there is a good deal of evidence for the "looking-glass self" and for the larger view that the self develops in social interaction. At the same time, the self is also influenced by an individual's achievements and abilities. Moreover, because of the availability of objective measures of certain qualities and because communication is less than perfect, there is also room for the self to be more than just a reflection of the appraisals of others.

Common-sense explanations falsely assume that people "turn out"; that is, that after a given number of years, they are fully formed and will never change in any significant way. This view has been aided by the Freudian conception of personality, according to which most of socialization occurs during the first six years of life. Most social psychologists now argue instead that people never stop "turning out"; that the process may continue throughout life. In fact, if there is some underlying theme to this chapter, it is that the self is always in flux, or, at least, has the potential for change. True, people tend to prefer consistency across situations and time. But it is equally true that the self is flexible and responsive to changes in social relationships.

Chapter 3

Others

Her hair had been shoulder-length and straight, and her clothes conservative, slightly more formal than most of her high-school friends; she preferred to wear slacks rather than jeans. Then, one day, she was seen coming around the corner of her school accompanied by her new friends. Like them, she was wearing spiked jewelry, had a ring inserted in her nose, had dyed her hair a shocking purple, and was wearing a studded black-leather jacket. Her attitudes had also changed dramatically: she became cynical about the media, about politics, about her parents' middle-class lifestyle. After school, she spent hours listening to punk-rock music and reading magazines about the punk lifestyle. She was totally consumed by a desire to copy her idols, the punk-rock musicians whose style, dress, and behavior her parents found thoroughly crude, vulgar, and offensive.

A 9-year-old boy spent his after-school hours alone, shooting baskets in the driveway of his suburban middle-class home. Neighbors were not sure what to make of his behavior. After each and every basket, he threw his fist into the air, shouted to himself, and pranced around the driveway accepting the congratulations of invisible teammates. He referred to himself as Larry Bird and modestly recounted how he made the winning shot in the championship game.

A 19-year-old college student was thoroughly depressed by her grade of B+ on an English exam. Her well-intentioned friends tried to console her by pointing out that her grade was the highest in the class and that most of her classmates got Ds and Fs. It was all to no avail. She could not shake the thought that her parents would say, as they always had, that "nothing less than perfection is good enough." For her, anything lower than an A was absolute failure.

How are we to make sense of such behaviors? Why would a young girl change her style of dress and attitudes so suddenly and so completely? Is the young basketball "star" a bit nutty to make believe he is Larry Bird, or is this merely a childish fantasy? What about the college student who is so miserable about a grade with which most of her friends and classmates would be happy? What all three have in common is that their behavior is very much influenced by other people—other people like the girl's new friends, whose punk way of life provided a powerful model for conformity; other people like Larry Bird, who served as a sports idol for the 9-year-old's practice sessions in his driveway; other people like the parents of the college student, who carried to the campus not only clothes and books, but the standards of academic performance her parents had drilled into her from an early age.

Looking Ahead

In the last chapter, we discussed the importance of the "social group or organized community that gives people their unity or disunity of self," which G. H. Mead (1934) called the "generalized other." Mead's concept of the generalized other is extremely abstract, taking into account the broadest impact of the entire "language community" on our behavior, attitudes, and definition of self. This is, of course, an extremely general context within which people orient their social behavior. In this chapter, we focus on precisely how particular individuals and groups within this "language community" can influence our attitudes and behavior. In this regard, we will use the term *reference other* to mean any person or group of people, real or imagined, present or not, to which human beings orient themselves. We begin our examination where reference others are perhaps most visible and obvious: in the immediate situation. We focus our attention, first, on conformity to group pressure and, second, on obedience to legitimate authority. We ask: To what extent can "normal" individuals be expected to yield to group pressure or authority demand? We then expand our discussion to include the relationship between conformity, on the one hand, and culture and deviance, on the other. We ask: Just how pervasive is conformity in everyday life? And is conformity something always to be avoided? In the second major section of the chapter, we look beyond the immediate situation to locate reference others in groups to which an individual does and does not presently belong. This directs our attention to the role of retrospective and anticipatory socialization in everyday life. Next, we turn our attention to three major functions which reference others perform for the individual. We learn that the individuals and groups who serve as reference others may help to shape or reinforce our norms and values, provide information about social reality, or serve as a standard of comparison for judging our abilities, opinions, or achievements. Finally, we ask whether the idea of "reference other" is actually an oversocialized concept. Do individuals willingly comply with the demands of other people? Are there standards of comparison available to the individual that are not social? As individuals, are we mere replicas of the larger society in which we reside?

The Influence of Others Who Are Present: Conformity

Social psychologists who emphasize the impact of the immediate social situation on an individual have focused their attention on the concept of *conformity*—any change in behavior or belief as a result of real or imagined pressure from other people. From the situational perspective, conformity is primarily a matter of yielding to pressure, so that individuals act differently from the way they would act if they were alone (Kiesler and Kiesler 1969). For example, a shopper riding alone in the elevator of a large department store might stand on one leg, hum a popular tune under his breath, and play with the elevator buttons; but the same shopper riding in a crowded elevator would more likely stand perfectly still, face the elevator doors, and remain silent. If the difference in the behavior of our hypothetical elevator rider is actually a result of the presence of other passengers, then we can say that he has conformed.

Yielding to group pressure In 1936, Muzafer Sherif conducted a laboratory experiment to discover how group norms are developed.

This became a classic study of conformity as it occurs in an ambiguous situation. Specifically, Sherif's experiment took advantage of an optical illusion known as the *autokinetic phenomenon*: the fact that a stationary pinpoint of light will appear to move when viewed in an otherwise totally darkened room. (Try it yourself. Punch a tiny hole in one end of a shoebox and place a lighted flashlight in it aimed at the hole. Make sure the room is totally darkened, and you should see the dot of light moving when projected against a distant wall.)

To determine how they would act when alone, Sherif first asked his subjects individually to view the pinpoint of light and report its apparent direction and range of movement. (Don't forget, of course, that the light only seemed to move and was entirely stationary.) The first subject, for example, took a seat in a room completely without windows. The door was shut tightly and all lights turned off. A moment later, a tiny pinpoint of light appeared on the wall directly in front of the subject. After a few seconds, the light "moved" in erratic fashion and finally disappeared. The subject was then asked to estimate the distance traveled by the light. He offered "4 inches." All the other subjects were tested individually in the same way.

The day after the original experiment in which individual judgments were measured, the same subjects returned. This time, however, they were placed in groups of three or four where they viewed the light together. This allowed Sherif to measure the effects of conformity.

Sherif found that the estimates of how far the light had moved tended to cluster around an overall group judgment. For example, perhaps individual A had initially seen the light as moving 4 inches, whereas individual B had seen it moving 6 inches, and individual C had seen it moving 2 inches. But when they viewed the light together as a group, they came to a compromise agreement: all of them saw the light as traveling 4 or 5 inches!

Sherif's use of the autokinetic phenomenon created an ambiguous situation in which subjects were asked to form their judgments. The completely darkened room left no guidelines, no structure, no standards of comparison—except for those which could be found in the judgments made by other subjects. No wonder conformity prevailed.

Years later, Solomon Asch (1952) set out to address a different question concerning the circumstances for conformity. If asked to make a simple, clearcut, and obvious judgment, would subjects still yield to the pressure of other people? That is, would they still conform in an unambiguous situation?

In the first of his studies, Asch presented a set of eight individuals with three lines of different lengths. The subjects were then asked to match the length of a fourth line with one of these three comparison lines.

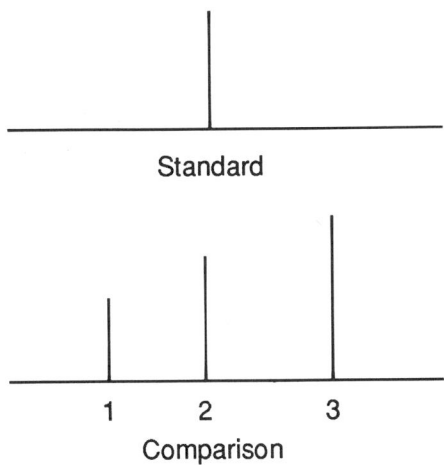

His specific instructions were as follows:

> This is a task which involves the discrimination of lengths of lines. You see the pair of white cards in front. On the left is a single line; on the right are three lines differing in length; they are numbered 1, 2, and 3 in order. One of the three lines at the right is equal to the standard line at the left—you will decide in each case which is the equal line. You will state your judgment in terms of the corresponding number. There will be 12 such comparisons. As the number of lines is few and the group small, I shall call upon each of you in turn to announce your judgment, which I shall record here on a prepared form. Please be as accurate as possible. Suppose we start at the right and proceed to the left.

All judgments were made out loud and in order of seating in the room. As you can see in the diagram of the original lines we have reproduced here, the correct answer is quite obvious. Asch was curious whether subjects would conform after others in the group gave blatantly incorrect answers. Would they actually abandon their own judgments about the relative lengths of the lines?

Actually only one participant in the Asch study was a naive subject; all of the others were really confederates of Asch who had been instructed beforehand to respond incorrectly when asked to match the length of the lines. The naive subject was seated second-to-last in the row, so that he or she always heard six of the "other subjects" give their inaccurate estimates before it was his or her turn. Over a number of trials with different groups, approximately one third of the naive subjects made incorrect estimates, conforming to the public, but inaccurate, judgments of the other group members. Almost all of these subjects had previously given correct estimates when they were tested alone—that is, without being subjected to the bogus estimates of the majority.

Asch was surprised that he had uncovered so much conformity among "reasonably intelligent and well-meaning" subjects who were "willing to call white black" in what should have been an obvious and simple judgment of fact. His follow-up interviews with the naive subjects who conformed by responding incorrectly were revealing. Some actually misperceived the length of the lines, or so they claimed. Others were able to identify the correct lines but doubted their own judgment ("How could I possibly be right? They must know something that I don't"). Many of his subjects, however, neither misperceived the lines nor doubted the evidence of their own judgment; instead, they conformed in order to avoid appearing different from the other group members, and admitted as much.

The results of a recent replication of the "Asch effect" suggest that many of the subjects may have been lying. In fact, when their responses were highly public and therefore subject to the scrutiny of others, 4 to 5 times as many subjects engaged in "conscious falsification of perception" than experienced "genuine perceptual change" (Jennings and George, 1984). Many people conform because they are in doubt as to what is correct and seek information from others; but many others conform simply to be accepted by other members of their group (Deutsch and Gerard, 1955).

Just how many reference others must be in the majority to achieve the greatest degree of conformity? As the number of people in the majority increases, do we get corresponding increases in conformity? Asch's (1952) original research reports that a majority of either 8 or 16 persons does not produce more conformity than a majority of only 4. This figure may be slightly low, as indicated by more recent studies which suggest that maximum conformity requires a majority of 6 people (Gerard et al. 1968; Valenti and Downing 1975). Whatever the optimum size of the majority for the production of conformity, however, it is clear that large numbers of people are not necessary, and may in fact reduce conformity responses (Stang 1976).

You can imagine that after hearing six statements that differ from your belief, you might find it very difficult to say what you wanted to say. But what if just one of those six had said what you were thinking? What happens when group unanimity is broken by a lone dissenter? In a variation of his original experiment, Asch (1952) found that the rate of conformity dropped dramatically from 32 percent when there was a unanimous majority to less than 6 percent when a lone dissenter gave support to the naive subject. Apparently, conformity can be produced by a very few people and reduced by even fewer.

Yielding to legitimate authority So far, we have focused on the way an individual's judgment can be affected by pressure exerted by a number of reference others in a situation. Beginning in 1963, Stanley Milgram conducted a series of studies in which he looked at a different aspect of conformity. He was interested in the influence that can be exerted by a single person—specifically, someone in a position of authority—on the behavior, rather than the attitudes, of an experimental subject. So Milgram's studies differ from those of Asch and Sherif in at least two ways: first, he studied conformity to individual rather than group pressure and, second, he used a behavioral measure of compliance.

Indeed, Milgram's behavioral measure was both dramatic and powerful. He wished to discover whether volunteer subjects could be induced to administer severe electric shocks to total strangers merely because an authority figure ordered them to do so. Here's how the original study was conducted.

Milgram took an advertisement in a New Haven, Connecticut newspaper offering four dollars to volunteers to participate in a one-hour "study of memory." In each experimental session, there were three participants: (1)

the experimenter, dressed in long white lab coat, holding a clipboard and presenting an imposing image of authority; (2) the subject, the person who responded to the ad who was always given the role of "teacher" and was instructed to administer a shock to a "learner" for every incorrect response he gave in answer to a quiz; and (3) a "learner," played by a confederate of the experimenter, who intentionally gave wrong answers to the quiz and pretended to suffer from the electric shocks. Naturally, no shocks were really administered by the "teacher," but Milgram went to great lengths to convince subjects that they were actually giving shocks to the "learner."

The "teacher" was seated at an elaborate electronic console featuring a panel of thirty switches labeled with increasing levels of voltage from 15 volts at the low end to 450 volts (ominously labeled XXX) at the high end. To make the equipment believable, the "teacher" was given a sample 45 volt shock, the only real connection on the board.

For every incorrect answer that the "learner" gave, the "teacher" was told to punish the "learner" with a shock, proceeding from the lightest to the most severe with every wrong response. Seated in an adjoining room, the learner responded over a microphone to the shocks he was supposedly receiving according to a script. For example, at 120 volts, he yelled about the pain and groaned; at 150 volts, he demanded to be released from the experiment; and, beyond 330 volts, he stopped responding altogether as though he had passed out or died. Throughout the study, the experimenter who served as the authority figure prodded the "teacher" with commands such as "It is absolutely essential that you continue" and "You have no choice. You must go on." Nothing else was used to induce "teachers" to administer the shocks.

Imagine how you would react to the authority of the experimenter. Would you punish a total stranger with electric shocks for incorrect answers to a quiz merely because an authority figure in a lab coat urged you to do so? If you think you might, how severe a shock do you think you might administer before you defied the authority figure by refusing to go on? When Milgram asked a group of subjects just like those who had served as "teachers" what they might do, they overwhelmingly predicted that they would not administer shocks at all. Even a panel of psychiatrists made the same prediction.

If you are like us, the results of Milgram's study might astound you. In the version of the experiment we described, over 60 percent of the "teachers" continued shocking the "learners" right to the very end of the scale—the end marked XXX at 450 volts. Just in case you think this result occurred because the "teachers" thought the "learner" wasn't actually harmed, you should know that Milgram ran the experiment another time with the learner screaming through his microphone (at 195 volts) that he had a heart condition and that it was hurting him. In spite of this added factor, over 60 percent of the subjects continued to obey the authority of the experimenter at all times, punishing the "learner" for incorrect responses right to the end of the voltage scale. Even when the "learner" was brought right into the room with the "teacher"—in fact, seated right next to and touching the "teacher"—30 percent of the "teachers" administered maximum shocks.

▶ Perspective:
The Effect of the Immediate Situation

Conformity outside the lab   Could it be that Milgram's study is merely a lab experiment that has no application to real life? Many people may think that conformity as extreme as this could only be produced in a controlled laboratory setting. Unfortunately, they are wrong!

A tragic example was the Jonestown, Guyana, massacre—the mass suicide and murder of 913 people. On November 19, 1978, men, women and children—all members of the People's Temple—lined up to sip a fatal dose of cyanide-laced Kool Aid. Most were dead in five minutes.

To account for the murder/suicide of so many people, we must refer back to the principle illustrated by Milgram's study of obedience to authority. The Temple's 47-year-old, self-styled dictator, Jim Jones, exerted absolute control over the daily activities of his followers. His authority was greatly enhanced by the fact that Jonestown was a social environment located literally in the middle of nowhere, cut off from family and friends, and totally isolated from outside reality. The one and only "reality" for the followers of Jim Jones was the power of Jones himself, whose charismatic sermons and rantings against the evil of the outside world were the tools with which he fashioned total compliance.

The real-life situation with which Milgram was originally concerned was the obedience to the authority of Adolph Hitler and the rise of Nazism in the 1930s and 1940s. The world tried to make sense of the horrors of the death camps by arguing that the Nazis had been "madmen" who actually enjoyed destroying life and causing pain. Yet the results of Milgram's studies provide an alternative explanation. Like the "teachers" who were willing to administer shocks merely because an authority figure told them to do so, many Germans acceded to the demands of the Nazi regime.

Even the Nazis themselves yielded to pressure from other people. According to Dicks (1972), the process whereby they were socialized to kill extended over a long period of time, facilitated by strong and continuing group pressure and indoctrination. The constant marches and uniformed processions, the all-day group singing of the Party's anthem, and the required cheering—all of these conspired to enhance the group bond. The Nazis were finally conditioned to believe that no "right-thinking German patriot" could stand to deviate from their doctrine. ■

Conformity and culture It is important to recognize that conformity does not always, or even typically, result in the disastrous behavior such as that of Nazis or followers of Jim Jones. In fact, we depend upon conformity to the culture—the norms and values—of a group for the stability of everyday life, and indeed would be completely lost without it. Think, for example, of how dangerous it would be to drive a car if you couldn't count on others to conform to the rules of the road such as driving on the correct side of the street and stopping at stop signs. What if people failed to conform to moral norms such as the prohibition against murder? In the absence of conformity to culture, society as we know it would disappear, and we would be left with "the war of all against all."

More benign evidence of the existence of conformity in everyday life is found in the way that people dress. Many fads and fashions represent nothing more than compliance with widespread standards for how people should look. They can be very short-lived, as in skirt length (minis, maxis, and everything in between), or hair styles (crew cuts, Beatle style, punk, and ponytails), or more long-lasting, as in wearing a suit and tie to a formal occasion or wearing a long dress to get married (Davis, 1984).

Teenagers are especially sensitive to changes in fads and fashions which might impress their peers. Conformity usually means acceptance by others, whether shown by owning the "right" stereo equipment and listening to the "right" music or by having the "right" haircut and wearing the "right" clothing.

Teenage conformity has been strong for at least the last 65 years (Anastos 1983). In the 1920s, teenagers everywhere consumed crossword puzzles, yo-yos, roller skates, and Hi-Li. They competed in round-the-clock dance marathons, flagpole sitting, and gum-chewing contests. By the late 1930s, attention had shifted to the latest craze: goldfish swallowing. At St. Mary's University, a college sophomore set a record by eating some 210. Some students graduated to eating phonograph records! In the '50s, college students tried to stuff themselves into anything from Volkswagen Beetles to phone booths. Panty raids invaded the college campuses and Hula Hoops became a national form of exercise. Fads of the '60s included Frisbees, skateboards, psychedelic T-shirts, and posters. In 1974, young people (and later some older people too) took off their clothing to "streak" through police stations, libraries, football stadiums, and parties. One particularly enterprising streaker made his television debut by streaking across the stage during the televised presentation of the Academy Awards. Many teen fads of the 1980s are a reflection of the new electronic era: portable headset stereos, digital clocks and watches, video games, MTV, and personal computers. What will be next? The only thing we know for sure is that new fads are just around the corner. By the time this book is published, we could be swallowing goldfish again.

Obviously, people conform in different ways in different cultures, and the styles of conformity change over time. It is less obvious, however, that the degree of conformity itself varies within and between cultures. When Asch's conformity experiments were replicated in other countries, a number were found to have rates of conformity similar to the 32 percent originally reported for Americans (e.g., 31 percent in Lebanon, 34 percent in Brazil, and 32 percent in Hong Kong). By contrast, among the Rhodesian Bantu, whose culture emphasizes conformity and severely punishes deviant behavior, the conformity rate was a whopping 51 percent (Whittaker and Meade 1967). More recently, replications of the Asch procedure have discovered lower rates of conformity in both the United States and Britain than the 32 percent reported decades earlier (Larsen 1974; Perrin and Spencer 1980).

Even within a culture, there are variations in the ways different groups conform. One such issue that has really fascinated social psychologists has been gender differences. Given the traditional distinction between role definitions for men and women in our society, it is easy to understand why researchers, just like the rest of us, would expect females to conform more readily than males. Milgram (1974) certainly thought so when he repeated his original studies in obedience, this time using females as the "teachers." Surprisingly, he found that females were no more compliant than males in administering electric shocks.

Milgram's results are not out of line with other research. Recent reviews of the literature of social psychology find little evidence to support the contention that women conform more readily than men (Eagly 1978; Cooper 1979). In fact, Eagly and Carli (1981), in comparing male-female conformity rates, describe the gender difference as "barely visible to the naked eye."

Does this mean that men and women always conform to the same extent? Not necessarily. In fact, a recent study by Pugh and Wahrman (1983) suggests that it very much depends on the specifics of a situation. The researchers asked subjects who worked in pairs to make judgments about an ambiguous stimulus. Specifically, they had to decide whether a triangle had more black or white area (actually, the triangle in question had exactly equal areas of black and white). After making their initial decisions, subjects were told that their partner's decisions had differed from theirs, and that they had the opportunity at that point to change their minds. Conformity was indicated when a subject yielded to the judgment of the partner.

There were three conditions for matching partners by gender: both male, both female, and mixed. In the same-gender pairings, women were no more likely to conform to the decisions of their female partner than men were to conform to the dicisions of their male partner. In mixed-gender pairings, however, women deferred to men more often than men deferred to women. Apparently, then, men and women do not differ in susceptibility to pressure from other people at all times and in all situations. Sex-role expectations are relational: we are taught that women ought to defer, but only because men are thought to be more competent. The recency of these findings suggests that sexism is still very much with us.

Conformity in disguise The influence of pressure from reference others on our behavior and attitudes may be even greater than we know or, at least, are willing to acknowledge. Much of conformity may take "disguised" forms; what passes for independence or individuality may instead be a subtle or unexpected result of another person. We might, for example, meet a student whose dress and appearance are so much at odds with conventional campus fashion that we are convinced he is totally oblivious to what his fellow students expect him to wear. We conclude: "Here is a student who couldn't care less about what others think or demand. His long hair, beard, and hippie attire are at least ten years behind the times. Maybe someone should wake him up and tell him this is the 1980s."

Actually, our bearded, long-haired student may be very much influenced by social pressure, though not in a way that we expect from many college students. After getting to know him, we might indeed discover that he is acutely aware of "proper" dress on his college campus. He knows, for example, that short hair is in style and that the long-haired, bearded look is regarded as old-fashioned. In fact, this is the very reason for his choice of dress and appearance. He senses what is expected and does just the opposite: In short, though we may call him a rebel, he is actually showing another face of conformity; that is, *anticonformity*.

Many people value their sense of freedom and autonomy. They despise extreme forms of social pressure and prefer to project a confident and effective self-image (Baer et al 1980). When coerced to "go along with the crowd" so that their sense of freedom is threatened, they may react by going in the opposite direction—on some campuses, long hair, beards, and sixties' clothing may be a result.

Reactance theory predicts that people will indeed act to protect their sense of independence when they feel their personal freedom being restricted (Brehm and Brehm 1981). The rebellious response can take the form of a "boomerang effect" (Gamson, Fireman, and Rytina 1982).

Even those people who want to conform to the demands of reference others may not be able to do so. Beginning with Stryker (1956), we have known that individuals differ with respect to their role-taking accuracy.

Some are adept at picking up the cues from their interactions with others and correctly understand what is expected of them in particular social situations. Others, however, lack social sensitivity: try as they might, they are simply unaware of what other people think are the correct rules for social behavior.

At the extreme, psychologists talk about the *idiosyncratic personality* whose lack of role-taking skills makes him or her a constant social embarrassment. Everyone seems to have been in a situation with a person like this, although it isn't always obvious at first. You begin to get the idea when he continues shaking your hand long beyond the point you are accustomed to letting go; he laughs much too loudly at a joke that deserves only a smile; he stands so closely that you feel like backing away; and, despite all your hints that you are in a hurry to leave, he fails to withdraw gracefully from the conversation as you expect anyone else would.

You might think that, like the rebel, the idiosyncratic personality is beyond the rules of conformity. Once again, however, conformity is operating in an invisible way. Like most of us, he wants to conform to what is expected of him and thereby gain the acceptance of others; however, he simply doesn't know how.

It is not always clear where an idiosyncratic personality got his strange set of rules for social behavior. From the point of view of more socially skilled individuals, he or she seems to be "marching to the beat of a different drummer." When you think about the behavior of the anticonformist and the socially inept individual, you can see why social psychologists may be compelled to look beyond the immediate social situation for the reference others who are influencing behavior.

For example, in Sherif's (1936) studies using the autokinetic phenomenon, he illustrated how individuals yield to pressures in the immediate social situation. You might think that once a research subject left the experimental situation, the group judgment as to the movement of the light would no longer have much effect. Over time, you might expect it to disappear entirely. To find out, Sherif retested the same subjects a year later, only this time individually rather than in groups. Surprisingly, his subjects' judgments about the movement of the dot of light continued to conform to the group norm established a year earlier. Sherif's original experimental group continued to serve as reference others even though they were no longer in the immediate situation and much time had passed.

Conformity and deviance Behavior that violates norms is called *deviance*. At first glance, it might appear that conformity and deviance are diametrically opposed to one another: you either confrom or you deviate; you either obey the rules of society or you don't...or so it might seem. In the field of abnormal psychology, this point of view is reflected in the concept of the sociopathic or antisocial personality—a character disorder in which an individual is considered undersocialized and therefore feels little or no guilt (Levin and Fox 1985).

By contrast, sociologists argue that deviance can and often does arise out of socialization itself—in the acceptance of deviant norms and values. Based on this view, Sutherland (1924) long ago proposed a social learning approach to the study of juvenile delinquency which he called *differential association* theory. According to Sutherland, how we behave depends on how our intimate associates or friends want us to behave. Therefore, boys become delinquents when their attachments are to others who engage in and approve of violating the law. Through differential association, delinquents learn both the specific techniques and the general norms for committing crime. They come to depend on their delinquent friends for the rewards—attention and respect—they were not able to secure elsewhere (Burgess and Akers 1966).

In some cases, differential association may lead to the emergence of a *counterculture*—a group whose members totally reject the important values of the dominant society and attempt to develop an alternative set of values by which to guide their lives. Such countercultures have included the hippies and political radicals of the '60s as well as the punks of the '80s.

From the point of view of middle-class conventional Americans, members of countercultures engage in deviant behavior which may threaten the very existence of a "mainstream" way of life. Although this may be true, the members of the counterculture also conform. For example, hippies of the '60s could often be identified by their long hair, bell-bottom jeans, and love beads. Punks similarly can frequently be identified by their mohawks, spiked jewelry, and paramilitary clothing. Members of youth countercultures such as hippies and punks also express a shared system of values emphasizing expressive activities such as art and music and a preference for living in the present (Levin and Spates 1970; Lamy and Levin 1986).

The Influence of Others Who Are Absent: "Different Drummers"

To this point, we have focused our attention on the influence of reference others in the immediate situation, whether group members or representatives of legitimate authority. But social psychologists who emphasize a sociocultural perspective often look beyond the immediate situation for their understanding of conformity. From this point of view, an individual is never really "alone." The 9-year-old boy who was shooting baskets in his driveway was physically by himself, but socially accompanied by his reference idol, Larry Bird. The 19-year-old college student was also accompanied by others, in this case, her parents in the form of impossibly high standards for academic performance.

This is, of course, far from unusual; indeed, even the sanest of us may be influenced by people who aren't in the immediate situation—people we admire, fantasize about, or despise. On occasion, all of us "march to the beat of a different drummer." That "drummer" may be next door or thousands of miles away, real or imaginary, admired or dreaded, dead or alive, existing in places we wish we could be or have left.

Clearly, then, reference others may be located in any group to which individuals orient themselves, whether or not they are members of it (Hyman 1942). This gives the concept of reference other its special usefulness. After all, there are many concepts in social psychology (including, as you have already seen in this chapter, conformity) which tell us that we are influenced by other people in the immediate situation; but the concept of reference other also emphasizes that we can be very much influenced by others, even when they aren't anywhere around. They may be in groups we used to belong to, groups to which we want to belong at some future time, or even groups which exist only in our imaginations. In other words, our membership groups need not contain our reference others. This idea is very much a part of the distinction between retrospective and anticipatory socialization.

Influences from the past: Retrospective socialization
What social psychologists call *retrospective socialization* occurs when a person's behavior or attitude is affected by a group to which he or she used to belong but no longer does. Earlier in the chapter, you saw that a full year after subjects had conformed to group judgments in Sherif's original study, they continued as individuals to use the group norm. Since the group influencing their judgments was no longer present, we can say that retrospective socialization was operating.

People move around so much nowadays that it is easy to find examples of retrospective socialization as they go from home to home or job to job. One of our students, for example, told a story in class about her experiences when she was 10-years-old and her family moved from Chicago to Phoenix, Arizona. She had a terrible time adjusting to the change. She said she refused to make new friends, although there were many children her age on the new block. She spent entire days in her room sulking and, in her best moments, pretended that her old friends were still with her for company. She even dressed the way she had.

The way she tells it, this might have gone on even longer had her parents not gotten a phone bill of almost $200 for the many long-distance calls she had made to her old friends. She was experiencing retrospective socialization with a vengeance.

Her parents, meanwhile, were also experiencing their version of retrospective socialization. The move to Phoenix had been to much higher paying jobs for both of them. Although their standard of living had increased greatly, they continued to live extremely modestly. They maintained their former habits of dress, entertainment, voting, and budgeting, even hiding their new wealth from their Chicago friends. Old habits die hard—especially when they are supported by old reference others that continue to be appealing.

Plans for the future: anticipatory socialization Not all our behavior is oriented to the past, of course. Many of us act like the people we hope someday to become—like the reference others we aspire to join. Social psychologists call this phenomenon *anticipatory socialization*, because an individual's behavior or attitude is influenced by the group he or she anticipates joining at some future date. The group we aspire to join sometimes has a greater effect than any group in which we presently hold membership.

O'Kane, Barenblatt, Jensen, and Cochran (1977) report, for example, that the attitudes of the working- and middle-class adolescents they studied were explained more by their class of destination (the social class they would likely join as adults) than their class of origin (the social class into which they were born; their family's social class).

In a similar way, we hear repeatedly from our students that once they were accepted to colleges during their senior year of high school, they began anticipating what it would be like to be college freshmen. Many remember buying sweatshirts with the name of the college they were going to attend. One male student admitted he learned (with some discomfort) how to smoke a pipe, because that was part of his image of a real college student.

Undoubtedly, many high-school seniors who expect to go to college do start behaving as though they were already college freshmen. Some may begin to dress differently or to hang around with a different set of friends; others may study harder or try the drugs they think college students use.

As indicated in Chapter 2, medical students also anticipate their social futures. Indeed, an important part of medical training includes anticipatory socialization: The medical students learn that they have to cut corners in order to meet the demands of their schedule and that their original idealistic motivations to enter medicine have to be tempered to the realities of their profession. In everyday practice, these medical students come to expect to be called "doctor" long before they actually have their diplomas (Becker et al. 1961).

The Functions of Reference Others

Both membership and nonmembership groups may influence our lives in any number of ways. In the socialization process, their members provide us with norms for behavior, information about the world, and the ability to evaluate our performances and beliefs. That is, in the language of social psychology, reference others serve normative, information, and self-evaluation functions.

The normative function   Many reference others serve a *normative function* (Kelley 1968; Shibutani 1972). As a source of norms and values, they tell us what is right and proper and what is wrong and improper: whether to eat with chopsticks or fork and knife; how to comb our hair; what political ideas to adopt; where to go on a date; when to study; whether or not to wear pleated pants; and so on. According to Felson and Reed (1986), this normative function even produces shared expectations about how favorably the people in a group should evaluate themselves. If they appraise themselves at a level too much above or below their reference others, they may violate an important group norm.

In his classic study of American social character, David Riesman (1950) showed that the selection of normative reference others differs between those people he called "inner-directed" and those people he called "other-directed." For the *inner-directed* type, the family is an important source of norms and values throughout life. As a young child, the inner-directed person learns appropriate and inappropriate behavior—what is morally and socially right and wrong—because his parents teach him. Even as an adult, he possesses an internal sense of what is right, proper, and moral. He continues to behave in accordance with what his parents have taught him, regardless of the expectations of individuals he happens to be with at a particular time, whether on the job, at home, or at play.

The Hollywood version of inner-directedness is provided by Clint Eastwood's portrayal of Dirty Harry, the big-city cop who refuses to bow to underworld pressure, refuses to kowtow to his boss, refuses to play political games, refuses to obey the rules, refuses to follow either the letter or the spirit of the law—so long as it interferes with his deeply internalized goal of apprehending a criminal. He urges a slimy holdup man to "Go ahead and make my day," drawing his gun and waiting for an excuse to blow the "creep" to smithereens. He applies twenty karate chops and a kidney punch to another suspect who refuses to reveal the identity of an accomplice. He places a cocked, loaded Magnum revolver to the forehead of his archenemy. This is inner-directedness par excellence, because the character Eastwood plays knows with unshakable certainty what is "right" for him to do.

Riesman contends that we once were a nation of inner-directed people. But that all changed by the mid-20th century, as everyday life became more and more bureaucratized and "getting along with other people" became a major concern. Americans everywhere shifted their reference others away from family and toward contemporaries. In Riesman's words, we became *other-directed*, operating out of a need to be approved and accepted by our peers, friends, coworkers, classmates, roommates, or dates. A fixed, rigid sense of morality would no longer do. Instead, other-directed individuals became flexible in terms of what they believed was right and wrong—moral behavior was determined more by what peers expected than by what parents taught during the first few years of life.

In our view, the most compelling recent illustration of other-directedness is Woody Allen's fictional film character Zelig. This "human chameleon" was purported to have changed his attitudes and even physical appearance to match those of the people with whom he was interacting. Using sophisticated cinematic special effects, Allen actually showed Zelig's transformations: When he was with a black man, his skin darkened. When he was with a rabbi, he suddenly grew a beard and discussed religious issues. And when he was with an Asian, his eyes changed shape and his hair straightened and darkened. Zelig's psychiatrist in the film (played by Mia Farrow) determined that he had an overppowering need to be liked, which led him to do whatever was necessary to fulfill the expectations of others. Zelig's extraordinary skill at other-directedness made Allen's film a metaphor for the times—a period in history during which Riesman claimed we became other-directed as a culture.

Believe it or not, many college students are permanently effected by their years at college. As social psychologist Theodore Newcomb (1943/1967) pointed out many years ago, the college campus can be an important source of norms and values which continue to influence how a student thinks and behaves long after he or she has graduated.*

---

*Like some other social psychologists, Newcomb used the term *reference group* to describe the influence of others (Hyman 1942; Sherif and Sherif 1969; Shibutani 1972; Merton 1957a; Hyman and Singer 1968; Singer 1981). In fact, a variety of terms have been emloyed for the same or slightly different purpose. These include "reference relationship" (Rose 1962), "comparison-other" (Festinger 1954), and "reference idol" (Hyman 1960). In his exhaustive review of the use and history of these terms, Schmitt (1972) strongly suggested the use of the inclusive term "reference other." For consistency's sake, we will continue to use this term to refer to the effects of both groups and individuals.

Between the years of 1935 and 1939, Newcomb conducted a detailed study of all the students at Bennington College; which, at that time, was a small women's school in Bennington, Vermont. he quickly learned that many of the students at Bennington became more and more liberal as they went through their four years of school. On the average, even those seniors who had grown up in wealthy, conservative homes were much less conservative about public issues of the day than they had been as freshmen. At Bennington, students whose attitudes were nonconservative also had the respect of their fellow students and participated extensively in college activities. They were the students who had "school spirit."

Of course, not all of the women at Bennington were liberalized by going to college. In fact, some of them remained staunchly conservative throughout their four years. These students tended to be the relatively few "malcontents" on campus—the ones who were least popular with their classmates and who usually stayed away from college activities. They didn't have much "school spirit."

More than 20 years later, Newcomb again interviewed most of the former students he had originally studied at Bennington. They were now middle-aged women who typically had become at least "fairly well-to-do" members of their communities. For example, many could afford to send their children to private schools. Most enjoyed a relatively high standard of living. Considering only how much money they had accumulated, we might expect these Bennington alumnae to take a pretty conservative political position. Instead, they maintained the same liberal point of view about public issues that they had acquired during their undergraduate days some 20 years earlier. Few of them had reverted to their conservative backgrounds.

How in the world had these women managed to maintain their recently acquired liberalism upon leaving Bennington? After college, had they chosen to associate only with people who supported their nonconservative stance? Newcomb thinks that this is exactly what had happened. In fact, he found that many of his Bennington alumnae had selected husbands, friends, and associates who shared and encouraged their liberalism. Wouldn't you have an easier time maintaining your beliefs about, for instance, having children, the value of religion, or voting for a particular candidate, if all of your friends believed the same way?

Newcomb's Bennington study says at least two important things about reference others: first, that the individuals in groups to which a person actually belongs—his or her membership groups—are not always used as reference others. For many of Bennington's conservative seniors—those who hadn't been shaken from their conservative point of view—the liberal students and teachers around them failed to have much, if any, impact on their attitudes. Instead, it was the conservative perspective of their families that continued to make a difference, even if they no longer lived with their parents or had much contact with them beyond an occasional visit or letter.

The second thing that Newcomb's study tells us is that we may be very much influenced by a group, even though it is not a positive point of reference. In fact, we may even behave in such a way as to avoid being associated with its members. Hence, the influence of *negative reference others*. For example, have you ever known people who are so vile or repulsive that you go out of your way to be different from them? Have you ever felt embarrassed to learn that a group of people you consider to be "dumb" or "backward" share your opinions about a certain issue? Have you ever found yourself "rebelling" against a group by taking a position at odds with theirs?

For some of Bennington's more liberal students, the people on their campus were an important positive point of reference. These students tried hard to be liked by fellow students and faculty members, and were proud to be part of the Bennington College community. At the same time, many of them were also oriented to home and family, but only in the most negative sense. Some actively rebelled against their parents' ultraconservative politics and adopted a more liberal position in opposition to what they were taught to believe at home. (Shades of reactance theory!) Just the opposite was true of those students who maintained a conservative posture. For them, home and family—and not their "misguided" and "ill-informed" fellow students or instructors on campus—remained a positive point of reference.

Newcomb's research suggests that reference others help people to define themselves by providing them with norms and values which may be accepted or rejected. At Bennington, political attitudes were influenced by family, academic community, or both.

An alternative view of the way normative reference others operate is found in Goffman's (1959) work on the presentation of self in everyday life. As we saw in Chapter 2, he regards much of everyday interaction as an elaborate ritual of self-presentation—a theatrical stage on which the actors play their roles so as to project an appropriate image of themselves to the members of an audience. Could certain individuals make use of reference others purely for reasons of self-portrayal rather than self-definition?

This is precisely the question that Carver and Humphries (1981) had in mind in their study of Cuban Americans' attitudes toward relations between Cuba and the United States. The researchers reasoned that the Castro regime in Cuba represents an important negative point of reference for Cuban Americans in the United States, the vast majority of whom had fled from Cuba after the Communist Revolution in 1959. Many had left their homeland with little more than the clothing on their backs, abandoning lifestyles that had been both comfortable and secure. To them, the Castro government is an army of occupation which will someday be overthrown. Among Cuban Americans, therefore, there is a general desire to identify themselves as being opposed to the political leadership in Cuba.

Carver and Humphries tested this reasoning by asking Cuban American students for their opinions on issues concerning the relaxation of hostility between Havana and Washington (for example, ending the economic blockade against trade with Cuba and reestablishing diplomatic relations). Subjects were randomly assigned to either the reference-other or the no-reference-other condition. In both situations, subjects were asked to respond to a questionnaire containing items about Cuban–U.S. relations. But only in the reference-other condition did subjects read statements attributed to an official of the government in Havana before they were given the opinion questionnaire. Concerning the economic blockade, for example, subjects read: "We in the Ministry of economics of the Republic of Cuba announce our commitment to ending the so-called 'economic blockade' of Cuba by other countries in the Western hemisphere. People in other countries, such as the United States, can only benefit from reopening trade with our country. As Castro himself has pointed out, we will provide them with an important new market for their products, as we can also supply them with materials they have been lacking since the blockade began."

As expected, subjects in the reference-other condition were more opposed than subjects in the no-reference-other condition to the relaxation of hostility between Cuba and the United States. That is, subjects' opinions were more opposed to such liberalization when a representative of the Cuban government was quoted as favoring it than when no quote was presented.

Having demonstrated that the Castro government indeed represented a negative reference other, Carver and Humphries next turned their attention to the distinction between self-definition and self-presentation. In a second experiment, subjects again gave their opinions after reading the favorable opinions of members of the Castro regime. This time, the experimenters also tapped their subjects' level of private and public self-consciousness by means of a paper-and-pencil measure called the Self-Consciousness Scale (Fenigstein, Scheier, and Buss 1975).

People who are high in *private* self-consciousness are especially aware of their own feelings and beliefs. They are said to be "in touch" with their most private and personal concerns. By contrast, people who are high in *public* self-consciousness are extremely aware of the social "other-directed" aspects of the self. That is, they are concerned with what Goffman emphasized about everyday interaction—the impression they are making on other people.

Carver and Humphries found that opposition to relaxing hostility between Cuba and the United States was correlated with public but not private self-consciousness. In other words, subjects who were high in public self-consciousness—who were very concerned about making a good impression on others—were also especially influenced by the statement they read by an official of the Castro government. This was not true of subjects who were high in private self-consciousness—those who were aware of their private feelings and beliefs.

According to Carver and Humphries, this finding indicates that their Cuban American subjects used their opposition to the negative reference other for self-portrayal rather than self-definitional purposes. By rejecting the opinions of Castro's regime, they tried to establish a favorable impression of themselves in the eyes of their peers. Their opposition to the Cuban leadership was meant to tell other Cuban Americans that they identified with the mainstream of the exiled community in the United States.

The information function So far, we have looked at how reference others serve as a source of norms and values. But a second important function must be considered as well. Reference others give us basic data about reality. In the words of Shibutani (1972), they provide us with a "perspective."

▶ Perspective:
The Effect of Social Definition

Second-hand experience Much of what we think we know about the world is based on second-hand information. Take, for example, our understanding of what the People's Republic of China is like. Before the mid-1960s, China was almost entirely unknown to Americans. We come from different parts of the country (Bill from New York and Jack from Texas); but growing up we had the same narrow reference source for information about China. We had both read Pearl Buck's *The Good Earth*, and that was all we had. Along with the rest of America, our first direct look inside the Great Wall was through the network television cameras that accompanied President Richard Nixon on his historic trip there. Our reference source had changed. We saw architecture unlike anything in our country, citizens sweeping snow from the sidewalks in the predawn hours, and ping-pong tournaments in which it apparently did not matter who won! From that point, our selection of reference sources for learning about the People's Republic has expanded tremendously.

Though most Americans still have never been to China, they now have a definite idea about what life in China is like. We can now choose from among a variety of documentaries about Chinese society; we may read about China in novels, newspapers, and popular magazines; or we may even talk with people who have visited China or with Chinese people in the United States. ■

Many people come to see the world, including China, through the eyes of a group. This is the information function that reference others serve: the perspective of a group becomes the perspective of the individual. So, for example, if a group of people defines everyday life as violent and dangerous, then the individual will see everyday life as mean and threatening. If a group of people defines our society as one in which poverty has been totally eliminated, then the individual will believe that poverty no longer exists.

For most of us, our very first informational reference others consist of our family, especially our parents. At least initially, we uncritically accept their world view. As young children, what alternative do we have?

But since the 1950s, another source of data about the world has rivaled, and perhaps even surpassed, the importance of the family as a way that children learn about the world. After all, we have for decades been a "boob-tube" society addicted to television. By the mid-1960s, 93 percent of all American families already owned at least one television set. And by 1972, the majority of American families had a color set.

American families watch plenty of TV—more than 6½ hours daily. And much of what they watch is violent to an extreme: George Gerbner (1980) reports that incidents that hurt, kill, or threaten to injure human or humanlike beings occur in more than ⅔ of all prime-time programs and in 9 out of 10 weekend morning programs. In television dramatic series, 63 percent of all major characters engage in some type of violent conduct. The exciting climax seems inevitably to involve a bloody fight scene in which "our hero" pulverizes this week's version of the enemy of justice and humanity. Tonight, it might be members of the A-team; tomorrow Crockett, Spencer, or Magnum P.I. The names may change, but the violent theme remains the same: television: "good guys" using violence to bring their culprit to justice. (Have you ever noticed that TV heroes are actually more violent than the criminals they apprehend?)

Gerbner argues that television veiwing scares children by giving them a *mean world view*. Heavy viewers tend to have a "heightened sense of fear and mistrust...manifested in their typically more apprehensive responses to questions about their own personal safety, about crime and law enforcement, and about trust in other people" (p. 206).

Some analysts have suggested that the impact of television on our society is pervasive. Others have argued that the impact of television is instead limited to a small number of cases of "copycat" delinquency in which specific children imitate television behavior. True, very few children have been killed trying to fly like Superman; even fewer have killed their neighbors in the style of their favorite episode of Magnum P.I. But it may also be true that millions of children who grow up addicted to TV tend to overestimate the proportion of whites in the world population, the proportion of Americans, the proportion of males, the amount of wealth in our society, and the amount of violence. Why? Well, if Gerbner is right, it is because the typical prime-time episode is overpopulated by white American male characters who have lots of money and use plenty of violence. Television may provide a caricature of our society; but, according to Gerbner, for many children, it is society.

Does television violence inevitably lead to a violent society? Probably not (Hughes 1980). In Japan, for example, TV series are much more violent than ours, but the amount of violence in the streets is relatively low. Unlike the situation here, the family has maintained much of its importance as a source of reference others in the daily life of the Japanese. So television messages to Japanese children are usually monitored, censored, and interpreted by parents, grandparents, or siblings. The presence of an adult member of the family who sits with children while they watch their favorite violent program may be a key to reducing the harmful effects of TV. In our society, such supervision is often missing; in Japan, it is an ordinary part of everyday life.

You might be wondering how we can treat television as a source of reference others. After all, isn't it only an electronic machine? Apparently not in the minds of the millions of people who consider the nightly anchorman on ABC, CBS, or NBC a close friend ("Martha, it's time to watch Dan"). Apparently not to the millions of housewives, retired men, college students, and preschool children who faithfully watch their favorite soap opera on a daily basis; who follow their soap opera heroes and villians into their bedrooms at home and their office at work; who know more about the cast of "General Hospital" and "Days of Our Lives" than they know about their real neighbors next door.

The self-evaluation function So far, we know that reference others can be a source of norms and values as well as information about the world. We turn now to examine a more personal function: *self-evaluation*.

That is, reference others provide us with a standard of comparison when we evaluate our goals, opinions, or abilities.

Active and spontaneous forms of social comparison have been found in the behavior of children as young as age 3 (Mosatche and Bragonier 1981) and tend to increase through adolescence into the college years (Davis 1966; Marsh and Parker 1984). We have never handed back an exam to our students without seeing many of them comparing their grades. When we ask about this, students consistently say that their grades are meaningless without knowing how others in the class have done. "A 78," said one student, "could be an A if everybody else got in the 50s or 60s. It happens all the time in math courses that a 35 is the highest grade on an exam." Students have come to expect to be graded "on the curve," with success and failure a purely relative matter. For this reason, when given the choice, many college students would like to have their grades in percentile form; that is, indicating how well they did relative to other students in their class, their school, or across the nation (Levin and Levin 1973).

The process of social comparison is not limited to the classroom. Someone in business or industry who reflects on how well he or she is doing might well compare salary, profits, or income with those of others in the same company or industry. On every block, there are people who compare against their neighbors the greenness of their lawns, cost of their cars, and straightness of their children's teeth. This kind of social comparison is a way of life in American society.

Accurate feedback. Notice that in the examples above, our college student, businessperson, and neighbor compared their own success with that of others in the same classroom, in the same business, or on the same block. This seems to happen quite often: people tend to compare themselves with similar others or, in the case of abilities, with those who are equal or slightly better (Goethals and Darley 1977). According to Festinger's *Theory of Social Comparison* (1954), we do this to get honest, accurate feedback about our abilities, achievements, or opinions. He says we want very much to know where we stand, how we are doing in life. So we compare ourselves with reference others—not just any reference others—but specifically with those who are roughly similar to us on the characteristic being evaluated. For example, we sometimes play tennis at a local club where there is a well-established ranking system (from 2.0 to 9.0) for the evaluation of how well a person plays. In tournaments and arranged matches, people tend to play others with the same numerical ranking. That way, players have a good idea about how well they are playing in comparison with others of like ability. A comparison of our game (at 4.5) with that of Boris Becker (at 9.0) would be not only meaningless but depressing.

For an explanation of why this is true, we can return to the work of Leon Festinger (1954). According to him, the larger the gap between an individual and his reference other, the less valuable a comparison is likely to be. That is, you simply can't get honest, accurate information about your abilities, achievements, or opinions, if you decide to compare yourself with some who is very different from you.

The idea that people compare themselves with similar others is not new. Hyman, in 1942, talked about the tendency to make comparisons with friends. Robert Merton (1957) later contended that a perception of status similarity may be a precondition for making any comparisons at all.

Festinger takes this notion a step further. He argues that the need for honest feedback about the self motivates individuals to close the gap between themselves and their reference other. Imagine, for example, that two people are playing tennis. One is much more talented than the other. Now, according to Festinger's Theory of Social Comparison, there will be a great deal of pressure on the better player to play a poorer game than his or her ability would predict. Some research does indeed suggest that pressure to close the gap may exist. But why? Is it, as Festinger claims, because the better player desires more honest information about his or her talent for tennis—information only available by closing the gap? Or, for example, does the better player feel sympathetic toward the less talented player and so attempts to help the opponent to "save face"?

Self-protection. As suggested by Festinger, there is a powerful motivation for many individuals under many of the conditions of everyday life to seek accurate self-appraisal (Strube et al 1986). Just as clearly, however, people aren't always interested in getting honest, accurate information about themselves. In fact, there are occasions when many of us would prefer hearing something flattering than something true. Sensitivity groups and therapy sessions exist in which honest feedback is given and received. But the very presence of these special sessions for being honest must mean that we aren't always so honest in everyday life.

Goffman (1959) has observed that we often want other people to believe that we are competent members of society. In fact, we may go to elaborate lengths to project a positive image of ourselves in public situations. Many of us also would like to think highly of ourselves; but that is not always possible. Sadly, there are times when our self-esteem may be seriously threatened, and a person doesn't have to be a perpetual failure for this to occur. It happens all the time. For example, even good students sometimes get poor exam grades; competent workers can lose their jobs when an industry declines; or a well-liked person can be rejected by someone he or she wishes to keep as a friend. When our self-image is being threatened, we may be more receptive to favorable than to accurate information about our abilities or achievements (Gruder 1977; Sachs 1982). Rather than compare ourselves with a similar other, we prefer to make a *downward comparison* — a comparison with a person or group we perceive to be inferior on that characteristic being evaluated. This may explain why students who have done poorly on an exam prefer to compare their own score with a classmate whose score is even lower (Hakmiller 1966). For Hakmiller, this finding reflects the operation of defensive social comparison, "the function of comparison in this situation of sustaining or reasserting the favorability of the individual's self-regard" (p. 37). In another study, Wilson and Benner (1971) set out to examine the idea that people with high self-esteem would choose a "comparison other" to maximize the information they obtain about themselves, whereas people who have low self-esteem would try to avoid a potentially threatening comparison. After receiving their scores on a "leadership test," Wilson and Benner's subjects were given the opportunity to compare their leadership ability with that of another student. The expectation was clear: subjects with low self-esteem should want to compare themselves with someone lower in ability and should avoid a high-scoring "comparison other." Results of the study by Wilson and Benner tended to support their prediction. In a public condition, significantly more high-self-esteem males chose the highest scorer as a comparison other than did low-self-esteem males. For female subjects, self-esteem influenced choices of comparison other in a private condition, where sex-related competition was minimal.

Self-improvement. As comfortable as a downward comparison may be, there are also times when we prefer to compare our abilities or achievements with those of an individual whom we perceive as superior to us on a particular characteristic. If our motive is self-improvement, we might make an *upward comparison* (Nosanchuk and Erickson 1985).

Strauss (1968) studied the social comparison choices of 197 totally blind respondents. Festinger's Theory of Social Comparison woud predict that blind people compare themselves with similar others—that is, with other blind people they know. After all, blindness would seem to be a characteristic which greatly helps determine what an individual can and cannot attempt to do. But Strauss found instead that on ability to learn, appearance, and moral character, the majority of her blind respondents claimed to compare themselves with sighted, not blind, reference others. Apparently, many had not given up trying to live an independent existence; they refused to be limited by their disability. For them, sighted individuals served as "reference idols," whose everyday accomplishments (for example, dressing themselves, crossing the street alone, and holding a decent job) were regarded as realistic personal goals.

Upward comparisons can help an individual who strives to improve his or her status in life, but at some cost. Upwardly mobile persons may get carried away, thinking strictly in terms of reference others who are vastly superior. The undergraduate student who always compares his ability in science with Albert Einstein's may get good grades in physics courses; but he or she also risks the possibility of being tremendously frustrated. One of our students, in fact, used to talk enthusiastically about his future as an important scientist. He even spoke seriously about winning the Nobel Prize. Naturally, we did not want to discourage him, but we also did not want to support false expectations. Perhaps we should have tempered his dreams, for when he started taking higher level physics courses, the C's and D's he earned were devastating to him. He had chosen reference others so far above his abilities that the fall to reality was harder than it need have been. Parker and Kleiner (1968) have shown that people with mental disorders tend to compare themselves with reference others far above them on various status characteristics. As a result, the mentally ill have profound feelings of personal failure and loss of self-esteem.

The presence of television in the living rooms of most Americans may represent a profound source of upward comparisons with respect to both social status and physical attractiveness. As we have seen, the world of prime-time television is largely a middle-class world, in which extreme poverty is all but absent. One must ask what is the impact of viewing this middle-class world on a daily basis, especially on audience members who are themselves poverty stricken and can see no legitimate sources of upward mobility.

Regarding the effect of television on perceptions of beauty, there is greater evidence. One study found that after male college students watched "Charlie's Angels" (a program which featured highly attractive female central characters), they evaluated a female student as being less attractive than she had otherwise appeared to be (Kenrick and Gutierres 1980). Even the importance of beauty itself can be influenced by media portrayals. Tan (1979) exposed young women between the ages of 16 and 18 to 15 television commercials for beauty preparations. A control group of teenagers watched 15 commercials for products having nothing to do with beauty. All of the young women later were asked to rank the relative importance of 10 characteristics such as intelligence, sex appeal, a pretty face, and so on. The women who viewed the beauty commercials were more likely than those from the control group to consider beauty-related characteristics more important than other attributes.

According to a series of recent studies by Silverstein, Perdue, Peterson, and Kelly (1986), television may promote eating disorders such as obesity and anorexia nervosa, which are more common among women than men, by depicting an unrealistically thin standard of comparison for female attractiveness. In one of their studies, this standard of attractiveness among popular television characters was found to be slimmer for women than for men. Specifically, whereas 69 percent of the female characters were rated by independent judges as thin, only 18 percent of the male characters were so rated. Thus, a message that women may receive from comparing themselves with characters on television is that they are supposed to be slim and must chronically diet to stay or become attractive.

Before leaving the topic of self-improvement, allow us to complicate matters a bit more. There are some instances in which an upward comparison—at least comparing our ability with those who are in fact slightly better than we are—can actually improve self-esteem. Cialdini et al. (1976) refer to this phenomenon as "basking in reflected glory" or "borrowing status." It occurs because an individual who identifies with a group of people comes to regard their achievements as his or her own. By association, for example, the children of successful parents may feel a personal success; the students at a prestigious college may feel positive self-regard because they are enrolled in a school with "smart students." Of course, this positive effect of the reference other's performance by association may also be offset somewhat by negative thinking about the self produced by upward comparison with a superior other, especially if an individual suffers from poor self-esteem (Felson and Reed 1986).

Whatever the psychological disadvantage overall, there is reason to believe that certain people under certain conditions make all of their comparisons upward. For example, Nosanchuk and Erickson (1985) recently studied a local unit of the American Contact Bridge League, a group of individuals whose primary objective is to foster the game of bridge in North America. In the situation of this competitive game, its highly committed and serious players made upward comparisons, whatever their motives. In fact, even self-protection or ego-defensive comparisons were, for these individuals playing bridge, upward, although not to the same degree as comparisons they made to obtain information about the game. Apparently, under conditions of intense competition, even a slight upward comparison can be a psychological relief from the information-seeking behavior of those who attempt to improve their game or, perhaps, their status in a group.

Groups vs. categories as reference others It must be emphasized here that the concept of reference other is a very broad one, including both groups and individuals. In reality, we refer not only to *groups*—a set of individuals who interact together and who regard one another as members—but also to individuals who share common characteristics but who do not necessarily interact with one another. In the strictest sense, they are not truly groups. Social psychologists call them *social categories*. For example, the Bridgewater Beagle Owner's Club is a group because they meet regularly (interact), think of one another in terms of their group membership, and share certain goals and rules for interaction. By comparison, red-headed Americans constitute a social category. Although they share more than one characteristic, they do not necessarily interact nor do they share conscious membership, goals, or rules for interaction.

Merton's (1957a) analysis of *relative deprivation* among World War II soldiers illustrates the importance of social categories as a standard of comparison. Among those soldiers inducted into service, married men were more likely than their single counterparts to maintain that they "should have been deferred." This unwillingness of married soldiers to serve can be explained in terms of relative deprivation: comparing themselves with unmarried draftees, the married soldiers could feel that they sacrificed more by their term of service to the Army. After all, they were leaving their brides and, in some cases, their children as well. The single soldiers were, by comparison, relatively free of civilian responsibilities. Comparing themselves with married civilians, the married soldiers also felt relatively deprived. From their point of view, married men at home had managed to escape all of the family sacrifices that those who served their country were asked to make.

Merton's analysis of World War II soldiers also illustrates the influence of membership group as a point of reference. A sample of soldiers was asked, "Do you think a soldier with ability has a good chance for promotion?" Based on common sense, we might predict some relationship between actual opportunities for promotion and the perception that opportunities for promotion exist. Thus, we would expect soldiers in a branch of the service where rates of promotion were high to be satisfied with their opportunities for obtaining a better position. Conversely, we would expect soldiers in a branch of the service having low rates of promotion to be dissatisfied with these opportunities.

Actually, the opposite was found by researchers: "The less the promotion opportunity afforded by a branch or combination of branches, the more favorable the opinion tends to be toward promotion opportunity." For example, there were numerous promotions in the Air Corps, yet members of the Air Corps were critical of their chances for promotion. By contrast, the Military Police gave fewer promotions than any other branch of the Army, yet Military Policemen were relatively satisfied with their promotion opportunities.

Why was there only dissatisfaction where there apparently should have been happiness and contentment? The research team who studied World War II soldiers argued that a high rate of promotion among the soldiers in a particular branch of the service gave them excessively high expectations for promotion. Comparing their achievements with "others in the same boat with them," members of this group may have felt a sense of frustration with their present position and impatience with prospects for mobility into a better position. Hence, the concept of relative deprivation is used to explain a finding that might otherwise have made no sense at all.

What happens when a person uses more than one group as reference others? Suppose that the viewpoint expressed by the members of one group is opposed to the viewpoint expressed by members of another. For example, how will a person's sexual morality be influenced when his religious group and his socioeconomic status (a social category) operate at cross purposes? Research has shown that church attendance is associated with conservative sexual attitudes; research has also shown that high socioeconomic status is associated with liberal sexual attitudes. What happens to the sexual attitudes of a person who has high social status but who identifies closely with the viewpoint of his or her religious group? Which frame of reference will win, religious group or socioeconomic status category?

Bock, Beeghley, and Mixon (1983) examined sexual attitudes (attitude toward abortion, sexual permissiveness, birth control, and pornography) in a national cross-section of white adults. In addition to sexual attitudes, the researchers also examined each of their respondent's socioeconomic status (occupational prestige) and religiosity (church attendance and strength of religious identification). They found that religious group involvement had greater impact on sexual attitudes than did socioeconomic status category. Specifically, the more people with high status were involved with their religious group, the more their religiosity influenced their sexual attitudes: they had more conservative attitudes about abortion, sexual permissiveness, pornography, and birth control—regardless of high socioeconomic status. If Bock, Beeghley, and Mixon's findings can be generalized, we might conclude that when the values and beliefs of a group and a social category are opposed to one another, an individual is more likely to conform to his or her group's values and beliefs.

Just because a group seems to have greater influence than a category doesn't mean that social categories don't have any influence at all. As we saw earlier, American soldiers' satisfaction with Army life may have been profoundly affected by their choice of a reference category. Another example of the power of social categories is found in the effect of age denial on the sense of personal competence among elderly people. For many older Americans, their contemporaries constitute a negative point of reference—numerous Americans over the age of 65 or 70 actively attempt to deny their own aging by referring to themselves as "young" or "middle-aged," dying their hair, and applying youth-oriented cosmetics. Is this denial of age necessarily "bad"? Not if you believe that older people ought to remain active members of our society for as long as they possibly can. During his presidential election campaigns, Ronald Reagan went to some lengths to avoid the stigma of old age. His campaign advertisements depicted him as an outdoorsman who loved to ride horses and chop wood. Some insiders claimed he even dyed his hair! In American society, association with old age is a liability, and no politician can afford to be seen as old, regardless of his chronological age.

An important consequence of accepting the status of "old," "aged," or "elderly" is the tendency to also accept the nastiest stereotypes about older people. In conducting some of our own research on the subject of age-related stereotypes, we had many opportunities to speak to people concerned with problems of aging. For example, we heard from health-care professionals, nursing-home activities directors and people who had family members who were growing older. One story we heard repeatedly concerned the aging individual who, after the sudden loss of a job or spouse, felt compelled to accept the status of old age. In far too many cases, a rapid decline in activity, optimism, and health soon followed. Sadly, such people are likely to do what many younger people expect: withdraw from society, sit in their rocking chairs, and wait for death (Levin and Levin 1980).

Is "reference other" an oversocialized concept? We must be careful not to leave an *oversocialized conception* of the effects of reference others; that is, the belief that once a person is socialized, he or she becomes an automatic role player who simply does what society expects (Wrong 1961). In reality, many people conform not because they wish to do so, but only because they are coerced by the fear of negative sanctions being imposed on them. Young children may comply with the demands of their parents in order to avoid their punishments. Adults may conform with the demands of a political or economic system because the alternative is a stiff penalty or imprisonment. Every society has its mechanisms of social control to assure a degree of conformity. In simple, closed communities, gossip and scandal are frequently enough of a threat to reduce deviant behavior to a minimum. In modern societies, formal mechanisms of social control as found in courts and prisons serve the same purpose (Merry 1984).

Even individuals who are enthusiastic in their willingness to conform are not precise replicas of the society in which they live. Mead emphasized the importance of the Me phase of the self through which conformity is achieved; but he also recognized the existence of the I which is innovative, impulsive, and not yet under the direct guidance of a group's norms and values. Everyone has a choice as to how to behave and a wide variety of choices as to what others to use as a point of reference (Wrong 1961).

At least for some purposes, individuals can get along just fine without any reference others. It is often assumed, for example, that students universally form self-concepts about their academic ability by a process of social comparison—that is, by comparing themselves with their schoolmates. In fact, Davis (1966) once used the metaphor of the campus as a "frog pond" (it is better to be a big frog in a little pond than a small frog in a big pond) to argue that students may develop low levels of aspiration if their schoolmates are extremely capable (an upward comparison). Recent research suggests, however, that "school climate" (variations in average ability by school) has only a weak effect on self-concepts of academic ability, self-esteem, or long-range educational attainment (Bachman and O'Malley

1986). What really seems to count is a student's ability to get good grades and perhaps to receive praise from teachers and parents, regardless of how well other students do. Perhaps being around schoolmates with low ability does give a slight boost to a student's self-concept; but, more than social comparison, it is a student's actual ability that makes the big difference.

In Strauss's study of social comparison among the blind, she was surprised to find a number of her respondents who said they never compared themselves with other people, either blind or sighted, when it came to evaluating their ability to learn, appearance, and moral character. These respondents Strauss labeled "noncomparers," because they claimed to use no reference others at all.

You might wonder how it is possible ever to find out how we are doing without the help of other people as a standard of comparison. There are other, nonsocial standards as well. For one thing, some individuals have an absolute standard which is unaffected by the relative successes or failures of other people. During the early 1960s, it was common at the Harvard Graduate School of Business to evaluate success in terms of a person's ability to "make his or her age." What this meant was that to be a financial success, a 28-year-old should be making $28,000 a year or more, and so on. Of course, today with inflation, the scale has changed; and now, they speak of doubling your age. Such evaluations are absolute and therefore independent of reference comparisons. In the classroom, the serious and intense college student might not care at all how her classmates do on their final exams. She too has an absolute standard of success. As far as she is concerned, only an A will do. Less than that is total failure! Whether or not she uses her family for normative guidance, there is every reason to assume that she does not use a social standard of comparison for evaluating her grades.

There is another nonsocial standard of comparison that may be more often used by everybody. comparing one aspect of self with another aspect of self. For example, many of us evaluate our ability to do something today in comparison with our ability to do the same thing earlier in time. A friend of ours who builds harpsichords started out making very elementary instruments from kits. They turned out fine, but they are nothing in comparison with what he builds today: beautiful 17th-century replicas of dual-keyboard classics. He says that in order to keep improving his work, he must use his most recent production as a standard of comparison.

It is also possible to evaluate an ability to do something by comparing it with an ability to do something else. Child psychologists who are confronted with an adolescent suffering from low self-esteem frequently advise parents to emphasize that nobody can be good at everything and to stress the specific talents their child has shown. For a 15-year-old who has some social problems but gets As in school, the comparison of one ability with another may provide a basis for raising self-esteem. (The trick is to get the kid to do it without external encouragement.)

▶ Perspective:
The Effect of Social and Cultural Forces

American competition for morality As a final idea, we raise the possibility that the use of reference others may actually vary from culture to culture. In our society, there is great competition for power, status, and wealth. Because of our open-class system, many individuals are anxious about where they stand, whether they are "keeping up with the Joneses," how they might improve, or at least not reduce, their social status.

According to Jack Douglas (1970), Americans are concerned in all situations with their moral value relative to the moral value of other individuals. He characterizes the evaluations we make of ourselves as a *zero-sum game*. Each American gains in moral worth and status only to the extent that others lose in moral worth and status, and vice versa. Given a zero-sum definition of the situation, Americans are therefore committed to a "competitive struggle" to upgrade themselves by downgrading others. Downward comparisons are commonplace. As a result, reference others provide an important standard of comparison for evaluating our achievements.

By contrast, societies where social standing is largely inherited and fixed at birth have no need for everyday standards of comparison, at least not of social status. In such societies, status is built into social institutions in the form of castes. Most individuals are not anxious about their status: indeed, they know exactly where they stand in relation to others, and there is little if anything they can do about it. Perhaps that is why newcomers to American society who assimilate—adopt American values and interact with middle-class native Americans—quickly come to compare their abilities, opinions, and achievements with those of other people (Levin and Leong 1973). They learn what Americans already know: that status in American society is very much determined by the reference others they select. ■

Looking Back

In this chapter, we have focused on the way others influence the behavior and beliefs of individuals. We have referred to such others as "reference others" in order to include any person or group of people, real or imagined, present or not, to which human beings orient themselves.

Individuals often conform to reference others in the immediate social situation. In classic laboratory experiments, subjects will frequently yield to group pressure when asked to make a judgment in either an ambiguous or a clear-cut situation. Moreover, a surprisingly high percentage of subjects yield to the demands of an authority figure to do something they would ordinarily find morally repugnant (for example, to administer shocks to a total stranger). Even outside the lab, forces for conformity are evident in extreme social behavior, such as that demonstrated in the Jonestown Massacre and the rise of Nazism.

But conformity isn't always negative; it also occurs in the ordinary circumstances of everyday life, in the norms and values that individuals agree to share. In fact, society wouldn't be possible at all without the presence of conformity. However, the degree of such culturally based conformity differs by culture and over time.

Conformity is pervasive, taking disguised forms that pass for independence or individuality. These include the anticonformity of the rebel, the socially inappropriate behavior of the idiosyncratic personality, and the enigmatic behavior of the individual who conforms to reference others who are absent from a social situation.

Social psychologists who emphasize the sociocultural perspective often look beyond the immediate situation for their understanding of conformity.

Reference others may be located in any group to which human beings orient themselves, whether or not they are members of it. These reference others serve at least three functions. First, they are a source of norms and values which provide guidelines for everyday life (the normative function). Many students learn from reference others on their college campus political and social norms that they maintain for years after graduation. A second function of reference others is that they provide basic data about reality (the information function). Not only people, but also the mass media can serve this function. It is possible that millions of children have a distorted perception of social reality because of the world view they see on television. Lastly, reference others provide us with a standard of comparison when we evaluate our goals, opinions, and abilities (the self-evaluation function). Festinger's Theory of Social Comparison argues that the major motive for social comparison is to receive accurate, honest feedback about ourselves. In contrast, other motives for social comparison have been identified. These include self-protection, in which an individual selects from reference others only flattering or favorable feedback, and self-improvement, in which an individual compares him or herself upward with a reference idol.

Despite the important presence of conformity in everyday life, individuals must not be thought of as automatic role takers who simply do what society expects. Actually, individuals differ a great deal in the way and degree to which they use reference others, and some seem to use no reference others at all. We must also remember that many people do not willingly comply, but go along in order to avoid the negative sanctions that others can bring to bear on someone who deviates.

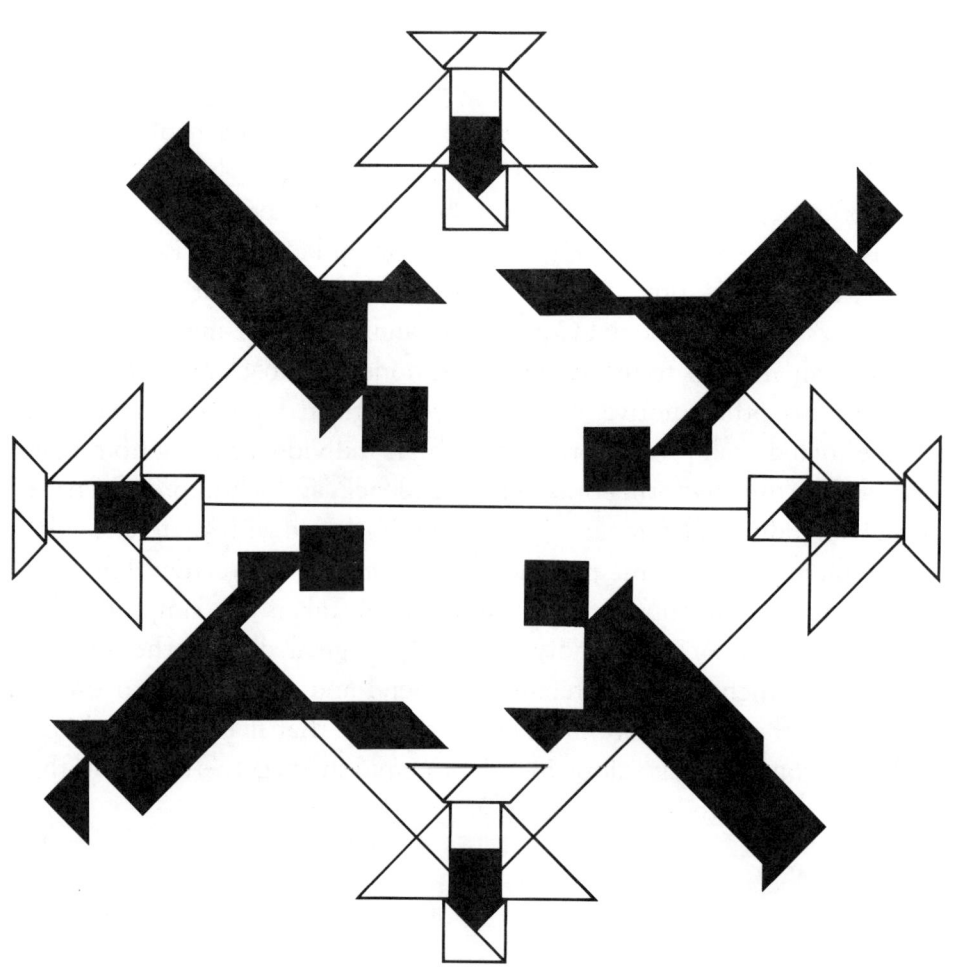

Chapter 4

Communication and Language

OUR PARENTS MAY HAVE TOLD US that "Sticks and stones may break your bones, but words will never harm you," but we can recall many times when words hurt deeply. One overweight 5-year-old was nicknamed "Lump" by his classmates and it outraged him for years. To this day, though he is now trim and almost 40 years old, he is sensitive about his weight and hates for anyone to make fun of another person's physical appearance. In high school someone started a nasty rumor that a girl in the school was pregnant and was going to have to drop out. Though it was not true, she felt branded for the two years until she graduated and left for college. And as teachers we have seen numerous cases in which a bright child who stammers or has an accent is labeled stupid by other children. Often the targeted child tries to withdraw into silence to avoid the taunts, and suffers increased problems overcoming the original difficulty.

When this happens, parents want to tell their children that words are in some sense less "real" than physical objects like rocks. But the truth is that they are both very real. The physical world is made up of the objects we can sense, while the social world is made up of the agreements among people, expressed in words, about what is true. In the words of W. I. Thomas, "If men define situations as real, they are real in their consequences" (Thomas and Thomas 1928, p. 572). To the extent that this is true of human social life, communication and language are at the root of our ability to deal with one another, because agreements among people must be arrived at through communication. Thus, if children decide to label a newcomer as "one of us," then that is what he or she becomes. But the decision to label the same child as different in a negative way (as fat or stupid) is just as real in its social effects. In this sense, words are as real as rocks.

Looking Ahead

In this chapter we examine some of the most elementary pieces of the human puzzle, communication and language, as they operate in creating and maintaining human social organization. We ask: How do human and nonhuman forms of social order differ? And is the human capacity for communication and language really unique? In order to answer the latter question, we explore the character of language and the way in which it is acquired. We also look at important variations in styles of communication between and within human social groupings, and treat differences in language between cultures, social classes, and sexes and over time. We ask, for example: Do differences in language exist between men and women, between blacks and whites, or between middle- and lower-class individuals? If so, what are the implications of such differences? Lastly, we examine important nonverbal forms of communication to determine how it is possible to communicate through body language, gestures, and the management of space. Is it possible that individuals often communicate more by what they don't say than by what they do say to others?

Communication and Social Order

In its simplest terms, *social order* is merely the ability to predict another person's behavior and what he or she expects for our behavior. We draw on a number of sources of information to do this, such as the quality of the immediate situation in which we are interacting, our past experiences in such situations, the clues conveyed by the statements we hear, the appearance and behavior of the other person, and so on. In short, we need information to know how others will behave and how they expect us to behave in return. The process by which this information is conveyed between people is called *communication*.

All communication is social, since any attempt to transmit information must take place between at least two individuals. Social communication is at the core of everyday human interaction, because in order to deal with one another on any social level, we must transmit information and intentions to others.

As an example, think of two strangers who are in an elevator. For a few floors they travel in silence. Then one says, "I hate elevators," to which the other replies, "Me too." Then both get out at the first floor and smile quickly to say goodbye. Because they interacted so briefly, we could not really say they had developed what we think of as a social relationship. However, without the communication there would have been no interaction, and without that, no possibility of a relationship in the future. Even so brief an exchange as the foregoing has all the core elements of human communication: (1) sociality, (2) reciprocity, (3) abstraction, and (4) intentionality (Luckmann, 1984).

Sociality Communication is social in that it is an exchange of information between individuals which structures and regulates the nature of their relationship and interactions. In the case of the elevator conversation, what we know to be polite conversation between strangers never touches on serious topics (neither is expected to ask about belief in God, for example), and a certain congenial tone is struck. Had either participant communicated differently (asked too personal a question, such as the contents of a package, for example), the nature of the relationship would have changed, probably becoming more distant and awkward. Notice that sociality does not necessarily mean amiability. Communication is social since it regulates relationships, whether they are amiable and comfortable or not.

Reciprocity Communication is based on exchange of information with the resulting establishment of, literally, a common ground for interaction. The mechanism for this sharing of information is a shared language. One person (the source) who wishes to communicate an idea encodes it in a form (the signal), which he or she thinks will be understood when decoded by another person (the destination). Participants in a conversation provide feedback to one another, which confirms that what each has intended to communicate is what was understood. So, using the model developed by Schramm (1972), the act of communication with feedback might look like the diagram below.

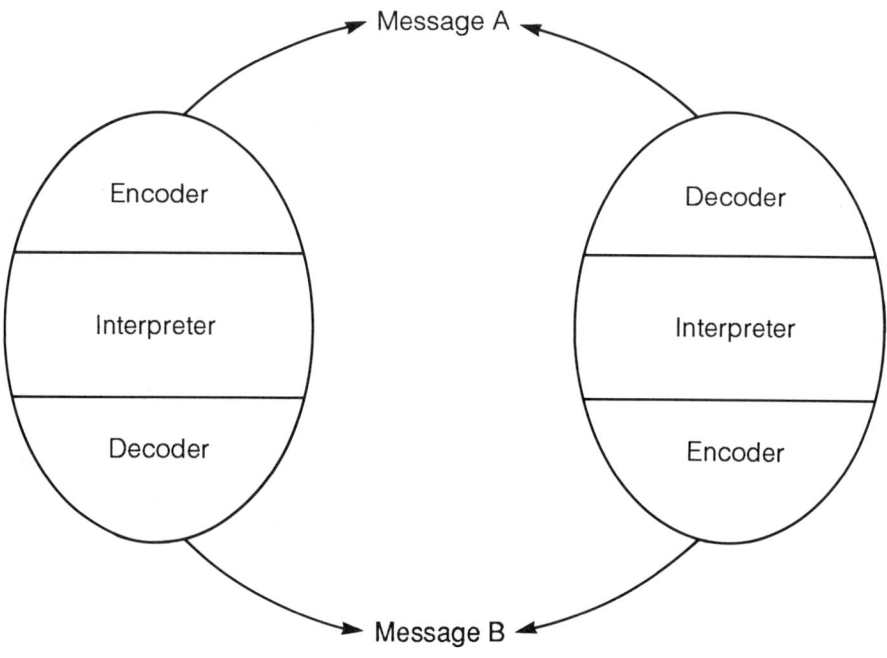

A person wishing to communicate a certain idea "encodes" the information as a signal ("message A"), which is then decoded and interpreted by the person who is its destination. In response the second person may then become the source of a second message by encoding and sending as a signal the information he or she wishes to convey ("message B") which is, in turn decoded and interpreted. Message B provides the feedback which informs the original communicator whether or not message A was understood.

For example, the reply to the statement "I hate elevators" not only conveyed information ("Me too"), it also showed that the opening statement was understood and interpreted as polite conversation. In the absence of further clarification by the person who spoke first (for example, "I mean I'm going to be sick"), the participants can agree that the exchange has reached a satisfactory conclusion.

Abstraction *Abstraction* is a characteristic that is probably unique to human communication. It consists of the ability to refer in conversation to objects, actions, or ideas not present in the immediate situation. For example, the word "hate" is an abstraction. It refers to a strong negative emotion which was not apparent in either of the people in the elevator. The fact that neither of the people was yelling or grimacing suggests that both understood the special meaning of "hatred" as it applied to their situation. In fact, your ability to understand from the words on this page what it is like to have such a conversation in an elevator means that you have understood an abstraction of the event. You were not there, and need not have been, to have had its meaning successfully communicated to you. Later in this chapter we will deal in more detail with this special quality of human communication.

Intentionality Communication is a purposeful act. That is, it is engaged in for the purpose of exchanging information and, thus, conducting social relationships. We can, within certain limits, decide what information to transmit and can decide whether or not to communicate with others. Each of the people in the elevator had it within his or her power to speak or not and to choose the content of the messages. As you will see later in this chapter, what we communicate is not always what is understood by others, and we sometimes communicate to others without knowing we are doing so.

Meaning, Symbols, and Language

When humans communicate with one another they are able to exchange information about characteristics of the immediate situation (the average age of people in the room, for example), about situations in another place (the average age of people in another country), or time (what the average age of Americans was in the 18th century), or even about situations that do not now and may never exist (speculation about what it would be like to live forever). Animals other than humans can communicate about experiences in their immediate environment, for example, warning one another of some danger. But humans are apparently uniquely able to conceptualize beyond the immediate situation. This is because in comparison with other animals, humans have an advanced capacity for abstraction, the process whereby meaning is attached to some object or experience.

Meaning The concept of meaning has been of intense interest to philosophers and theologians, who have often focused on questions such as the meaning of life itself or whether meaning exists. But social psychologists, especially G. H. Mead and the symbolic interactionists, have developed a different and more limited understanding of the concept of meaning.

For Mead (1934), *meaning* is what is established by the relationship between individuals and the events in their lives. That is, the environment presents people with conditions to which they must respond in everyday life. These challenges range in complexity from simple acts such as sitting on a chair, to complex ones such as maintaining multiple relationships in a family. From the social psychological point of view, no object, action, idea, or set of relationships has a meaning apart from human experience. Events have meaning only to the extent that individuals respond to them.

Look around at the objects that surround you. You may see walls, a chair, a painting, or a range of other items. In what sense can you say that they have meaning? In its common use, the word "meaning" has come to suggest "importance," as in the expression "a meaningful relationship." Certainly mundane objects do not have meaning in this sense. But they all have meaning as abstractions. That is, we have attached names to them which stand for the qualities they have in common in terms of human experience.

For example, a chair is an object with certain physical properties (legs and seat) and a human use (to be sat upon). The color, size, materials, and construction of chairs can differ and they will still be recognizable to us as chairs. In the same way, we can abstract the characteristics of a behavior such as running and successfully distinguish it from closely related behaviors such as walking or jogging. We can even create abstracted labels for a number of types of relationships, such as friends, lovers, or family. In every case, a meaning is created out of human interaction in the environment, which, of course, includes other humans.

So human experiences in the environment are mediated by meaning. We do not behave directly toward some object, but in terms of its meaning to us. Thus, our reactions to the appearance of a harmless garden snake are determined by our understanding of its meaning, and in our culture, snakes are generally thought to be dangerous and even evil. Meaning can mediate human behavior so powerfully that an object that is physically present can actually be defined out of existence. Take the following instance.

A friend of ours came back from a trip to South Africa in the 1960s and told the story of a trip she took into the countryside with her white hosts. When their car overheated they got out to wait for it to cool. Our friend looked into the distance and saw a group of black people standing in the shimmering heat alongside the desert road. Pointing, she asked her hosts, "What are those people doing there?" They looked, but apparently could not see them. "What people?" they asked. "Those people!" our friend said again. Finally, after more pointing and exchanges, the white South Africans understood. "Oh, the blacks." Because our friend had used the word "people," her hosts, who did not call blacks "people," had actually not seen them. By the same principle that some objects qualify by human experience to be recognized as chairs, even humans can be subjected to the process of definition.

Meaning and Symbols

Meaning is not attached to objects or experiences in isolation. Such meanings are shared by communities of people. In fact, they are generated out of interaction with one another. It becomes a matter of agreement that, for example, a chair is an object with a set of physical characteristics and a specific use, and that it will be called a chair. Mead used the word *symbols* to refer to items (especially words) to which meanings are attached by members of a group. The word "chair" is a symbol, as are all other words in the dictionary. They are not the objects themselves, but shorthand representations of them which allow us to evaluate and exchange abstracted information about experiences. Even when we do not communicate our experiences to one another, symbols are present. This is because the private evaluation of experience, *thinking*, is essentially the mind "talking to itself." If this is true, then without words (symbols) one cannot think.

To illustrate that this is the case, try thinking without using words. Perhaps you could review what you did last night or plan what you are going to do after you finish reading this. Do you "hear" the words in your mind? Most of the time, of course, you are not consciously aware of the role of symbols in thought, just as you are not usually conscious of the existence of the tongue in your mouth or of your breathing. But the words are there every time you think.

Human vs. nonhuman communication Humans communicate and interact at the symbolic level. Mead contended that humans live in the realm of symbols to an extent unmatched in the rest of the animal world. Our patterns of cooperation depend on our ability to communicate the meaning of our experiences to one another via symbols. Using symbols, we can do this after or in anticipation of such experiences and, thus, are free to create a social reality by agreement. To understand the distinctiveness of our symbolic form of interaction, consider the level of communication which other animals employ.

The social organization of animals other than humans is, in large measure, inborn. The patterns of cooperation which we see in their ways of feeding (wolves hunting in packs, for example), procreation, and care of their young (geese forming mating pairs for life), or protection against predators (musk oxen forming a protective circle with the young packed in the center against attacking wolves), are the product of many thousands of years of evolution. The instructions for such behaviors are transmitted genetically from one generation to the next.

The social organization of nonhuman animals, then, is primarily genetic rather than symbolic. They lack the need or the ability to convey to others of their kind abstracted information about their environment and their experiences in it. This does not mean that they lack the ability to communicate. Though they are limited to communication about events that are present in their genetic instructions or in their immediate environments, animals can respond to and communicate at the level of signs, cues, or stimuli which indicate something directly. They engage in what Mead called a *conversation of gestures*. For example, the sight of a lion is a sign which triggers in monkeys an immediate and automatic (that is, unthinking) response (shrieking in fear) which communicates a warning to other monkeys in the area. Another example is the squawking of birds when their nests are approached. Patterns of response to signs may be implanted genetically or by training, as when a dog is taught to howl or bark ("speak, Fido") or a porpoise is taught to click and squeak for food rewards (Miller 1981).

Whatever their origins, such forms of communication are *adaptive*; that is, they are aids to survival within specific environments. When monkeys shriek in fear or birds squawk in warning, such communications help these animals (and their kind) to escape predators. Trained animals which vocalize on cue earn rewards or avoid punishments.

We can also see adaptive forms of communication in animals which teach their young a variety of survival skills. Lion cubs, for example, must learn how to hunt and, though the bulk of the teaching is by example rather than by verbal communication (the mother lion growling when the cub strays), we are sometimes tempted to see some parallels in such behavior with the way humans communicate. It is common to see this occur in television and film programs such as the Jacques Cousteau series, in which animal behavior is sometimes interpreted in human terms, a process called *anthropomorphism*. When a narrator says that a sea otter "seems to want to make friends with Phillips," he is attributing to the animal an understanding of a human meaning, friendship. Also, many of our students over the years have insisted that their dogs "think they are people" or that their cats "think they are dogs." The danger in equating human and nonhuman communication is that nonhumans have a severely limited capacity for abstraction.

Until relatively recently, most researchers concluded that animals other than humans were totally incapable of abstraction. That is, all their communication was assumed to be exclusively at the level of signs. Thus, it would be beyond the capacity of a dog or chimpanzee to recognize that different objects can be grouped by the properties they have in common. It would also, therefore, be beyond them to communicate with one another at this symbolic level.

In order to discover whether animals can symbolize we need a method to communicate with them. Early efforts focused on teaching chimps and apes to speak. But these animals lack the physical structures to form human-style speech, so all the tortured manipulations, including pinching their nasal and throat regions, came to naught. It was not until the 1960s that researchers began to take advantage of the excellent manual dexterity of chimps and apes to try to teach them the system of symbols contained in American Sign Language. In the most celebrated of these studies a female chimpanzee named Washoe was taught hundreds of signs which she was able to use with her trainers (Gardner and Gardner 1971). She could indicate that she was thirsty or hungry by signing, or ask to be tickled (which she did frequently). She learned the sign for "dirty," then used it appropriately when she spread peanut butter on herself. But was Washoe using symbols, or was she merely displaying an impressive repertoire of stimulus-response patterns? That is, when she asked to be tickled, did she understand the meaning of "tickle" in the abstract sense that a human does, or did she merely associate the signing of "tickle" with the pleasant consequence?

The researchers reported a number of instances in which they contended that Washoe's behavior showed the ability to abstract experiences. For example, Washoe learned the sign for "open" with a particular door. She later correctly applied it to a variety of different objects, including jars, drawers, boxes, and so on. In other words, she could generalize the qualities of opening one container to others, despite their differing sizes, shapes, and methods of opening. Such generalization is a critical element in the process of symbolizing and of symbolic communication. Lucy, another chimp who was taught to sign, on several occasions showed the ability to abstract experiences when she used the characteristics of objects with which she was unfamiliar in order to give them names. For example, she named watermelon with the signs "candy fruit," and radishes with the signs "cry hurt food."

Researchers have differed in their interpretations of these data. Gardner and Gardner have been enthusiastic in their belief that such behaviors indicate the ability of apes and chimpanzees to symbolize, even though it has been suggested that this ability is limited to that of a 1- or 2-year-old human (Brown 1973). On the other hand, critics (Terrace 1984) have concluded that the chimps in these studies learned the combinations of signs by imitation and for rewards such as food and affection. Accordingly, what looked to some like abstract thinking was merely complex sets of stimulus-reward patterns. In either case, even if apes, chimpanzees, or other animals have limited ability to abstract experiences, it is generally agreed that no animal has the capacity of humans to attach abstract meaning to experiences or to express them in symbols.

Forms of symbolic expression Though most of the symbols we use to communicate take the form of spoken or written words, we also communicate by means of *gestures*, physical actions which carry meanings shared by a group. For example, lifting one's shoulders and spreading one's hands, palms up, means "I don't know." (There is also a word that describes this act: a "shrug.") Clapping hands indicates approval, while the "thumbs down" means disapproval.

The rich variety of meanings which can be expressed by physical gestures is illustrated by American Sign Language. It is possible to convey as complex a set of abstractions with the hands as with the voice. With the development in the 19th century of sign language, many hearing- and speech-impaired people were given their first opportunities to enter the world of meaningful human interaction.

In her autobiography, Helen Keller (1904), who had been blind and deaf since early childhood, explained that before she was taught through signing to attach labels to experiences, she was like a drifting ship, unable to make sense of the events of her life or share them with others. Seemingly simple acts like holding a doll and spelling out the word "doll" with her fingers gave shape to her experiences because she could now communicate with others.

Variations in symbols and meanings Symbols are, in a sense, arbitrary. That is, it does not matter whether the object we refer to as a chair is called by that name or some other. The truth of this statement is demonstrated by the fact that different languages successfully use their own words to refer to a single object. A horse in English is *una caballo* in Spanish, and though there may be confusion between the languages, there is none within each language. All that is required is that the members of a social group agree to use the same symbol for an object, experience, idea, and so on.

The extent to which people share such symbols varies by region, context, and over time. Regionally, for example, large sandwiches are variously called "heroes" in New York City, "hoagies" in Philadelphia, "poor boys" in New Orleans, and "submarines" in Boston. Some years ago they were called "Dagwoods," after the cartoon character Dagwood Bumstead who favored them. Words meant to refer to "something good" have also changed over the years. What was once "23-skidoo" (no kidding), became "peachy," "neat," "cool," "groovy," "out of sight," "bad," "excellent," "awesome," and then "radical." The context in which a symbol is used can also change its meaning significantly. For example, if you eat a friend's lunch in a cafeteria, you are consuming his or her food. But on the basketball court, a player who has had his "lunch eaten" has been taken advantage of, embarrassingly, most likely by an opponent's convincing fake, as in "That guy ate your lunch."

Clearly, the way a symbol is used can be highly variable. Take the word "light." Depending on the way it is used it can refer to the energy we know as the opposite of darkness ("Is it still light out?"), the object that converts electricity into light ("Turn on a light in here"), a relative lack of weight ("I'll carry the box if it's light enough"), or a characteristic of a person ("He's a real mental lightweight").

Using this social conception of meaning, we can appreciate how humans attach a range of meanings to a symbol. One important distinction between two types of meaning is that between denotation and connotation. *Denotative meanings* are those you find in a dictionary—meanings which attach specific and concretely delineated characteristics to a symbol. The denotative meaning of a symbol is the widely shared core of its definition in a culture. For example, a heart is defined as a collection of muscles arranged in such a way that they can pump blood throughout an organism. Everyone in a culture who is old enough to have learned the word "heart" knows these to be the core, objective characteristics of the object. However, "heart" also carries the connotative meaning of emotion and will. *Connotative meanings* transmit more than just what an object is; they suggest how we evaluate the object or how we as a people feel about it. Thus, "heart" denotes a mass of muscles with a specific function, but it connotes warmth and spirit as well.

The process by which we attach meanings to experience and label them with words is *communal*. That is, we must come to agreement as a community what word will refer to what experience. For example, we have come to agree to call a stone a stone. The same process operates in the creation of connotation. We can actually identify some of the sources of new connotations in a culture by looking at its most inventive users of words, such as poets. In his play *Julius Ceasar*, William Shakespeare had the character Marullus address a crowd of commoners with the words "You blocks, you stones, you worse than senseless things." He did not mean that these people were literally (denotatively) blocks, but that they had the qualities of a block. By such a metaphoric use of words, the language gains connotation. It is possible that the connotative meaning of "block" has survived to our day in the form of the term "blockhead," but if the example from Shakespeare seems a bit outdated to you, consider the following more recent connotative uses. Referring to someone as a computer connotes analytical skills and, perhaps, lack of emotion, while saying someone is a rocket connotes speed.

▶ Perspective:
The Effect of the Immediate Situation

Criticism and praise to fit the situation Just as we can adapt our behavior to suit the demands of changing social situations, so we can change how we communicate. For example, R. A. Birdwhistell (1964) noted that Fiorello LaGuardia, the popular mayor of New York City in the 1930s, could speak standard American English, Yiddish, and Italian. And not only did the mayor change the language he used to fit the group to whom he was speaking, he also changed the nonverbal cues to suit the language he was using. So the hand gestures he used with Yiddish were different from those he used when speaking Italian.

Even if we do not realize we are changing styles of communication to fit varying situations, such changes can have important effects on others. For example, Van Oudenhoven and Siero (1985) divided elementary-school students into "bloomers" (those students who the teacher thought were not performing up to their potential but would begin to do so during the school year) and "nonbloomers" (those students who the teacher thought were performing up to their potential). They then observed the way the teachers communicated with bloomers versus nonbloomers.

Their results indicated that teachers displayed significantly more negative nonverbal communication (for example, shaking the head to indicate that the student's answer was poor) toward those students who were thought not to be able to improve (nonbloomers) than to children who the teachers expected to improve (bloomers). However, the teachers also gave nonbloomers approximately twice as much verbal praise as they gave to bloomers. In other words, the style of communication used by teachers in situations involving one group of students was very different than that used with the other. Children thought to be working to their potential received more nonverbal criticism and more verbal praise from their teachers than did the children who were thought to have room for improvement. ■

Language If a group of people share the meanings of an interrelated set of symbols, it is possible for them to communicate complex sets of meanings. For example, when a child comes home from school and tells her parents what happened that day, she can explain in words (the symbols in this case) how the teacher showed them a garden snake. She describes its shape, color, movement, and texture and, if she is talented at storytelling, her parents can picture the events in some detail. Because they also went to school, and because they share with their child an understanding of the symbols she is using, the parents can also fill in details about such school events for themselves; the way the children gathered in a circle around the teacher, the way some of the children probably cringed or giggled at the thought of touching the snake, the way the teacher must have reassured them that there was no danger, and so on.

Notice that all this information can be transmitted without the participants (or you, the reader) having to be in the classroom or having a snake in the room with you. The events of the day are abstracted. That is, they are recreated with symbols that are combined in such a way that they can stand for the event. Its reality is possible because we share *language*, a network of what G. H. Mead called *significant symbols*, symbols which are used as forms of expression in words and gestures, and whose meanings are agreed upon by a group of people (Lauer and Handel 1977). In language we see the culmination of all that has been said so far in this chapter about the way humans abstract the meanings of their experiences into symbolic expressions that can be communicated with others.

The specialized study of language called *linguistics* focuses on: (1) the sounds that are used in languages (*phonetics*) and the way these sounds are combined to form words (*morphology*), (2) the meanings attached to words (*semantics*), and (3) the rules by which words are combined within languages (*syntax*). But social psychologists are less concerned with the internal mechanisms of language than with the relationship between language and human social life (Fishman 1972).

Paralanguage Just as human experiences vary greatly, so do the forms of linguistic expression. For example, *paralanguage* refers to those variations in linguistic expression that are achieved by varying how we say something, rather than what we choose to say. Such nonsemantic manipulation of meaning can be achieved by variations in pitch, volume, stress, and so on (Key 1975).

Consider the statement "Sure, go right ahead." Read it with no strong variations in emphasis on any one word and it means just what it says. The speaker is giving someone else permission to do something. However, the meaning of this sentence can be reversed entirely without changing one word, that is, with no syntactic manipulation. First, emphasize the word "Sure" by (1) adding volume, (2) stretching the duration of the word's pronunciation, (3) changing the pitch of your voice during the pronunciation of the word so that it begins with a lower note, rises to a higher note, then falls again, and (4) pausing after the word. Second, in completing the sentence, emphasize the word "right" and stretch it out for a full two seconds. The same words now convey the message "I don't want you to do what you said you wanted to do."

Nonverbal language Though the bulk of our communication is accomplished through the use of spoken words, we can also communicate without them. *Nonverbal communication* includes any form of behavior which communicates meaning without the use of spoken or written words. Examples of nonverbal communication include sign language, gestures, and body language.

American Sign Language is a complete and formally documented system of nonverbal language which, as you have already read, provides those who lack hearing and/or verbal speech with the ability to "say" with their hands essentially all the meanings that a person with no such disabilities can express. "Signing," then, is a formalized version of nonverbal language.

But you don't have to know sign language to express yourself nonverbally. For example, everyone uses gestures such as nodding the head to indicate agreement or understanding, or the "thumbs down" gesture that means disapproval. These differ from sign language because they are not part of a formally structured nonverbal language system, but they are widely understood and consciously used in society. We know what we mean to convey when we shake our heads to indicate "no."

However, we humans also exhibit a wide range of behaviors which carry symbolic meaning, though we are often unaware we are doing so. Sometimes called *body language*, these forms of nonverbal communication include many physical behaviors such as body position or facial expression which communicate meaning, often unintentionally (Harrison and Knapp 1972). For example, we may not realize we are sending a message when we widen our eyes suddenly during a conversation (showing surprise), or knit our brows (concern or confusion), or place hands on hips (impatience), but the message can be quite clear to others, even if they are not consciously aware of its having been conveyed.

Whether its forms of expression are verbal or nonverbal, formally structured or not, widely or regionally shared, and intentional or unintentional, language serves as a foundation for our interactions. After discussing how humans come to acquire language, we will look more closely at both verbal and nonverbal forms of language, and at their varying operation in social life.

Acquiring Language

Children are not born speaking in sentences. In fact, infants can do little more than gurgle, cry, or scream. But over time, language skills show up in normal children at fairly predictable rates. The following is a summary of the average ages at which certain language skills appear.

1) *4 months* — Child responds to stimuli such as play with adults by cooing or chuckling.

2) *6–9 months* — Child "babbles" and produces repeated, rhythmic "nonsense" words such as "gagagag," or "babababa."

3) *12–18 months* — Child uses a limited number of words ("Ma," "Da") and can respond appropriately to the meaning of others he or she does not yet use, such as "no."

4) *18–21 months* — Child can construct sentences of two or three words such as "Me want it."

5) *24–27 months* — Child has a vocabulary of 300–400 words from which he or she composes somewhat longer sentences.

6) *30–39 months* — Child's vocabulary grows in size and his or her sentences become longer and more complex in structure, like an adult's. (Wood 1981)

By the time children are about 3 years old they can talk in well-formed sentences and express themselves about pretty much any experience they may have had. That is, they have something like 80 to 90 percent of the language ability they will ever need to get along in society. But where did this ability come from?

Studies of the acquisition of language have tended to fall into one of two major schools of thought; the first arguing that language, like many other skills, is learned through experience in the environment, the second contending that we are born with much of the capacity for speech already in us, and that language appears naturally during development.

Language is learned The best-known argument that language is learned was proposed by the psychologist B. F. Skinner in his classic language text, *Verbal Behavior* (1957). He proposed that language is learned by imitiation of adult language coupled with a system of reward and punishment called *operant conditioning*. That is, children produce their own sounds naturally, and imitate the sounds they hear adults make. Their parents select certain of these from among many other behaviors to be reinforced (by the achievement of a desired end or by a reward of food or affection, for example), and so it is more likely for these behaviors to be repeated. A behavior that is not rewarded or is punished (by the failure to achieve a desired end, withdrawal of food or affection, or active punishment such as scolding) is less likely to be repeated. Accordingly, language is acquired by a sequence of learning events in which parents reinforce those verbal behaviors that they consider desirable (those that fit the adult language system they use) and extinguish by punishment those they consider undesirable (verbal behaviors not considered part of their adult language system). In Skinner's terms, language is acquired when "relatively unpatterned vocalizations, selectively reinforced, gradually assume forms which produce appropriate consequences in a given verbal community" (1957, p. 31).

As an example of how this works, consider how parents act toward their 14-month-old. The child, who is already using the word "ma" for "mother," picks up a banana and says "na," twice. It sounds to mother like "nana," which she thinks is an attempt to say "banana." Is it? Certainly, the child has heard the word "banana" hundreds of times because every time an adult in the family gives this child a banana, his favorite food, the word is used. "Here's a lovely banana." "Want a banana?" And so on. From Skinner's point of view, it does not matter if the child intended to say "banana" and missed by a bit, or whether the vocalization was a repeatedly inaccurate effort to say "ma," or whether it was merely random babbling. The important fact for Skinner's learning theory of language is that the parent who was there picked up on these sounds because they were recognizable as part of standard, adult language and reinforced them by kissing the child, laughing, and making a big fuss over the "new word" baby has learned.

For Skinner, the words in a language, and the rules by which they are put together into sentences, are merely bits of knowledge which can be learned by the process of operant conditioning. Sounds that approximate the standard language behavior of the adult community are selected for reinforcement, and each time they are repeated, the adults encourage closer and closer adherence to adult language standards. The first statement of "nana" may be rewarded, but subsequent uses of "nana" are corrected, with the reward withheld until some effort at compliance is achieved. The parent holds the banana in front of the child and says "Say *banana*," emphasizing the missing first syllable, then gives the food to the child as a reward for any attempt at making the "b" sound.

Though this procedure of operant conditioning may seem to make sense for the learning of a vocabulary, what about the very complex rules for syntax, the way words are combined in a language? According to Skinner, though they are more complex, rules for sentence structure are learned by the same process of successive approximation of adult language through conditioning. A child who is frightened of a tractor may say simply, "Tractor no!" and grab onto mother's leg. The meaning is clear. Mother picks up the child and says "You don't like the tractor," or asks "Don't you like the tractor?" The child may not learn either form of the correct syntax immediately, but some element of it appears in her next statement, "Me like it tractor, no." Thus, just as increasingly accurate expressions of vocabulary can be conditioned in children over time, so can syntactic structures.

Biological bases of language   In 1959, Noam Chomsky, a psycholinguist, criticized the learning theory of language in an influential review of Skinner's book. Chomsky contended that the trial-and-error process of learning theory was inadequate to explain the complex capacity for sentence formation in a 3-year-old. Given the essentially limitless number of combinations of words that are possible in sentence formation, there would be inadequate time in a hundred lifetimes, not to mention in the first three years of one life, for the processes of imitation and reinforcement to implant the unique sets of word combinations we observe in children. That is, learning theory cannot account for the creativity in language use that children develop so quickly.

Chomsky also noted that adult language often seems unrelated to children's language. For example, the way adults actually speak provides children with a poor model for the child to imitate, since adults hesitate, reform sentences, and "edit" themselves constantly. And if children get their models for language from adults, why do they tend, at given ages, to form sentences such as "Me no want," or "Me runned." They did not hear these from adults.

Lastly, Chomsky believed that the differences in languages across the globe are superficial, and that beneath these differences are universal principles of linguistic performance shared by them all. For example, all languages employ subjects, verbs, and objects in sentences and allow for the expression of declarations, questions, and denials. He proposed that the commonalities in languages can be explained by the existence in all humans of biologically based structures for the learning of language.

Chomsky identified two levels of language structure, both of which are contained in every sentence. *Deep structure* consists of those universal rules for the expression of meaning which are biologically implanted in the brain. The deep structure of a sentence is contained in its meaning. By contrast, *surface structure* is the shape that an individual sentence takes. Languages differ in surface structure (the words and ways they are combined to express meanings), but not in deep structure.

To illustrate the differences between deep and surface structure, consider the following two sentences. "I sold my car." "My car was sold by yours truly." The surface structures of these sentences differ, but they mean the same thing, so their deep structures are the same. Or, compare the surface and deep structures of different languages. The German sentence "*Ich muss jetzt essen*" means exactly the same as the English sentence "I have to eat now," though the surface structure of the German is actually in the form "I have now to eat." The fact that, unlike English, German sentences often end with the verb, does not change the characteristic relationship between subject ("I") and verb ("eat") which is established in deep structure.

Deep structure may be in all of us from birth, but the surface structures of language differ, and within one language there are many acceptable ways to express one idea (varying surface structures). Therefore, it is apparent that children must have some way of acquiring the rules for surface structure which dominate in their group. Chomsky called this mechanism the *Language Acquisition Device*, or *LAD*.

The LAD consists of underlying linguistic rules for the construction of phrases and sentences. According to Chomsky, the child's brain is "pre-wired" with neural connections which predispose him or her to put words together in ways that satisfy the demands of deep structure for meaning. There is a variety of combinations of words which will satisfy the demands of deep structure. Thus, a child who says "Me like it tractor, no!" can be assumed to have obeyed the demands of deep structure in expressing herself, though there is no model for such a surface structure in the child's experience.

Chomsky recognized that in order to develop language, a child must have contact with the environment. Language does not spring fully formed from the brain of a child. But where Skinner claimed that all of language is acquired by contact with the environment (adults), Chomsky claimed that hearing language merely serves to provide vocabulary and activate the LAD mechanisms for transforming deep structure into surface structure.

Which came first, language or thought? Chomsky's work is based on the assumption that deep within each of us are principles for thinking which predispose us to express ourselves in ways that may differ superficially (such as in vocabulary and syntax), but which have in common certain core, universal linguistic characteristics (such as subject, verb, object relationships). According to Chomsky, then, thought gives rise to and shapes language.

If this is the case, then we must conclude that the differences in the languages that people speak are superficial, and that everyone must think in basically the same ways. But is this true? According to Benjamin Whorf (1956) it is not. His work in this area, which has come to be called the *Whorfian hypothesis* or *Linguistic Relativity*, suggested that language shapes the way people think.

Whorf compared the linguistic forms of expression in a variety of languages and saw differences which seemed more than simple variations on a common, underlying theme. They appeared to reflect genuinely different ways of thinking about the world. Most of his evidence was presented in the form of comparisons between the ways in which languages describe natural objects and events. For example, he noted that while English has one word for snow, Eskimo languages have several, each of which reflects a different characteristic of snow such as snow which is falling versus fallen, packed versus loose, dry versus slushy, and so on (Whorf 1956). But his analysis went well beyond differences in vocabulary. Consider his comparison of the descriptive English phrase "It is a dripping spring," with its equivalent in the Apache language:

> Apache erects the statement on a verb "ga": "be white (including clear, uncolored, and so on)." With a prefix "no-" the meaning of downward motion enters: "whiteness moves downward." Then "to," meaning both "water" and "spring" is prefixed. The result corresponds to our "dripping spring," but synthetically it is "as water, or springs, whiteness moves downward." How utterly unlike our way of thinking (Whorf 1957, p. 241).

Whorf's conclusion is that the structure of the Apache language shapes the way Apaches can think about the world, just as the structure of English shapes the way we think about the world. To a speaker of English, a dripping spring is a coherent object. The fact that there is water involved is implied by the words "spring" and "dripping," but not specified. For the speaker of Apache, however, the constituent elements of a spring, water, movement, and color are all specified. The form of the Apache language, with its flexible, synthetic combination of words delineating the elements of a situation, differs greatly from the structure of English with its separate, summary defining words. According to Whorf, the characteristics of the two languages lend their speakers to perceive and think about the world differently. Accordingly, Apaches would tend to see events and objects as related in fluid and unfixed ways, while speakers of English would tend to categorize and compartmentalize events and objects in stable, fixed relationships.

Some critics of Whorf's work contend that the basic ideas are sound, but that the influence of language on thought has been overstated. They point out that while languages differ in the way they express experiences, these differences are merely matters of degree. For example, Eskimo languages may have many words for snow and English just one, but by making some additional effort, the different qualities and uses of snow can be expressed in

English. We may have to say "wet, wind-blown, sticky snow" to get the description exact enough, but it can be done. The more moderate, or "weak" version of the Whorfian hypothesis, then, is that language makes the expression of certain types of experiences easier or more efficient.

▶ Perspective:
The Effect of Social and Cultural Forces

Male and female voices   Norms or rules for social behavior in America differ for different groups. Norms differ by sex, race, age, economic well-being, and so on. Such differences are also evident in the way people communicate. Women, for example, have been shown to use different linguistic constructions than men, such as "tag questions" (e.g., "don't you think?") and the word "so" as an intensifier (Lakoff 1975; Holmes 1986). Even in preschoolers the spontaneous use of "thank you" is significantly greater in girls than in boys (Becker and Smenner 1986).

The differences in language used by males and females may be more than just a surface reflection of differences in politeness. According to Carol Gilligan (1982) differences in male and female ways of speaking are reflections of their profoundly different experiences in the social world. In general, men are taught to value independence and autonomy and the aggressiveness that maintains them, while women learn to maintain a continuing balance between their responsibilities to others and their commitment to themselves. For Gilligan, women have a "different voice," because they lead different lives. And because the experiences of men have been used to establish the standard for "normal" experience, those of women have typically been described as deficient or inferior.

In a recent study examining the differing "voices" of females and males, Wood (1986) analyzed how women and men described relationship crises. She found that most women tended to concern themselves with relational issues and personal identity. For example, relational issues included problems in communication, liking, sexual compatibility, and so on. Personal identity focused on issues like maintaining one's sense of self within the relationship and the extent to which both partners felt and expressed commitment to the relationship. Thus, women were much more likely than men to describe a relationship crisis with statements like "I felt smothered," "He would not say how he felt about me," or "It seemed his work was more important to him than I was."

By contrast, male descriptions of relationship crises did not focus on the quality of the relationship or on personal identity, but on the failings of the partner or on external forces as the source of the crisis. Blaming the woman included the claim that she did not understand his needs or that she was boring, demanding, or uncommunicative. Males also blamed external forces such as the failure of specific plans to be fulfilling (e.g., a job not becoming available that would make it easier to see one another) or other people intruding in the relationship (e.g., her interest in another man).

The contrasts between the way females and males talked about their troubled relationships were consistent and clear in other areas as well. In discussing what they were proud of, females tended to focus on the way they tried to help the relationship, their care for others, and their responsibility to themselves. By contrast, men were proud of their adherence to sets of formal, external rules for decent conduct, such as "sticking to the marriage vows or the original agreements between a couple."

According to Wood, these differing ways of talking about relationships reveal that men and women experience social life in very different ways. The differences between the male search for autonomy and the female desire to strike a balance between self and social caring are reflected in their different voices. ∎

Language in Everyday Use

So far we have looked at a number of relatively abstract issues such as the relationship between communication and social order, between meaning and symbols, and between language and thought. But language is more than an abstraction; it is also a practical, everyday tool for communication. People speak to one another in order to get things done, things ranging in complexity and importance from morning greetings to a presentation at work to the President's State of the Union Address before Congress. Though there are common threads in the way people use a given language, there are also apparent differences. By listening even briefly, it is apparent that the use of English differs by sex, race, and social class.

It is interesting to study such differences simply to gain an understanding of the rich variety of language use that is possible. But for the social psychologist, it is more important that attention to the way people speak to one another provides a "window" on their relationships. The language people use in communicating reveals much about the way they perceive themselves and others, and much about the way they make sense of the world and their place in it (Hudson 1981).

Differences in language patterns

Gender. Men and women not only speak differently; they are spoken to (and written to) differently. For example, did you notice that the previous sentence started with the words "men and women"? That use seems more natural to most readers than "women and men," just as it seemed more natural not too many years ago to leave out the female reference entirely. In a sentence that read, "A child needs his vitamins," the word "his" was understood to refer to both male and female children. But it is by no means more "natural" in the sense that it inherently sounds better to our ears to say "men and women," than "women and men."

Specific linguistic constructions are taught as elements of a culture and reflect its social-organizational patterns. In fact, language serves to transmit and enforce patterns of all forms of inequality, including that between the sexes (Thorne and Henley, 1975). For example, if we grow up hearing the word "chairman," then the word "chairperson" sounds awkward or unnatural. If the head of a committee is always referred to as a "chairman," then it is possible to conclude that committees should not be, and are not, headed by females. If in every reference to both sexes (e.g., "men and women") the males are mentioned first, then it is easier to believe that men have primacy in a general sense as well. The language we use not only reflects the social arrangements of a people, it creates social opportunity (Kramarae, Schulz, and O'Barr 1984).

One way to illustrate the differing semantic treatment of the sexes in America is to compare gender-linked terminology. As we can see on direct examination, the terms we use to refer to women are consistently more negative than those for men, or simply leave women out of the issue entirely (Key 1975; Schulz 1975).

1) A male who never marries is called a "bachelor," which connotes freedom and possibly an intention to enjoy himself. However, a woman who never marries is called a spinster or old maid, both of which are terms that connote lack of choice and failure.

2) In marriage ceremonies the classic, closing line has traditionally been "I now pronounce you man and wife." Parallel construction would have the line read either "man and woman," or "husband and wife" (not to mention that, as usual, the male reference is first). The second-class status of the female is shown in the fact that from the moment they are married, he is still the man he has been, while she is transformed into an extension of her husband.

3) It has been accepted style to address letters to a family in the form "Mr. and Mrs. Rupert Jones," in which case Mr. Jones survives as an identifiable individual but Mrs. Jones does not, or even in the form "The Rupert Joneses," in which case Mrs. Jones has disappeared entirely.

4) The title "mister" remains the same for males throughout their lives. However, a female who is single, whatever her age, has traditionally been titled "miss" only until she marries, at which point she is referred to as "misses."

In each of the examples above, the language used differs by gender, and in each case the language suggests female inferiority, since her standing depends upon her marital status, while that of the male does not.

Not only does the language used to refer to the sexes differ, but styles of speech differ between females and males as well. If the way men and women speak reflects and reinforces the inferior status of women in society, then speaking "like a lady" serves to identify the speaker as subservient to some degree and to perpetuate that status. The following are some of the specific sex-linked differences in speech that researchers have examined.

Lakoff (1973, 1975) found male speech to be typically direct, assertive, and adult, while female speech was immature, exaggerated in its politeness, and passive. In drawing these conclusions, Lakoff used a number of characteristics she recognized in her own and others' speech habits.

1) Female word choice differs from male. Females are much more likely than males to use "empty adjectives" such as "nice," and "sweet," and "attractive words" which carry no strong meaning. Males, on the other hand, tend to use more active, powerful words like "great" or "super."

2) Females use the "tag question" and the voice intonation of a question (voice rising at the end of a sentence) to soften the impact of a statement that a male would leave declarative. For example, where a male would say "It's a boring movie," a female would be more likely to say "It's a boring movie, isn't it?" This passive construction allows the speaker to avoid the responsibility for an assertion, but also causes the speaker who uses tag questions to be perceived as less intelligent and having less knowledge (Bradley 1981).

3) Females make more frequent use of modifiers such as "sort of," or "probably," or "I think" than men do, and also use the word "so" more often than men. Each of these uses makes statements less direct and assertive.

4) Lastly, Lakoff suggested that females use the rules for polite address much more than men, resulting in "flowery" speech that seems more useful for the establishment and smoothing of relationships than for the utilitarian transfer of information.

Lakoff's conclusions about female speech patterns were based on her subjective evaluations of her own speech and that of acquaintances. But a number of her propositions have been tested objectively by others. For example, in two experimental studies Crosby and Nyquist (1977) found that females used the "female voice," those styles of speech which Lakoff described, significantly more than did males.

The first study was a laboratory experiment in which undergraduate students were asked to engage in one-to-one conversations on the topic of "the merits of Boston." All conversations were "same sex" (female-female, male-male) and were taped for later analysis. To measure the extent to which Lakoff's description of female speech patterns occurred in any conversation, the researchers counted the frequency of characteristically female words (e.g., empty adjectives, so) and constructions (e.g., tag questions and hedging devices). The results indicated that in those conversations between females there were significantly greater frequency of the "female voice" than in the conversations between males. In the average female conversation, there was a mean frequency of 5.16 such constructions, while in the male conversations their mean use was only 3.08.

In a second experiment, the researchers were interested in discovering whether the "female voice" might also appear in men who found themselves in positions of social dependence, since these patterns of speech were believed to be associated with lack of social power. For the period of a week they had an observer code conversations which took place in a police station between the male officers and clerks who worked there and 45 male and 45 female citizens who came in to conduct a variety of business as clients. These conversations were analyzed for the frequency with which Lakoff's female speech patterns had been used by either participant.

Their results revealed that, as in the previous study, female speakers used the characteristic "female voice" that Lakoff described significantly more frequently than did male speakers. This result persisted whether the female was speaking to another female or to a male. What was more interesting, however, was that both male and female clients used the female speech patterns more often than the police personnel. That is, the "female voice" was used by anyone in the role of inferior as a way of showing passivity, dependence, and/or subservience. This suggests that just as it does not pay for a female to seem to be challenging a male, it does not pay for a male to seem too assertive or challenging to a police officer from whom he may need help.

Another series of studies has examined conversational interruptions as linguistic indicators of differences in sex and social power. Zimmerman and West (1975) proposed that the ability to change the topic of a conversation by interruption is an indication of social power, as is the ability to violate the broad cultural norm for "turn taking" (Goffman 1971). Within the specific context of conversations it has been established that people take turns in talking (Duncan 1972), but it is also true that people do interrupt. To find out whether males and females differ in this regard, Zimmerman and West recorded conversations between adults in a variety of ordinary places such as coffees shops and private homes. Their sample of conversations consisted of 11 male-female conversations (mixed sex), and 20 same-sex conversations (10 male-male and 10 female-female).

Analysis of the interruptions (speech overlaps) in the same-sex conversations revealed that the frequency of interruptions was the same in male-male as in female-female conversations. That is, males did not interrupt one another any more often than females interrupted one another. However, the conversations between males and females revealed an entirely different pattern. In cross-sex conversations, males were found to have interrupted females far more often than the reverse. In fact, of all 48 interruptions identified in the 11 cross-sex conversations, 46 of them, or 96 percent, were initiated by males.

As in the studies conducted by Crosby and Nyquist, Zimmerman and West were interested in discovering whether the specific sex-linked speech pattern of interruption occurred in situations of differential social power unrelated to gender. They conducted a second version of their earlier study by recording five conversations between parents and children in a physician's waiting room and coded the conversations for interruption (West and Zimmerman 1977). Of the 14 interruptions they discovered in the five parent-child conversations, twelve, or 86 percent, were initiated by the adult. These results suggest that, like the "female voice," interruption is a style of speech that differs between males and females not because of any inherent linguistic tendency in either sex, but because of the different levels of social power that characterize the two groups in America.

Race. So far, we have focused on the linguistic differences between males and females in America. These differences seem subtle and slight in comparison with the differences between white and black English. Black English vernacular has often been treated as a dialect of the standard form of English that dominates in the culture (Labov 1972). Just as the female voice has been found to mark the speaker's social standing, the use of black English has been found to establish in the listener expectations that the speaker is inferior (Labov 1982). In fact, during the 1960s and 1970s both black and white observers of racial differences in language tended to take the position that "black dialect" was "impoverished" and the cause of poor academic performance by Blacks (Grubb 1986).

What are the linguistic patterns that are used in black English in America? From the studies of black teenagers in California in the late 1960s conducted by Folb (1980) and Labov's examinations of *sounding* or verbal dueling (1972, 1974), we can identify at least the following elements of black English:

1) *Vocabulary*—Many words and phrases used in the black dialect were wholly absent from standard English. Here are just a few examples taken from her extensive glossary: "ace," for best friend; "bat," for unattractive female, "Charlie," for white male; "dagger," for lesbian; "fall out," for laugh uncontrollably; "hully," for obese person; "number one," for first-degree murder; "oil," for liquor; "put it in the wind," for leave; "rugy," for unattractive; "sack mouth," for one who talks too much; and "yacoo," for a racist or as a derogatory term for a white person.

2) *Metaphor*—As the list of black vocabulary above shows, many terms are metaphoric. The term "bat," for example, which refers to an unattractive female, might derive from a number of sources, such as "ugly as a bat," "an old bat," or "so ugly she must have been beaten with a bat." Whatever its origin, the term "bat" is used as a metaphor for the target.

3) *Lyricism and rhythmic patterning*—Sentences are often formed of rhythmic, lyric combinations of terms and phrases, such as "Take it slow / And go for what you know," with the voice used to emphasize patterns as in a song or poem.

4) *Verbal dueling, variously called "sounding," "cutting," "the dozens," and "signifying," among other terms*—This form of verbal play consists of ritualized insults fired back and forth within a group in rapid-fire style with speed, fluency, and creativity emphasized and valued. Naturally, printing an excerpt from such a conversation, with its speed, fluidity, and rhythm does it no justice, but at the risk of losing most of the flavor of sounding, one person might begin by saying to another, "Your father got brick teeth," to which the immediate response is, "Aw your father got teeth growing out his behind," and so on (Labov 1972, p. 296). According to Kochman (1983),

personal insults and defenses against them can be expressed within the framework of sounding without inevitably violating the boundary between play and nonplay.

The characteristic differences in black English (vocabulary, metaphor, lyricism and rhythmic patterning, and verbal play) do not merely distinguish black from white English; they also mark the user as inferior. In a celebrated trial brought in 1977 in Ann Arbor, Michigan, the court was asked to decide whether a number of black children who had been labeled by school officials as "learning disabled" and "emotionally disturbed" were, in fact, normal and healthy and that they had been treated badly by the school merely because they spoke a different type of English. Testimony focused on whether the black English vernacular speech which the children used was actually inferior for the expression of ideas. The judge in the case concluded that whatever language difficulties there were in the classroom were caused by the unconscious biases of teachers toward the children who spoke black English (Labov 1982).

Class. There is such a large overlap between race and social class in America, people often think black vernacular is equivalent with lower-class language. However, there has been a good deal of research into the language patterns of poor people independent of their race. In sum, studies have concluded that "lower-class speech is less explicit in verbally communicating meaning" (Jewson, et al. 1981). As with the speech of women and blacks, the differences in vocabulary are important, with words like "ain't" and words that express "tough talk" more common, and with specific constructions like double negatives ("I didn't do nothing") and place fillers ("you know") also more frequent than in middle-class speech.

As with the reactions to black English, many of the problems faced by speakers of lower-class English are due to the negative reactions of teachers to their way of talking (Baratz 1972). In fact, looking back over the discussions of language differences by gender and race, it seems clear to us that there are important commonalities in the fact that groups differ linguistically within a culture. It may be interesting to note how vocabularies, syntax, or patterns of voice inflection vary. But such a focus misses the critical fact that wherever there is a dominant or standard form of a language, all variations from it are defined as inferior (Nichols 1984).

Those who are taught nonstandard language patterns and employ them in everyday life are labeled by that use and experience dimished opportunity as a result. Recall that language is the prime tool by which humans define the meaning of their experience, and, therefore, the value of them. Those who determine what forms of expression are to be valued in a culture can cause the experiences of those who do not use approved forms of language to be devalued. Thus, a job candidate who says he is "favorably impressed with the facilities of a business" is much more likely to be taken seriously than one who is "blown away by the stuff you got here."

Universals and Variables in Nonverbal Communication

To this point we have focused on the way communication is accomplished through what we say (*verbal language*) and how we say it (*paralanguage*). However, a great deal can be communicated nonverbally, that is, without making a sound. During conversations our body language (e.g., posture and gestures), the distance we stand from the other person, facial expressions, and even how dilated our pupils are can all send information. Grouped under the general heading of *nonverbal communication*, such factors may actually carry more than 60 percent of the meaning we convey in a conversation, a higher percentage of meaning than is carried by what we choose to say in words (Birdwhistell 1970).

From the listener's point of view we sometimes know, without understanding how, that what a person has said is not what he or she means. We know there is a gap between what is said and what is meant because we can unconsciously pick up nonverbal signals from the speaker. From the point of view of the speaker, the transmission of nonverbal information, though often unconscious, is a critical element of the communication process. Just why this is the case may be made clear by looking again (as we did in the chapter on the self) at Erving Goffman's comparison of human social interaction with stage performance.

We talked a good deal about Goffman's (1959) conception of the self in

Chapter 2. He proposed that by staging performances, people attempt to project specific images of themselves, depending on the way they define the situation in which they find themselves. As with actors on stage, only a portion of the management of the impressions conveyed in everyday interaction is due to the lines people deliver. We all "interpret" the roles we play with words plus gestures, facial expressions, movements, and so on. Much is conveyed by nonverbal techniques, many of which Goffman and others have examined closely.

Nonverbal forms of communication, though they vary greatly, are found in all cultures. For example, Eibl-Eibesfeldt (1974) has documented the existence in a wide variety of cultures of physical gestures that accompany greetings. "When greeting over a distance people smile and nod; and if very friendly they raise their eyebrows with a rapid movement, keeping the eyebrows maximally raised for approximately ⅙th of a second." This *eyebrow flash* is observed to differ somewhat across cultures, being suppressed in Japan, for example, where it is considered indecent. However, its commonality across cultures is more impressive than its variations. In fact, it has even been observed in nonhuman primates (Weitz 1974).

Another widely distributed nonverbal indication of greeting involves hand gestures. For example in many Western cultures we greet one another by waving one open hand near the shoulder. By comparison, in many Eastern cultures greeting is accompanied by the placing together of hands before the chest or face, palms or fingertips touching in the "prayer," while some primitive societies such as Dahomeans greet one another by snapping their fingers (Argyle 1975). Another pattern of nonverbal communication which Eibl-Eibesfeldt finds widely distributed is the indication of embarrassment by hiding one's face or mouth behind one's hand.

The similarities and differences in meaning of the nonverbal behaviors in various cultures have been of special interest to anthropologists and students of comparative linguistics. However, social psychologists have focused on the way nonverbal communication techniques operate in the relationship between people within a culture. Let us examine more closely the nonverbal communication techniques of (1) body language, (2) facial expression and gaze, and (3) the management of space and territory.

Body language *Body language*, sometimes called *kinesics*, consists of those physical actions such as posture, the placement of hands, arms, and legs, and all gestures which communicate meaning, whether consciously exhibited or not. Although they are sometimes included within discussions of body language, we shall treat facial expression and the management of space separately. Take the example of a conversation in which one participant becomes impatient. Without ever saying a word or changing facial expression he expresses his impatience by several varieties of body language. He may lean backwards and cross his arms across his chest, then begin tapping his foot on the ground rhythmically, and finally put his hand up with the palm flat and facing the other person in the gesture that unambiguously means "stop" in many cultures. Using such forms of body language is critical to our social performances and our ability to influence the performances of others.

For example, Eckman and Friesen (1969) classify forms of nonverbal behavior as emblems, illustrators, or regulators. Each is used in a different way to influence communication. *Emblems* are gestures which carry direct meaning. For example, nodding the head means "yes" and circling one's index finger around an ear means "crazy." Emblems, then, are essentially words that are expressed nonverbally.

Illustrators are movements that are coordinated with speech and used to emphasize or clarify verbal meanings. Clenching one's fist or chopping down sharply with an opened hand provides emphasis to the words that are said during the actions. A number of experiments have been conducted in which messages are either heard and viewed, or only heard. The results consistently show that more information is conveyed more accurately when a speaker's illustrative body language can be observed (Bull 1983).

Regulators are used to influence the way a conversation proceeds, including who is to speak, for how long, and when subjects are to change. For example, by simply turning one's head away from a speaker and toward another person in a group, it is strongly suggested that the speaker should stop talking, and the person to whom attention has been directed should begin. Several other examples of regulative body language were discovered in a study conducted by Knapp, Hart, Friedrich, and Schulman (1973), in which subjects were asked to conduct an interview with someone else "as quickly as possible." Given the task of getting out of the conversation quickly, the subjects were observed to use a variety of nonverbal regulating tactics, including breaking eye contact, pointing the feet and legs toward the door, nodding the head, and leaning forward.

Studies of nonverbal communication in job interviews have found that a variety of these cues can directly influence the impression a candidate makes. In fact, some interviewers are aware of body language to the extent that they actively look for candidates to use specific nonverbal cues. For example, from his observations of many job application interviews, Raffler-Engel (1983) found interviewers to want candidates who did not fidget or gesture excessively, nor were so still and stiff that they "seemed to be hiding or controlling something." What the interviewers wanted was a candidate who showed controlled aggressiveness by leaning forward while maintaining a basically upright posture and who employed "appropriately animated gestures."

More recently, research on the effects of nonverbal communication during job interviews has suggested that such forms of communication can be used with good effect, or can be overdone. Baron (1986) had confederates of his take part in interviews for entry-level management positions and employ a series of positive nonverbal cues such as nodding and smiling to the interviewer, using perfume, or both. The interviewers' ratings of the job candidates revealed that the use of positive nonverbal cues of nodding and smiling had a significant positive effect on candidates' ratings, as did the use of perfume. However, when both nonverbal techniques were employed by candidates (nonverbal cues and perfume), interviewers' ratings declined significantly. Baron concluded that the negative effect of the combined nonverbal cues was due to the sense of the interviewer that he or she was being manipulated. These results seem similar to those of Raffler-Engel that the way a person communicates nonverbally can make it seem that he or she is "trying too hard."

In another study of nonverbal behavior in job interviews, Gifford et al. (1985) found that some nonverbal cues seem to be used for making specific sorts of judgments. Thirty-four job applicants' interviews were taped and shown to 18 expert judges who had extensive experience in employment interviewing. Careful examination of the taped interviews revealed that judges used the candidate's style of dress, frequency of gesturing, and time spent talking in evaluating his or her social skills. That is, those candidates who dressed more formally, talked more, and gestured more frequently were thought by judges to be more socially skilled.

Clearly, body language can be used to influence others. However, those who use it can also be influenced. For example, Riskind (1984) conducted an experiment in which subjects were asked to perform a task and then, at random, either failed or were given good grades on their performances (failure versus success conditions). Simultaneously, the subjects in each of the failure and success conditions were, at random, placed in either upright or slumped postures. The results indicated that when the slumping posture was appropriate to the situation (i.e., the subject had failed the task), the body language minimized feelings of helplessness and loss of motivation. However, when the body language was inappropriate (slumping after doing well on a task) significant losses in motivation and feelings of control were discovered. These results suggest that as with verbal communication, nonverbal messages such as body language are "heard" by the people who send them, even if they do so subconsciously. If we know that messages influence their targets, we also know that messages influence those who send them.

▶ Perspective:
The Effect of Social Definition

Communication and gender identity In this chapter we have presented a good deal of data about the way males and females differ in styles of communication. But how are we to explain differing styles of communication within each group? Not all men speak the same way, nor do all women. As the interactionists have demonstrated so clearly, each person brings to each social interaction a unique set of understandings that influence how she or he will define the situation and behave within it. This is also, it turns out, true of communication.

In a recent study of this issue, Drass (1986) began with the realization that one cannot assume that a person's physical gender automatically determines his or her gender identity. Drass argues that gender identity is "the set of meanings individuals attribute to themselves as males or females," and that a male's sense of self may vary as to the degree of "maleness" and that a female's sense of self may vary as to the degree of "femaleness."

Using a scale for the measurement of gender identity developed by Burke and Tully (1977), Drass had 56 male and female college students make a series of self-evaluations for gender-related characteristics such as emotionalism, power, bravery, individualism, ambition, and sensitivity. Each student was then asked to engage in a conversation with a person of the same gender. These dyadic conversations (male talking to male and female talking to female) were recorded and analyzed later.

The results showed that those students who defined themselves as having "male" qualities such as independence, ambition, strength, and assertiveness displayed significantly greater rates of conversational overlaps (talking while the other person is still talking) and interruptions (breaking into and taking over the conversation). This was true whether the student whose self-definition was more "male-like" was physically a male or a female. That is, if a person's definition of self is dominated by traditionally male characteristics, he or she (physical gender does not matter) will use the patterns of speech that are characteristic of males in American culture. The opposite will be true of individuals whose self-concepts are more "female-like." To understand speech patterns, then, we cannot ignore the concepts and definitions which individuals bring to their social interactions. ■

Facial expression and gaze Given that most of our attention is directed at the face of the person with whom we are talking, it should be no surprise that the face and eyes are powerful and direct sources of nonverbal communication (Harper et al. 1978). Researchers have cataloged the primary facial expressions of emotion including anger, happiness, fear, surprise, sadness, disgust/contempt, and interest (Osgood 1966). In fact, we can see strong similarities in the expression of emotions in various cultures, and even in animals (Darwin 1872). For example, pulling the lips back from the teeth shows anger in humans and a range of other animals such as dogs, lions, and so on. Also, a direct, prolonged gaze shows threat and power while looking away shows deference.

Many studies have attempted to discover which of the facial expressions of emotion is the easiest to recognize, and what categories of people are best and worst at perceiving such emotions. Using photographs or drawings of facial expressions of emotion about which a large number of judges agree, subjects are asked to identify the emotion depicted in each. It has been found that those emotions which subjects tend to identify with greatest accuracy are happiness and sadness, while those about which people are least accurate are disgust, contempt, and surprise (e.g., Levitt 1964). Other studies report that sex and race can both influence the accuracy with which the facial expression of emotion is communicated. For example, females are often found to be more accurate in producing and judging the facial expression of emotion than males (Harper et al. 1978).

One famous person who has been identified prominantly in terms of his ability to communicate, and whose political successes are often attributed to that ability, is Ronald Reagan. In a study of his ability to evoke emotional reactions in viewers, researchers videotaped excerpts from the President's speeches representing his facial expressions of (1) happiness/reassurance, (2) anger/threat, and (3) fear/evasion. These excerpts were shown to subjects in visual-only and sound-plus-vision formats. Results indicated that the subjects smiled during happiness/reassurance displays by the President and frowned during both the anger/threat and fear/evasion displays. These reactions were even more strongly present in reaction to the visual-only presentation (McHugo et al. 1985). For those who have sought an explanation for this President's exceptional ability to gather popular support in the face of what polls say is widespread disagreement with his specific programs, it is possible that his actor's skill with the facial expression of emotions has been critical.

Like facial expression, gaze is a powerful communicator. Eye contact has been consistently shown to be an important indicator of the nature of a social relationship (Argyle and Dean 1965; Goffman 1971). In some cases extended gazing may indicate emotional warmth and closeness, as in the gaze that lovers exchange (Rubin 1970), while in others extended eye contact is used as a communicator of power, as in "staring down an opponent" (Rosa and Mazur 1979). In Goffman's terms, eye contact (gazing) is an example of a *tie-sign*, an act that makes apparent the nature of a relationship. Two fairly recent studies illustrate the way gazing operates as a form of nonverbal communication.

In one study, the female members of 96 male/female couples were interviewed by either male or female interviewers while standing on line outside movie theaters in New York City. While the interviews were being conducted with the female, the male partner's behavior was watched to see if he displayed *tie-signs*, that is, indications of his relationship with his date. These included one form of verbal cue (amount of talk) and two forms of nonverbal cue (direction in which his body was turned and the direction of his gaze). Analysis of the behavior of the male partner indicated that when the subject of the interviews became more intimate (e.g., personal questions about the respondent's childhood memories) the males exhibited more tie-signs, including more talk, aiming his body directly at his partner, and gazing directly at his partner. Such tie-signs were also produced at a greater rate when the interviewer was male rather than female. The implication of this finding is that when the character of a relationship seems threatened, a variety of forms of communication, including talk, body language, and eye contact are employed to maintain and reaffirm social closeness (Fine et al. 1984).

Eye contact can also be used to signal to others whether we expect to have an advantage over them (social power) or not. Ridgeway and her colleagues (1985) recorded the nonverbal behaviors of subjects as they were brought together in same-sex and mixed-sex pairings to work on a small task. It has been well documented in other research that, despite the recent changes in sex roles in America, males continue to expect to have social power advantages over the women with whom they interact, and females share this expectation for males (Eagly 1983). It was therefore assumed by Ridgeway et al. that males who had been told that they would work with females would expect to enjoy a power advantage over them. The researchers predicted that males would communicate this expectation by sending specific nonverbal signals to their partners. This is precisely what happened. Males maintained significantly longer periods of eye contact on first meeting their female partners than did males who worked with other males. Males who worked with females also took significantly less time to take their turn in talking (called *verbal latency*) than did males with male work partners. In other words, both duration of eye contact and shortness of verbal latency are used to signal one's expectations for social power in interaction.

The management of space in interaction   One of the most subtle forms of nonverbal communication is the way we arrange ourselves physically in a space in relation to others. We have been aware for centuries of the territoriality of animals as they mark their areas with scents or simply fight off intruders in a hunting ground. But the systematic examination of human territories, sometimes called *proxemics*, has been fairly recent (Hall 1966). According to Edward Hall, people unconsciously control the amount of space left between interacting individuals. The amount of space allowed differs by culture, sex, social setting, and a variety of other factors. For example, as a general rule, Mexicans tend to stand closer to one another in normal conversation than do white Americans, who, in turn, tend to stand closer to one another than do black Americans (Argyle 1975). In addition, Hall observed that within a given culture, the distances maintained between individuals have consequences for the type of communication taking place between them. He identified four such "distance zones":

1) *Intimate distances* are closest (ranging only to a maximum of about 18 inches) and are used only in intimate relationships. Talk as a form of communication is of minimal importance, and the senses, including touch, sight, and even smell are most important.

2) *Personal distances* begin at about 1½ feet and range to a maximum of about 4 feet. Physical contact is still a distinct possibility, but sensory communication diminishes greatly in comparison with intimate distance. At this distance low or moderate voice volume is most typical, and relationships may range from intimate to fairly close, with proportional effects on distance.

3) *Social distances* range from 4 to a maximum of about 12 feet. These distances are used for interaction with people who we might know,

but not intimately or as social friends, that is, people with whom business might be conducted or more formal social interaction. At social distances, sight and hearing are the dominant channels for communication.

4) The *public distance* is the farthest, ranging from 12 to 25 feet, and is reserved for interaction with noted "public figures," such as a film actor or office holder. Communication is accomplished by broad indicators such as gestures and body posture; even speech, which must be at a relatively high volume, can be indistinct.

Erving Goffman (1971) extended our understanding of proxemics beyond the simply physical distances Hall studied by identifying a number of kinds of *territories of the self* which we use to regulate our everyday interactions:

1) Goffman began with the notion of *personal space*, the area around a person whose boundaries form a sort of ellipse shape. This territory goes from close behind a person, extends a little farther away around the sides, and then stretches out in front for a distance that depends upon where the person is, or what he or she is doing. The way to determine the shape of an individual's personal space (including yours) is to have another person approach until the "target person" begins to feel uneasy.

Personal space changes shape and size when we sit in a chair (the ellipse shortens dimensions in back and on the sides) and when we begin to move (the ellipse extends in the direction of our movement, depending upon speed). The effects of sitting in a chair and of moving lead us to other categories of Goffman's territories of the self.

2) The *stall* is a form of territory consisting of a space to which an individual must make an "all-or-none" claim, such as a chair or telephone booth. In normal interaction, only one individual can occupy such a territory, and any suggestion of sharing it is interpreted as an invasion.

3) *Use space* is that territory to which an individual lays claim because she or he expects to make use of it. For example, a person who is running extends his or her personal space by the use space stretching in front. The faster the running, the greater the expanse of use space, and the greater the possibilities of territorial invasions.

4) The *sheath* is that set of objects that make contact with one's body, such as skin, clothing, hair, and so on. The sheath forms the final territorial boundary for social distance in close quarters. In a crowded elevator, for example, personal space shrinks to the minimum, but contact with clothing, hair, skin, and so on is still considered a violation in American cultural behavior.

5) The *turn* is the order in which an individual gets to do what she or he wishes. It is a territory better measured in space than in time. For example, a person in a crowd of people at a service counter expects to be taken care of "in turn," though there may be no physical way of identifying whose turn it is. When we stand on line, we are creating a physical ordering of the turn, and those who "cut in" may be yelled at for their violation.

6) There are many varieties of territory which we use in interaction, too many for us to discuss here. However, here is a last one: *eye contact*. Though we classed it as an element of facial expression, it can also be seen as a territory of the self, since whom we look at, and who we allow to look at us, indicates whether we wish to interact at all. Consider a student who is sitting in the college library reading. She looks up from her book and "sweeps" the room with her eyes. During the "sweep" she notices that a male student across the room is looking at her. She now must decide whether he too was simply looking around or whether he was actually staring at her. She waits a few seconds before discretely looking up, only to discover that he is still looking right at her. She has the power to control the territory of eye contact; all she need do is not look again. However, if she wishes to make possible any further social contact, she can look again, and hold eye contact this time. Thus, without saying a word, we can communicate nonverbally in a wide range of ways.

Looking Back

As we have seen, communication is intimately related to social order. In fact, it can be argued that without communication, no forms of social cooperation between humans would be possible. While nonhuman animals do communicate, human communication is uniquely abstract. That is, we attach meaning to our experiences and to objects in the environments whose reality is due only to our agreement about that meaning.

The expression of abstract meaning through symbols, which is dominated in human behavior by spoken language, is richly varied. Cultures differ in the languages they use, and groups within cultures also vary. Variations include differing meanings for the same word and variations in styles of verbal expression.

Communication is not only verbal. Nonverbal communication includes forms of sign language (formal systems for attaching meaning to gestures) and informal signing, such as body language, facial expression of emotion, and gaze and the manipulation of territory or space. Such forms of nonverbal communication may actually convey more meaning than what we choose to say to others in words.

Communication and language do indeed represent basic elements in understanding the human puzzle: they play an essential part in the development of the self. As we shall see in the next chapter, communication is also an important aspect of the roles that we come to play in everyday life and of the conflicts that develop between the individuals who play those roles.

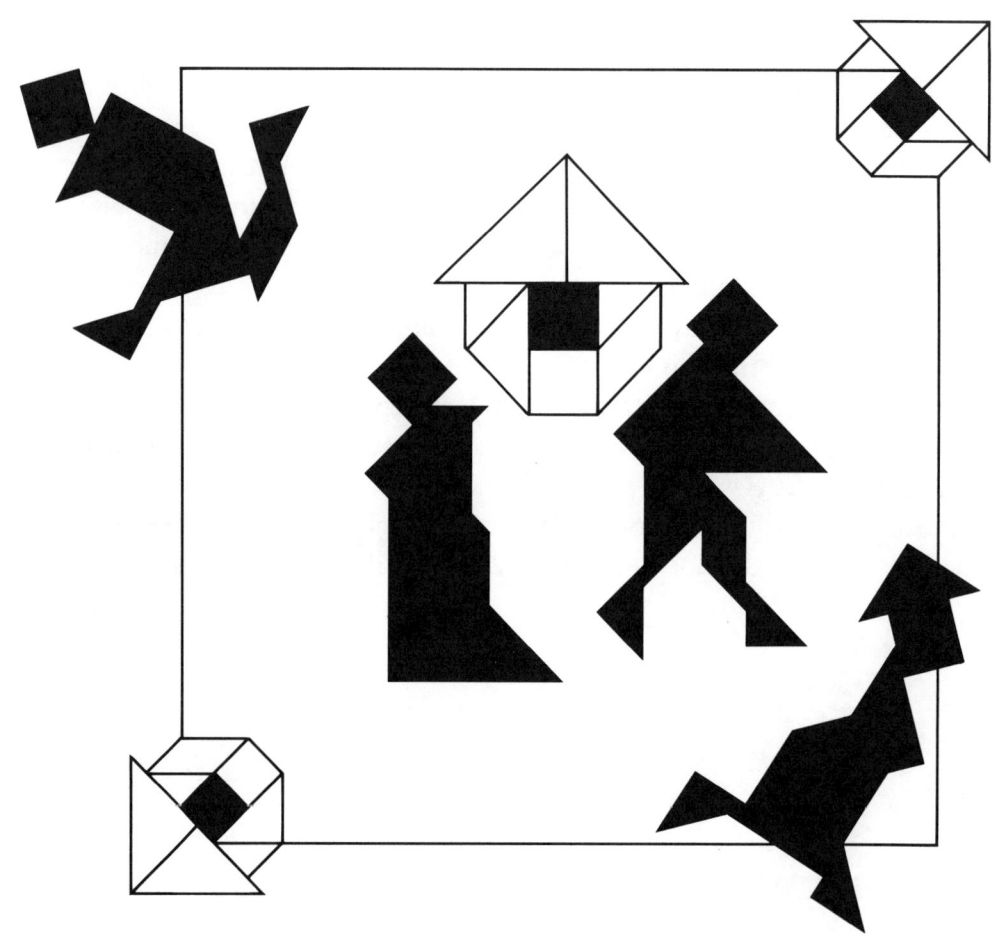

Chapter 5

Roles

CONSIDER THE FOLLOWING INTERACTION. You are in a busy department store to buy a shirt, but the shirt you are interested in is in a glass case and there is no sales clerk in the area. You start to look for some help, but it is not obvious at first glance which of the people in the area works for the store. How do you know which of the people to approach? Perhaps the employees wear uniforms or name tags. Perhaps they behave differently than customers, arranging items on shelves or hangers or looking around at customers rather than at merchandise. Finally, you pick out a person who seems to work at the store. You ask if you can get some help with the shirts, only to have the person respond that he does not, in fact, work there, and would also like to find someone who does.

At the beginning of the conversation you might have felt some embarrassment at misidentifying this person as a store employee. However, as soon as he reveals that he is not, and that he is, like you, looking for help, the interaction settles into a more comfortable pattern. You are now both clearly defined as customers who can, for example, complain about the lack of efficiency in the store. In such a situation you might expect to hear lines like "You can never get help when you want it," or "You could just walk out of the store with something and not pay."

Though interactions like these are common, we typically do not make such mistakes. We are more likely to correctly identify the customer as a customer because we usually wait for clear indications of how to act toward people in specific situations. The critical element in this process is termed the *role*—behavioral expectations for what an individual "should" do (Heiss 1981). Sometimes the expectations are clearly established for a well-structured situation such as the department store example. At other times the situation is not familiar or its character is unclear and participants must create, on the spot, an agreement about what behaviors are appropriate (Turner 1986). In either case, roles allow social interactions to proceed according to rules that make them predictable, orderly, and understandable to the participants. That is, roles allow people to vary their behaviors to fit the demands of social situations, and so to anticipate and satisfy the expectations of others (Zurcher 1983).

Looking Ahead

In this chapter, we shall examine a concept that is central to the literature of social psychology yet is much disputed by those who use it. Almost everyone seems to agree that roles are behavioral expectations for what a person should do in specific social situations. But some assert that such expectations are part and parcel of the social structure to which an individual must adjust, whereas others argue that individuals are often free to make their own roles. This theoretical split was seen in previous chapters between those who saw a self determined by unconscious or cultural forces, and those who saw an active self molded by the individual. The same split was also represented in the debate between those who attributed an external reality to reference others which is linked to an individual's behavior and attitudes, versus those who saw reference others as created in the individual's imagination.

The roles we play provide us with "lines" to deliver that inform others of the part we play in a given social interaction. Unlike the actors in a theater, however, we live in a society where we must improvise in order to stage an effective scene. Nothing is entirely fixed; little is permanent. When change becomes the norm, tremendous ambiguities and conflicts develop with respect to what we are expected to do. Role strain is uncomfortable; but it also makes possible the social changes which benefit our society as a whole.

Social Behavior by "Script"

In William Shakespeare's play *As You Like It*, the character Jaques begins a famous speech with the lines:

> All the world's a stage,
> And all the men and women merely players;
> They have their exits and their entrances;
> And the one man in his time plays many parts.

Social psychology has borrowed directly from theater in describing the concept of role (Biddle and Thomas 1966). In films or plays the author sets the part in a dramatic situation and provides the actors with a script of lines to deliver. In real life, as illustrated by the interaction in the department store, we take on a role we are expected to play, depending upon how we define the situation in which we find ourselves. Once we have done this, what we say and do—in short, how we play a part—is pretty much established. But there are some differences between the way roles operate on the stage and the way they operate in real life.

In everyday interaction the lines are not specifically set out as they are in a script. There is a range of statements within a role which will fit the situation and satisfy the expectations of others. For example, a sales clerk can say "May I help you?" or "I am not in the shirt department, but I'll find someone for you." Either would be appropriate for an individual playing the role of department store employee.

In addition, social situations are not always known beforehand by the participants as they are by stage actors. In real life people must often develop some sort of agreement as to the type of interaction they will have. For example, in the department store interaction, the participants started out defining the situation as an exchange between customer and sales clerk, then redefined the situation as one between mildly dissatisfied customers. The "lines" you would expect would be different for the two situations.

The Qualities of Roles

It should be clear by now that the roles people play are determined by the situations in which they find themselves. The very same person is expected to play one role at home (perhaps the role of father) and another role at work (perhaps the role of teacher). The situations at home and at work can be seen to have *structure*. That is, each consists of a stable set of relationships that can actually be charted, the way a business might display its organizational structure. For example, below is a simplified picture of the structure of a workplace, in this case a college.

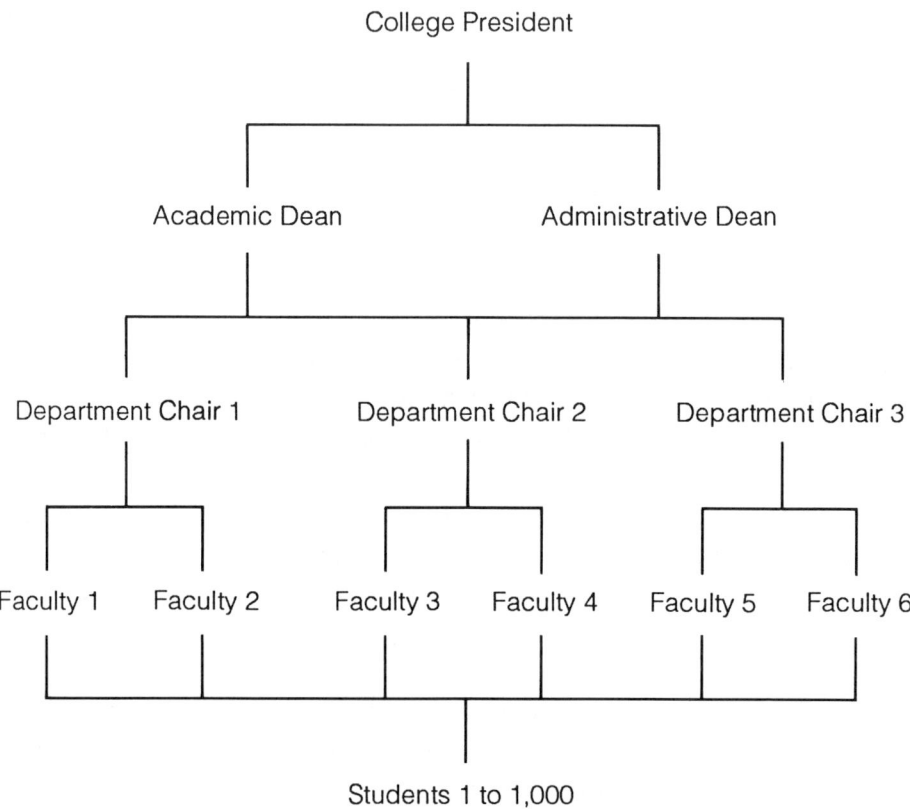

Like any structure (a building, for example), a *social structure* is composed of component parts which are related to one another in consistent ways. Each place within the structure is called a *status* or *social position*. Social statuses make sense only in the context of some social structure. So a faculty member has an organizational status, or place within the structure of the college, which exists in relation to the other statuses (for example, students and department chairs) in the structure.

Social structure and social status are terms that are useful for describing relationships, but do not focus on behavior. That is the emphasis of the concept of role. Recall that roles are behavioral expectations for what an individual "should" do. The way Ralph Linton (1936) described the process, roles are behaviors expected of individuals because of the social structural statuses they occupy. In short, roles are statuses in action. Thus, I occupy the status of teacher (a position within the social structure of a college), but my role consists of the behaviors expected of a person in that status.

Roles are relational and reciprocal Roles then, like statuses, are *relational*. That is, they make sense only in the context of the other roles in a given social situation. Ralph Linton, who did much of the early work in defining these ideas, put it this way: "the position of the quarterback is meaningless except in relation to the other positions. From the point of view of the quarterback himself, it [the role] is a distinct and important entity. It determines where he shall take his place in the lineup and what he shall do in the various plays" (Linton 1936).

The relational character of roles is critical in making sense of everyday behavior. A person whose behavior might be defined as odd, or even dangerous, can be understood and accepted as totally banal when enacted in the appropriate social setting. In the appropriate setting, a total stranger can ask you to sit down so he can put his hands in your mouth and poke around with a pointed tool. This is sensible, even appropriate behavior by a dentist in his or her office, but eccentric at the very least for a sociology professor in a classroom, or even by a dentist at a dinner party. Context is everything in gaining acceptance for social behaviors.

The enactment of any role is also, therefore, *reciprocal*. When an individual decides what behavior is expected in a given situation, he or she automatically orients that behavior to the demands of some other role. For example, the customer at a store plays that role toward a sales clerk. A teacher's behavior is oriented by the expectations of students. A physician plays the role with a patient's expectations in mind. To the extent that the expectations of each participant are fulfilled (I do what you expected me to and you do what I expected you to), the roles have made the interaction stable and meaningful for the actors.

This would be true no matter what the roles involved, as long as the participants share a definition of the situation, of the roles appropriate to that situation, and of the behaviors expected in those roles. For example, a couple we know sees their marriage as a sort of partnership, rather like a business. They spend a great deal of time apart but like one another and claim that there is a variety of reasons for being married, including tax advantages, increased social contacts, and the ability to own a nicer home than either could afford alone. The fact that they define the roles of husband and wife differently than most of the rest of the society does not necessarily diminish the usefulness of the marriage roles they play. It is only necessary that their expectations for one another's behaviors be shared and fulfilled.

Roles exist independently of their occupants Roles like teacher or student are played by a variety of individuals and are more enduring than any role occupant. For example, though currently many Americans strongly associate Ronald Reagan with the presidency of the United States, the role of president existed long before he was born and will likely remain long after he leaves the office.

Roles are features of the social situations in which they occur. The role of pitcher, for example, is a consequence of the structure of a baseball team. We know what behavior is expected of a pitcher only to the extent that we understand how the pitcher fits into the game of baseball. It is the set of relationships, then, that demands our understanding. Once such an understanding is in place, we can predict what each participant will do, independent of which particular individual happens to be playing a role. Though they were on different teams during the 1986 World Series, Boston pitcher Roger Clemens was expected to play the role of pitcher in much the same way as New York Mets pitcher Dwight Gooden. It is the stability of the role of pitcher over time that allows baseball fans to make comparisons between the players of the past and those in the game today.

In a sense, roles are more "real" than the people who occupy them. A teacher friend named Lou tells the story of a visit from his brother, who was at the time an accountant. The brother claimed that he could easily pass as a professor with very little preparation, because he knew how they acted. The following day, wearing his brother's "professor outfit" (worn corduroy jacket and tie) he entered one of Lou's classes with the announcement that he was a guest lecturer and proceeded to give a 50-minute talk (much of which, we were told, was pure invention), but which the students took very seriously and accepted thoroughly as material for which they would be held responsible. Clearly, from the point of view of the students, Lou's brother *was* a professor because he acted like one.

Role sets If you look back at the diagram of the structure of a college, you can see that there is a variety of positions within the organization. In fact, our version is much simplified in comparison with a real college. We left out, for example, distinctions between ranks of faculty members, between graduate and undergraduate students and between the years from freshman to senior, the positions of various staff members, and so on. And if there are so many statuses, there must also be a wide range of roles being played in any social structure. Since this is the case, any one actor within the college setting must be capable of orienting his or her role behavior to the expectations of a variety of other roles. In fact, though we have been using the term role, the term *role set* more accurately describes the way we must be capable of performing in social situations. A role set summarizes all of the role relationships in which an individual is involved by virtue of occupying a single status (Merton 1975b).

Take the example of a faculty member. He or she is a member of a fairly complex social structure and so must be able to fulfill the expectations of a variety of other role players. Students expect a faculty member to behave a certain way toward them, while the president of the college may expect a very different sort of behavior from faculty members. The role set of a faculty member, then, includes sets of behavior expected of him or her by a variety of other role players within the social structure of the college. On the next page is a diagram depicting the nature of the role set attached to the status of a faculty member. Individuals who occupy any of the other roles in the college expect different behavior of a faculty member, depending on the particular role relationship.

Any other member of the college will have a role set for his or her status in the social structure. The role set of a student includes expectations for his or her behavior by other students, faculty and staff members, and so on. Sometimes these expectations vary widely from one another. For example,

Role Set for a College Faculty Member

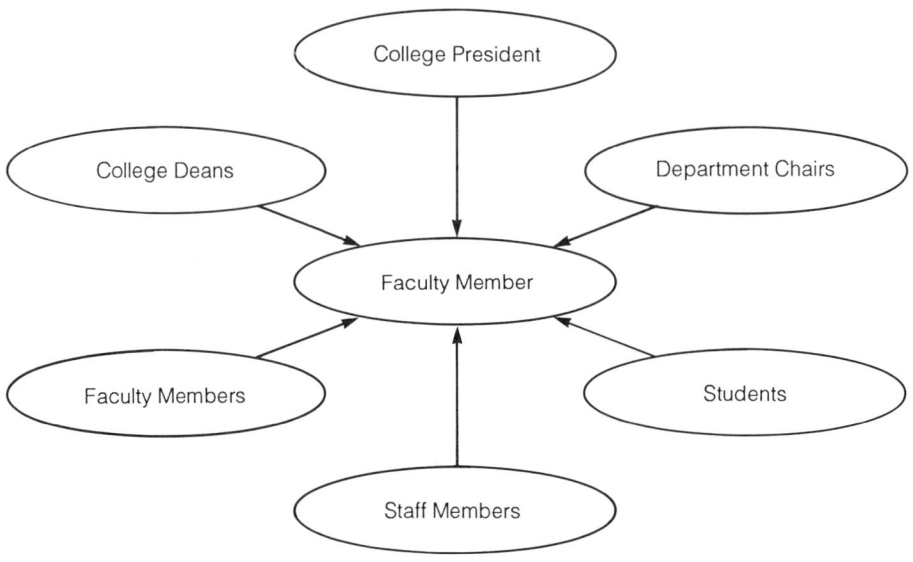

a college senior is normally expected to act very differently towards the president of the college than towards a sophomore at the same school. At other times different expectations for role behavior are barely distinguishable (a college senior normally is not expected to behave much differently toward a sophomore than toward a junior).

Multiple Role Sets In a given day, an individual commonly takes part in a number of different social situations. Waking in the morning, he or she may have a role set within a family (in relation to mother, father, wife or husband, daughters, sons, brothers, sisters, etc.). Then at work the role set attached to an employee is taken on (in relation to bosses, customers, and coworkers). On the way home, a visit to a store calls up the role set of a consumer (in relation to store employees, store owner, other customers). If guests are invited for dinner the role set of host applies (in relation to cohosts, guests, children of hosts, and, in affluent circumstances, servants). In short, every individual is called upon to shift from one role set to another at short notice, each time matching his or her behavior to the expectations of the various role players within a new situation.

Teaching in college, we have seen an increasingly common example of the expansion of multiple roles in some of our students; namely, women who have returned to school to complete or begin delayed college educations. Often they add the role of student to their roles as mothers, job holders, and homemakers. As you will see later in this chapter, piling on such multiple roles can create problems for these women (Gerson 1985).

Role Taking

Actors on the stage know what to say because they are told by the director what each scene in the play is about, and because the specific lines are printed in a script. However, playing a role in real life requires the active involvement of individuals in the creation of a sort of "social performance." This is certainly the case when we enter social situations with which we are unfamiliar, such as the first day in college classes or the first day at a new job.

But even social situations in which we find ourselves day after day, such as college classes or visits to a department store, can be interpreted in varying ways by their participants. For example, when you walked into a high school class to find that the regular teacher had been replaced by a substitute teacher, did you redefine somewhat the meaning of the situation? If your school was anything like the ones we knew, many students did, at least enough did to make things difficult for the substitute in ways that the regular teacher would never have tolerated. The processes by which people actively interpret the meaning of their social interactions so as the establish and enact satisfactory role relationships are termed *role taking* and *role making*.

Role taking (Mead 1934; Blumer 1953; Turner 1956, 1962; Sherohman 1977) can be defined in simple terms as the ability to assume the viewpoint of another person. That is, in interaction, an individual imagines how others are going to act by guessing how they define the specific social situation. To know how we are expected to act, we must try to "get inside" the minds of others and see ourselves from their point of view. In order to make accurate guesses, we use the clues that are available in a specific situation whose meanings we have learned by experience.

To illustrate, imagine an employee who has been asked to go to the boss's office. On the way to the appointment, she may have few or no clues as to the boss's intentions, and, therefore, cannot know what the situation will be like. How should she act? Perhaps she asked fellow employees if they know what is "going on," or tried to recall how the boss was behaving earlier in the day. If these attempts to predict what role she is to play provide no information, she enters the meeting looking for her first clues. Does the boss come to the door to greet her with a smile and handshake, or remain seated at her desk working without looking up? What are the boss's first words, and what sort of expression does she have on her face? Is there anyone else in the room? The employee would certainly draw different inferences from the presence at the meeting of her close friend and colleague than from the presence of a competitor in the organization. Having collected clues from such sources, the employee guesses, before the interaction really begins, how she is expected to behave, then acts accordingly.

The early development of the idea of role taking comes from the work of G. H. Mead, who contended that our ability to take into account the perspectives of others is at the very source of social order and the development of the human self (see chapter 2 on the self). According to Mead, role taking is basic to human cooperation and social organization, since it provides the mechanism whereby we can take into account the intentions of others and, thereby, adjust our actions to them. But role taking should not be thought of as a one-way process, in which a single actor takes the role of some other person. Role taking is an interactive and mutual act, in which all participants in a social situation simultaneously use clues to infer one anothers' intentions (Blumer 1953). It is the mutuality of the process of role taking that makes possible the social cooperation of which Mead wrote.

Children see others in interaction and take part in social life themselves. By the process of socialization they learn a repertoire of behaviors for a variety of social situations, and how to recognize what Mead called the *significant symbols* that identify such situations. By the time a child is just a few years old, he or she is expected to know how to act differently at home with the family than when "company" comes, and how to greet an adult friend of the family as opposed to an adult stranger (Watson and Amgott-Kwan 1984).

Role-taking ability and accuracy Social psychologists have emphasized the way role taking results in shared definitions of social situations and patterns of successful communication. However, as is the case in all human behavior, there is evidence of error in role taking. As was made clear in the chapter on the self (Chapter 2), the socialization process is far from uniform in society. Individuals have widely divergent experiences from which to learn, and also differ in their ability to imagine the intentions of others, that is, to take the role of others (Lauer and Handel 1977). In addition, the clarity of social situations varies widely, the most ambiguous of which pose problems for the accuracy of role taking by participants (Sherohman 1977). Thus, if in a given interaction the participants make inaccurate guesses about one anothers' intentions, the source of such inaccuracies might be the role-taking abilities of the individuals or the problems posed by the situation.

Role-taking ability and the individual Consider some of the factors which might influence a person's ability to take the role of others. It is apparent that those who are more attentive to the behavior of others will, since they can gather more cues, excel at role taking. For example, David Riesman (1950) distinguished between "inner-" and "other-directed" personality types in America; the former typically relies upon deeply internalized sets of beliefs as guides for behavior, while the latter attends closely to the beliefs of others in determining how he or she is to believe and act. To the extent that the "other-directed" person pays more attention to the beliefs and actions of others, such a person should be a more able role taker (see Chapter 3).

In an empirical study of married adults and their parents, Stryker (1956) examined how *role-taking accuracy*—the ability to correctly assume the viewpoint of others—is influenced by factors such as degree of interaction, sex, and similarity of interests. He measured the attitudes of a sample of adult married couples and their parents on a range of issues, and asked each to predict one anothers' attitudes on these same measures. The difference between an individual's attitudes and the predictions for those attitudes by some other family member provided the measure of role-taking accuracy. Stryker found that role-taking accuracy was greater (1) between blood relatives (son and father, for example) than between in-laws (son and father-in-law) and (2) between individuals of the same sex than between individuals of different sex. It is possible that these results can be explained by the fact that blood relatives and people of the same sex interact more frequently, and so develop common interests and ways of acting and thinking. Perhaps men and women (and members of different families) are socialized differently enough so that they develop greater or lesser skill at role taking. In either case, data like Striker's suggest that accuracy in role taking may become a quality of an individual.

Role-taking accuracy and the situation A number of social psychologists have also focused on the way role-taking accuracy is influenced not by the characteristics of individuals, but by the situation in which they interact. The accuracy of role taking is likely to be diminished in situations in which there is a great deal of distracting and inaccurate information or in which participants lack clear information on which to base predictions. Perhaps key actors wish to hide their intentions, or are unsure themselves how to act. A common example of such a situation is the beginning of a dating relationship. Vernon and Stewart (1957), for example, found that the more frequently a couple dated, the more accurate was their role-taking ability with one another.

▶ Perspective:
The Effect of the Immediate Situation

An experiment in cruelty How can we make sense of cruel behavior? After the world became aware of the atrocities committed by Nazis in the concentration camps during World War II, the questions tended to focus on what type of people could commit such acts. Were they monsters or moral degenerates? But at their trial at Nuremberg for "crimes against humanity," Nazis leaders looked so ordinary, though they were eventually found guilty of having organized and carried out mass executions. We tend to ask the same sort of questions about a criminal who kills or about a police officer who beats a prisoner. Are they, by nature, violent and cruel people?

Is it possible for people who are not, by nature, cruel to act cruelly? A number of studies have provided evidence that social situations can lead ordinary people to behave in ways that we might expect only from violent and sadistic individuals. One of the best known of these was conducted by Philip Zimbardo and some colleagues at Stanford University in the early 1970s, and it almost got out of hand (Zimbardo, Haney, and Banks 1973).

Zimbardo and his associates transformed the basement of one of the university buildings into a mock prison, putting cots into a series of rooms and providing them with locks and bars. They conducted lengthy interviews with 75 university student volunteers and chose for the study approximately 20 of the most mature and stable ones. They then randomly assigned about half of the students to play the role of "guard" in the mock prison, and the remainder to play the role of "prisoner." Remember that the interviews had been conducted to eliminate from the study any unstable individuals whose statements revealed them to be prone to violent or cruel behavior. So the investigators intended to discover whether violent or cruel behavior by prisoners and guards is a product of the roles they play in a structured situation rather than of their personalities.

To increase the reality of the situation, the experiment began with "arrests" of the prisoners at their homes by city police. They were searched, handcuffed, read their rights, charged, and driven to "jail" in police cars. There they were stripped of their clothes, sprayed with disinfectants against body lice, issued uniforms, and put into "cells."

You might imagine that since all the participants knew the exercise was make-believe, and that it was scheduled to end in two weeks, the guards and prisoners would play the roles for the purposes of the experiment, but not realistically or wholeheartedly. However, after only a few days, both the guards and the prisoners were playing their roles all too convincingly and energetically. The guards did not merely try to keep order in the prison; they actually began to do things to humiliate and dominate the prisoners personally. For example, they subjected the prisoners to petty and demeaning orders such as making them sing, laugh, or be silent on command. They intentionally made messes of the prisoners' cells so they could order them to clean up. In short, they asserted their power over the prisoners to no purpose other than to force the prisoners to bend to that authority.

For their part, the prisoners became increasingly passive and obedient. They resented their treatment but felt powerless to fight back. As the guards became more authoritarian, and the prisoners obeyed orders, their roles as inmates became entrenched. Before a week was up, four of the prisoners suffered episodes of such anxiety, rage, or depression that they had to be excused from the study by the researchers. In fact, the entire experiment was cut short after only six days when it became apparent that the guards had become abusive and domineering and the prisoners emotionally and psychologically at risk.

In interviews with the participants after the study both "guards" and "prisoners" expressed surprise and shame at how they had behaved. Guards would not have predicted that they were capable of such cruelty nor prisoners that they were capable of such acquiescence. Unless the preliminary interviews failed to reveal personality disorders in the study's participants (and no subsequent criticisms of the study have convinced us of such a flaw) then it can only be concluded that the cruel behavior that is common in prisons is a consequence of the roles created by the structure of the situation, and not necessarily a result of the personalities of the actors involved. ∎

Role Strain

In this chapter we have tried to show how roles allow people to vary their behaviors to fit the demands of the countless varieties of social situations in which they might take part. But it should have become clear by now that roles are not so clearly defined nor consistent from day to day as the role an actor plays on a stage. Recall that a role such as student should be considered a role set, since any role actually consists of orientations to the expectations of a series of other roles. In addition, because our daily lives put us in contact with a range of social structures such as families, school, work, businesses, and government agencies, we must be capable of moving easily from one set of role expectations to another. Lastly, even though social situations are often repeated, such as going to work each day, they can vary in important ways, requiring adjustments in the way roles are played. Though the members of a culture typically become quite skilled at the demands of role performance, it should be apparent that all these complexities can pose problems.

Role strain is a general term for "the felt difficulty in fulfilling role obligations" (Goode 1960). That is, an individual who for any reason experiences problems in playing a role can be said to be experiencing role strain. The major sources of role strain are role conflict and role confusion. *Role conflict* is the condition of strain in which an individual feels subjected to incompatible expectations for his or her behavior. *Role ambiguity* is the condition of strain in which an individual enters a social situation for which no clear role is established.

Role conflict Any time you sense that you are "torn" between two sources of action, it is possible that you are experiencing role conflict. Here are a few examples, each of which illustrates a different source of role conflict:

1) An executive in a company is asked by her boss to work late on a project one night, knowing that if she agrees to do so it will greatly help her chances for a promotion and raise. However, she has promised her daughter that she will be home that night to attend her dance recital, knowing that she wants badly for both her parents to be there.

2) A supervisor at an assembly plant is given a memo from management which calls for changes in work procedures which will increase production, but will also endanger the workers in his area.

3) A male nurse finds that he is unsure of how to act when he is at work with the other nurses, almost all of whom are female, and is uncomfortable when he meets someone who asks what he does for a living.

In each of these situations, role conflicts are evident in the need to make uneasy choices about how to act. In the first case, the role conflict is created by incompatible demands *between* two role sets, or interrole conflicts. In the second, the incompatibility of demands is generated from *within* one role set, or intrarole conflicts (Gross, McEachern, and Mason 1966). In the third, the incompatibility of demands is between a role set that is learned (the role of student, for example, is acquired by experience) and one that is ascribed (the role of female, for example, is assigned to an individual at birth). Let's look at these types of role conflict in order.

Role conflicts between role sets The first case is an example of conflicting expectations between two role sets. The woman is both an executive and a family member. Each role set places demands on her to which she must adapt. When she is at work, she is expected to "act the part" of an executive, producing good work and forwarding the aims of the company. At home, she is expected to act like a mother and wife. If her schedule can be arranged so that the two role sets are isolated, conflicts can be avoided. However, as the example illustrates, this is not always possible. The demands of the two role sets become incompatible when the boss wants her to work late but family members want her home to take part in family activities.

This problem has become common as women have increasingly taken on full-time careers in addition to their family roles. How have they dealt with the role conflicts that have inevitably resulted? In a study of 97 women in dual-career families (both wife and husband had full-time jobs) who also had preschool children, Elman and Gilbert (1984) examined how these women managed the conflicts between their professional and family roles.

The investigators measured the degree of role conflict in the subjects' lives by asking them to rate on a 7-point scale the degree of conflict ". . . you typically experience between your parental and professional roles." Subjects were also asked to rate on a 7-point scale the degree to which they felt they were ". . . managing the conflict between your parental and professional roles." Lastly, subjects responded to a series of questions designed to measure the extent to which they employed each of five different strategies for coping with role conflict. Following are descriptions of each of those coping strategies which Elman and Gilbert identified and their findings as to the effectiveness of each.

1) *Increased role behavior* — In this strategy, working women simply decided to "do more." That is, they attempted to spend more time at each of the roles and to be more efficient in each so that neither role would suffer. This might entail getting up earlier to spend time with their children and husbands, make good lunches for the kids, and still get to work on time. Then they might plan to bring work home to do after the children were asleep. This pattern has been dubbed the "supermom" syndrome.

Elman and Gilbert found that this strategy was the most effective one in coping with the subjects' role conflicts. That is, the women who were measured as employing high rates of increased role behavior as a coping strategy also reported high scores for coping effectiveness. In addition, increased role behavior was also the coping strategy most strongly endorsed by the subjects. That is, the women in the study felt that "doing more" to satisfy the demands of both roles was the best of the five coping strategies to employ.

2) *Cognitive restructuring* — This strategy involves changing attitudes about the meaning or importance of the role conflicts. For example, a woman might decide that the conflicting demands on her are not very important ("It could be worse") or that the conflicts are not at all unusual ("Everyone must face this. It's natural to feel like this.") The data showed cognitive restructuring to be the second most effective coping strategy after increased role behavior, and it was also the second most strongly endorsed.

3) *Structural role redefinition* — In this case, women tried to get others to change their demands so as to reduce confict between the roles. For example, an employer might be asked to change work hours so as to accommodate the woman's family plans, while children and husband might be asked to take on more responsibility in the home, such as preparation of meals. Elman and Gilbert's data revealed that this strategy (and the remaining two strategies) were essentially unrelated to successful role conflict management. That is, employment of this strategy neither increased nor decreased with scores for coping success. Of the five coping strategies studied, it was the fourth most strongly endorsed method.

4) *Personal role redefinition* — This strategy entails making a choice as to which of the conflicting roles, family or career, is more

important. Once such a choice is made conflicting demands can be resolved. However, it is apparent that such a choice is not only difficult, but also creates further problems, since other family members or colleagues at work cannot be expected to accept such a decision readily. Personal role redefinition was found to be unrelated to effective management of role conflict, and was the third lowest in endorsement by the subjects.

5) *Tension reduction*—This last coping strategy is characterized by subjects' attempts to reduce the unpleasant tensions produced by role conflicts by doing things to take their minds off their problems. This might include indulgent eating or drinking, overt complaints about the situation, or energetic exercise programs. Like the personal and structural role redefinition, tension reduction was found to be a poor coping strategy. Employment of this technique was unrelated to level of coping effectiveness. It was also the least endorsed strategy of the five.

If we were to try to apply the findings of Elman and Gilbert to the realities of everyday life, it would seem that some strategies make more sense than others. But why? Notice that the five strategies differ in terms of who is called upon to make changes in their expectations and whether situations will change at all.

The tension reduction strategy changes nothing in the situation. It is merely a method of temporarily reducing the unpleasantness of role conflicts by acts (such as physical exercise, overeating, or complaining to friends) unrelated to the source of the frustration. If this strategy were the only one employed, the sources of the role conflict would remain in place, creating a continuing need for tension reducing behavior.

Cognitive restructuring also does nothing to concretely change the demands of the two roles. However successful an individual might be in redefining the importance of the conflict, she can still expect her family members and boss at work to define their demands on her time as important. Her redefinition of the situation is bound to be disputed by others in her life. Further, others in both her family and workplace are likely to be displeased if, having diminished the importance of the conflicts, she makes choices between competing demands at random.

Personal role redefinition, like cognitive restructuring, is likely to displease others in her life. However, this strategy can result in less role conflict, since a choice is made as to which role is more important and so provides a mechanism for deciding whose expectations to fulfill. The problem is, of course, maintaining a satisfactory relationship with the role relationships which have been devalued. To the extent that one's career depends upon putting company goals ahead of family goals, an employee (especially a female employee) can lose a job for making the "wrong" choice. The same is true for maintaining a successful family relationship. Women are still expected, even more than men, to devote time to the care of the home and the raising of children.

Structural role redefinition, if it can be accomplished, seems to be a promising strategy, since it actually alters the demands on the time of a working family woman. Assuming she can negotiate flexible hours and work limits with her employer and/or home responsibilities and schedules with her husband and children, a woman can concretely reduce the sources of her role conflicts. The problem here is in the negotiations. Is the family willing to accept less from her than they had in the past, and is an employer willing to accept less than he or she thinks is available from another employee?

Lastly, increased role behavior seems like a good strategy, but only for those individuals who have the energy and organizational skills to "do it all." If the family or job makes more demands, simply fill in somewhere by careful planning and use of time, or make more time by getting up earlier and staying up later. For anyone who has tried to do this, it is common for the demands to catch up in the form of physical or emotional problems.

▶ Perspective:
The Influence of Social and Cultural Forces

Sex-role expectations An important theme in this chapter has been the way people search for clues about how they are expected to act in specific social situations. The chapter opened with an illustration in which discovering whether a given person was a store employee or another customer determined the type of role behavior appropriate to the situation. In the same way we look for clues such as the marital status, political opinions, social class, gender, and other characteristics of individuals.

Knowing whether a person is male or female can help us guess how they expect us to behave, but anyone who has been paying attention to changes in American culture knows that sex-role expectations are very different today than they were a few decades ago. Through the 1950s and into the 1960s, there seemed to be broad acceptance in America that females were expected to be concerned with the raising of children and the care of a home, while men were expected to focus on making a living to support their families. To the extent that these "traditional" sex roles were accepted by males and females, it was possible to predict how a female might expect a male to behave toward her (open the door, pay for meals, compliment her appearance, talk about children, homes, and neighborhood issues, and so on), and how a male might expect a female to behave toward him (express concern for his comforts, admire his accomplishments, ask for his help in technical matters, and so on).

It is not surprising, especially if you are a female, if you find this description of America's recent sex-role expectations laughable or offensive. Not too long ago our culture shared clear and narrow sex-role expectations, but things have changed. America is in the midst of a sex-roles revolution. The evidence shows that by the early 1970s younger female Americans were seriously questioning the culture's norms for female behavior and that today, especially among younger females, those norms are broadly rejected.

In a recent study Tallichet and Willits (1986) measured the sex-role attitudes of a sample of Pennsylvania high school sophomores in 1970 (when they were 16 years old) and then again in 1981 (by which time they were 27). The research focused on the attitudes of 294 females who responded to both questionnaires. They were asked to respond on a 10-point scale ranging from strong agreement to strong disagreement to a series of statements about the role of females. Some of the statements were: "The best place for most women is in the home"; "If a man and woman are equally able to handle a job, the man should still get hired"; and "No woman can be completely happy unless she has children of her own." Thus, the lower a respondent's scale score, the more traditional her attitude toward sex roles, and the higher the score, the greater her disagreement with it.

Here is a summary of the average scores for the respondents on the seven attitude items:

CHANGES IN WOMEN'S ATTITUDES TOWARD ASPECTS OF THE TRADITIONAL FEMALE ROLE, 1970 TO 1981

Item	1970	1981
1) A college education is more important for boys than for girls.	5.92	8.57
2) Every girl should get married if she possibly can.	6.27	8.57
3) The best place for most women is in the home.	6.16	8.62
4) A woman should leave the major family decisions to her husband.	5.40	8.57
5) A married woman should not work outside the home.	7.32	8.95
6) If a man and woman are equally able to handle a job, the man should still get hired.	5.98	8.35
7) No woman can be completely happy unless she has children of her own.	6.04	8.27
Composite Score (for all seven items)	6.16	8.56

As you can see from the table of results, the responses to every one of the seven items was significantly more negative in 1981 than in 1970. (Keep in mind that lower numbers indicate greater agreement with the traditional role of female.) In 1970 these women were already questioning the traditional sex-role norms for women. Their composite score for all seven items was 6.16, indicating something like neutrality or very mild disagreement with the statements on average. But by 1981 their composite score for the items was 8.56, indicating that they consistently disagreed strongly with the assumption that a woman's place was in the home, raising children, and not in competition with men for jobs.

For anyone looking to predict how to act toward a woman today, especially a young woman, it would be best to keep in mind that though the culture does establish broad norms for sex-role behavior, such norms change. ∎

Role conflicts within role sets The second example of role conflict describes a supervisor who is asked by management to change work procedures which will speed up production but also endanger workers. This is an instance of role conflict in which a person is subjected to conflicting demands from within his role set. Recall that any role consists of behaviors expected by a variety of others within a social setting. So a supervisor in a company must fulfill differing expectations for his boss than for the workers he oversees. The conflict in this case can be severe, since the supervisor, by deciding whether to implement the new procedures, may be choosing between the safety of his workers (one responsibility of the job) and the job itself (if he fails to please management).

Such role conflicts are common. Imagine, for example, a 10-year-old child in a family who discovers that her older sister is experimenting with drugs. Her role set in the family includes the expectation from her older sister that she will be loyal and not "tell on" her to their parents. But it also includes the expectation from her parents that she protect family members from danger, even if it requires "telling."

In a now classic study of role conflict, Gross, McEachern, and Mason (1966) studied 105 Massachusetts school superintendents. They responded to a questionnaire in which they indicated how they thought other people expected them to act when deciding about raising teachers' salaries. Superintendents were found to experience clearly defined role conflicts in this area (88 percent of the respondents reported feelings of conflicting expectations from a variety of sources). As you might have guessed, teachers expected their superintendents to act one way in the setting of teacher salaries, while taxpayers expected them to act quite differently. The data showed that superintendents clearly perceived the conflict: 99 percent reported that they felt teachers expected them to recommend the highest salary possible, while 75 percent of the superintendents felt taxpayers' associations expected them to recommend the lowest salaries possible.

The researchers found that the superintendents employed a range of strategies to deal with the role conflicts created by the issue of teacher salaries.

1) The *clear-choice strategy* was a decision in favor of one side or the other (recommend high salaries versus recommend low salaries).

2) The *no-choice strategy* was a decision not to be involved in the decision at all (make no recommendation on teacher salaries).

3) The *compromise strategy* was a decision to try to reduce the level of conflict by one of a number of techniques such as: (a) work to negotiate a settlement between the teachers and those who wanted to limit their salary increases; (b) work to get just one of the groups to modify its demands; (c) make a compromise proposal for limited salary increases without trying to get either group to modify its demands.

But how did each superintendent decide among these strategies? Gross, McEachern, and Mason concluded that the strategy chosen depended upon the way a given superintendent defined the situation in terms of (1) the legitimacy of the demands of each group (was a group seen as having the right to make demands?) and (2) the power of each group to apply sanctions against the superintendent (was a group in the position to reward or punish the superintendent for his or her actions?). Using legitimacy and sanctions as the basis on which superintendents define their situations, the authors identified three possible orientations toward the conflict resolutions:

1) The *moral orientation* was taken by those superintendents who were concerned only with the relative rights of competing groups to influence the decision about teacher salaries. Thus, if a superintendent who applied the moral approach believed that only teachers had the right to influence salaries, he or she could be expected to recommend the highest salaries possible. If, on the other hand, the superintendent felt that only taxpayers' associations should legitimately influence the decision about teacher salaries, then a low salary level would be recommended. (Notice that both of these decisions are examples of the clear-choice strategy.)

If the superintendent using the moral perspective felt that both competing groups had the right to influence salary levels (or that neither did), then he or she could be expected either to try to work out some sort of compromise (the compromise strategy) or to avoid making any decision (the no-choice strategy).

2) The *expedient orientation* was taken by those superintendents who decided the issue in terms of which of the competing groups were believed to be in a position to deliver punishments or rewards. Thus, a superintendent taking the "expedient" approach would recommend high salaries for the teachers if he or she felt that teachers could make life difficult, or low salaries if the perception was the taxpayers were in a position to deliver more misery for an "incorrect" decision. (Notice that either the moral or the expedient orientation could result in a clear-choice decision, depending on how the superintendent defined the situation.) Of course, an expedient superintendent might take the no-choice or compromise approach if the teachers and taxpayers' associations were seen as being equal in their power to punish or reward.

3) The third type of orientation to conflict resolution was identified as the *moral-expedient*, taken by those who gave no greater weight to legitimacy or sanctions, but weighed both factors in coming to an estimation of net balance. That is, a moral-expedient might decide that both competing groups have the right to influence a decision, but that only one has the power to apply sanctions. In this case, the clear-choice approach would be taken in favor of the position of that group perceived to have more sanctioning ability. A moral-expedient might also take a clear-choice approach if the competing groups are thought to have similar amounts of sanctioning ability, but only one is thought to have legitimacy in the issue. Lastly, evaluations of legitimacy and sanctions that come out roughly equal would be expected to result in compromise or no-choice decisions by the moral-expedient.

The researchers went beyond merely identifying the types of factors which might influence a person's strategy for coping with role conflict. They tried to measure these factors among their superintendents and then predict the type of coping strategy they would employ. Once they knew how a superintendent evaluated the relative importance of legitimacy and sanctions, and how he or she perceived the distributions of legitimacy and sanctions for the competing groups, the researchers were able to make accurate predictions about the superintendents' decisions in 91 percent of the cases of role conflict on the issue of teacher salaries.

Role conflicts between learned and ascribed roles Most of the roles we have discussed to this point have been *learned roles*. That is, roles that we take on during life as a result of our effort and experiences. For example, a person learns what is expected of a husband or wife by experience in social life and takes the role on voluntarily in most cases. The same is true for roles like teacher, superintendent, executive, and so on. However, a number of the roles we play are *ascribed*. That is, they are imposed upon the life of an individual involuntarily, often at birth. For example, the roles of female or of black American are ascribed. The role of old person, though it does not occur at birth, is also ascribed, since it is imposed upon individuals by the passage of time.

The behaviors expected of people in ascribed roles are less flexible than those associated with learned roles. For example, a teacher may choose from a range of behaviors in fulfilling the role of teacher. We may, within limits, be formal and strict or informal and personal and still satisfy the expectations of students, deans, and so on. But an ascribed role is typically more narrow in its defined expectations. The role of female, for example, has for some years allowed for little deviation from the culturally expected behaviors associated with home and child care.

When ascribed and learned roles conflict, the difficulties presented are particularly challenging. The male nurse experiences conflicting expectations for his behavior since a nurse (a learned role) is expected to be nurturing, obedient to physicians, and supportive (classic expectations for the role of female), while his ascribed role as male includes expectations of assertiveness, independence, and toughness. Another example of such conflict between ascribed and learned roles is the female executive. The typical expectations for female behavior listed above conflict with the expectations for toughness and independence in an executive. As the roles of female and male in America change (Tallichet and Willits 1986), we can expect the frequency and severity of such role conflicts to diminish. However, there is still evidence that these role conflicts persist.

Wexler (1985), for example, studied the role conflicts created by competing demands in the lives of female police officers. If a woman acted as police officers are expected to act (tough and aggressive), how was she to maintain a sense of identity as she had learned it from the larger culture? Wexler found that female police officers used one of four strategies for dealing with this role conflict:

1) The *neutral-impersonal style* involved being as businesslike as possible on the job while attempting to avoid all issues related to sex-role styles of behavior. The approach was that gender basically has nothing to do with police work.

2) The *semi-masculine style* involved taking on some of the characteristic behaviors of males in the performance of the job. This included a belief in "being physical and winning."

3) The *feminine style* was characterized by acceptance by female officers of the difference between male and female characteristics on the job. This included a concern with attractiveness, the acceptance of special treatment by male officers, and a sexual undertone to the relationships between female and male officers.

4) The *mixed style* consisted of using elements of each of the first three styles. A female officer might, therefore, sometimes try to avoid the issue of gender, sometimes display typically male characteristics, and sometimes display typically female ones.

One of the best-known students of the way roles operate, Louis Zurcher (1966) studied another example of role conflict between a learned and ascribed role. Two of his senior students were hired as "hashers" to perform kitchen jobs for a sorority. They were expected to do the dirty work of cleaning pots and pans, carry out garbage, serve dinner and clear plates, and perform any other odd jobs that sorority sisters might request.

The conflict was between the lowly role of hasher, with its lack of power or dignity, and the role of male college student, with its expectations of ambition, aspiration, and independence. Zurcher's students observed the behavior of other hashers and reported on their own reactions, and reported that hashers had a number of techniques for dealing with the role conflict they suffered:

1) *Rationalization*—Hashers sometimes explained why they had taken such a demeaning job by contending that it was only temporary or that they did it to meet women (despite the fact that the sorority had a rule that sisters not date hashers).

2) *Denial*—Hashers often tried to prevent friends and acquaintances outside the sorority from finding out that they held such jobs. Sorority sisters were considered "good kids" only if they did not treat a hasher like an employee if she met one outside the sorority house.

3) *Projection*—Projection is the tendency to attribute to others traits that a person senses in himself but which would be painful to acknowledge. Hashers sometimes accused the sorority sisters of being of "low birth" or inferior.

4) *Aggression*—Hashers often referred to the dining room as the "pig pen" and even served food that had been dropped on the floor or sabotaged with grass, marbles, salt, or blood from an accidentally cut finger.

5) *Withdrawal*—To distance themselves from the unpleasantness of the role conflict, hashers drew distinct boundaries between the dining room and the kitchen, reserving their space for horseplay, jokes, and other methods of pleasant ways of passing the time at work.

6) *Compensation*—The hashers tried to make up for their feelings of inferiority by creating "balancing" roles, such as the claim that they were great lovers or students outside the sorority house.

▶ Perspective: The Effect of Social Definition

The emergence of roles for extraordinary circumstances
Roles may be seen as determined by the social situations in which they occur, especially when the situation is highly structured. The role of a soldier during basic training is a good example. Virtually every expectation

for the behavior of new recruits is established by tradition and enforced by the military chain of command. But few situations are so well defined. We are often called upon to fill in details of role expectations or modify those that exist. And, though less commonly, we sometimes find ourselves in circumstances in which there are essentially no previously existing definitions of the situation and, therefore, no set of role expectations. When this occurs, the participants must come to agreement about how to define the situation and what role each person will play, even if no such roles ever existed before or will ever exist again.

The social psychologist Louis A. Zurcher (1983) found himself in just such a circumstance when a tornado ripped through Topeka, Kansas, just a few blocks from his home. For the next three days he joined with a number of other citizens fighting to clear the debris, and he also took advantage of the rare opportunity to observe the emergence of role definitions among his work crew.

It was almost 36 hours after the tornado struck before a number of "voluntary work crews" (VWC's) began to form in the city. According to Zurcher, the delay was caused by the need of citizens who were not previously assigned to establish emergency relief organizations to deal with the demands of their primary role obligations as family members and friends. Once the safety of family, friends, and one's own home was attended to, however, many individuals felt the need to "do something" about the destruction. But what? Most had no experience or official role to play in such a disaster, so they wandered off in search of a way to help. One of these people was Zurcher.

On the first day people satisfied their need for "activity," to "do something" by feverishly hacking at the fallen trees and debris with no attempt at organizing their efforts. Zurcher found himself working next to a few others, but almost no interaction took place between them. Eventually these men would form one of the VWC's, but for the time being, the focus was on private, physical labor. In interviews he conducted a few days later, Zurcher found that in these first hours, workers were grateful for the company, but no recognizable roles could said to have been created, since there was no interaction.

On the afternoon of the first day one of the workers found a truck that was fitted with an A-frame, like the ones used on tow trucks. It was apparent that this piece of equipment (later dubbed the "monster" by the crew members) could be extremely useful in clearing fallen trees. Zurcher identified the arrival of this truck as the key element in the formation of roles among the workers. It formed the focus of the group's organization, since it created a series of specialized work roles designed to take advantage of its capacities to do jobs. One man became the driver, or "monster-man," another his assistant, two specialized in saving, two in climbing, and two in roping. Lastly there was a rigger who dealt with the winch operations of the truck, and contact man (Zurcher). By the end of the first day silence and personal labor were still the rule, but the presence of the "monster" had begun to cause these specialized roles to begin to emerge.

On the second day the men, who less than one day before had been strangers, met by arrangement and went off with the truck to work. By this time a sense of cohesion, of being a distinct group, had developed, and during the day the work roles emerged with increasing clarity. But unlike a typical, full-time work crew, this group decided, rather spontaneously according to Zurcher, not to develop a hierarchy. A few boy scouts and their troop leader came by to see if they could help and asked "Who's the boss here?" but were told "We're a team. There is no boss." The crew members agreed with this assessment, claiming there was too much work to do to spend time on bosses. In keeping with the lack of hierarchy, none of the crew members used last names or referred to members' careers outside their disaster relief roles.

On the third and last day of the group's existence, the members began to focus on using their newly developed skills most efficiently. They felt they were best qualified to know which jobs required their time and the "monster," so they ignored those job assignments given them by the central disaster relief office which they felt a waste of time. They also seemed to enjoy certain types of challenges. It became a matter of group pride to tackle the removal of particularly large trees that threatened property directly. By the end of the third day, when the group disbanded (most of the relief work was done), the volunteer work group was a highly efficient coordination of organized work roles.

What Zurcher had observed was the emergence of roles in a "role void."

At first, there were no work roles, no group, no social organization, only a sense that there was work to be done. Each person worked alone. Within three days the members of the crew had created roles around the capacities of the "monster" and the nature of the work to be done. Who can guess how often unique roles are created for special circumstances, never to be enacted again? ■

Role ambiguity The role conflicts previously discussed are instances in which clearly defined roles such as teacher, student, female, or supervisor create conflicting expectations for behavior. However, as indicated above, it is also common for people to enter situations in which expectations for behavior are unclear or entirely absent called *role ambiguity*. For example, in the 1960s a number of Americans experimented with communal living arrangements. Reports from these communes told of various problems, one of which was the lack of precedents for how residents should behave towards one another. Since a typical aim of these settlements was to eliminate hierarchy, all the expectations for behavior that were generated by ranking (for example, the role of boss or of parent) were not available. Early in these experiments, and for newcomers along the way, roles were ambiguous. How were they expected to behave?

Since the people who began the experiments with communal living had virtually no guidelines for role behavior, this was an extreme case of ambiguity. But milder levels of role ambiguity can occur when some elements of an otherwise well-defined role are missing or unclear. For example, a student who had been hired by a local company to train in their marketing division came back to visit and reported that he was given a lengthy and detailed job description on his first day at work. It looked as though the role he was to perform was clearly defined. However, he soon found that he was asked to perform a variety of tasks not in his job description, and that these requests came from people more senior than himself from offices outside his area. While the bulk of his work role was clear and stable, he did have to assert himself in order to clear up the ambiguous boundaries of his responsibilities.

In the case of this former student, the role ambiguities were uncomfortable. They might even have resulted in trouble at work if some senior employee decided that his effort to limit the scope of his responsibilities showed a lack of cooperation or energy. On the other hand, some role ambiguities can be used to one's advantage. For example, when a job is poorly defined, an individual might use the ambiguities as an opportunity to exchange undesirable tasks for more desirable or influential ones. In either case, role ambiguities require the person performing the role to "fill in" the behaviors that are missing or unclear. For the employee in a company this process might be a matter of limited shaping of the role, while for the members of a newly formed commune, it might entail the creation of a role "from scratch."

Role Making

When social situations are seen as clearly defined by participants, role taking is relatively uncomplicated, even when some ambiguities occur. It is merely a matter of gathering information from the social environment as to the behaviors expected in a role, then "stepping into" the role and playing it. However, in those cases where situations are vaguely defined or wholly new to participants, roles must be shaped or created if meaningful interaction is to proceed. It is in such cases that social psychologists speak of the process of *role making*, the process of shaping or creating a role to eliminate or reduce its ambiguities (Turner 1962). So just as role ambiguities may range from minor gaps in information about how to act to entirely absent guidelines, role making may require anything from slight modification of roles to their wholesale creation.

Given the flexibility inherent in the process of taking on a role, it is merely a matter of degree to distinguish between the processes of role taking and role making. As Turner states the issue, "Roles 'exist' in varying degrees of concreteness and consistency, while the individual confidently frames his behaviors as if they had unequivocal existence and clarity. The result is that from time to time to make aspects of the roles explicit he is creating and modifying roles as well as merely bringing them to light; the process is not only role taking but role making" (p. 22).

The relationship between role taking and role making is nicely illustrated in Louis Zurcher's study (1983) of priests and felons who transformed the roles to which they had become accustomed. Each had played a well-structured role for a very long time, and each was forced by circumstances to remake it. How did they do this?

The priests in the study had "fully enacted the traditional priestly role." That is, they had followed the dictates of the church hierarchy, performing their roles according to long-established patterns. But during the 1960s, a time of widespread social protest and liberal thought in America, some of the priests in the San Antonio, Texas, archdiocese rebelled against their archbishop's conservative and authoritarian leadership. These dissident priests were searching for a way that the church could become more socially active in the areas of inequality and civil rights. As Zurcher reports, these people risked serious consequences, including excommunication, to remake the role of priest from its traditionally established patterns to one more like that of the social activists of the day.

The felons in Zurcher's study began with roles even more clearly defined than that of the traditional priest. They had been in prison, during which time their every behavior was established and monitored by the official prison authorities and the second authority structure within a prison, the prisoners themselves. Expectations for prisoner behavior, then, was exceptionally clearly established. The need to remake their roles was brought about by release from the prison.

Once paroled out of prison, the role of felon still applied, but the differences were between the incarcerated felon and the paroled felon. The role outside prison was much less clearly defined than it was inside. The world seemed strange and unpredictable. Though a paroled felon was technically free, each knew that there were restrictions, some of which could not be anticipated. The label of "ex-con" could appear at any time, such as during a hiring investigation into an employment history. Those who managed to successfully remake their roles required the support of others such as family and friends to complete the transition.

For both priests and prisoners, their roles encompassed or supplanted the multiple roles associated with work and family, roles which normally contribute to the way most other people see themselves. Since the roles they had played for years were pervasive in the lives of both the priests and prisoners, it is understandable that their self-concepts were almost entirely constructed out of these roles. In the case of both the priests and the felons, Zurcher concludes that successful transformation of their roles by the process of role making resulted in profound changes in each individual's self-concept. To understand how this process occurred, let us examine more closely the relationship between roles and the self.

Roles and the Self

In Chapter 2 (The Self), it was argued from the work of Mead and others that one's sense of self is strongly influenced by social interaction. Since social interaction is mediated through the roles people play within social situations, it is possible to see the self as the combination of an individual's "role identities" (Turner 1978).

As illustrated above, an individual may be called upon to play any of a range of roles, such as mother, worker, artist, consumer, and so on. Each of these may contribute to her overall sense of self. However, it is also likely that each is not of equal importance to her. That is, "some role identities are more a part of the self than others and consequently have a variable effect on the self-concept" (Callero 1985).

In an examination of how roles contribute in varying degrees to the sense of self, Callero (1985) defined salient role identities as those that are most influential in structuring a self-concept. Typically, we would expect role identities such as family membership, religion, work, and political affiliation to be most salient in one's self-concept. However, Callero found that for some people, relatively unusual role identities can have important effects.

He obtained questionnaire responses from a random sample of 658 blood donors. Their answers clearly showed that giving blood was an important part of their self-concepts. In fact, he found that those individuals for whom blood donation was most important to their sense of self (1) defined themselves in terms of the role identity of blood donor, (2) tended to evaluate others in terms of whether they gave blood, (3) had more friends who were also blood donors, and (4) perceived others as expecting them to give blood.

While Callero acknowledges that other role identities such as work and family can still be expected to be most salient to one's self-concept, each individual is capable of constructing a unique self out of the wide variety of roles he or she is called upon to play, and the varying salience attached to a particular role identity.

Self and role distancing Sometimes an individual is called upon to play a role which is at odds with his or her sense of self. In order to make it clear to anyone who might be present in such a situation, the individual may behave in such a way that it is clear that the role performance does not represent his or her self-concept. This process is called *role distancing* (Goffman 1961). In a sense, role distancing can be understood as an expression of role salience. Just as some roles may be vital in the creation of a sense of self (occupational or family roles are two that were suggested by Callero in the study just reviewed), others may be low in salience (the role of neighbor, for example). Still other roles are not just low in salience, they are actually contrary to one's sense of self. Role distancing sends the message to others and to one's self that such roles are not part of our self-conceptions.

For example, a teenager is asked to babysit his 10-year-old brother, and agrees to take him to the movies to see a cartoon feature. On the way into the theater he meets some of his friends whom he immediately informs of the fact that he is babysitting and that he is not really interested in going to see the cartoons for himself. By distancing himself from the role of "cartoon watcher," he protects his self-concept as he and his friends might perceive it.

A colleague of ours tells a similar story about herself. She was doing some research for an article she wanted to write on the extent to which pornography contributes to sexism in America. For the first time in her life she went into a store to buy some pornographic magazines and video films. She told us that as she put her purchases on the counter she suddenly felt compelled to tell the cashier that "This stuff is not for me. I'm doing research." You might imagine that the store employee had heard that one before, and our friend knew it the minute she "explained herself." But her self-concept as a researcher and feminist was threatened by the need to purchase the pornographic materials, and, though only she and the store clerk were present, she felt she had to engage in a little role distancing.

Looking Back

By providing us with a way to fulfill one another's expectations for social behavior, roles make interaction proceed more smoothly. The roles we play provide us with "lines" to deliver that inform others of the part we play in a given social interaction, and establish reciprocal relations between interacting individuals.

Any one role is oriented toward the expectations of a range of other people. Playing a given role, then, different behavior can be expected of one depending on the role from which the expectation comes. Thus, a teacher can be expected to act one way toward a student and another way toward a colleague. There is nothing "unnatural" about this state of affairs; indeed, almost everyone must, on a daily basis, play out the expectations for multiple role sets.

Roles have been conceived as varying in flexibility. Those who view roles as elements of stable social structures speak of structured roles and see little room for individual interpretation of role expectations. Those who emphasize the process by which individuals create or negotiate role expectations according to the demands of the situation speak of role as process. This latter view is congruent with, and probably stems from, the work of social psychologists who argue for the existence of an active self. They tend to minimize the structural aspects of role in favor of role making.

In a rapidly changing society, individuals often experience role strains, difficulties in fulfilling role obligations. There may be conflicting expectations for the performance of roles in two role sets (such as between mother and career woman), or within a single role set (for example, the military chaplain). In addition, conflicts between learned (nurse) and ascribed (male) roles can and often do occur. Such role conflicts do indeed make people uncomfortable, because they do not know what is expected for their behavior. A world without role strain would be psychologically more secure, since individuals could predict one another's behavior. However, such a world would also be sterile, rigid, fixed, uniform, and unchanging.

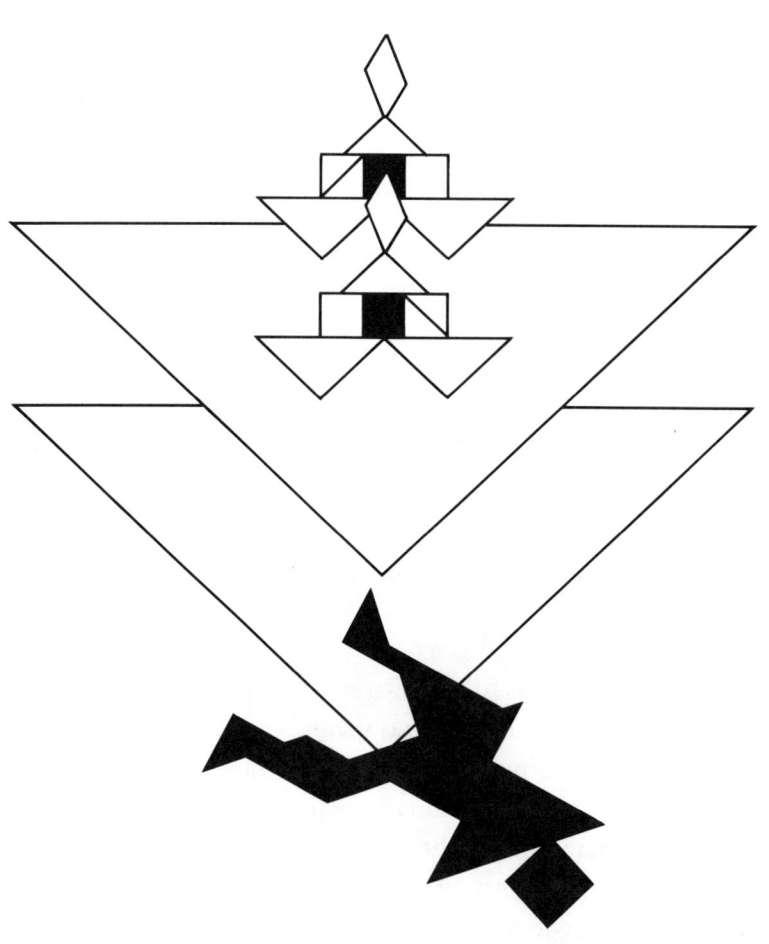

CHAPTER 6

Aggression and Violence

EVERY YEAR, APPROXIMATELY 20,000 PEOPLE ARE MURDERED IN AMERICA. Who knows how many hundreds of thousands more are pushed, slapped, or punched over disputed parking spaces, differences of opinion in bars or at parties, and affairs of the heart.

Beginning in ancient times, philosophers and social thinkers have recognized that societies can help protect us from one another, from someone who "goes berserk," killing at random, from another who cold-bloodedly picks out a target for revenge or profit, or from another who simply seems to enjoy humiliating his companions. We have police, courts, laws, and everyday rules to help prevent such aggressive behaviors, or at least punish them when they occur.

It would obviously be wonderful if we were able to remove the sources of what we call aggression. Needless to say, human misery and suffering would be greatly alleviated. It is not surprising, therefore, that many social psychologists have turned their attention to investigate the causes, conditions, and consequences of aggression and violence.

Looking Ahead

In this chapter, we explore the causes and consequences of aggression and violence in everyday life. We examine the role of frustration as a factor in aggression. Are there certain elements in a situation which might provoke aggression when people are frustrated? For example, are frustrated individuals more aggressive at the very sight of a gun or a knife? We also ask: Do human beings have an essentially aggressive biological nature? Or is aggression something that we learn as members of society? Those who take the former view also argue for the effectiveness of catharsis in reducing human aggressiveness. They believe that competitive sports, such as boxing and football, actually serve a "safety-valve" function for society by draining off excessive aggressive energy that might otherwise result in war. We ask: What is the relationship between sports and violence? Are people actually less aggressive after they watch a hockey game? Does hockey prevent war?

What Is Aggression?

We define *aggression* as any behavior whose intention is the injury of a human being, even if it is an injury to oneself. The most extreme forms of aggression are termed *violence*. The harm may be physical, as when men fight in a bar or kill each other in war. Or aggression may be more psychological and subtle, as when a prankster plays a practical joke in order to scare or humiliate someone in front of friends or relatives. Moreover, aggression may occur on the individual level, as, for example, when a man opens fire on the patrons in a crowded restaurant or one barroom customer punches another in the mouth. Aggression may also occur on the group or institutional level, as when one country wages war against another.

Though broad, this definition of aggression immediately narrows the scope of the behavior we wish to describe and explain. First of all, the injury must be intentional rather than accidental. A man who carelessly crashes his automobile into another car on the highway should not be regarded as acting aggressively, no matter how much damage he might cause (unless, of course, he has purposely chosen to injure the people riding in another vehicle). In the same way, a major-league pitcher whose fastball gets away from him and hits a batter may not be considered to be acting aggressively (unless, of course, he has purposely decided to bean the batter). Second, the injury must be to human beings rather than to inanimate objects. A woman who smashes a mirror against the wall of her bedroom should not be considered to be acting aggressively (unless, of course, her intention is to destroy someone else's property).

Understanding the intention of an aggressive person is an essential element in defining aggressive behavior. Accidents don't count. Yet it is not always possible, and frequently difficult, to "get into someone else's head" to determine his or her precise motivation. How do we know, for example, whether an automobile "accident" really lacks purpose or planning? Could it actually be a carefully concealed act of suicide or of anger directed against society in general, if not against a particular individual? Phillips (1979; 1980) suggests, for example, that automobile "accidents" involving a single vehicle and small airplane "accidents" may frequently be disguised forms of suicide which are precipitated by a well-publicized suicidal act. Similarly, a vase thrown against a wall may be simply that: a vase being smashed to smithereens. But it could also be a symbolic act of aggression directed against a tyrannical boss or a frustrating lover. How are we to know?

The situation determines what we call aggression The interactionist perspective alerts us to an important problem with applying our definition of aggression: namely, that the meaning of any behavior will vary a good deal depending on the situation in which it occurs. Behavior regarded as aggression under one set of circumstances may not be regarded as such under a different set of curcumstances. For example, two children are rolling on the ground in an animated version of a televised episode of "The A-Team." They throw pretend punches to the head and kicks to the abdomen; they scream and shout at the top of their lungs; they chase one another around the yard. At what point does their "playing" end and their "fighting" begin? Are they being aggressive or just having fun?

The answer depends upon the way the children defined their situation. From the point of view of an observer (especially an adult unfamiliar with the television program on which the play was based), the behavior is likely to be labeled aggressive. But as long as the children intended no harm to one another, even if one was accidently hurt, the play should not be considered aggression. Of course, if real fighting began, it would reflect a changed set of definitions between the children.

Our ability to understand the way people define situations can have much higher stakes than deciding whether children are merely playing.

Sometimes we must determine degrees of punishment for aggressive or violent behavior.

Much courtroom testimony is directed at discovering motive and intent. For example, a thief breaks into your home while you are sleeping. You wake up and hear the intruder and grab a baseball bat as the stranger climbs the stairs. When he reaches the top stair, you hit him, knocking him over the bannister to the floor below where he dies.

In many states, your defense counsel must show that, in your mind, you felt your life was in danger. If the jury is convinced that this was your definition of the situation (and, incidentally, that you had done all you could to get out of the predicament), you will be found innocent. If not, you can be found guilty of manslaughter and sentenced to prison.

▶ Perspective:
The Effect of Social Definition

How do we define an aggressive situation? The problems of deciding whether or not a particular behavior constitutes aggression is also illustrated in the perception of sex between people on a date. Courts are increasingly being called on to determine whether the sex that took place between dating individuals was, as she claims, a rape, or as he claims, essentially voluntary.

As many as one-half of all rapes and attempted rapes may occur between acquaintances rather than between strangers (National Crime Survey 1981). Many of these instances of rape apparently occur on dates. For example, a series of studies by Kanin (1957, 1967, 1971) and Kanin and Parcell (1977) determined that between 20 and 25 percent of the college women they studied reported that their dates had forceably attempted sexual relations. These women typically had responded by crying, pleading, screaming, and fighting back.

When a stranger forces his victim to engage in sex, you can expect overwhelming agreement that it should not be called sex at all but rape, a crime of violence. But are there any circumstances in which the aggressive pursuit of sexual contact is not normally defined as rape in American society? The data from some studies may make you uncomfortable.

According to Shotland and Goodstein (1983), because the dating relationship is viewed as "a consensual social encounter," there is a good deal of confusion as to when rape has or has not occurred. The norms governing sexual behavior on a date can be used by aggressive males as a convenient rationalization for treating their dates as sexual objects. First, men often share the belief that a woman communicates her sexual intentions in subtle or symbolic ways. For example, her very presence in a man's apartment or her willingness to engage in sexual foreplay may be taken as signs of her consent to have sexual intercourse. Second, a woman is at the same time expected, as part of the dating ritual, to resist her date's sexual overtures, regardless of whether she ultimately consents. Therefore, "no" is sometimes taken to mean "yes." And finally, some men believe that women enjoy being sexually and physically dominated, including the preference to be "roughed up."

Shotland and Goodstein (1983) studied the variables involved in deciding that sex during a date was actually rape. A detailed account of a date was read by 141 male and 146 female college students, in which the male used either less ("Lee answered, 'Relax Diane, don't worry'") or more ("Lee slapped her across the face again") force to obtain sex, after the female began to protest either early, moderately, or late during foreplay. Her protest consisted of only pleading ("Diane said again, 'Stop, Lee, don't'") or pleading while physically struggling ("and slapped him across the face").

According to Shotland and Goodstein, subjects were more likely to blame the woman (that is, the sex was not defined as rape) when her date used low force to obtain sex and when she began to protest late during foreplay. Moreover, the man's behavior was considered more violent (i.e., defined as rape) when he used more force, and when the woman's protest was early and physical. When is sex during a date defined as "rape," a violent crime? In the case of forced sex on a date, it depends on the way the situation is defined. ■

Two types of aggression Despite serious problems of definition and application, social psychologists continue to be drawn to the concept of aggression. To clarify their subject, some distinguish between two distinct types of aggression. On the one hand, they talk about *instrumental aggression*—intentional injury as a means to some other end, as a way of achieving one's goals and satisfying one's desires. On the other hand, *expressive aggression* occurs when injury is an end in itself. The aggression is carried out for its own sake—out of a need to express anger, irritation, or hostility—rather than for its usefulness in achieving some other end.

Mass murder can be used to illustrate the essential differences between instrumental and expressive aggression. In this crime, the perpetrator kills a number of victims either all at once or one at a time over a period (serially) ranging from days to years. Many mass murders are instrumental: their purpose is to protect a killer from being discovered and apprehended by the law. Thus, Ronald Piskorski and Gary Shrager were recently found guilty of an armed robbery which ended in the shooting of six residents of New Britain, Connecticut. The unfortunate victims had been employees and customers who happened to be present during the robbery of Donna Lee's Bakery and could have identified their assailants. So Piskorski and Shrager committed the murders in order to silence the six witnesses to their crime. They were probably not angry or irritated with their victims.

By contrast, serial murders often are examples of expressive aggression. The killer exercises a sadistic need to express his anger by sexually assaulting, torturing, and finally killing his victims. For this reason, a serial murderer rarely shoots his victims; a gun would only serve to distance him from the physical contact he desires. Instead, he prefers strangling, beating, or clubbing to death. In such cases, a killer has nothing to gain except the "pleasure" he derives from his crimes. Serial killer Ted Bundy provides an apt example. He is suspected of having killed dozens of young women in four states. His many victims were bludgeoned, strangled, sexually molested, and then buried. For Bundy, killing was an end in itself (Levin and Fox 1985).

Is the aggressive crowd expressive or instrumental? An act of aggression often contains both expressive and instrumental motivations. In crowd behavior, the distinction can break down completely. A purely *expressive crowd* has no particular goal, but it provides a release of tension for its members, often through applause, dancing, or singing. By contrast, a purely *acting or instrumental crowd* has a goal and follows a plan of action in order to attain it (Blumer 1939; Miller 1985).

An interesting example of a "hybrid" in crowd behavior—one containing both expressive and instrumental components—is found in the largest mass lynching in American history, an event that occurred in the aftrmath of the brutal murder of the police chief of New Orleans in 1890. Chief David Hennessey was cut down by five unknown assailants who opened fire with shotguns and pistols. By the next morning, millions of people across the nation read in their local newspapers that the prominent police chief had been shot down by the "Mafia," a conclusion based only on the word of a captain in the New Orleans Police Department who claimed that his dying friend had whispered only that his assailants were "dagos."

According to Gambino (1977), this charge fed directly into a widespread fear among local residents about the pervasive influence of the Mafia in the life of New Orleans. Without evidence, the mayor made public a list of "94 Mafia murders" in the city. He failed to mention, however, that these murders had taken place over a 25-year period and that the list was compiled by including every homicide in New Orleans with an Italian-sounding name. He also failed to indicate that 91 of the murders were still unsolved. Indeed, the mayor's assumption that the killers were Italian and Mafiosi was pure speculation.

Nineteen Italians were arrested for Hennessey's murder. The trial of the first nine defendants ended in a mistrial for three men and a verdict of "not guilty" for another six. Even before the second round of trials could begin, 12,000 citizens met in the central business district to listen to speeches by New Orleans' community leaders concerning Hennessey's murder. After being stirred to a frenzy, the crowd became an angry mob which then stormed Parish Prison, where the defendants were being held. They slaughtered 11 Italians, three of whom had been previously acquitted, three whose court appearance had ended in a mistrial, and five more who had never even been tried. Another eight men escaped by hiding themselves in closets or under mattresses in their cells.

What had begun as an expressive crowd quickly beame an angry mob with a purpose. But the mass lynching cannot be attributed strictly to "crowd madness." According to Gambino, there was, instead, a deliberate plan on the part of those who stood to gain to eliminate the competition from Italians in local agriculture and industry. Plantation owners were alarmed that Italians who originally worked the sugar fields for slave wages were suddenly buying up cheap land. Moreover, Sicilian fishermen and peddlers, shortly off the boats from the Old Country, were seen by local business leaders as monopolizing the fruit, oyster, and fish industries of the City.

The violent behavior of the crowd actually had its roots in events of the morning after the jury's verdict was given to the court. At that time, local newspapers carried an advertisement inviting the citizens of New Orleans to attend a mass meeting "to remedy the failure of justice in the Hennessey case." Among the sponsors of the ad and leaders of the meeting were wealthy land owners, political leaders, and a political boss with a long history of violence. They were able to convince the citizens of New Orleans, most of whom would ordinarily be incapable of murder, of the righteousness of taking the law into their own hands. The result was a mass killing.

What is it about crowds that makes their participants so easy to manipulate? Why can crowd members be made to behave in ways that would probably be unimaginable to them as individuals? In his classic work, *The Crowd*, LeBon (1896) suggested that the anonymity of members of a crowd protects them against external controls and frees them psychologically to express their "savage, destructive instincts." More recently, social psychologists have attempted to explain crowd aggression with the broader concept of *deindividuation*—a state of reduced self-awareness in which anonymity plays an important part (Zimbardo 1969; Mann, Newton, and Innes 1982). For Diener et al. (1980), for example, deindividuation occurs when attention becomes focused completely on the group rather than its individual members. As a result, individual self-awareness is reduced enough so that the members of a crowd, without thinking, react to emotions, cues, and motives of the moment.

The Causes of Aggression

As we have seen, aggression takes a variety of forms and can be inspired by a variety of motives and circumstances. In their search for constancy in aggressive behavior, social psychologists have attempted to locate factors in all aggressive acts which might explain why they occur. We now turn our attention to these causes of aggression. We ask: What role, if any, does biology play in the development of aggressive behavior? How does frustration predispose an individual to be violent? And, finally, can aggression be learned?

Is aggression biological? Many people believe that aggression is instinctual—an inborn, unlearned element in the biological makeup of all human beings. It is important that we examine this viewpoint, because it is often employed in support of the opinion that human nature is basically negative and that human beings are essentially evil. What is more, to the extent that aggression is inborn and unlearned, it is also fixed. This would give us little reason for hope of ever developing effective strategies for reducing aggressive or violent behavior.

Freud (1949) supported the biological view when he proposed that human beings have "an active instinct for hatred and destruction." Freud argued that there were two opposing instincts which motivate human behavior: the life instinct called *Eros* and the death instinct known as *Thanatos*. In the Freudian view, Eros is a positive force responsible for all behavior aiming to further life. By contrast, Thanatos has as its essential aim the destruction of life. When directed outward and turned on other people, it is, according to Freud, the source of all aggression in human beings, including murder and war.

Freud argued that the death instinct has to be expressed in one way or another. Otherwise, it builds up within an individual until it is discharged either in an explosive outburst of aggression against other people or in self-destructive behavior (suicide). Of course, society does not usually permit the expression of unbridled aggression. (Indeed, society could not exist at all under such conditions.) But there are *sublimated*, that is, more socially acceptable methods for reducing aggressive energy; they tend to be subtle, symbolic, or ritualized. They are methods for "letting off steam" without destroying social order. Sublimated forms of aggression such as boxing, football, and violent television programs may provide temporary expression of Thanatos, but they are not always enough. From time to time, the death instinct "swells" to a point where only mass rebellion or war will do.

The importance of sublimated forms of aggression is illustrated in a Freudian analysis of cannibalism. According to Sagan (1974), the practice of cannibalism as a social custom is an extreme form of aggression which finds sublimated expression in less obvious forms of ritualized behavior.

During times of war, cannibalistic tribes will literally "eat the fruits of their victory" by cannibalizing warriors from enemy tribes.

Sagan (1974) reports the observations of a G. Turner, who in the mid-19th century spent almost 20 years among the Polynesian Islanders, some of whom were cannibals. The members of one group had the custom of dragging the bodies of enemies they had slain back to their village for roasting in stone ovens. The cooked hands of the vanquished had special ceremonial importance and were reserved for consumption by the priests. The overt form of aggression is, of course, the killing of the enemy. Its sublimated form is seen in the ceremonial consumption of his remains.

Where eating human flesh is prohibited, ceremonies involving human sacrifice and head hunting replace cannibalistic activity. In more "civilized" societies, even these extreme forms of aggression are eliminated and cannibalism is symbolically represented in "dog eat dog" competitiveness. Sagan claims that all such sublimated forms—whether human sacrifice, head hunting, or extreme competition—have the same end: to "eat them up alive," "to chew them up and spit them out." Perhaps you recognize these sayings from cheering at American sports events like football and hockey. In our experience, they can even be heard in the offices of corporate America, where competition is at least as fierce as it is on the playing field.

According to Sagan, some societies have also practiced *affectionate cannibalism*, whereby the remains of deceased persons are eaten by relatives, usually as part of an elaborate funeral ceremony. The purpose of such affectionate forms of cannibalism is to maintain the presence of a loved one who has died (think of the saying "You are what you eat"). However, there may also be an aggressive motive in affectionate cannibalism. Just as a young child may feel abandoned by a loved one who has died, so an adult may feel some anger associated with the death of a relative, anger which is discharged in a cannibalistic ritual.

Sagan argues that even affectionate cannibalism has its sublimated forms. Rather than directly devour the corpse, members of some societies will eat the remains of an animal placed next to the corpse. In 1924, John Roscoe reported such a custom among an African tribe known as the Bagesu. Members of this group did not eat the corpse of a loved one, but sublimated this desire. They would kill a cow and wrap the body of the deceased in its skin, then ceremonially cook and eat the meat of the animal. Several days later they repeated the process. In less obvious versions of the same phenomenon, relatives will maintain the presence of the deceased by wearing his bones or hair, keeping his ashes, or eating and drinking in the presence of the corpse (for example, at a wake).

Freudians are not alone in their emphasis on inborn, biological factors in explaining aggression. Proponents of the field of *ethology*—the study of animals in their natural environment—have also supported the existence of an aggressive instinct—a natural urge to violence. Prominent ethologist and Nobel prize winner, Konrad Lorenz (1966) has presented a large amount of evidence that animals are aggressive by instinct. He describes, for example, the battles between male animals as they compete for females, or the defensive behavior of a group of animals whose territory is invaded by another animal of the same species. He describes the massacre that ensues when different colonies of insects or rodents are mixed together. They will literally tear one another apart.

Lorenz argues that we have evolved from violent animals and so must have inherited their destructive dispositions. He denies the possibility that behavior is primarily a reaction to environmental conditions and argues instead that it results from internal and spontaneous sources. Thus, the aggressive instinct can and often does build up in the individual, swelling to a point where it can only be effectively released through an explosive outburst of violence. External stimulation is unnecessary.

Lorenz assumes that aggression gives animals an advantage in the struggle for survival and that he can explain human aggression in the same terms. There is little doubt that animals do in fact engage in the kinds of aggressive behavior which ethologists have reported. The question is whether Lorenz and other ethologists are correct in the meaning they attribute to some of this behavior. For example, does aggression among males during the mating season actually give them a sexual advantage?

Lila Leibowitz (1978) argues that it does not. She reported on the mating behavior of the temperate-zone woodland deer. As among other antlered species, the male deer or stags during the breeding season constantly engage in violent contests, in which they repeatedly smash into one another's antlers. However, the winners of these battles do not necessarily win the females of the herd. In fact, they are frequently too exhausted and scarred from the long, stalemated battles to engage in sex at all. Instead, while the fights are in progress, the less aggressive stags herd off as many females as they can. In this case, aggression turns out to be distinctly disadvantageous for the combatants.

Fromm (1973) has suggested that Lorenz may have been only half right in another respect. He argues that instrumental aggression may indeed have its roots in our biological heritage, being necessary for our survival as individuals and as a species. Instrumental aggression is, after all, a means to an end. It is therefore self-defensive, protective, and necessary. Aggression for its own sake (expressive aggression) is, in Fromm's view, another story altogether. What he calls *human destructiveness*—sadistic aggressive behavior as an end in itself—is not instinctual, but completely learned, in response to human circumstances. Specifically, destructiveness results from a society's failure to satisfy the basic human needs of its members. According to Fromm, destructive aggression increases to the extent that society becomes "civilized" and therefore more out of touch with the basic needs of its citizens.

Fromm reminds us that instrumental aggression—aggression as a means to an end—can be found among all primates. The Great Apes are extremely aggressive toward one another in the interest of securing food or maintaining dominance. In sharp contrast, however, he also claims that only human beings engage in destructive aggression—we are the only primates who, sadly enough, kill one another for the pleasure of it.

The effect of frustration on aggression In 1939, a group of Yale University psychologists—Dollard, Doob, Miller, Mowrer, and Sears—focused on the effect of *frustration*—an unpleasant psychological state resulting from the failure to satisfy some need or desire—on aggression. They suggested that frustration and aggression are inextricably connected. More specifically, in what came to be known as the "frustration-aggression hypothesis," they argued that frustration always causes some form of aggression, and that aggression is always preceded by frustration. Thus, anything that interferes with behavior toward a goal—whether something as minor as waiting for a red light to change or as major as failing to earn enough money to feed one's children—will inevitably lead to aggressive behavior.

Clearly, we now know that this is not entirely true. Many people deal with the frustrations of daily life without resorting to aggression or violence. Indeed, people are more likely to wait patiently for a light to change or find a faster route home than to shout obscenities or get out of their car and punch out another driver. They are more likely to change jobs or seek further training for higher-paying work than to beat the boss or take it out on family members. Frustration does not always lead to aggression.

Just as clearly, every aggressive action is not preceded by frustration. There must be countless examples of aggression which occur in the complete absence of frustration; for example, a child who picks a fight with friends after watching his favorite TV characters pulverize one another, or soldiers who go off to combat essentially because they are ordered by their commanding officer to do so.

Although the original frustration-aggression hypothesis was overstated, it is not without validity. Aggressive behavior does *tend* to increase when people are prevented from reaching a goal they expect to reach. People do yell at their children after a bad day at work or punch the wall after stubbing a toe. But the tendency is greater if the frustration is severe; that is, if people are deprived of something important that they were absolutely certain of getting—for example, being promised a promotion that falls through at the last moment. The tendency is also greater if people feel they can "get away with" being aggressive—if they do not anticipate being punished in return or being rejected by their friends and associates. For example, a child is more likely to bully his playmates if he thinks that none of them will stand up to him and that parents will not find out (Goldstein 1986).

Animals certainly tend to respond aggressively after they are deprived of a reward they are accustomed to receiving. Azrin and his associates (1966), for example, conducted an experiment in which pigeons received food every time that they pecked at a key. Once the birds had learned this behavior, the experimenters then suddenly withdrew their reward: no more food was administered even if the pigeons pecked appropriately. As expected, the birds responded by attacking other pigeons in the experimental chamber.

Of course, pigeon behavior is one thing; human behavior, quite another. Do people attack one another when their goals are blocked and they can't get what they want? In 1960, Stuart Palmer studied 51 convicted murderers to determine whether severe frustrations suffered during childhood might have led them to commit murder later in their lives. Needless to say, murder is an extreme form of aggression.

To provide a "control group" of similar men who had not committed murder, Palmer also studied the nearest-in-age brother of each murderer. He found the 51 convicted killers had indeed experienced more intense frustrations than had their "control" brothers who weren't convicted of murder. Specifically, the convicted murderers were more likely to have been dissatisfied with their prestige or status, to have suffered physical defects, to have done poorly in school, and to have had fewer friends. In sum, they had led "dismal, unprestigeful, frustrating lives" (p. 37).

An examination of the life of a particular killer will help to make the point (Levin and Fox 1985):

> James Ruppert looked normal, but a close look at his biography reveals that he actually led a life of frustration. When James was a young boy, the Rupperts lived in a long barn-like structure which lacks indoor plumbing and running water. His father raised chickens and squabs in the rear of the house. At the same time in his life, James began to suffer from a case of asthma—an allergy to dust and feathers—which left him sickly and limited many of his physical activities for the rest of his childhood. He simply couldn't perform like other children his age. He walked hunched over from illness, so sickly that he was not permitted to take gym at school or to play sports with the neighborhood kids. Even without asthma, his frail appearance and short stature could have severely limited his success in competitive sports.
>
> James Ruppert was regarded a "sissy" by the other kids in the neighborhood. He remembered being a shy, introverted child who, from his earliest years in school, was routinely teased by other children and had few, if any, friends. Until his junior year in high school, James remained pretty much a loner, avoiding extracurricular activities, rarely attending ballgames or going to dances, and never dating girls. The events of childhood had a lasting effect: Try as he did, James Ruppert was impotent; he was never able to have sexual relations with a woman, except as they occurred in his rich fantasy life.

It didn't help that Ruppert's five-foot eleven-inch 36-year-old father died of complications from tuberculosis when James was only 12 years old, forcing him to assume adult responsibilities from an early age. Ruppert told psychiatrists that, after his father's death, his mother would beat and taunt him and would encourage his brother Leonard to do the same. From James's viewpoint, his mother had made very clear to him that his presence was a mistake; that she had wanted a girl, not another boy in the family. At the age of 16, things at home got so bad that Ruppert ran away and later attempted suicide by hanging himself with a sheet. Though he failed in this attempt, the thought of suicide was something that stayed with Ruppert for decades to come.

Ruppert's mother showered love on her older son, who became a constant reminder to James of his own inadequacies. Leonard was the male head of the household after their father's death, whereas James always felt like an outcast in his own family; Leonard played sports while James sat on the sidelines; James was very conscious of being five inches shorter than his brother; James's math and science teachers always compared him with his older brother whose grades in the same classes had been superior; Leonard graduated from night school with a degree in electrical engineering, whereas James flunked out of college after two years; Leonard became a successful engineer with General Electric, whereas brother James went from job to job; Leonard was happily married with eight children, whereas James never married, was jilted by his only fiancee, and continued to live with his mother. Moreover, James had dated the woman whom his brother would later marry and had even introduced them to one another.

Given the severity of his frustration, it may not surprise you to learn that on Easter Sunday, 1975, James Ruppert shot to death his brother, Leonard. At the same time, he also murdered his mother, his brother's wife, Alma, and their eight children — eleven people all together.

On the collective level, the effect of frustration on aggression can be seen in a *revolution*, where a group of people attempt by violent means to overthrow the institutions of a society. Examining the circumstances under which revolution is likely to occur, one gains a strong impression that frustration is not always so obvious. True, revolutions hardly, if ever, occur in societies where most of the members are happy and content with their institutions; but neither are revolutions an inevitable consequence of extreme or prolonged impoverishment and oppression. Instead, revolution seems to occur most often when the members of a society experience severe *relative deprivation*—a sense of dissatisfaction in comparison with either their own history or the advantaged situation of another group (See Chapter 3).

Thus, the concept of relative deprivation pinpoints the source of frustration, even when it is less than obvious. By emphasizing the difference between actual and felt deprivation, we look for the preconditions of revolution in any group whose members *feel* disadvantaged or exploited, regardless of their actual economic or political circumstances. By any measure, colonial Americans like Paul Revere and George Washington could hardly have been considered objectively poor, yet they provided the driving force for revolution to overthrow British rule. In the 1960s, the children of middle- and upper-middle-class Americans formed much of the protest and rebellion against the Vietnam War, racial inequality, and "the establishment" generally.

▶ Perspective:
The Effect of the Immediate Situation

Can a situation release aggression? We noted that frustration does not always lead to aggression. Recent versions of the frustration-aggression hypothesis attempt to explain why. Berkowitz (1962) suggested that aggression follows frustration only when the appropriate external conditions for aggression are present. In other words, for aggression to be expressed, certain *external releasing cues* (any of various signals in the environment) must be present in a situation. In the absence of such cues, an individual's behavior will not be aggressive (Boyanowsky and Griffiths 1982).

What are the releasing cues for aggression? They can be people, objects, or settings. For example, James Ruppert may never have killed his eleven relatives if his brother, Leonard, hadn't walked into his house at precisely the moment he felt most frustrated. All it took was Leonard to ask, "How's your Volkswagen, Jimmie?" for James to unload 33 rounds of ammunition on his unsuspecting guests. Apparently, the aggression was there, just waiting to come out. And just seeing his brother was the signal that released it.

Cues to release aggression often have a basis in our culture. Sadly, there are certain groups of people whose members are too often chosen as targets of hostility, and they often serve as releasing cues. Many of us are taught by parents, teachers, peers, and the mass media that the physical or symbolic presence of these individuals is an appropriate occasion for the expression of aggression. Thus, some midwestern farmers have recently expressed anger toward "Jewish bankers," whose policies and procedures they perceive are to blame for intensely frustrating economic conditions which promise to eliminate the small farmer. Similarly, white parents during the '60s were incited to violence at the sight of black Americans who "invaded" their segregated neighborhoods and schools. Also, during the 1960s, long-haired hippies who wore beads and carried flowers seemed to provide releasing signals for police violence at the Democratic National Convention in Chicago and numerous other protest sites.

Objects also serve to release aggression aroused by frustration. In a controversial study, Berkowitz and LePage (1967) considered the interesting possibility that weapons serve as releaser cues; that an individual who is frustrated is more likely to be aggressive if a knife or gun is present in the situation. Please do not misunderstand: Berkowitz and LePage are not suggesting here that angry people are more likely to pick up a weapon when one is available (although this is probably true as well). Instead, they hypothesize that merely seeing a gun or knife increases the likelihood that frustrated individuals will punch, slap, and fight one another. In this view, guns literally trigger aggression!

Berkowitz and LePage had 100 undergraduate students from the University of Wisconsin take part in an experiment, in which half were made angry and half were not. All the students in the study were asked to solve a problem. At random, half the subjects were chosen to receive negative evaluations for their solutions in the form of a series of seven electric shocks (the anger conditon). The other half of the subjects received less negative evaluations in the form of only one electric shock (non-anger condition).

At this point, subjects were given an opportunity to "get even" by administering from one to ten shocks to the individual who had evaluated their solution. Each subject was seated at a desk containing a shock key which operated a mechanism for administering punishments. But some also found a 12-gauge shotgun and a .38 caliber revolver; others found a badminton racquet rather than any weapons; and still others found nothing on their desk but the shock key.

The result supported Berkowitz and LePage's contention: angered subjects (subjects who had received seven shocks) were significantly more aggressive in giving retaliation shocks when in the presence of the weapons than when in the presence of badminton racquets or the shock key alone. For non-angered subjects (those who had received only one shock), the presence of weapons made no significant difference at all.

Just like people and objects, social settings can also serve as releasing cues for aggressive behavior. The newspapers are replete with stories about violent episodes in lounges and bars. As an extreme example, a distraught customer who had spent his evening drinking in a Dallas, Texas, bar later returned with an automatic rifle and massacred the patrons inside. Clearly, aggression is much more likely to erupt among people in bars, pubs, and alleyways than in churches and restaurants (Goldstein 1986). ■

Is aggression learned? Those who argue that aggression is learned rather than instinctual point to the fact that the form of aggression varies tremendously from culture to culture and that it doesn't occur at all in some. If aggression were totally inborn in humans, how would such cultural variations occur in the absence of genetic differences for aggression across groups? In the institution of the "potlatch," the Kwakiuti Indians conquer their opponents, not with physical punishment, but by giving away or destroying more of their own personal property (for a people to whom spirituality is paramount, material possessions only increase one's vulnerability). Among the Indians of Santa Marta, contestants fight by striking a rock or tree with a stick until it breaks. In Eskimo culture, arguments are resolved in a contest in which opponents sing nasty songs about one another (Boring, Langfeld, and Weld 1939).

Even in our own society, forms and amount of aggression vary considerably. For example, the southern states have traditionally had more than their share of one-on-one, single-victim murders, but less than their share of mass murders. By contrast, California, Texas, and New York have recently experienced a disproportionate number of mass murders, including the grisly serial killings by the Hillside Stranglers, the Night Stalker, and Son of Sam that have made page-one headlines across the nation. Crimes of violence are much more likely to be committed by men than women and by young people than their elders (Levin and Fox, 1985).

If aggression were purely instinctual and therefore in uniform need of being expressed, we would not be able to locate important social factors to explain it. But Wolfgang and Ferracuti (1967) have proposed that higher rates of homicide among young men, in the lower classes, among blacks, and in the South may have a cultural basis—they are a result of a *subculture of violence*, in which violent behavior is regarded as an appropriate response to any menacing situation—a threatening glance, a jostle, an insulting comment, or the presence of a weapon. In this subculture, violence is a norm to which everyone is expected to comply. Those who do not are ignored, ostracized or victimized by other members of the group. Conversely, those who gain a reputation for toughness and aggression are accorded high status. Aggressive models abound.

Cohen (1955) applied the subcultural viewpoint to his study of delinquent gangs. He described what he saw as a delinquent subculture which taught its members norms including "...malice, an enjoyment in the discomfiture of others, a delight in the defiance of taboos... (p. 27). Gang members, according to Cohen, learn and act on these subcultural rules in order to gain acceptance and status among their peers.

Most persuasive of the argument that aggression is largely learned is the finding that the members of some societies apparently express no aggressive behavior. The Arapesh of New Guinea, the pygmies of the Ituri rain forest, the Lepchas of Sikkim, and the Australian Aborigines apparently display few if any signs of violence. They live for long periods of time at peace with one another, lacking everyday expressions of anger or even words in their language for weaponry or defense. In the absence of evidence that these and other peaceful groups are genetically abnormal, we are forced to reject the view that aggression is a necessary and inevitable element of our biological makeup. Unless aggression is universal, it is difficult to argue that it is instinctual (Goldstein 1986).

The Catharsis Hypothesis

The catharsis hypothesis represents one of the most significant issues dividing social psychologists who believe aggression is learned from those who take an instinctual point of view. According to proponents of the instinctual view, aggression that goes unexpressed inevitably accumulates in the individual until it results in an explosive outburst called a *catharsis*. According to the *catharsis hypothesis*, in order to "drain the reservoir" of aggression before it is too late, it is important that society provide diversions for the expression of aggression—socially acceptable channels for discharging aggression.

The catharsis hypothesis apparently receives widespread support in the public mind, especially as it applies to spectator sports. It is not unusual to overhear a conversation between friends at a cocktail party in which boxing, hockey, and football are justified on the basis of their "safety-valve" or cathartic effects. (For example; "If it weren't for vicarious participation in NFL football, the average guy would probably beat his wife. After all, how else could he let off steam?")

Research by David Phillips (1983) suggests just the opposite. He examined the homicide rates in America immediately following televised heavyweight prizefights and found a brief but sharp increase in homicides, an overall increase of 13 percent. This effect seemed to peak on the third day after the prizefights, especially following heavily publicized events. The biggest third-day peak occurred after the fight that received the greatest publicity: Muhammad Ali and Joe Frazier's "Thrilla in Manilla."

Phillips' study can be used to support the contention that aggression is learned; more specifically, that some people imitate the aggressive behavior of their heroes on television and the movies. But what about the actual spectators to aggressive athletic contests? Perhaps the catharsis effect actually does work for the fans in the stadium, arena, or ballpark who vicariously participate with the players on the field. If so, then, spectators should be less aggressive, less angry after cheering on their favorite football players as they pulverize members of the visiting team on the field of play. Because of the opportunity to have a catharsis, then, spectator hostility should diminish after observing aggression between wrestlers, boxers, football players, hockey players, or soccer players.

Front-page headlines would make one cautious about accepting the validity of the catharsis interpretation of the calming effect of athletic contests. In 1964, a riot at a soccer match in Lima, Peru, claimed the lives of 300 spectators. In 1977, Guatemalan soccer spectators attacked fans of the visiting team with machetes, hacking five people to death. In a soccer contest between Italy and England in 1985, 37 fans were trampled to death. Violence is not, of course, restricted to the game of soccer, although it has been especially visible in that sport. There have also been violent outbursts or riots among spectators at boxing matches, hockey contests, and football games—indeed, at any body contact sport that draws large numbers of fans (Mann 1979; Lewis 1982).

How can we begin to connect the angry outbursts of spectators with the aggressive actions of athletes on the field of play? Smith (1979) did exactly that in his archival study of violence among hockey spectators. Specifically, he learned that some 74 percent of all angry outbursts among onlookers followed extreme outbursts of violence among the players. Apparently, the fans in the arena imitated their heroes on the field of play (Russell 1983).

Even more convincing evidence against the catharsis viewpoint can be found in a field study by Goldstein and Arms (1971), which they carried out at the annual Army-Navy football game. Both as they entered the stadium before the game and immediately afterwards, male spectators were approached and asked to take a paper-and-pencil measure of hostility. Contrary to the catharsis hypothesis, Goldstein and Arms report that hostility increased among supporters of both teams, Army and Navy, among the winners and the losers alike who had witnessed the contest. But measures of hostility for males at a nonaggressive "control" event—a competitive gymnastic meet—did not differ before and after the competition.

The heightening of hostility among spectators leaving the football contest, but not the gymnastic meet, may in fact be a result of observing a violent confrontation between players on the football field. But it might instead reflect any of several uncontrolled variables in the study. For example, perhaps people who attend football games are more explosive than people who attend gymnastic meets. Or perhaps spectators at football games consume larger amounts of alcohol than spectators at gymnastic meets, and alcohol makes people more volatile.

A more recent study attempted to deal with these issues. Arms, Russell, and Sandilands (1979) brought their own subjects—127 female and 87 male college students enrolled in introductory psychology—to a sporting event. One-third attended an ice hockey contest (realistic aggression), one-third attended professional wrestling (stylized or fictional aggression), and one-third attended a swimming competition (nonaggressive control). All of them were escorted to a spare dressing room, either before or after the contest, where they were asked to complete a set of measures indicating their feelings at that time, including their level of hostility.

In this way, the researchers were able to hold constant some of the variables that may have influenced the results of Goldstein and Arms' original study of spectators to a football game. Because all subjects in the second study were assigned on a random basis to one of the sporting events, it could be assumed that spectators at the hockey match were initially no more aggressive than spectators at professional wrestling or the swimming contests. Moreover, drinking alcoholic beverages could not be blamed for results, since alcohol was not present at these events.

Results obtained by Arms, Russell, and Sandilands were every bit as convincing as those obtained in the original study. Significant increases in hostility were registered among subjects who attended hockey and wrestling, but not among spectators assigned to observe the swimming competition. Apparently, both male and female spectators become more hostile after observing an aggressive sporting contest, whether that aggression is realistic as in football and ice hockey or a spoof as in professional wrestling. Final score: Imitation 2; Catharsis 0.

Another approach to the question of the cathartic effect of aggressive athletic contests is cross-cultural. If these violent confrontations in competitive games like football and hockey really do "drain" hostility, then they should be common in peaceful societies, where the expression of aggression is inhibited, but relatively scarce in warlike societies, where aggression is discharged directly (Storr, 1968).

To find out, Sipes (1973) examined 20 different societies around the world; 10 could be classified as warlike and 10 could be classified as peaceful. He also examined the popularity of combative contact sports in each of these societies. His results were contrary to what would be predicted by the catharsis hypothesis: 9 of his 10 warlike societies but only 2 of his peaceful societies actually had combative sports. According to Sipes, these results indicate that combative sports could hardly be regarded as an alternative to war for the reduction of pent-up aggression. Instead, societies whose members are very aggressive in one area of life tend to be aggressive in other areas of life as well. Indeed, competitive contact sports like football and hockey may actually teach youngsters to express aggressive behavior in later life, including preparation for warfare.

Once again, the evidence suggests that violent sports are not generated within societies in order to provide spectators with a safe means to vent their feelings of hostility. The catharsis notion does not seem to work. It makes more sense, in the light of these data, to see violent sports events as expressions of values of an aggressive, competitive culture and as arenas in which spectators are provided with models for their own aggressive acts.

▶ Perspective:
The Effect of Socal and Cultural Forces

Family Roles and Family Violence When we think of the family, we may have an image of love and tranquility, peace and acceptance, intimacy and mutual respect. Ironically, when it comes to violence, there really is "no place like home." Every year, 50,000 parents use guns or knives against their children; 175,000 siblings use guns or knives against a brother or sister; and 100,000 husbands and wives use guns or knives against one another (Gelles 1985). No wonder, then, that 14 percent of all murders occur right in the family unit, one spouse killing another, a child killing a parent, a parent killing a parent, and so on (Mones 1985). The family is probably the most violent group or institution that a typical member of our society is likely to encounter (Straus et al. 1980).

Part of the problem of family violence is a result of the very things we may cherish most about family life. For one thing, we spend a great deal of time together with family members in relationships which may cause great tension and stress. Parents are responsible for satisfying the needs of screaming, crying infants; siblings often compete with one another for the attention of their parents; spouses must handle problems related to paying their bills, satisfying their partner's sexual desires, and accepting a compromised lifestyle (Bourne and Levin 1983).

Adding to the likelihood of family violence is the fact that the family is regarded as a place where we can "be ourselves." That is, we are permitted in the family context to behave in ways we would otherwise consider unacceptable or abnormal. We don't have to "put up a front" or "play a role" the way we do at the office or with friends. As a result, we feel less need to hide our anger or hostility. In the family, we are permitted, and even expected, to scream, act depressed, be nasty, even lash out at others. "In no other context are persons as free from external restraint: husbands can yell at their wives; fathers can scream at their youngsters; employees cannot show hostility towards their bosses" (Bourne and Levin 1983, p. 257).

Further, the special nature of family roles is deeply implicated in aggressive behavior of family members toward one another. Parents usually expect to have power over their children and to set limits on their behavior. If children challenge the authority of their parents by refusing to obey, parents may feel justified in spanking or hitting their children in order to "teach them a lesson" or "show them who is boss." Generally, the rule in a family is that "if someone is doing wrong and 'won't listen to reason,' it is OK to hit. In the case of children, it is more than just permitted. Many American parents see it as an obligation" (Straus et al. 1980, p. 16). Between 84 percent and 97 percent of all parents use some form of physical punishment on their children (Straus, et al. 1980).

Sex-role expectations also encourage family violence. In the traditional view, men are to be dominant and powerful, whereas women are to be dependent and submissive. To fulfill the masculine cultural image means to demonstrate superiority over women, to show them "who's boss." In the family, battering of women may be used by men to prove their masculinity and, at the same time, to put and keep their wives "in their place."

Outside the family unit, it is rarely permissible for a man to hit a woman. But, for some men in America, "the marriage license is a hitting license." When a wife challenges her husband's authority, the husband may retaliate physically (Straus, Gelles, and Steinmetz 1979). Although husbands and wives kill each other in almost equal numbers, wives are seven times more likely than their husbands to kill in self-defense (Wolfgang 1958; Gelles 1985). ∎

Social Learning and Aggression

As we have seen, research on the effect of combative sports on spectator violence consistently supports the view that aggression is learned; more specifically, these studies suggest the validity of *social learning theory*

(Bandura 1977). In this view, most aggressive behavior—for example, combat, football, or dueling—involves detailed skills that must be learned. In fact, we learn aggression not only from being directly rewarded and punished. We also learn it through the role models we imitate. Clearly, other people may serve as models of learning in many other areas of life. In Chapter 2, we explored in some detail the influence of parents in early socialization of the child. If imitation occurs in the acquisition of language and gestures and in the internalization of career and educational goals, then we should not be surprised that it also occurs in learning aggressive behavior. For example, parents who employ aggressive solutions to their problems tend to have children who favor aggressive methods for dealing with others (Hoffman 1970).

Bandura (1977) suggests that the mass media generally, but television in particular, provide a powerful source of models for aggressive conduct. Findings obtained in a large number of studies on the effects of televised influences on behavior support this argument: they show that television can serve as a tutor in teaching aggressive styles of behavior (Comstock et al. 1978; National Institute of Mental Health, 1982).

To demonstrate the power of social learning on aggression, Bandura and his associates (1963) asked nursery-school children to watch a five-minute videotape on a television monitor in which a woman was shown aggressively punching and kicking a plastic Bobo doll. One-third of the children also saw a scene showing the woman being rewarded with candy and soft drinks for her aggressive behavior. Another third of the children saw the same woman kicking and punching the doll, after which she was punished for her aggressive behavior. The remaining one-third of the children saw only the woman's aggressive behavior, in the absence of reward or punishment.

After the children viewed the television monitor, all of them were led into a playroom containing a number of toys, including a plastic Bobo doll. The experimenter observed and recorded the number of aggressive acts committed by each child. Bandura's results indicated that the most aggressive children were those who had seen the television model rewarded; the least aggressive children were those who had seen the model punished.

Bandura's study of children's reactions to media portrayals of aggressive behavior suggested, among other things, that television dramatic series in which aggressive behavior is routinely rewarded (for example, the star character beating a suspect in order to secure a confession and solve the case) may increase the aggressive behavior of children in the audience. If so, then children who watch lots of violent television should be more aggressive than children who don't.

In 1972, McIntyre and Teevan studied the relationship between television-viewing behavior and aggression in a sample survey of 2,300 teenaged boys and girls. All the youngsters in their study were asked to indicate their favorite television programs and also to report any of their antisocial behaviors (such as serious fights at school, vandalism, trespassing, and so on). Not surprisingly, McIntyre and Teevan found that teenagers whose favorite programs were very violent were also more likely than the less frequent viewers of such programs to commit antisocial acts.

Looking Back

We began this chapter with a series of questions concerning the nature of aggression and violence. At first glance, the easiest question to answer might seem to be: What is aggression? How will we know it when we see it? Yet, what is considered aggressive behavior in one situation may not be in another. According to the social definition perspective, how a situation is defined determines whether or not a behavior will be labeled aggressive and whether aggressive behavior will be considered appropriate to a situation. For example, a hockey player who body-checks an opponent may not be regarded by spectators as having acted aggressively. It's within the rules of the game which provide its definition of the situation. The same behavior on the street, of course, is clearly seen as aggressive.

The biological view of aggression proposes that aggression is simply born into human beings, and that internal tension is diminished by the catharsis of aggression. If this were true, then we would have little hope of ever developing effective measures to reduce aggression. We would be forced to depend on the effectiveness of football, boxing, and other competitive sports to serve as safety valves for reducing feelings of frustration in a socially acceptable way. The evidence supporting the catharsis is, at best, very thin.

Social psychologists acknowledge the link between frustration and aggression, but also realize that frustration does not always lead to the expression of aggression. The situational perspective helps explain the conditions under which frustrated people will act aggressively. The presence in a situation of specific objects, people, or settings serves as releasing cues for aggression. For example, when angry people are in the presence of guns or knives, they are more likely to strike at one another.

There is a great deal of evidence to support social learning theory as an explanation for aggression and violence. Apparently, models for aggressive behavior teach or reinforce the lesson that aggression is an appropriate way of solving life's problems. Perhaps the behavior of a parent who uses aggression in this way, or even a bully on the block, is imitated by a child who concludes that aggression in some sense "works."

Models for aggressive behavior, according to the socio-cultural view, also exist on a much broader level. There are symbols in our culture through which we learn shared norms for behavior. Just as the heroes in Horatio Alger's American success stories symbolize the norms for hard work, so mass media images like Sylvester Stallone's Rocky and Rambo teach norms for aggression and violence.

Our culture also teaches roles, a secondary effect of which is to increase the likelihood of aggression and violence. In the American family, for example, it is expected that individuals will spend a great deal of time together and be permitted to express extreme emotion. In addition, parents are expected to discipline children and males are expected to prove their masculinity and authority. In combination, these cultural expectations greatly increase the likelihood of aggression and violence in the family, a fact that is borne out by the statistics for domestic violence.

CHAPTER 7

Prejudice and Discrimination

EVERY SEMESTER, we ask for several of our students to volunteer to participate on a "prejudice panel" whose members meet together several times to discuss personal issues related to prejudice and discrimination. During the past few years, numerous students from almost every conceivable race, religion, gender, national origin, and sexual preference have participated.

Aside from their shared status as undergraduate students, all of the panelists have one thing in common: They have experienced prejudice and discrimination. Sometimes it is obvious and blatant; other times, it is more subtle and is disclosed only after a probing conversation. The panel that we ran last year was typical. In the first group meeting, a young man in a wheelchair voiced his resentment that able-bodied students sometimes treated him like an "invalid" by their excessive helpfulness. He also disliked being called a "cripple." A few minutes later, a female engineering major related an incident on her summer job in which she was snubbed by male engineers on the grounds that she was doing "man's work." In the same session, a black student complained that he had been stopped by local police on several occasions while driving through his hometown for no other reason than the color of his skin. The next week, a gay student told us that since our last meeting, he had been harassed by football players in a local bar. Also in this session, a Chinese student explained that the hostility felt by his parents and grandparents toward the Japanese could be traced to the invasion of China by Japan. In the third session, a white Catholic student asked the black members of the group why so many of them seem to separate themselves from white students in the cafeteria and other places on campus. A white Anglo-Saxon Protestant student confessed that he had grown up in a home where his parents routinely told insulting jokes about the many different minority groups they despised. During our fourth meeting together, a black student discussed his unfulfilled ambition to be a great trumpet player. As a young child, however, his white music teacher had suggested that his lips were simply too thick to ever play the trumpet, so he gave up. Towards the end of our last session, a woman of Armenian descent disclosed feeling like a victim of prejudice from other Armenians because they disapproved of her "non-Armenian" blonde hair, blue eyes, and fair complexion. And on and on it went....

Looking Ahead

Clearly, prejudice and discrimination are hardly confined to the experiences of college students; they exist to some degree anywhere and everywhere there are people who differ from one another in terms of such characteristics as age, sex, race, or national origin. In this chapter, we shall examine the elements of prejudice and discrimination, their causes, and the factors which play a part in their reduction. We shall also look at the relationship between prejudice and discrimination to discover whether prejudice causes discrimination, or vice versa. Our point of view is that of functionalism: We argue that prejudice and discrimination exist because of their consequences for certain groups and individuals, and we examine those consequences in some detail. Finally, we turn our attention to factors, both personal and institutional, which have been strongly implicated in the reduction of prejudice. We ask: To what extent can prejudice and discrimination be reduced by law or by intergroup contact? Are there psychological strategies that might effectively reduce the need for scapegoating the members of other groups?

The Elements of Prejudice and Discrimination

Prejudice and discrimination are actually two words for the two sides of the same phenomenon: the hostility that is directed against human beings based on their group membership. *Prejudice* refers specifically to an individual's negative attitude toward the members of a group, whereas *discrimination* refers to how an individual behaves toward the members of that group. Major forms of prejudice and discrimination in our society have traditionally been based on an individual's race (racism), sex (sexism), and age (ageism).

Like many other attitudes, prejudice can be regarded as consisting of the following three basic components or dimensions which predispose an individual to relate to the members of a group in a negative way: negative beliefs or *cognitions* (also known as stereotypes), negative feelings or *emotions*, and *behavioral intentions* (the tendency to discriminate at some future time) (Ehrlich 1972).

Negative beliefs. In the words of journalist Walter Lippman (1922), stereotypes are "pictures in our heads," beliefs that we hold regarding the members of a category. In a pioneering study of ethnic stereotypes, Katz and Braly (1933) sought to determine those "pictures" of a number of different racial and ethnic groups held by 100 Princeton University undergraduates. Their findings indicated a high level of agreement—sometimes reaching 75 percent—among the Princeton students that

> Jews are "shrewd," "mercenary," and "industrious"
> Blacks are "superstitious," "lazy," and "happy-go-lucky"
> Turks are "cruel," "very religious," and "treacherous"
> Chinese are "superstitious," "sly," and "conservative"
> Italians are "artistic," "impulsive," and "passionate"
> Irish are "pugnacious," "quick tempered," and "witty"

Negative feelings. Stereotypes regarding a particular group of people may be accompanied by negative emotions—hatred, revulsion, fear, contempt, or envy—evoked by the symbolic or actual presence of outgroup members. When prejudice involves the emotional and the irrational, it may become a more or less persistent characteristic of an individual, one that begins in early childhood and is deeply rooted in his or her personality (Rosnow 1972). Under such conditions, even the idea of eating at the same table or drinking from the same water fountain as someone who is, for example, black or Hispanic may create feelings of anxiety and fear (Vander Zanden 1983).

Negative behavioral intentions. The disposition on the part of a prejudiced individual to discriminate against members of a particular group has often been studied in the concept of "social distance." Since Bogardus developed his Social Distance Scale in 1925, numerous researchers have asked such groups as native white businessmen, schoolteachers, Jews, blacks, and white female college students to which level of the following scale they were willing to admit the members of various groups:

1) to close kinship by marriage
2) to my club as personal chums
3) to my street as neighbors
4) to employment in my occupation
5) to citizenship in my country
6) as visitors only to my country
7) would exclude from my country

Studies of social distance have yielded amazingly consistent results across groups: a general unwillingness among Americans of diverse backgrounds, regions, and socioeconomic positions to have close relations with people of color and a widespread preference for individuals of English and German descent (Derbyshire and Brody 1964; Simpson and Yinger 1986). More specifically, Americans are relatively unwilling to admit someone who is black, Chinese, or Japanese to close kinship by marriage, to their clubs as personal chums, or to their street as neighbors.

Has prejudice declined? There is some evidence that younger generations of Americans may be somewhat less reliant on stereotyped thinking and prejudiced feelings about ethnic and racial groups than their older counterparts in former generations (Karlins, Coffman, and Walters 1969; Taylor, Sheatsley, and Greeley 1978). Condran (1979) found that from 1963 to 1972 there was "unambiguous evidence of generally liberalizing attitudes in our society" (p. 474), and Grabb (1980) reported that whites, since the 1960s, have increased their tolerance for racial integration.

At the same time, however, Condran also determined that between 1972 and 1977 the liberalizing process slowed down greatly in certain areas, stopped completely in others, and, in attitudes toward integrated neighborhoods and general black assertiveness (called *intrusion*), actually began to reverse in the direction of intolerance. Grant and Holmes (1981) provide persuasive evidence that stereotypic beliefs continue to have an impact on judgments made about individuals coming from various ethnic backgrounds. The blatant "rednecked" form of prejudice may have subsided, but it apparently has been replaced by a more subtle and indirect version, in which a prejudiced individual attempts to preserve a nonbigoted self-image (Gaertner and McLaughlin 1983; Katz 1981; Sears and Allen 1984). A recent study by Frey and Gaertner (1986) demonstrated, for example, that white subjects were just as helpful to a black as to a white person when their failure to help a black person might have been seen as a sign of bigotry. However, when their failure to help could be easily justified (that is, when the individual's need for help was caused by his own failure to work hard), subjects gave more help to the white than to the black individual.

Even if the tendency to attribute negatively stereotyped traits has faded somewhat, the tendency to see one's own group as possessing superior traits continues in full force. In one study, for instance, whites were regarded as more ambitious, smarter, and cleaner than blacks; but blacks were not rated as lazier, dirtier, or stupider than whites (Gaertner and McLaughlin 1983).

There may also have been some substitution of new stereotypes for traditional ones. Karlins, Coffman, and Walters (1969) compared the stereotypes held by Princeton undergraduates in 1967 with those found in the earlier study by Katz and Braly (1933). The findings of Karlin, Coffman, and Walters failed to support the contention that stereotypes have been fading. Instead, traditional stereotypes that declined in their frequency of usage seemed to have been replaced by other stereotypes, in many cases resembling the original ones. For example, the traditional image of blacks as "superstitious" and "lazy" gave way to the view that they were "musical," "happy-go-lucky," "lazy," and "ostentatious." Similarly, rather than stereotyped as "pugnacious" as in the 1930s, the Irish were seem as primarily "quick-tempered" and "extremely nationalistic."

Particular prejudices also grow or decline over time. During the colonial era, for example, older members of society were generally respected and admired. Many people would actually powder their hair in order to give it the color of age (Fischer 1977). The prestige of the aged was also extremely high in many preliterate societies (Cowgill and Holmes 1972).

By contrast, the last few decades have witnessed a decline in the status of older people and a growth of ageism in the United States directed against the elderly (Levin and Levin 1980). In 1975, for example, a Harris survey found that the majority of adult Americans believed that the elderly were not very sexually active, not very useful members of their community, not very bright and alert, and not very good at getting things done. In 1977, researchers compared jokes dealing with the elderly with jokes about children. Their study suggested that whereas more than 70 percent of the jokes about children were positive, more than 66 percent of those dealing with the aged were negative (Richman 1977). More recently, Levin (1987) had college students from California, Tennessee, and Massachusetts evaluate a number of characteristics of a 25-, 52-, or 73-year-old man from his resume and a photograph of him taken at the three different ages. Results revealed significantly more negative evaluations of the older target person than either the middle-aged or younger condition by students in all three regions of the country. The students in California, Tennessee, and Massachusetts agreed that the older man was less active, less competent, less intelligent, less reliable, and less energetic than he had been during his youth or middle age.

Are women really the gossip mongers of society?

Many stereotypes assume the status of cultural truisms—they are accepted as part of the natural order of things and are rarely, if ever, seen as needing confirmation or proof. For example, many people believe that women gossip more than men—that females generally spread nasty, derogatory, even scandalous information about the lives of others. This stereotype has been repeatedly used to belittle women, though the evidence to support the allegation is sorely lacking (Rysman 1977).

Levin and Arluke (1985, 1987) recently studied sex differences in gossip mongering among male and female college students at a large northeastern university. They had trained observers overhear conversations in the student lounge, a central area of the university in which large numbers of undergraduates congregate to talk, study, and read. During an 8-week period, 3 hours daily, the two observers listened to and recorded 194 instances of gossip in the conversations of 76 male and 120 female students.

Do women actually gossip more than men? In this sample of college students, observers estimated that female students actually did devote a larger proportion of their conversations to discussions of other people than did the male students. Specifically, 71 percent of the women's conversations, compared with 64 percent of the men's conversations, were spent talking about others. Before accepting the validity of the stereotype that women are "gossips," however, let us not forget that gossip has a pejorative meaning in its popular usage. If this popular view is correct, then female conversations should be more negative than the conversations of their male counterparts. Levin and Arluke found instead that both male and female conversations contained the same percentage of clearly positive and clearly negative references to others. For instance, both male and female talk concerned favorable and unfavorable references to personal habits, manners, appearance, and role performance of students and instructors on campus.

Targets of gossip also varied by sex of student: consistent with their sex roles, women focused more on intimate friends and relatives, whereas men talked more about distant acquaintances and media celebrities. At the same time, however, men and women did gossip about many of the same topics as well, especially dating, sex, and personal appearance. Only for the topics of sports and coursework did significant differences by sex emerge, with males talking more about sports and females talking more about the courses they were taking. Overall, the conversations of men and women in this study—all of them college students—could not have been predicted from the stereotyped images widely believed to apply to gender. Instead, men and women often talked about many of the same topics and with the same tone. Women were no more likely than men to spread nasty and malicious gossip.

How does prejudice influence discrimination? The traditional sex-role stereotypes for women are incompatible with leadership and management roles (Powell and Butterfield 1979; Offerman 1986). Some research indicates that women may have little chance to be regarded as leaders even when they behave in a manner that would be enough for men to be perceived as leaderlike. Research conducted by Berndt and Heller (1986), for example, indicates that children tend to expect girls to display stereotyped behavior even when they have previously behaved in a manner inconsistent with gender stereotypes. More to the point, Porter and Geis (1980) showed that when the sex-role stereotype—men lead while women follow—disagrees with a situational cue—a woman seated at the head of the table—raters use gender and not situation to determine leadership status. In other words, even when a woman is seated in the chair identified with leadership, the man is still regarded as the leader and the woman is seen as the follower.

More recent research is, however, somewhat more optimistic regarding reactions to women in leadership positions. Offermann (1986) had students enrolled in introductory psychology view a videotape of a three-person mixed-sex group working on a joint class project. All of the students watched a tape showing an individual behaving like a group leader—that is, sitting at the head of the table, talking more than the other members, speaking first and after each pause, contributing the largest number of novel ideas to the group, and supporting the ideas of others. Half of the students saw a male leader; half saw a female leader.

Offermann's reults indicate that success in the leadership role can partially overcome the sex stereotype. Specifically, subjects were no more likely to identify the male than the female in the videotape as a group leader. Moreover, sex of the leader did not appear to influence subjects' ratings of the leader: Compared with the male, the female in a leadership role was evaluated just as highly for such qualities as leadership, dominance, intelligence, competence, industriousness, and supportiveness. Unfortunately, these positive evaluations did not extend to the subjects' predictions of future group performance. Under certain conditions, subjects expected the group to be more successful in the future when it had a male rather than a female leading it.

Perhaps Offermann's subjects sensed something that had been reported by social psychologists some six years earlier. In 1980, Sanders and Schmidt set out to establish whether discrimination against women in leadership positions can take an active form by actually interfering with their accomplishments and sabotaging their successes. Students at the University of Iowa, both males and females, participated in an experiment which was much like the real-life experience of someone in business who works on a project whose goal is established by a supervisor at a higher level. Specifically, all subjects in the experiment were asked to sort cards into categories according to a quota previously set by "an engineering student" at the University. One-half of the subjects were told that the quota setter was a male; the other half that the quota setter was a female.

Sanders and Schmidt found that subjects did less work when they believed the quota was set by a female rather than a male. This "sabotage effect" tended to be stronger for male than for female subjects, although it was present to some extent even in females. If these results can be generalized to "real life" situations, we might conclude that women may be less successful than men in obtaining support for their projects. "In turn, this relative ineffectiveness would produce less successful projects, which could be taken, erroneously, to reflect upon the ability of the project designer" (p. 487).

A second finding in the Sanders and Schmidt experiment deserves comment. They found that even their female subjects worked harder when they believed the quota was set by a man as opposed to a woman. Apparently, some minority members actually come to accept the validity of stereotypes about their own group. In 1968, for example, Goldberg asked a sample of college women to read a number of professional articles and to rate them for persuasiveness, value, and so on. One-half of the women were told that the articles were written by "John T. McKay," whereas the other half were told that the same articles were written by "Joan T. McKay." Regardless of the field with which it dealt, the article attributed to a female author was rated less favorably by the sample of college women.

Of course, Goldberg conducted his study in the '60s, at least a few years before the women's movement had had a chance to "raise the consciousness" of American females concerning prejudice and discrimination based on gender. In a sample of 294 young women between 1970 (as high school students) and 1981, Tallichet and Willits (1986) report that these women shifted their attitudes dramatically away from traditional sex-role ideas. By 1981, the majority rejected the notion that education and work are more important for men, and that every woman should marry, stay home to raise children, and leave the major decisions to her husband. Also indicative of a long-term change in the sex-role perceptions of women, there is evidence that women who continue to support traditional sex roles tend to be older and less educated (Morgan and Walker 1983).

Does discrimination cause prejudice... and vice versa? Which comes first, prejudice or discrimination? The question of the direction of cause and effect between these two important variables is part of a larger issue concerning the primacy of attitudes versus behavior. Some social psychologists argue that attitudes cause behavior; others contend that behavior causes attitudes (Ajzen and Fishbein 1980; Zanna et al. 1982).

At first glance, it may seem obvious that attitudes always precede and determine the manner in which individuals behave. After all, isn't discrimination simply a reflection of the prejudice that people hold toward the members of different groups? From this viewpoint, in order to predict who will and will not discriminate against a person of Puerto Rican descent, all you have to do is measure their attitude toward Puerto Ricans. Actually, however, many studies have uncovered inconsistencies between prejudice and discrimination, between attitude and behavior. They have found prejudiced people who don't discriminate, people who discriminate without being prejudiced, and so on. For example, Robert Merton's (1957) "fair-weather liberal" can be regarded as someone who may not have negative feelings or beliefs about the members of a particular minority, yet is ready to discriminate against them in order to gain social approval or financial reward. This type is illustrated by individuals who deny being prejudiced against their black classmates but refuse to befriend any of them for fear they would offend their bigoted white peers. Another possibility is the "timid bigot," an individual who harbors negative feelings or beliefs about the members of a minority but who is not predisposed to break the law in order to take action against them.

These inconsistencies between prejudice and discrimination were first detected in a classic study conducted by Richard LaPiere (1934), who accompanied a Chinese couple on a lengthy automobile tour of the United

States. In the 250 hotels and restaurants which they visited during their three-month trip, LaPiere and his companions were refused service only once. Some time later, LaPiere wrote to each of the establishments he had visited, asking whether it would or would not accept a Chinese customer (during the '30s, there was strong prejudice against individuals of Asian descent). Ninety percent of those who responded said they would not serve someone Chinese—yet they had!

LaPiere's study has often been used to demonstrate that you cannot predict whether an individual will discriminate based on knowledge of his or her prejudiced feelings about a particular group of people. The study has also been criticized by social psychologists who point out, for example, that the person who refused the reservation by mail may not have been the person who served the Chinese couple upon its visit. Whatever the merits and deficiencies of LaPiere's early work, a number of more recent studies has found the same inconsistency, leading many social psychologists to reject the concept of attitude as a causal variable and focus exclusively on behavior (Eagly and Himmelfarb 1978; Feagin and Feagin 1978; Wicker 1969).

There are at least two important social psychological theories from which it is possible to support the primacy of behavior over attitudes and to explain why some prejudiced individuals often also discriminate. According to Festinger's (1957) *theory of cognitive dissonance*, a person who makes a decision that is inconsistent with his or her beliefs is liable to experience the unpleasant psychological condition he calls cognitive dissonance. In order to reduce the dissonance, the individual will alter his or her beliefs to bring them into line with the behavior in question. For example, suppose that an individual places a bet on a horse based on a friend's tip that the horse is a "sure thing." Before he actually places the bet, the individual may have mixed feelings about the horse in question. He may, for example, consider the track records of all the horses in the race as well as the quality of their jockeys. After examining the odds, he might read the racing section of the local newspaper or ask friends who frequently place bets. Once he actually makes his bet at the track window, however, his attitude toward the horse immediately changes. He has now made an irreversible decision which he seeks to justify. Rather than continue to weigh the positive and negative qualities of chosen and unchosen horses and jockeys, he immediately becomes absolutely convinced that he has made the best decision, that he has chosen the fastest horse, and that he is a sure winner. His attitude follows his behavior.

From this point of view, prejudice is an attitude that is developed and used to justify discrimination. We first make a decision to discriminate against an individual based on his or her racial identity, and develop attitudes consonant with our behavior. Once the prejudices are entrenched in our culture, they act on a collective level to perpetuate such discriminatory treatment.

From Daryl Bem's (1970) *self-perception theory*, we can also predict that attitudes will follow behavior, but for an entirely different reason. According to Bem, we often do not really know what we feel or believe until we are forced to develop an attitude when asked for our position. When asked what we believe, we then tend to evaluate ourselves as we evaluate others — by examining behavior and inferring an attitude. If, for example, someone reads the *New York Times* on a daily basis, we infer that she must like the *New York Times*. If someone always has eggs for breakfast, we infer that he must like eggs. By a similar process, if someone asks how we feel about a particular group of people whose members we have always gone out of our way to avoid, we might infer that our feelings and beliefs are negative. Rather than read our attitudes directly, we "cheat" by taking our clues from the same behavior that others look at to determine our attitudes. Unconsciously, we use the way we behave to infer how we feel and what we believe to be true. This we call our attitude.

There are also many social psychologists who continue to believe in the primacy of attitudes over behavior, prejudice over discrimination. They point out that it was naive, as some early social psychologists did, to expect a perfect correlation between attitude and behavior, between prejudice and discrimination. Prejudice, they contend, is one (although one of the most important) of the variables that go to determine whether discrimination will occur. For one thing, a particular behavior may be influenced by more than one attitude (Wicker 1969). For example, an individual who decides whether or not to discriminate against Italians may be influenced, to some extent, by her attitude toward Italians; she may be influenced even more, however, by her attitude toward money or friendship. If discriminating against someone of Italian descent means losing either money or friends, she may decide not to do so, even though she is prejudiced against Italians. Second, there is often some degree of inconsistency between the cognitive (belief) and affective (emotional) components of an attitude (Raden 1985). The effect of attitudes is generally stronger when these two components of an attitude are consistent; when they are inconsistent, the predictive power of the attitude is diminished (Liska 1984). For example, an individual who grows up feeling a profound dislike for Asians and believing that they are superstitious and sly is more likely to discriminate than someone who believes the stereotypes but does not have a negative feeling toward Asians. Third, as suggested by Ajzen and Fishbein (1977), attitudes are more predictive of behavior when they are directed at the same target and involve the same behavior. If so, then, attitudes toward specific behaviors will best predict the outcome of a single incident. For example, the reaction of someone who is white to the first black person who moves into the neighborhood might be predicted by asking him for his attitude toward this specific situation rather than his attitude toward black people in general. Finally, attitudes are likely to be predictive of behavior when an individual sees some personal relevance in the behavior being predicted (Sivacek and Crano 1982). For example, attitude toward Vietnamese-Americans is likely to be consistent with discrimination against Vietnamese-Americans for an individual fisherman who must compete with the newcomers in order to earn a living. By contrast, there may be less consistency between attitude and behavior for someone who has never met a Vietnamese-American and does not have a "vested interest" in controlling their relationship.

Concerning the relationship between prejudice and discrimination, Simpson and Yinger (1986) probably summed it up best when they suggested (1) there can be prejudice without discrimination, (2) there can be discrimination without prejudice, (3) discrimination can be among the causes of prejudice, (4) prejudice can be among the causes of discrimination, and (5) probably most frequently they are mutually reinforcing.

The Functions of Prejudice and Discrimination

We contend that prejudice and discrimination persist because they have some extremely important functions for certain members of our society (Levin and Levin 1982). By *function*, we mean a consequence that aids in the adaptation or adjustment of a system (Merton 1957). What, for example, are the functions of college? How does it aid in the adjustment of individuals and the culture of which they are a part? For one thing, we expect college to raise self-confidence and to allow its graduates to adapt better to their careers and general lifestyles. A college education may also help perpetuate the values of progress, science, independence, profit, future-time orientation, and so on.

To conclude that something is functional is not to conclude that it is therefore good in a moral sense. That judgment depends on how one feels about the system for which it is functional. For example, there is no disagreement with the assertion that the human heart is functional for the operation of the body as a system. In a functional sense, then, the heart is functional for the human organism, regardless of our judgment of the goodness of the specific human being. Therefore Adolf Hitler's heart was functional and still evil in a moral sense, because it contributed to the maintenance of a person we believe to have been evil.

Some of the functions of prejudice can be seen clearly in the factors which are discussed below. At the personality level, prejudice reduces the annoying uncertainties of everyday life and permits displacing aggression to a group of people whose members are entirely innocent of imposing frustrations on the individual. As a trait in the authoritarian syndrome, prejudice satisfies a psychological need to bolster or protect self-esteem at the expense of powerless individuals who are stereotyped as inferior. Prejudice is also functional at the social level: It has consequences of a political or an economic nature that aid in the maintenance of the majority group *qua* group and of its advantaged position in a society. This function of prejudice occurs when there is competition between groups for scarce resources.

The need for structure   Every individual has the need "to give adequate structure to his universe" (Katz 1960, p. 170). Prejudice operates in the lives of many people to "define the situation," provide order and clarity, and reduce the cognitive and emotional uncertainties of everyday experiences. Culturally supported prejudices provide ready-made expectations in terms of which individuals can be categorized. What people often do is to fill the gap in their knowledge of others with oversimplified and distorted preconceptions, many of which are based on group membership. Thus, a prospective employer who knows little about a black job applicant, save from his limited contact in an interview situation, might use a stereotype about blacks in order to form a conclusion regarding the applicant's abilities (Katz 1960). Although stereotyped categories narrow the amount of information necessary for decision making to occur, they also expand the scope of available information (Ehrlich 1972). The interviewer who judges an applicant on the basis of his or her racial identity immediately gains much information about characteristics that the applicant is presumed to share with other members of his or her race. Thus, stereotyping individuals by their group membership may in part have a benign motive, though a harmful effect.

In fact, some social psychologists have proposed that stereotypes are no more or less than attributes that we associate with category labels such as race and sex and impute to individuals much as attributes of categories of objects are imputed to individual objects (Hamilton et al. 1980; Taylor 1981). From this point of view, stereotyping is a means whereby people organize the social environment into social categories in order to organize the process of social interaction (Taylor and Falcone 1982).

As a response to this need for structure, stereotypes may be used to categorize and label individuals from groups that are valued as well as groups that are deprecated. Jones, Wood, and Quattrone (1981) had the members of four Princeton University "Eating Clubs" for undergraduate upperclassmen rate the members of their own club and then the members of the three other clubs on each of the following pairs of opposites: introverted–extroverted, refined–crude, athletic–nonathletic, arrogant–humble, deep–superficial, laid-back–uptight, optimistic–pessimistic, and low socioeconomic status–high socioeconomic status. The researchers' findings indicated that the students rated the members of their own club as more heterogeneous on these personal characteristics than they rated the members of the other clubs. In other words, they tended to see wider individual differences among their own club members and more uniformity among the members of the other three clubs. This was true regardless of their degree of preference for the members of their own club. Apparently, members of other groups "all look alike," even if an individual doesn't despise them.

Despite their universal appeal in everyday life, stereotypes concerning the members of minority groups cannot always be explained as originating in a benign need simply to structure the social environment. Taylor and Falcone (1982) report that those people who organize information about an individual based on his or her group membership may not be the same people who express stereotyped beliefs about that individual. These researchers had 20 subjects listen to a tape of 6 speakers—3 males and 3 females—discuss the topic of "how to increase voter turnout." After the tape had ended, subjects were asked to evaluate each of the speakers and to recall which speakers said what. Overall, subjects rated the male speakers as more savvy, influential, interesting, and effective than the female speakers—even though objectively the male and female speakers had been matched on these characteristics beforehand. Moreover, subjects who could not recall precisely which speaker had given which arguments were able to recall whether the speaker was a male or female. There was, however, very little overlap between those who recalled arguments by sex and those who rated male speakers as more competent than female speakers. In other words, subjects who categorized speakers' arguments by sex were not necessarily the same subjects who devalued female speakers.

Stereotypes apparently have a special attraction for extremely prejudiced members of society. Prejudiced individuals seem to be especially intolerant of cognitive and emotional ambiguities (Martin and Westie 1959; Steiner and Johnson 1963; Triandis and Triandis 1972). According to the authors of *The Authoritarian Personality* (Adorno et al. 1950), this aversion of highly prejudiced persons is a generalization of their intolerance of the affectual ambivalence that exists when both love and hate are felt for a parent. From this viewpoint, prejudiced individuals want absolute and unequivocal feelings about themselves and others; aided by a series of stereotyped polarities—black versus white, strong versus weak, good versus evil—they suppress any awareness of their own weaknesses and the weaknesses of their parents. Instead, their anger is externalized. Members of their own group are glorified and idealized, whereas culturally designated outgroups become targets for displaced aggression.

As adults, extremely prejudiced individuals may become inaccurate role takers, people who are not capable of accurately estimating characteristics of other individuals from the cues they give in interactional settings. For example, Koenig and King (1962) found that students opposed to racial integration were significantly less accurate in predicting the responses of other students on campus than were students who espoused attitudes favorable to racial integration. Presumably, students who are poor role takers might instead rely on stereotyped preconceptions in order to form judgments about their fellow students on campus.

Experimental evidence for the existence of *intolerance of ambiguity*, a particular dislike of unclear situations, among prejudiced individuals was first uncovered by Block and Block (1951), who tested 65 college students over 100 trials as follows: Each student was placed in a darkened room where he or she was asked to estimate the distance that a pinpoint of light had moved. Actually, of course, these subjects were exposed to the autokinetic phenomenon (See Chapter 3), so that the light really never moved but only appeared to do so. Block and Block reported that highly prejudiced students were quicker than their more tolerant counterparts to establish a norm for themselves regarding the movement of the light. They quickly reported the light as moving in a constant direction and to a constant number of inches from one trial to another, whereas the tolerant students could better accept not having a clear-cut answer and so took much longer to establish a norm regarding the movement of the light.

In a more recent test, Quanty, Keats, and Harkins (1975) discovered that anti-Semitic subjects were more willing to label a face as Jewish on the basis of limited information than were unprejudiced subjects. When asked to identify a number of photographs as Jewish or non-Jewish, the anti-Semites thought that they saw more snapshots of Jews, but were also more inaccurate than their unprejudiced counterparts. Perhaps as a result of their need to define the situation, the anti-Semitic subjects made numerous erroneous guesses: "They seem more concerned with correctly identifying Jews than they are with falsely labeling a person Jewish" (Quanty, Keats, and Harkins 1975, p. 454).

The displacement of aggression As we saw in Chapter 6, frustrated people often lash out against those who are perceived to be the cause of their troubles. Yet hostility is not always directed against the true source of their frustration, for the source may be vague and difficult to identify (for example, bad weather or a bad economy) or much too powerful to be safely attacked (for example, the boss) (Williams 1947; Berkowitz 1962). Moreover, it may be difficult to justify retaliating against the true cause of a frustration when we know that his behavior was accidental or, at least, out of his control (Burnstein and Worchel 1962; Geen 1972).

For example, have you ever been knocked down or bumped by someone who admits that he didn't see you and is extremely apologetic as a result? If you're like most people, it may be difficult, and even less satisfying, to strike out or get even with him. After all, he didn't mean to hurt you, and you know it. Under such conditions, an individual who has experienced frustration may attempt to locate a more vulnerable and visible enemy against whom his hostility can be directed with relative impunity. After having an accident on the highway, a frustrated driver might, for example, go home and take it out on his spouse or his children. He might also be more impatient than usual the next day with his fellow workers. This process is called *scapegoating* or *displaced aggression*: the aggression generated by a frustrating event is displaced or redirected to an innocent target.

Given their powerless position in society, American minorities have often served as targets for displaced aggression. Historically, blacks have acted as scapegoats, because they have been not only vulnerable to attack but also visible by virtue of their skin color and physiognomy. Until 1930, for example, the frequency with which southern blacks were lynched increased as the price of southern cotton decreased. Much of the blame for economic hard times during this period was focused on blacks, even in the face of irrefutable evidence that they had nothing to do with the falling price of cotton. More recently, the shortage of energy and economic recession that characterized much of the period of the 1970s and early 1980s brought with it a rapid rise in anti-Semitic activities as well as renewed incidents involving the Ku Klux Klan (King 1979). During the mid-1980s, as much of the nation was recovering from a severe recession and as energy prices fell, anti-black and anti-Semitic sentiment became concentrated where levels of frustration continued to be high—among some midwestern farmers who were eager to place the blame for their economic depression in the midst of national prosperity.

Early experimental evidence for the presence of displaced aggression as a factor in prejudice and discrimination was provided by Miller and Bugelski (1948), who required 31 young men in a vocational training camp to take a battery of lengthy and difficult tests that was scheduled so as to prevent them from attending the most interesting camp activity of the week. Both before and after these exams were administered, Miller and Bugelski measured the attitudes of their subjects toward Japanese and Mexicans. This was accomplished by asking the men to check a list of ten desirable and ten undesirable characteristics as being either present or absent in the average Mexican or Japanese. As predicted by the displaced aggression theory of prejudice, the men regarded Mexicans and Japanese less favorably after the frustrating tests than before they had taken them. From pretest to posttest, there was a significant decrease in the number of favorable traits checked and a slight increase in the number of negative traits checked. This finding has been replicated several times since Miller and Bugelski's classic experiment, either by means of paper-and-pencil questionnaires in which a set of subjects expresses aggressive feelings after being frustrated (Cowen, Landes, and Schaet 1959) or, more behaviorally, as the tendency to administer an intense electrical shock to another naive subject (Holmes 1972).

According to Coser (1956), scapegoating on a collective level may serve as a *safety valve*, whereby feelings of hostility are diverted to substitute objects, thereby protecting the leaders of a group from becoming the recipients of aggression. This phenomenon has been observed in the confines of the small-group laboratory. Burke (1969), for example, found that the displacement of hostility on a low-status member of a small group can become a mechanism whereby the task leader escapes the wrath of other group members.

Outside the experimental setting, the safety-valve function of displaced aggression may protect powerful individuals in a society from the anger of its members. Many frustrated people seem to avoid placing the blame for their economic troubles at the top rungs of national or corporate leadership. They seem often to direct their hostility to the poor, the downtrodden, and the marginal members of society.

In a classic statement, McWilliams (1948) argued that powerful people, understanding the advantage of displaced aggression, actually help the process along. For example, the anti-Semitism that emerged during the closing decades of the 19th century originated, according to McWilliams, with wealthy industrial tycoons who employed prejudice as a tactic for diverting attention from their own exploitive labor practices. As actively encouraged by these tycoons, anti-Semitism became a "mask for privilege" that quickly spread in scope to encompass wider and wider segments of American society. While the captains of industry were benignly regarded as "idols of production," the Jews were seen as greedy and mercenary "parasites." Also at the turn of the century, Italian newcomers to America similarly found themselves blamed for all of America's economic ills.

▶ Perspective:
The Effect of Social and Cultural Forces

Racism as colonialism   Blauner (1972) has argued that racial inequality became embedded in the structure of society, or *institutionalized* via colonization, a process not unlike that historically experienced by the third-world peoples of Asia and Africa in their relations with white Europeans. According to Blauner, American society has prospered because of the disposition to colonize its "subjects" on domestic soil—to defeat Hispanics, conquer Indians, and enslave blacks.

Blauner identifies an important distinction between the experiences of white immigrants and colonized people. Most white immigrants came to the United States voluntarily, although they may have decided to abandon their countries of origin because of extreme oppression. In most cases, therefore, white immigrants entered as part of a free labor force. Though exploited and disadvantaged upon entry, they still possessed a degree of independence, choice, and mobility that was simply not permitted to those who were colonial subjects of capture, conquest, or slavery. Thus, when the Irish felt trapped in Boston, they could pack their bags to farm in the Midwest or search for gold in California. If life in New York became too difficult, Jews moved to Chicago or Baltimore. Such opportunities were unavailable to black-, Asian-, and Mexican-Americans, who were not part of the free labor force.

Immigrants were also permitted to maintain their own cultural identity or to assimilate into the mainstream of American society on a voluntary basis. By contrast, the cultural heritage—and often the integrity—of colonized groups was frequently transformed or destroyed, breaking their resistance to outside influences and making it easier to dominate and control them. As a result, colonialism required that new institutions and lifestyles be imposed on those being colonized. ■

The authoritarian personality During the 1940s, at a time when fascism and anti-Semitism were major concerns throughout the world, a group of social scientists suggested that certain individuals were psychologically predisposed to displace aggression on or scapegoat Jews, blacks, and the members of other minorities. In their research, Adorno and his associates (1950) amassed a good deal of evidence for the presence of an *authoritarian personality structure*, a constellation of interrelated personality characteristics in which prejudice has a central position.

Adorno et al. took a Freudian view: They argued that the roots of the authoritarian personality could be traced back to the early socialization experiences of a child—in particular, in harsh and threatening forms of child rearing and clearly defined family roles imposed during the first few years of life. In an authoritarian family, the child is expected to be weak and submissive to the demands of the parents. In contrast, they assume a position of absolute dominance.

The child learns to comply in order to avoid being punished, but only makes a superficial and ambivalent identification with his or her parents, actually harboring much latent resentment toward them for his feelings of weakness and inferiority. As an adult, he comes to identify, albeit superficially, with those members of society who are regarded as strong and powerful (for example, Adolph Hitler) and to treat others in the manner he was treated as a child. He develops *ethnocentrism*—a general contempt for any and all members of society who are stereotyped as inferior and weak, whether they are blacks, foreigners, Catholics, Jews, or Hispanics. Scapegoating is a mechanism that an authoritarian individual employs in order to bolster and protect his fragile self-esteem, to feel good about himself in comparison with the allegedly inferior and weak minority members.

The symptoms of authoritarianism were identifed by the F (potential for fascism) Scale, a series of opinion statements to which individuals were asked to express their agreement or disagreement. For example, "authoritarian power and toughness" was measured by agreement with the item, "People can be divided into two distinct classes: the weak and the strong." "Authoritarian aggression" was indicated by an affirmative response to the item, "Homosexuals are hardly better than criminals and ought to be severely punished."

As suggested by the name given to the measure of authoritarianism (the F or potential for fascism Scale), only the politically reactionary or right-wing segment of authoritarianism was studied by Adorno and his associates. The original research into authoritarianism was conducted at a time in history when fascism was indeed of major concern to both social psychologists and laypeople, having been equated by many with World War II and German anti-Semitism. As Rokeach (1960) subsequently discovered, however, authoritarianism is not exclusive to those who hold a reactionary ideology, but may also be found among radicals, liberals, and moderates.

▶ Perspective:
The Effect of Social Definition

Attributing the causes of success How do we explain another person's accomplishments? Is it possible that we attribute the success of white men to ability while attributing the identical successes of blacks and women more to motivation or luck? In other words, do we think that successful blacks and women have to try harder in order to overcome their lack of skills?

In a study by Yarkin, Town, and Wallston (1982), 60 male and 60 female undergraduate students were asked to read a description of a highly successful banking executive. Subjects were led to believe that the banker was either male or female (named Bill or Alison) and either black or white (depending on whether the banker had attended Howard University or

American University and belonged to the NAACP or the Chamber of Commerce). All subjects then indicated the importance of each of four possible causal factors—ability, motivation, luck, and task difficulty—in explaining the banker's career accomplishments.

Results obtained by Yarkin, Town, and Wallston indicated that stereotypes about sex and race influenced the attributions which the students selected to explain success. Specifically, they attributed the white male's success more to ability and less to motivation and luck than they did any other group. Conversely, successful black men and all women were seen as less able and more motivated than their white male counterpart. Both women and blacks really are perceived as needing to try harder to achieve success in order to compensate for their relative lack of ability! ■

Culture and conformity Although several hundred research projects have followed the publication of the original work on the authoritarian personality, interest in this approach has waned in recent years. The authoritarian syndrome continues to be related to the approval of bigotry as expressed, for example, in identification with Archie Bunker of "All in the Family" (Chapko and Lewis 1975). However, the authors of *The Authoritarian Personality* treated prejudice as though it were part of an illness or disease which they called authoritarianism, as a pathological state—not unlike cancer or heart disease—that afflicts certain members of society because of the harsh manner in which they are socialized. In emphasizing the abnormal or pathological sources of prejudice, Adorno and his associates may have made a crucial mistake. They failed to give adequate recognition to cultural forms of prejudice.

As we have seen, prejudiced attitudes may be widely shared among the members of a group or society. Americans separated by virtue of differences in ethnicity, socioeconomic status, or region nevertheless express surprisingly similar beliefs regarding the members of various minority groups. What is more, prejudice often becomes an enduring characteristic of a society, being transmitted by its members from generation to generation, and receiving strong support in the form of custom or legal codes.

Far from always being deviant or abnormal, then, prejudice often becomes the normal and expected state of affairs in a society. It actually becomes an element of culture—the normative order—of the society in which it exists (Westie 1964). As such, we learn prejudice through our parents, peers, and teachers, just as we learn other conceptions of "what ought to be," such as motherhood, love of church, patriotism, and economic success. Therefore, it may be precisely those members of society who are most "socialized" or conventional and most willing to conform to society's norms who turn out also to be most prejudiced (Levin and Levin 1982). In 1952, for example, Christie administered the F-Scale to a group of inductees in an Army basic-training center both before and after they had completed six weeks of basic training. He found that recruits who fit well into Army life—those who were accepted by both fellow inductees and superiors—also became significantly more authoritarian during their period of training (Christie and Jahoda 1954).

According to Adorno et al., prejudice exists because it satisfies a psychological need in the authoritarian personality. If the residents of Mississippi turn out to be more prejudiced against blacks than are the residents of Connecticut, then Mississippians should also be more "authoritarian" and more prejudiced against a wide range of minorities.

But Pettigrew (1958) and, in a later study, Middleton (1976) found that residents of the South had a much higher level of antiblack prejudice than did residents of other regions of the United States. Yet the regions differed only slightly with respect to anti-Semitism, anti-Catholic prejudice, and authoritarianism (Middleton 1976). In fact, Pettigrew found less prejudice in the South than in the country generally. Apparently, regional and societal differences in prejudice cannot always be explained on the basis of authoritarian predispositions in a population which make some of its members hate almost everyone who is different. Cultural norms may be operating to produce prejudice directed against a particular group rather than against minorities generally.

The influence of competition In a classic study, Sherif and his associates (1961) demonstrated the relationship between competition and intergroup hostility in a series of experiments that took place in an isolated summer camp for 11- and 12-year-old boys. After spending a period of time getting to know one another, the campers were separated into two groups and placed in different cabins. When each group of boys had had a chance to develop a strong sense of group spirit and belonging, Sherif arranged to have them all participate in series of intergroup encounters—a tournament of competitive games such as football, tug-of-war, baseball, and a treasure hunt—in which one group could achieve its goals only if the other group did not. In other words, there could be only one winning team. Although the tournament began in a spirit of goodwill and friendly competition, it soon became clear that negative intergroup attitudes were emerging. The members of either group began name calling their rivals, in some cases completely turning against members of the opposing group whom they had selected as "best friends" upon first arriving at camp.

Sherif's findings shed light on the basis for intergroup hostility: When the status of one group depends on the subordination of another group, then we might expect that intergroup competition will become translated into prejudice and discrimination. In fact, one of the most visible determinants of prejudice may have its basis in *realistic group conflict*. The members of one group who attempt to secure a share of the scarce resources of their society meet resistance from the members of other groups who also seek their share of the economic pie. This may explain the strong relationship between the occurrence of antiimmigrant nativist activity and the incidence of economic depression. The newcomers to America are seen as competitors for the few jobs that exist during a shaky economic situation. Thus, during the depressions of 1893 and 1907, immigrants from Italy were regarded as "organ grinders, paupers, and slovenly ignoramuses" (LaGumina 1973). For similar reasons, perhaps, white workers who are in direct competition with blacks for employment in poorly paid, less secure jobs are more racially bigoted than are white workers in the better-paid and more secure segment of the labor market where there is little competition from blacks (Cummings 1980).

There may be an element of realistic group conflict in whites' opposition to busing. Bobo (1983) argued that whites who most oppose racial busing perceive that blacks pose tangible threats to their own interests. That is, they have children in public schools who participate in racial busing programs, and are most convinced that their own children will be bused. Sears and Kinder (1985) suggest instead that opposition to busing has a much more irrational basis. Its roots, they contend, reside essentially both in racial fears learned during early childhood and in deep-seated prejudice.

An important variant of competitive prejudice can be found in economic theories of intergroup hostility. Some theorists have claimed that white workers generally benefit in terms of occupational prestige and working conditions from the continued subordination of large numbers of blacks (Glenn 1963; Beck 1980). Other theorists have suggested instead that prejudice and discrimination against blacks increase income inequality among whites. That is, poor and middle-class white workers lose income, whereas wealthy whites get even wealthier (Reich 1972; Bonacich 1972). In this latter view, employers can depress the wages of white workers who fear competition from cheaper black labor. Racial divisions among workers also prevent black and white employees from uniting in the workplace and in the labor movement generally.

▶ Perspective:
The Effect of the Immediate Situation

Racial composition of desegregated classrooms   What is the effect of classroom racial composition on close friendships between black and white students? Does it help or hurt interracial friendliness when there is a majority of students who come from either group? Hallinan and Smith (1985) examined this question in a study of students in 18 desegregated classes. All from northern California elementary schools, the students were questioned over a school year regarding the development of their close friendships with classmates (for example, how many of their classmates who were originally "friends" had become "best friends").

Hallinan and Smith found that as the proportion of one racial group— either blacks or whites—increased, the popularity of that group with the students of the other race also increased. If there were relatively more blacks in the class, whites had more blacks as best friends; if there were more whites, then blacks had more whites as best friends.

According to Hallinan and Smith, friendliness between blacks and whites is affected by the number of opportunities students have for interacting with members of another race. Classrooms in which blacks are in the majority tend to promote white friendliness toward blacks, but at the expense of black friendliness toward whites. Similarly, white-majority classrooms promote black friendliness toward whites but are an obstacle to white friendliness toward blacks. When it comes to maximizing interracial friendships of both blacks and whites in desegregated classrooms, "racial balance" may therefore be the most effective mixture to achieve. ■

The Reduction of Prejudice

How do we go about attempting to reduce prejudice and discrimination? Activist civil rights groups often urge people to stop stereotyping others based on race, sex, or age and to judge individuals *qua* individuals. This strategy is based on the assumption that people know when they stereotype others, and have the capacity to change and the will to do so. Recent research indicates, however, that people who stereotype frequently lack introspective abilities: They may be totally unaware of their own propensity for stereotyping others and therefore may lack control over the many stereotyped images they employ in everyday life (Hepburn and Locksley 1983). Indeed, even those who consciously reject prejudice and discrimination on moral grounds may make use of stereotypes despite their intentions through what has been called *nonconscious ideology* (Bem and Bem 1970).

Moreover, if it is true, as we have suggested, that prejudice and discrimination provide gains for certain individuals and groups, then it seems unlikely that the recipients of such gains would be easily moved from their commitment to the status quo, regardless of the cogency of appeals to egalitarianism, humanism, or the like. On the psychological level, for example, social psychologists who test the effectiveness of moral persuasion on prejudice have reported obtaining what they call "boomerang reactions" to antiprejudice persuasive campaigns in which the persecution and victimization of minority-group members are depicted. At best, the most prejudiced individuals selectively avoid viewing these antiprejudice messages, for example, by turning to another channel on their TV sets. At worst, such content actually attracts prejudiced persons who seek vicariously to satisfy their hidden desire for carrying out cruel and sadistic forms of aggression on a scapegoat (Vander Zanden 1983; Vidmar and Rokeach 1974). A number of television movies over the past decade have portrayed the plight of exploited groups in society. Programs such as "Roots," "Holocaust," "The Autobiography of Jane Pittman," "King," "The Diary of Anne Frank," and "Against the Wind" may well have raised the consciousness of Americans regarding the history of various minorities. Sadly, however, they may also have fed the sadism of very prejudiced people (Levin and Levin 1982).

At the most fundamental societal level, we might begin by directing our efforts toward achieving a more cooperative, less competitive social environment, in which prejudice has less meaning for an individual's self-esteem or his life-chances. In such an environment, an individual would have less to gain by prejudice and discrimination. Most efforts at the reduction of prejudice have, however, been less ambitious and perhaps more realistic than to seek total cultural change. Instead, they focus on a particular institution in society—neighborhoods, schools, laws, and the like—where they believe change is a realistic possibility.

Effects of changes in the law Legal remedies have focused on reducing discrimination and its effects under the assumption that you can change behavior without first modifying attitudes. Indeed, by changing behavior (in this case, discrimination), you might also, in the long run, cause attitudes to change as well (that is, reduce prejudice). There is, of course, a limit to how much social change individuals will tolerate before they effectively resist it. In order for any social policy to be widely accepted, it must fall within the cultural framework of the values to which members of society conform (Allport 1954). There must also be some perception on the part of the members of society that measures are required in order to right a wrong, to reduce an inequity.

Smith and Kluegel (1984) have recently shown that barriers to opportunity may be more widely perceived in the case of women than blacks. Apparently, many people continue to take a "blaming the victim" stance regarding racial inequalities. Whitehead, Smith, and Eichorn (1982) report, for example, that lack of ability is more often used to explain failure on the part of individuals who are racially dissimilar than on the part of individuals who are racially similar. Given the strong trend away from traditional sex-role attitudes, some social psychologists predict a more favorable prognosis for efforts to achieve equal opportunity on behalf of women than on behalf of blacks (Smith and Kluegel 1984).

Beginning in the '50s, many government policies have attempted to remove restrictions based on race. Most noteworthy in this regard was Brown v. Board of Education (May, 1954), the landmark Supreme Court decision which provided a legal basis for desegregated education on a national level. This decision resulted from the situation of an 8-year-old black girl from Topeka, Kansas, who was required to be bused to a segregated black school located some distance from her home in order to avoid attending a local neighborhood school which was all white. Partly because of the evidence of social scientists, including social psychologists, as to the detrimental impact of segregation on black children, and partly thanks to the impact of black activism, the court decided that the doctrine of "separate but equal" had no place in public education. Segregation in the public schools was regarded as "inherently unequal" and therefore as unconstitutional (Burkey 1971).

Policies of affirmative action went a step beyond the Supreme Court decision of May, 1954. As found in the Civil Rights Act of 1964, such policies declared that the religion, national origin, race, and sex of individuals were not to be used as bases for discrimination or segregation in the areas of employment opportunities, public education, and voting, and in the use of public facilities. The Civil Rights Act requested the U.S. Commissioner of Education to conduct a survey investigating the extent to which public schools were segregated and failed to offer equal educational opportunities. But the act also put pressure on employers and educators to take some kind of positive action to narrow the gaps between blacks and whites. Penalties would be imposed when some employer or school district was found to be guilty of discrimination. The act created the Equal Employment Opportunity Commission to help implement its decisions with respect to employment. In addition, the Office of Education in the Department of Health, Education and Welfare was empowered to demand statistical evidence that integration was proceeding in a substantial way and to withhold federal money from school districts which failed to integrate. In 1968, the Supreme Court insisted that dual school systems be totally eliminated "forthwith." As a result, court-ordered busing became widely applied as cities were asked to desegregate their school systems.

According to Glazer (1976), federal policy aimed at achieving racial equality underwent a basic shift of emphasis beginning in the late 1960s and continuing into the 1970s, in a movement away from affirmative action and toward reverse discrimination. Civil rights laws as interpreted by government agencies and the courts became concerned with achieving equal "representation" rather than equal "opportunities." Thus, government guidelines to employers were increasingly addressed to "goals and timetables," to which the employers' efforts must be directed "to correct the deficiencies and thus to increase materially the utilization of minorities and women, at all levels and in all segments of his work force where deficiencies exist" (Bourne and Levin 1983, p. 32).

Intergroup contact From the standpoint of reducing prejudice, a number of social psychologists once believed strongly in the power of intergroup contact. It was argued that prejudice is merely a prejudgment — that is, a judgment that was made in the absence of knowledge about the members of another group of people. What is the best way to increase knowledge? It is, they contended, to make sure that individuals from different groups get to know one another as human beings. Much civil-rights legislation we have just discussed was based on this premise.

In an early study, Deutsch and Collins (1951) studied the effects of intergroup contact on prejudice in public housing projects where both blacks and whites resided. In one of the projects, black and white residents had been assigned to segregated buildings. That is, one of the buildings in the project was exclusively for white families; the other building was exclusively for black families. By contrast, residents in another project had been assigned to achieve integration: both black and white families resided in the same buildings. According to Deutsch and Collins, white residents in the integrated project became more positive in their attitudes toward blacks as compared with the residents in the segregated project. Apparently, contact between black and white residents who were roughly equal in terms of social status helped to reduce prejudice of whites against blacks.

Sadly, efforts at desegregating schools and neighborhoods over the past few decades have not always proven as successful in reducing prejudice as have the results achieved by Deutsch and Collins. In fact, there is some evidence that desegregation sometimes actually supports antiblack stereotyping (Stephan 1986).

One of the reasons why desegregation has not been more successful is that the contacts between black and white students are usually between groups of *unequal status*: typically, white students are middle class and black students are lower class. In many cases, group differences in behavior and attitudes which might properly be attributed to social class are instead seen by white students as racial in origin and, therefore, as confirmation of their stereotypes (Deutsch and Collins 1951; Cook 1972).

Another problem with intergroup contact as a method of reducing prejudice concerns the circumstances under which members of different groups come together. In school, they typically meet in desegregated classrooms in which they are likely to perceive one another as competitors for grades, popularity, and the like. Students generally tend to be encouraged in their efforts to exceed the achievement levels of classmates. Competitiveness is emphasized, whereas personal improvement tends to be ignored (Coleman 1963; Miller and Hamblin 1963).

From the standpoint of the reduction of prejudice, one of the most promising alternatives to competitive education can be found in Sherif's series of experiments with 11- and 12-year-old boys at a summer camp. After he had induced the intensely competitive tournament between teams of campers, Sherif was able to reverse their intergroup hostility by introducing a *superordinate goal*—a goal shared by all of the boys from both teams that could only be achieved by their cooperation. The result was that boys from different teams ended up liking one another again.

Sherif's concept of a superordinate goal may explain why the members of a team might be attracted to one another even if they are also competitors. On a football team, for example, the players compete to play particular positions; but they also realize that they must cooperate in order to achieve their shared goal of winning. As a result, members of a football team may actually like and respect their most talented competitors (Rees and Segal 1984).

The application of Sherif's concept of superordinate goal in an educational setting was demonstrated by Aronson (1975) in his *jigsaw teaching technique*. Based on the principle of the jigsaw puzzle, Aronson gave each child in a small "learning group" a piece of information that had to be shared with other classmates in order to put the puzzle together. For example, the lesson in one classroom concerned Joseph Pulitzer (after whom the Pulitzer Prize was named). Aronson and his associates wrote a six-paragraph biography of Pulitzer in which each paragraph developed an important aspect of his life: for example, how his family happened to come to this country, how and where he was educated, what his first job was like, and so on. Aronson cut up the biography into six sections and gave each student in the learning group one of them. In this way, every learning group had within it the entire biography of Joseph Pulitzer; but each student had one sixth of the story and so was dependent on his or her classmates to complete the entire story and get a grade. In Sherif's terms, they had a superordinate goal which could only be achieved by their dependence on one another.

After the students went off individually to master their particular paragraph, they then rejoined the learning group to teach one another all parts of Pulitzer's biography. What they soon learned was that cooperation, not competition, was their only means to a good grade in the course. Like the members of a successful football team, none of them would do well without the help of everyone else in the group.

Aronson tried his jigsaw method for a period of 6 weeks in school systems that had recently been desegregated by race. His results were impressive when compared against the outcome in traditional, competitive 5th-grade classrooms in which a superordinate goal was lacking: The children in the jigsaw groups liked their black and white classmates better, expressed more favorable attitudes toward school, had more favorable self-concepts, and performed at least as well on their exams.

Increasing insight and tolerance Individual and group forms of psychotherapy—to the extent that they can increase insight and self-acceptance on the part of a prejudiced individual—may serve as a springboard for individualized efforts to reduce prejudice and discrimination. Personal psychotherapy tends to be most effective in this regard when its overriding concern is the formation of a healthy personality. The reduction of prejudice is frequently an important by-product.

Allport relates the experience of an anti-Semitic woman who served as the respondent in a lengthy, in-depth interview regarding her values, attitudes, and feelings. Having reviewed her previous encounters with Jews, she finally said, "The poor Jews, I guess we blame them for everything, don't we?" (1954, p. 460). Her exchange with the interviewer had increased her self-insight to the point where she could trace her anger to its source and gain a new perspective on it.

Group therapy is another approach to the reduction of prejudice at the individual level. This form of therapy tends to be more efficient than its personal counterpart simply because several individuals can participate at the same time. Moreover, group therapy often operates to break down the support of prejudiced attitudes whose source lies in the norms of the group. Haimowitz and Haimowitz (1950) long ago provided evidence for the influence of group therapy on the reduction of prejudice. As the individuals in their group began to feel less threatened and better able to cope with the actual source of their frustrations, they also became less hostile toward members of various minority groups.

Rubin later suggested that sensitivity training was able to produce increased self-acceptance leading to a reduced level of prejudice. He noted that his conclusion might just as easily have been concerned with the influence of psychotherapy on prejudice: "Each provides the elements of psychological safety, support, and opportunities for reality testing assumed necessary to effect an increase in an individual's level of self-acceptance and consequently, by our model, decrease his level of ethnic prejudice" (1967, p. 238).

Recently, Langer, Bashner, and Chanowitz (1985) offered a method of "decreasing prejudice by increasing discrimination." Their assumption was that individuals frequently rely rather automatically and passively on distinctions about people they have previously drawn (that is, on stereotypes). They argued that active distinction making or "mindfulness" might reduce reliance on stereotyped distinctions about other groups of people and therefore also reduce prejudice against them.

Langer, Bashner, and Chanowitz tested the effectiveness of mindfulness on the perception of and reactions to children with physical disabilities. To train their subjects in drawing distinctions, the researchers operationalized mindfulness as the process of giving several different answers to one question about a disabled person. By contrast, low mindfulness was achieved by asking subjects only for one answer to a question about a disabled person, therefore assuring that they would make few, if any, new distinctions. For example, the high-mindfulness subjects were asked to write down four reasons why a blind female musician they saw depicted in a slide might be good at her profession and four reasons why she might be bad at it. By contrast, the low-mindfulness subjects were asked to indicate only one good and one bad reason.

Results obtained in a study of 47 6th graders from Cambridge, Massachusetts, supported the investigators' expectations. Children given training in mindfulness were more likely than those in the low-mindfulness group to recognize individual differences among disabled people and to see disabled people as sharing much in common with "normal" people. Subjects in the high-mindfulness condition were also more likely to recognize the specific competencies of people with disabilities. Most important, subjects who were trained in mindfulness were less likely to avoid someone with a disability.

Also at the individual level, some social psychologists have proposed techniques for reducing the authoritarian tendencies in personality, under the assumption that such a change would also reduce prejudice. Grossman and Eisenman (1971) placed a naive subject in a modified Asch-type conformity situation with three other students who were actually confederates of the investigators. The experimenter read the F-Scale items and asked the panel of "subjects" to respond out loud by either agreeing or disagreeing with them. As in the original Asch study, the confederates responded first and the naive subject last. Also as in the Asch study, the confederates' responses were prearranged: All of them either agreed or disagreed with the F-Scale items. With this procedure, Grossman and Eisenman were able to manipulate their subjects' F-Scale scores. When the three confederates agreed with F-Scale items, the naive subject scored more in the direction of higher authoritarianism; when the confederates disagreed with F-Scale items, the subject scored more in the direction of low authoritarianism.

In a more recent study, Griffitt and Garcia (1979) attempted to modify a characteristic of authoritarian individuals which was previously found in a series of jury-simulation studies by Mitchell and Byrne (1972) and Mitchell (1973). In these studies, authoritarian subjects who were asked to act as jurors consistently assigned harsher penalties to defendants they disliked than to defendants they liked. By contrast, the punishment decisions of low authoritarians did not express a personal bias—they were not at all influenced by their feelings toward the defendant.

Griffit and Garcia had their subjects—male and female introductory psychology students—participate in a simulated jury decision involving a defendant accused of negligent automobile homicide. During the "trial," testimony was introduced containing either positive or negative information concerning the defendant's character. Half of the subjects received positive information; for example, that the defendant was "a warm and sincere person who was quite friendly and cooperative during his interview." The other half received negative information; for example, that the defendant was "rather cold and insincere" and "impolite and uncooperative during his interview."

Before taking part in the "trial," subjects were divided into high- and low-authoritarian groups based on their scores on the F-Scale which they had taken earlier in the semester. Also prior to the "trial," half of the high-authoritarian subjects were given a verbal reinforcement/punishment procedure designed to lower their authoritarian attitudes, while half of the low-authoritarian subjects received reinforcement/punishment designed to raise their scores. The remaining high- and low-authoritarian subjects received no reinforcement or punishment and therefore served as a control group. Under the pretext that their original F-Scale scores had been lost, the verbal reinforcement and punishment procedure took place during the oral administration of the F-Scale. Among high authoritarian subjects, agreement with a prodemocratic statement was immediately followed by positive reinforcement (that is, the experimenter would nod his head positively, smile, and say "Mm-hmm") and agreement with an antidemocratic statement was followed by punishment (that is, the experimenter would shake his head negatively and frown). This procedure was reversed for low-authoritarian subjects.

According to Griffitt and Garcia, the reinforcement and punishment procedures above were successful in reducing the authoritarianism scores of high authoritarians and increasing those of low authoritarians. These procedures were also effective in dramatically reversing the patterns of subjects' behavior as jurors. By reinforcing and punishing their responses to F-Scale items, the usual bias found among high authoritarians was completely eliminated: Their sentence recommendations for the defendant were no longer influenced by whether they liked or disliked him. By contrast, reinforcement and punishment procedures actually created bias among low authoritarians where there had previously been none: Their punishment recommendations were now affected by their feelings toward the defendant. They tended to recommend a more lenient sentence when they liked him, a severe sentence when they didn't.

Education It is commonly assumed that formal education results in a more enlightened perspective that is less vulnerable to negative intergroup attitudes. In 1969, for example, Selznick and Steinberg reported finding an inverse relationship between anti-Semitism and amount of formal education, a relationship that could not be explained by differences in social class. Yet results claiming to demonstrate the impact of education on prejudice are extremely difficult to interpret and may demonstrate only that the educated members of our society have learned to express their prejudices publicly in subtle, more sophisticated ways (Stember 1961).

Few social psychologists continue to assert that formal education represents a powerful instrument for the reduction of prejudice, although many would probably agree that it has some impact. Jackson and Muha (1984) recently suggested instead that the well-educated members of our society may be the most sophisticated at justifying the status quo. Based on interviews with more than 1,900 respondents in a national probability survey of household residents age 18 and over, Jackson and Muha determined that college graduates were indeed more likely than individuals with only a grade-school education to support the general principles of racial integration, black residential rights, and women's job rights. They were not, however, more likely to agree with attitude items indicating support for the principle of equal rights and commitment to the elimination of inequalities between groups. According to Jackson and Muha, the training of the well-educated members of our society makes them the natural leaders in developing the principle of individual rights as a means of muting the demands of blacks and women. In other words, they are better than the rest of the population in justifying the status quo.

Looking Back

The relationship between prejudice and discrimination is problematic. Some social psychologists who believe in the primacy of behavior over attitude would have us eliminate the concept of prejudice; others argue instead that attitudes have an impact on behavior and that the concept of prejudice is an important one. There is evidence that, depending on other conditions, prejudice sometimes influences discrimination and discrimination sometimes influences prejudice.

Prejudice and discrimination have thrived and prospered across time and place, maintaining intensity in our present-day society, although often in more subtle and sophisticated forms. The tenacity of prejudice may indicate that it serves certain functions for individuals in society. For example, prejudice may satisfy a need for structure, provide an outlet for displaced aggression, enhance self-esteem, and reduce competition.

Policies to attack prejudice at the individual level have attempted to increase insight and tolerance, thereby hoping to reduce the need for displaced aggression and for self-esteem enhancement. Social policies at the institutional level have aimed directly to reduce segregation and therefore discrimination. Such policies have typically proceeded under the assumption that morality can be legislated, that behavior can change without first modifying attitudes. Antidiscriminatory legislation has had only partial success in the classroom. Many of the contacts between black and white students in desegregated schools have taken place between individuals of unequal status under extremely competitive circumstances in which they regard one another as opponents. Social psychologists have responded to the problem of intergroup contact in the classroom by experimenting with learning environments in which black and white students must be interdependent. That is, they must cooperate in order to complete an assignment and receive a grade in the course. Under such conditions, students come to like one another more, to respect one another as individuals, and to see one another as allies rather than enemies.

CHAPTER 8

Prosocial Behavior

JUST BY GOING THROUGH NEWSPAPER STORIES, it would not be difficult to make a case that people don't care about one another. In Milpitas, California, a teenager showed the corpse of his 14-year-old ex-girlfriend to more than a dozen high school classmates. Not one of them even bothered to call the police.... In Raleigh, North Carolina, a motorcyclist injured in an accident lay face down on a crowded highway. He counted 900 cars over a period of three hours before anyone stopped to help.... In Boston, Massachusetts, a third-year medical student was jumped by four teenagers while riding his bicycle home from the hospital. Lots of people watched, but none of them lifted a finger to help.... In New York City, a group of jeering and joking youths watched while a 30-year-old man was electrocuted on the third rail of the subway station at Times Square.... In Denver Colorado, Delores K. Brown was beaten, robbed, gagged and left in her car. Even her neighbors ignored her cries for help.... In Chicago, Illinois, no one stopped to help Mary Beth Hannigan when she was attacked and repeatedly stabbed on a busy exit ramp... and so on and so forth.

Social psychologists have long emphasized the destructive and callous side of human behavior. Based in part on the writings of Freud and, more recently, of ethologists such as Konrad Lorenz, they have focused on bystander apathy, prejudice, and violence and aggression—forms of behavior that are designed to move people away from or even to do harm to one another.

Whereas social psychologists have long studied antisocial behavior, they have only recently turned their attention systematically to questions of why people are attracted to one another, why they might help rather than harm others, why they are sometimes cooperative, friendly, kind, and generous, even at considerable personal expense. As though to confirm the saying that the question you ask determines the answer you get, the literature of social psychology seems suddenly to have made up for lost time. There is much recent evidence that human beings may not be so dastardly after all, and, in fact, may even be capable of genuine sympathy and compassion.

Looking Ahead

In this chapter, we shall explore some of those "newly discovered" admirable qualities called *prosocial behavior*, beginning with interpersonal attraction, then with helping behavior, and finally with altruism. In our examination of prosocial behavior, we must address a number of thorny, yet important questions: For example, what is it about beautiful people that makes them so well liked? Why do we prefer similar others? Are people who live in cities really less helpful than people living in rural areas? And, can we identify characteristics which make an individual a good samaritan? We begin with what might be regarded as the most superficial form of prosocial behavior, interpersonal attraction; we end with the profound form called altruism.

Why Do People Like One Another?

Under what conditions do individuals like one another? Why do they come to be attracted to one another as friends, dates, or marriage partners? Social psychologists have identified a number of factors which contribute to interpersonal attraction, including proximity, physical attractiveness, similarity, and an exchange of rewards.

Physical closeness When students in a classroom were required by their teacher to sit in alphabetical order, they tended to develop friendships with other students whose names began with the same letter—those who were seated close to them (Byrne 1961). Similarly, student-residents of a housing project were likely to make close friends, first with their next-door neighbors, and second with neighbors residing two doors away. By contrast, friendships almost never occurred between students separated by more than four or five houses in the project (Festinger, Schacter, and Back 1950).

Other things being equal, there is a tendency for people to like people who are physically close to them. College students are no different in this respect. They typically have closer friendships with other students who share their classes, are seated nearby, or live close to them in a dormitory or an apartment complex (Segal 1974; Priest and Sawyer 1967; Nahemow and Lawton 1975; Hays 1985).

Part of the influence of proximity is *mere exposure*; that is, we tend to become attracted to those persons we encounter most often (Brockner and Swap 1976; Insko and Wilson 1977). At the same time, mere exposure does not automatically ensure liking or friendship. Other, even more powerful, influences can overcome and even reverse the positive and friendly feelings generated by increased contact. In some cases, we may even grow to despise those people we know best. As the saying goes, familiarity may breed contempt for individuals who might, from a distance, be regarded in a favorable light.

More realistically, proximity only provides the opportunities for individuals to interact and, in a convenient way, to get to know one another (Priest and Sawyer 1967). Whether they will also like each other depends on a number of different factors, including their physical attractiveness, their similarity, and their ability to satisfy one another's needs.

Physical attractiveness During the freshman orientation week at the University of Minnesota, new students were given an advertisement inviting them to attend a "computer dance." Actually, the dance had been secretly arranged by social psychologists who wanted to study the importance of physical attractiveness on heterosexual attraction (Walster et al. 1966).

At the time they bought tickets to the dance, all students were asked to complete a questionnaire containing measures of their age, sex, height, religious affiliation, self-esteem, and so on. The physical attractiveness of each student was rated by a panel of judges who made their evaluations while administering the questionnaires. In addition, in order to estimate their academic achievement, the researchers gained access to the students' files containing their high school academic records and college board scores. Finally, dates were randomly assigned to all students who attended the dance.

Couples at the dance spent the first 2½ hours of the evening talking and dancing together, after which all males and females were interviewed separately and asked to evaluate their dates. Specifically, they were asked, "How much do you like your date?" and "How much would you like to date him or her again?" A few months later, students were again contacted to find out whether or not they had asked their partners for a second date.

How important were the factors of academic achievement, personality, and physical attractiveness in determining whether a couple would be attracted to each other during the evening? To their surprise, researchers discovered that attractiveness was extremely powerful—so powerful, in fact, that nothing else seemed to make a difference. Both male and female students liked attractive rather than unattractive dates, regardless of their own level of attractiveness and regardless of their dates' intelligence or personality. Both "beautiful" and "ugly" students preferred and desired to date again those students whom the panel had rated as being physically attractive.

This research suggests what has been consistently found in numerous studies: namely, that we actually do judge a book by its cover or a person by his looks. When it comes to dating, attractive people have a decided advantage. More surprisingly, perhaps, beauty also seems to have a major bearing on a person's success in many areas of life, not just one-night dates. Studies have shown that highly attractive individuals are more likely to be liked in long-term dating (Mathes 1974); to be popular with their peers as children (Mussen, Conger, and Kagan 1974; Dion and Berscheid 1974); to be cuddled and kissed as newborn infants (Berscheid 1982); to achieve higher grades in school (Clifford and Walster 1973); to be disciplined less severely by their parents (Berkowitz and Frodi 1979); to be recommended for a job after a personal interview (Dipboye, Arvey, and Terpstra 1977); to be regarded as a competent psychological counselor (Cash, Begley, McCown, and Weise 1975); and to have their written work judged favorably (Landy and Sigall 1974).

Why do we seem to be so attracted to beautiful people? One possibility is that physical attractiveness serves much like race and sex as a *status cue* which calls forth various cultural stereotypes and practices based on appearance (Webster and Driskell 1983). Clearly, attractiveness does indeed help determine what we believe to be true about other people (Deaux and Lewis 1984). We tend to think that *what is beautiful is good* and that good-looking people have good personalities (Dion, Berscheid, and Walster 1972). As children, they are expected to be smarter, more likable, and less problematic than their unattractive peers (Stephan and Langiois 1984). As adults, they are thought to have better mental health, more successful marriages, better sex lives, and higher social status (Cash et al. 1977; Dermer and Thiel 1975).

If attractive people of the opposite sex really have high status, then we might even gain prestige by being associated with them. That is, their advantage might "rub off" on us. Bar-Tal and Saxe (1976) tested this idea by showing subjects a set of slides depicting married couples who varied in their physical attractiveness. All subjects were then asked to estimate the income, level of career success, and intelligence of the husbands and wives portrayed in the slides they had seen. When paired with an attractive wife, the unattractive husband was rated as having the highest income, the greatest success in his career, and the most intelligence. By contrast, the unattractive wife paired with an attractive husband was judged strictly on the basis of her own degree of attractiveness. She did not benefit at all from being paired with her attractive spouse. If the results obtained by Bar-Tal and Saxe can be generalized, then only men gain in terms of prestige when their partner is highly attractive.

Is it also possible that the stereotype about good-looking people having good personalities actually contains an element of truth? This is not to say that attractive people are inherently superior; it is unlikely they are born with a superior disposition or temperament. More likely, what we expect of beautiful people later becomes a *self-fulfilling prophecy* by eliciting the behavior from them which confirms the expectancy.

This was cleverly demonstrated several years ago by researchers Snyder, Tanke, and Berscheid (1977), who had male undergraduate students participate in a study of "how people become acquainted with each other" by talking on the telephone for ten minutes to a female student they had never seen. Each male subject was given a packet of information, including a Polaroid photo which he was told pictured his female telephone partner. Actually, however, the subjects received a photo of someone else: half of them were given a very attractive woman; the other half got a relatively unattractive woman.

Snyder, Tanke, and Berscheid found that subjects who thought they were talking with an attractive woman rated her as more poised, more humorous, and friendlier. Moreover, outside observers listened to a tape recording of only the woman's side of the conversation, but were not allowed to see her photograph or to receive any information about her appearance. Based only on the tape-recorded conversations they heard, these outside observers rated the "attractive" woman as more confident, more animated, more attractive, and warmer. Keep in mind that the women whose voices they heard did not actually differ in physical attractiveness.

The experiment conducted by Snyder, Tanke, and Berscheid contains a self-fulfilling prophecy which may occur with some frequency in everyday life. When the male students talked with a woman they thought was physically attractive, they spoke to her in a positive way, a way that allowed her to express her most appealing, most admirable qualities. This was picked up by independent observers who were favorably impressed by the conversation of the "attractive" woman. The implications of this study may be far-reaching. In everyday life, attractive people may receive a large amount of positive feedback from the people with whom they interact. This positive treatment may, in turn, cause attractive individuals to think of themselves as "good," "friendly," or "appealing." Over time, attractive people may then begin to behave in a manner which reflects their very positive self-concept. They may actually become confident, animated, and sociable, thereby fulfilling the prophecy.

A final, perhaps more hopeful, note is in order before moving on: We have so far described studies demonstrating that physical beauty is a powerful determinant of attraction—that good-looking people are seen as having good personalities. Is the reverse also possible? Could an individual's personality actually help determine whether he or she is seen as beautiful? Is it conceivable that people with great personalities or great abilities also come to be regarded as having great looks?

To find out, Gross and Crofton (1977) gave a sample of male and female college students either favorable, average, or unfavorable personality descriptions of a woman. In addition to reading these descriptions, the students were also asked to evaluate the woman's attractiveness based on a photograph said to be of her which had been previously judged by an independent panel as being either attractive, average, or unattractive. As reported by Gross and Crofton, their subjects judged a woman as physically more attractive if they had been given a favorable rather than an unfavorable description of her personality. In fact, the woman perceived as most attractive by the sample of students received only average ratings from the independent panel of judges who had not seen her personality ratings. Clearly, perceptions of beauty are influenced by a pleasing personality description (Gross and Crofton 1977; Owens and Ford 1978).

Felson and Bohrnstedt (1979) studied the relationship between perceptions of ability and perceptions of physical attractiveness in a sample of girls and boys from 6th- through 8th-grade classes in a small midwestern city. Based on the earlier findings of Gross and Crofton, the researchers hypothesized that classmates' perceptions of a subject's physical attractiveness could be predicted by their perceptions of his or her ability to do sports or schoolwork.

Results obtained by Felson and Bohrnstedt supported their hypothesis: children who were attributed academic or athletic ability were also perceived as good-looking, even when objective levels of ability and appearance were controlled. Apparently, then, *what is good is also beautiful!*

Similarity There is a great deal of evidence that we tend to be attracted to people who are similar to us on a number of characteristics, including abilities (Zander and Havelin 1960), social status (Mehrabian and Ksionsky 1971), preference for activities (Werner and Parmalee 1979), and drug use (Kandel 1978). Nowhere can the relationship between similarity and attraction be seen more clearly than in the selection of a marriage partner. There is an overwhelming tendency for people to date and marry others who are similar with respect to their ethnic identity, education, religion, socioeconomic status, and age (Kerckhoff 1974).

Moreover, despite the widespread preference for a physically attractive date, which we discussed earlier in the chapter, individuals actually tend to choose dating and marriage partners whose physical attractiveness is similar to their own (Walster and Walster 1970; Murstein 1972; White 1980; Shanteau and Nagy 1979). Apparently, many of us fear being rejected by the beautiful people we prefer. Instead, we tend to choose our mates based on their likelihood of returning our interest and reciprocating our affection (White 1980).

Numerous studies have shown that we tend to prefer individuals as friends, dates, and mates who share our attitudes and values and to dislike individuals whose attitudes disagree with our own (Gonzalez et al. 1985; Newcomb 1961). Several different reasons have been advanced to explain this pervasive preference.

First, Byrne (1971) argues that *attitude similarity* serves to validate the correctness of our beliefs and values. It is therefore rewarding to hear our friends and acquaintances agree with our political and social views. Similarity makes us feel that our attitudes are correct (Festinger 1957; Newcomb 1961). Those who doubt the correctness of their beliefs are especially likely to choose a friend whose opinions are similar (Gormly 1974).

We may also like people who hold similar attitudes because we assume they will like us. To a person who is extremely concerned about being liked by others, this may be very important. Agreement may be taken as a sign of acceptance and friendship, whereas disagreement may indicate rejection (Walster and Walster 1963; Karylowski 1976).

Before leaving the topic of attitude similarity, we should note that individuals are not always attracted to others who share attitudes with them (Grush and Yel 1979; Russ, Gold, and Stone 1979). In fact, a person who strongly values uniqueness and individuality may actually feel threatened by, dislike, and go out of the way to avoid someone who is highly similar (Snyder and Fromkin 1980). Moreover, an individual who consistently agrees may be seen, at best, as dull and boring, and, at worst, as an obstacle to personal growth (Grush, Clore, and Costin 1975).

There may also be certain kinds of relationships to which the attitude similarity–attraction hypothesis simply does not apply. Most of the evidence linking similarity with attraction has focused on liking in peer relations such as friendships, dates, and marriages, rather than hierarchical role relations such as between boss and employee, or between parent and child.

Levin and Arluke (1983) sought to determine whether attitude similarity might also account for the interpersonal evaluations of parents and their adolescent offspring. They asked 85 mothers and their high-school-aged children separately to evaluate the other member of the dyad and also to fill out a questionnaire concerning their basic institutional values in politics, family, and social issues.

Results obtained by Levin and Arluke failed to support the notion that teenagers like parents whose values match their own or that they direct hostility toward parents whose values differ markedly from their own. In fact, attitude similarity was not a significant factor in these teenagers' evaluations of their mothers.

With reference to the mother's evaluation of her child, however, Levin and Arluke's results lent support to the similarity-attraction hypothesis. They found greater acceptance of children who were regarded by their mothers as similar in terms of values. The effect of similarity on attraction from the mothers' point of view may have reflected the traditional role of mother in our society, whose major obligation in the family has been associated with the socialization of children. Because of this role expectation, mothers may still regard degree of parent-child agreement as sort of a "yardstick" for judging their own competence as transmitters of norms and values to members of the next generation. If so, then, disagreement may symbolize personal failure and agreement may mean personal success. (By the way, if Levin and Arluke's study were repeated with fathers and their teenagers, we probably would not expect fathers to be so much attracted as mothers were to similar offspring. Despite the women's movement, male identity continues to be tied more into their careers than their families. We might also hypothesize that the evaluations of working mothers would be less affected by attitude similarity than those of mothers who are full-time homemakers. Unfortunately, we can only speculate concerning these possibilities, because Levin and Arluke's study has not yet been replicated.)

An exchange of rewards In explaining the impact of attitude similarity on attraction, we suggested earlier that to hear our friends and acquaintances agree with our personal views was frequently rewarding. Actually, many social psychologists have approached the more general question of why people are attracted to one another by suggesting that we like others who reward us and dislike others who punish us (Thibaut and Kelley 1959; Homans 1961, 1974; Blau 1964).

As discussed in Chapter 1, social exchange theorists have focused on the rewards people receive in the form of status, approval, money, or a sense of security, as well as the costs, such as embarrassment, inconvenience, and psychological stress. Many of the findings about attraction can be explained by this general principle. For example, we would expect friendships between people who are physically close because of their low cost in terms of inconvenience. We would also expect people to desire associating themselves with beautiful individuals in order to gain prestige in the eyes of others.

Research indicates that rewards may be more important than costs as predictors of interpersonal attraction, at least in dating and long-term friendships (Rusbult 1983). Hays (1985) compared "close" and "nonclose" friendships as they developed between college students during their first term as freshmen. Results showed that as close friendships progressed, so did the benefits accruing from their relationships. Reports of rewards such as companionship and emotional support were consistently higher between close friends than between nonclose friends and tended to increase as their friendships developed. Despite what would be predicted in a strict reinforcement approach (e.g., Clore and Byrne 1974), however, Hays found that costs were no greater for close than for nonclose friendships. In fact, certain dissatisfactions or costs—for example, emotional aggravation—actually increased as the relationships progressed. Such interpersonal costs may be "inescapable aspects of personal relationships and so, to some degree, may become immaterial. The critical factor in friendship satisfaction appears to be the amount of benefits received" (p. 922).

Despite the persuasiveness of exchange theory at an abstract level, it is not always so easy to determine what does and does not constitute a reward for those who are involved in a particular relationship. For example, praise is, under many circumstances, extremely rewarding; it is indeed something that many people like to receive. They also tend to like the person who flatters them. If, however, someone suspects that the source of praise has an ulterior motive and is being insincere, then a flattering comment will not be at all rewarding and the praiser will not be liked (Jones 1964).

When Will People Help One Another?

Prosocial attitudes contribute to prosocial behavior. Helping behavior occurs more often between people who like one another than between people who don't (Carnevale, Pruitt, and Carrington 1981). Moreover, all of the factors associated with liking—similarity, beauty, proximity, and reward—have been found to increase helping too.

Of course, just because we like someone doesn't necessarily mean we will come to their assistance when they need help. First of all, we may want to help but not know how to do so. For example, we may hear that a famous movie star whom we respect and admire is having trouble with an alcoholic son. As much as we might like to come to her rescue, there is probably little we can do. Even among our friends, there may be times when our helpful attitudes cannot be translated into behavior. Some people try to hide their problems; others simply prefer to deal with them independently. Moreover, in matters of medical emergency or finance, we may feel totally incompetent to intervene in an effective way.

The costs of helping The costs of liking someone tend to be relatively small. By contrast, those who intervene to help the victims of a crime or an accident may do so at some risk to their personal well-being. In July 1983, for example, a Florida man announced to the passengers of an airborne Northwest airliner that he was hijacking the plane to Havana.

Waiting for the appropriate moment to act, two passengers on the flight overpowered and subdued him.... In 1980, three Northeastern University hockey players chased and caught a purse snatcher after he had knocked down and injured an older woman.... In 1981, a 19-year-old woman in Cornwall, England, received gunshot wounds when she helped subdue a bank robber who had killed a guard in the commission of his crime.... In 1981, a bystander rescued a man who had jumped from the Dorchester Bay Bridge in Boston.... In 1984, Dr. David Munch of Denver, Colorado, saved a 2-month-old boy in an automobile accident, but suffered mangled legs in the process.

Given the costs, it is not hard to imagine why some people are unwilling to come to the rescue of someone in distress, especially when the need is vague. Emergencies aren't always clearly identified. This uncertainty sets the stage for would-be rescuers to instead rationalize their inaction.

Consider the costs to those who intervene to help the victim of a street crime. At the very least, they may run the risk of being inconvenienced, for example, by being late for an important appointment or by having to serve as a witness in a lengthy courtroom hearing. Even more serious, they may suffer physical injury or death as, for example, in an attempt to stop an assailant or mugger.

The costs are sometimes more subtle or psychological. Those who intervene unnecessarily run the risk of looking inappropriate or foolish; they may even be rebuked by their would-be victims. How does someone know that his help is actually wanted? How does he know that he possesses the medical competence or the physical strength to help rather than hurt the victim?

A final set of costs involves helping someone who is regarded as unpleasant—someone a witness might otherwise go out of his way to avoid—for example, a skid-row bum who falls to the pavement, someone who is severely disfigured or physically disabled, or a person of another race. Attitude toward a victim helps determine whether or not a bystander will decide to intervene in an emergency. If we are uncomfortable being around someone in trouble—for example, someone who is severely disfigured—we may be less likely to go out of our way to intervene on his or her behalf (Piliavin, Piliavin, and Rodin 1975). If we sense that someone has created his own troubles, however, we are more likely to ignore his plight. This may explain why a "sick man" carrying a cane who collapses on the subway is offered more help than a "drunk" who carries a bottle and smells of liquor (Piliavin, Rodin, and Piliavin 1969). We are also more prone to offer aid when a victim shares, rather than disagrees with, our important opinions and beliefs (Sole, Marton, and Hornstein 1975).

There are also personal rewards and costs associated with asking for help. Obviously, seeking the assistance of other people has its benefits for someone whose safety or well-being is threatened. Yet individuals often hesitate to seek help because of the associated costs, such as being forced to admit publicly that they are dependent and inferior (Shapiro 1980). This admission may be a threat to self-esteem because dependency is inconsistent with the values of self-reliance and individual accomplishment found in Western achievement-oriented culture (Nadler 1986). Individuals are more likely to ask for help in a society where the cultural emphasis is on communal achievement and cooperation, for example, among Israeli kibbutz dwellers (Nadler 1986).

▶ Perspective:
The Effect of Social and Cultural Forces
Are there norms of helpfulness? In 1960, Alvin Gouldner identified what he called the *norm of reciprocity*, a widely shared rule of behavior that says people should help those who have helped them and should not injure those who have helped them. According to Gouldner, some version of the norm of reciprocity is found in virtually all value systems and is therefore universal. At the same time, its expression in moral conduct varies by time and place.

The norm of reciprocity is a sort of "all-purpose moral cement," which can be applied to countless ad hoc transactions. In the Philippines, this norm tends to govern all relationships, even those which might be handled bureaucratically in our society. If, for example, one person pays his needy "compadre's" doctor bills, the latter may feel obligated to help his donor's child to get a job with the government. In the United States, such tendencies to repay indebtedness are weaker, though they apply to friendship, kinship, and neighborly relations and, less legitimately, to the informal network in bureaucracies as well. Many of us do indeed feel obligated to reciprocate when someone does us a favor.

According to Gouldner, the norm of reciprocity is conditional—people feel obligated to repay depending upon how much they value the benefit they have received from others. This value, in turn, depends on: "the intensity of the recipient's need at the time the benefit was bestowed ('a friend in need...'), the resources of the donor ('he gave although he could ill afford it'), the motives imputed to the donor ('without thought of gain'), and the nature of the constraints which are perceived to exist or to be absent ('he gave of his own free will...')" (Gouldner 1960, p. 171).

On the negative side, the norm of reciprocity may lead to neglect of the needs of those groups whose members are unable to reciprocate—for example, in relations with the mentally and physically disabled, young children, and powerless minorities. Fortunately, there are other norms, such as the *social-responsibility norm*, which urge us to help those who need help—the very people whom the norm of reciprocity would have us ignore (Berkowitz and Daniels 1963). And, in fact, people are especially likely to aid those who seem to be dependent on them. Still, there are many situations in which very needy members of society do not receive help. Most people are verbally willing to endorse the norm of social responsibility but do not behave in accordance with it (Piliavin et al. 1981). ∎

Are people in cities less helpful? In 1970, Latane and Darley attempted to find personality and background variables which would predict helping behavior. Only one factor—the size of the town in which a person had grown up—seemed to count. Specifically, people who grew up in small towns tended to be more helpful than those who came from larger towns or cities.

Several later studies confirmed Latane and Darley's observation. Takooshian, Haber, and Lucido (1977), for example, trained a young child to stand on a busy street in 4 large cities (New York, Boston, Philadelphia, and Chicago) and in 12 smaller towns in the surrounding areas. The child simply said to passersby, "I'm lost. Can you call my house?" During their experiment, 184 people—127 in the cities and 57 in the towns—were approached by one of the 14 children employed as confederates.

Results obtained by Takooshian, Haber, and Lucido indicated clear and consistent differences in the responses to the child between city and town residents. In the cities, only 46 percent of the subjects offered their help; in the towns, more than 72 percent did so. Moreover, regardless of whether they helped, all of the people approached in towns were sympathetic toward the plight of the child. In the cities, however, only a few among those who didn't help expressed their sympathy. Many just walked by quickly, while others gave the child a curt "no." One responded by snapping, "So what's your problem, kid? I'm lost too."

In a recent series of studies, Amato (1983) was able to examine separately the influence of various characteristics of city life such as population size, community disorganization, and fast pace of life on rates of spontaneous helping between strangers. He also looked at the effect on helping of differences by city in age and sex composition and level of social class. Amato uncovered persuasive evidence that population size was the strongest and most consistent predictor of helping. As population size increases, informal helping between strangers declines.

Stanley Milgram (1970) has tried to explain the lower rates of helping among urbanites by looking at the situation of city life rather than at the kinds of people who populate large urban areas. According to Milgram, city dwellers often experience *urban overload*: in New York City, Chicago, and Los Angeles, for example, they are bombarded on a daily basis by stimuli such as loud noises, bright lights, and crowded streets which compete for their attention. In order to avoid being completely confused and ineffectual, city dwellers must therefore be selective in terms of the stimuli to which they choose to respond. In this process, they may learn to ignore those factors in everyday life which do not seem to contribute to their personal survival or safety. Unfortunately, this may sometimes also mean being too preoccupied to notice people who are in need of help.

Laboratory research has supported Milgram's view by demonstrating that loud noise reduces helpfulness (Sherrod and Downs 1974; Yinon and Bizman 1980). Moreover, Korte and Kerr (1975) determined that people who live in noisy, congested neighborhoods tend to be less helpful than people living in quieter, less crowded environmental conditions.

The bystander effect Why is it that some bystanders fail to respond to the plight of others? Is it possible to identify elements in the situation of a crisis which reduce helping? Can we specify the social conditions necessary for the witnesses to an emergency to intervene? According to a model proposed by Latané and Darley (1970), for intervention to occur, a bystander must (1) notice the event, (2) define that event as constituting a genuine crisis or emergency, and (3) decide that he or she has some personal responsibility for intervening. At each of these stages, there is the possibility of a *bystander effect*—the presence of other witnesses may inhibit the willingness of any given bystander to lend a hand.

1) Notice the event. Suppose, for example, that someone is having a heart attack while walking during the crowded lunch hour in a large city. He clutches his chest in pain and slumps to the sidewalk. Will any passerby come to his aid? Not necessarily, according to Darley and Latané (1968). First, the bystander has to tear himself from his private thoughts and notice that something is going on. As obvious as it might seem, this may not always happen, simply because Americans consider it to be a breach of etiquette to invade the privacy of strangers in public places. According to a pervasive informal norm, it is "bad manners" to pry, stare, or listen intently while in the presence of strangers.

Norms respecting the privacy of others can be seen most clearly, perhaps, in a crowded elevator, where riders are strangers to one another. To uphold the norm of privacy riders are not supposed to stand too closely to one another, overhear anyone else's conversation, or talk to or even breathe on anyone they don't know. In fact, they are expected merely to stare straight ahead at the elevator door. (These norms do not operate when they are alone in an elevator, so riders are much freer to behave as they want). For the same reason, a witness to someone collapsing onto a crowded downtown sidewalk may simply not notice the victim or, observing that his behavior is unusual, may quickly turn away. As a result, people in a crowd are less likely to notice a potential emergency than if they are alone.

2) Define the event. This is, of course, not the whole story. Even if a witness observes an event, he or she must still decide that that event is truly an emergency before offering help. Smoke pouring from the walls of a house might indicate a raging fire that should be reported; but it might only be the exhaust smoke from a dryer or a backyard barbeque. A scream in the night might indicate someone in trouble who is calling for help; it might also be someone at a party having a very good time, a dog howling to the moon, or a heated but civilized family quarrel. Similarly, someone lying on the sidewalk may indeed be having a heart attack; but he may instead be sleeping off a drinking spree. He might appreciate your help, but he might also prefer to be left alone.

To define an ambiguous situation such as someone lying on a crowded sidewalk, a bystander is likely to look to other people in order to see how they are reacting to the same scene. If others appear to be excited, concerned, and upset, a bystander is likely to be excited, concerned, and upset. If others look calm and indifferent, however, a bystander is more likely to ignore the situation and continue on his way as though nothing of importance had happened.

The problem is that bystanders often look calm and indifferent, even when they feel excited, concerned, and upset; even if they are observing an emergency in which their assistance is sorely needed. Once again, an informal norm may get in the way of intervention: We are not supposed to react with intense emotion while interacting with strangers in public places. In fact, we tend to save our most extreme emotional outbursts for intimate conversations with family and perhaps close friends, where it is more appropriate to have them, and where we won't be embarrassed or rejected for doing so. As a result, individuals in public places are careful to "look cool" and not to overreact; they frequently appear to be less upset, less concerned, and less excited than they actually are.

This may explain why so many nervous people look so calm in dentist offices, airplane terminals, and hospital waiting rooms. It might also explain why people occasionally get trapped in burning theaters and nightclubs because they refuse to rush out while they still have the chance. It may also help explain why concerned bystanders don't come to the rescue of others. A crowd that seems passive and apathetic can imply to an individual that an event does not constitute an emergency or a crisis. Witnesses may be afraid that they will look foolish if they alone violate the norm and behave in an excited, emotional way. They will not, as a result, take a risk with their presentation of self and intervene by offering help.

To test the influence of the presence of others on definitions of an emergency, Latané and Darley (1970) set up the following experimental situations: A group of students who were waiting to be interviewed by a researcher in the next room were made to believe that they heard her climb on a chair. They then heard a loud crash and a scream as the chair collapsed and she fell to the floor. Then they heard her moan, "Oh, my foot...I... I...can't move it. Oh, I...can't get this...thing...off me." While overhearing the "accident," some of the students waited alone while others waited with another student. Out of the 26 students who waited alone, 70 percent offered to help the researcher. But among the 40 who waited in pairs, only 20 percent (eight people) came to her aid. In questioning later, the 32 students who hadn't offered their assistance told the investigator that they had believed that the researcher's accident wasn't serious. They described her injury as "a mild sprain." Some said, "I didn't want to embarrass her" or "I didn't think it was a real emergency."

3) Feel personal responsibility. Even if a person notices an event and defines it as an emergency, he or she will not intervene without feeling some personal responsibility to do so. Ironically, the presence of other bystanders may make an individual feel less personally responsible and, once again, less likely to give assistance. Darley and Latané refer to this phenomenon as *diffusion of responsibility*: If you breakdown on a crowded highway, hundreds of cars may pass without stopping to help you. If you break down on a lonely country road, however, the first person who passes may stop to lend a hand.

To test the notion of diffusion of responsibility, Darley and Latané (1968) set up an experimental situation which contained many of the elements present in the famous murder of a young woman in New York City during the 1960s. Kitty Genovese was stabbed to death in the middle of the night while many of her neighbors listened from their individual apartments. Though the victim screamed for help, and her assailant took almost 30 minutes to end her life, nobody even bothered to report the incident to the police, let alone leave the safety of their apartments to assist in fighting off Genovese's killer.

In the Darley and Latané simulation, subjects who were physically separated from one another heard a victim calling for help. Some thought that they alone could hear the victim's cries; some believed that other subjects could hear the cries too. Because they were not together in the same room with other subjects, their reactions could not have been influenced by the informal norms operating in stages 1 and 2 above (for example, they couldn't have been misled by other subjects who were really concerned but looked calm and indifferent).

Darley and Latané found evidence for the presence of a diffusion of responsibility, dependent on the number of individuals a subject believed to witness the emergency with her or him. Specifically, 85 percent of the subjects who believed they were alone with the victim offered their help; 62 percent of those who thought there was one other bystander offered help; and only 31 percent of the subjects who believed there were four other witnesses offered their assistance. As the number of witnesses to an emergency increases, the likelihood that any one of them will come to the rescue decreases.

▶ Perspective:
The Effect of the Immediate Situation

Reducing the bystander effect "Diffusion of responsibility" is generally discussed in terms of the potential of a witness to an emergency to be blamed for the victim's plight. When alone, a bystander is the one and only person who could be blamed by others if an emergency situation ends in tragedy. In the presence of many bystanders, however, the potential for blame is diffused or spread out over all of them. As a result, help may be delayed or reduced, since no one bystander feels personally responsible for intervening.

Studies that find a diffusion of responsibility have encouraged their subjects to feel a sense of anonymity by leading them to believe that they would never meet one another face to face. In setting up the experimental situation, the possibility of subjects blaming one another for not helping was therefore removed.

Gottlieb and Carver (1980) suggest that this sense of blame might be increased by making subjects anticipate that they would later interact with other witnesses to an emergency. If so, then, the anticipation of future interaction should cause the bystander effect to be minimized.

In Gottlieb and Carver's study, 98 female college students from the University of Miami were told either that they would have no personal contact with other subjects or that all subjects would be brought together later in a face to face discussion session. Each subject then took part in what appeared to be an anonymous discussion via intercoms with either one person or five persons who were seated in separate cubicles. During this session, one of the "subjects" (actually a confederate of the investigators) was heard choking, struggling for breath, crying out for help, and then falling silent.

As predicted, subjects offered help more quickly when they expected future interaction than when they didn't. Moreover, among subjects who did not expect to interact later, help was quicker in 2- than 6-member groups. When subjects anticipated face-to-face interaction with other subjects, however, the bystander effect was nearly eliminated.

Gottlieb and Carver's results are consistent with those of earlier studies in which the bystander effect was minimized when the other witness was a friend (Latané and Rodin 1969), when there had been a brief acquaintanceship between subject and victim of the emergency (Latané and Darley 1970), and when the victim explicitly requested help from the subject (Shaffer, Rogel, and Hendrick 1975). We are also more likely to help those with whom we have established a relationship than those who are total strangers. After a major disaster, for example, people tend to come to the rescue of family members first, friends and neighbors second, and strangers last (Form and Nosow 1958). This ordering of help-giving by relationship seems to apply to everyday events as well; even a superficial acquaintance seems to increase the likelihood of receiving help from others, although not to the same extent as a close relationship (Pearce 1980). All of these studies were able to place the burden of blame on the subject by indicating that his or her reaction (or lack of reaction) would be subjected to evaluation by the other persons involved in the emergency situation. ■

The role of personal competence Even if the bystander effect does not occur—when a witness notices an event, defines it as being an emergency, and feels personal responsibility for the fate of the victim—bystanders do not always come to the rescue. Social psychologists have argued that, under such conditions, a *sense of competence* or efficacy often helps determine whether or not a person will attempt a difficult or stressful activity (Bandura 1977; Carver 1979). People who feel they can cope are likely to do so; people who doubt their ability to cope are more likely to avoid the situation that makes them feel this way.

Personal competence clearly has an effect on helping. Huston et al. (1981) interviewed 32 individuals who had intervened in dangerous criminal episodes such as armed robberies and street muggings. Most had been injured in the course of intervening. As a typical example, when he stopped his car to help a woman who was being assaulted, one young man suffered a broken jaw in an exchange of blows with her assailant. In another case, a man was cut by pieces of broken glass during a scuffle with an intruder who had attempted at gunpoint to rob the owner of a grocery store.

Huston and his associates compared their sample of interveners with a group of individuals who had not directly intervened in either a crime or an emergency during the previous 10 years. These noninterveners were matched in terms of age, sex, education, and ethnic background on a person-to-person basis to be as similar as possible to the individuals who had intervened.

Surprisingly, the investigators report that their interveners were virtually indistinguishable from the comparison group of noninterveners in terms of personality characteristics such as humanitarianism, social responsibility, and social alienation. One factor that did seem to distinguish interveners from noninterveners was the presence of training for emergencies. Those who had come to the rescue during a criminal episode were significantly more likely than members of the comparison group to have been trained in first-aid, life-saving, and police work. In addition, crime interveners were significantly taller and heavier. When asked to describe themselves, they mentioned being physically strong, aggressive, emotional, and principled. According to Huston et al., these crime interveners acted out of a sense of competence rather than strong humanitarian purpose. They had the personal strength and training necessary to be injected into clearly dangerous situations.

Can competence overcome the bystander effect? Pantin and Carver (1982) tested this idea with the assistance of 92 female college students who either did or did not watch a series of public service films describing several first-aid procedures and arguing the importance of immediate first aid in response to a medical emergency. Those who saw the films were called High Competent; those who didn't were called Low Competent.

Three weeks later, the same college students participated in an experiment in which they all heard another "subject" (actually, a confederate of the experimenter) cry out for help while in the midst of a choking fit. Some of the subjects were made to believe that they were in a 2-member group (that is, that only one other subject heard the cries for help); others believed that they were in a 6-member group (that 5 other subjects heard the cries for help).

As in earlier studies of the bystander effect, Pantin and Carver found a diffusion of responsibility among Low Competent subjects—those who had not watched the films. These subjects were slower to respond if they thought themselves to be in a 6-member group rather than in a 2-member group. High Competent subjects acted differently: Those who had been exposed to the emergency-related films reacted quickly regardless of group size. Apparently, competence was enough to overcome the bystander effect.

The Roots of Altruism

Their destructive side notwithstanding, human beings also risk their lives for the sake of others, even when there is no particular advantage to be gained by their being helpful. We call their behavior *altruistic* and regard it as one of the most extreme forms of prosocial behavior.

Altruism is a value in virtually all human societies and forms the basis for most of the world's great religions as well as secular reform movements

(Rushton 1982). Hundreds of people, for example, donate one of their kidneys for transplantation into another human being and must live the rest of their lives with a single kidney to do the work of the two they originally had. Thousands more donate their blood at some personal expense and inconvenience. And in a less severe act of generosity, millions regularly donate money to their favorite charity in order to help those afflicted with poverty and illness. An agency looking for lost children got 2,000 phone calls after the airing of a nationally televised movie about Adam, a six-year-old boy who was kidnapped and killed.

In our society, we have institutionalized altruism by awarding medals for "outstanding acts of selfless heroism" as, for example, in the medals awarded by the Carnegie Hero Fund Commission or, during wartime, in the U.S. Army's awarding of the Congressional Medal of Honor.

A recent example of altruism is the behavior of Lennie Skutnik, the young man who was honored by first lady Nancy Reagan in 1982 for his heroic rescue of a survivor of an air Florida crash in the icy waters of the Potomac River. At the very least, Skutnik sacrificed his time and energy; he damaged his clothing and was late for dinner. More importantly, of course, he risked serious physical injury if not death. Yet Skutnik never hesitated to come to the rescue.

Is there a Good Samaritan? Social psychologists have long sought to locate factors in the socialization process to account for those who are altruistically disposed. London (1970) interviewed 27 Christians who during World War II had helped rescue Jews from their Nazi persecutors. He found three characteristics which were shared by many of these *Good Samaritans*. First, they tended to be adventurous types who had previously taken considerable risks with their personal safety. All of them now risked their lives in order to save the lives of others. Second, most were socially marginal people who hadn't fit well into the mainstream of German society or who themselves had been victimized. This experience of marginality may have sensitized the Good Samaritans to the plight of victims in general and of German Jews in particular. Third, and perhaps of greatest importance, most of the rescuers had at least one parent who served as a *model* of altruism—an intensely moralistic mother or father with whom the Good Samaritan strongly identified.

Essentially the same theme emerges in other studies of altruistic individuals. Rosenhan (1970) found identification with a moral parent among the civil-rights activists (called Freedom Riders) he studied, many of whom had given up their homes and jobs for the sake of playing an active role in civil-rights causes. Hoffman (1975) found the same modeling of a moralistic parent in altruistic children; and Barnett, Howard, King, and Dino (1980) discovered that college students who were extremely concerned about the welfare of other people had parents who were similarly concerned and affectionate.

▶ Perspective:
The Effect of Social Definition

The influence of role taking Hudson, Forman, and Brion-Meisels (1982) studied prosocial behavior in children as influenced by their ability *to take the role of the other*. These researchers identified 18 second-grade boys and girls as either high or low role takers based on their responses to structured questions about the intentions, thoughts, and feelings of other children and/or adults.

Each second grader was then videotaped for some 20 minutes teaching two kindergarteners of the same sex to make caterpillers with construction paper, scissors, glue, and crayons. From these 18 videotaped sessions, the following types of prosocial behavior were coded for each second grader in his interaction with the two kindergarteners: comforting, sharing, helping, friendliness, and social problem solving.

Hudson, Forman, and Brion-Meisels report that high role takers expressed significantly more prosocial behavior than their counterparts who were low role takers. Specifically, for example, high role takers were more helpful in terms of answering their kindergarteners' questions, more eager to lend them a hand, and more likely to provide options for problem solving. According to the investigators, these differences in prosocial behavior may have reflected the two groups' differing interpretations of the cues they receive from others. High role takers rarely overlooked indirect requests for help (for example, a kindergartener who glanced frequently at the tutor and strained in an exaggerated manner with the scissors). Given the same conditions, low role takers might have smiled at the kindergartener, but would have failed to volunteer their help. They were less able to fill in the gaps in meaning that resulted when communication from a kindergartener was incomplete or when his intentions were unstated. ∎

The interaction of biology and culture In the shallow waters of a small pond, a hungry northern pike edges closer and closer to the unsuspecting minnows feeding only six feet away. Before the predator can move in for the kill, however, a few minnow "scouts" abruptly leave the safety of their numbers to move in the direction of where the pike lies in wait. Upon spotting the enemy, they immediately swim back to warn the school of this menacing presence.

The sociobiological view of altruism is a modified form of Charles Darwin's concept of the survival of the fittest. Darwin had argued that "adaptive" genetic mutations—those random variations in the genes which give an organism some advantage in the "struggle for existence"—are retained through inheritance. That is, they are passed from generation to generation.

From a Darwinian point of view, then, selfish behavior would seem to be more adaptive than altruism because only the former enhances an organism's ability to survive. For example, minnow "scouts" would only risk their own lives if, by doing so, they also increased their own safety (for example, because they know where the danger lies and so have a better chance to escape the predator or because other minnows will surround and protect them when they return).

Sociobiologists have a much broader conception of survival of the fittest. They focus on behavior which improves the chances that an organism's *genes* will survive, even if the organism itself does not. They argue that organisms will be altruistic even at some risk to their personal safety in order to increase the likelihood that their genes will survive to be passed to the next generation. In this view, altruism rather than selfishness may be adaptive if the recipient of help also carries the helper's genes and can transmit them into the next generation. In other words, prosocial behavior occurs if the recipient of help is close kin (Dawkins 1976; Campbell 1975). A sociobiologist might argue, for example, that minnow "scouts" which perish in their attempt to warn their school of fish are increasing the probability that their close relatives—and therefore their own genes—will survive and reproduce. Minnow scouts thus actually benefit too: they live on by perpetuating their genetic identity in the group. This interpretation assumes that members of the school are genetically homogeneous, that their presence together is "a family reunion" (Fellman 1986).

Studies of social insects lend support to the existence of a "kin-specific altruistic impulse." For example, female worker bees are sterile, so they are unable to produce offspring of their own. Instead, they devote themselves to the task of caring for the offspring of the queen bee, in defense of which they have been known to sacrifice their own lives.

From a sociobiological viewpoint, the altruistic behavior of female worker bees may be a result of "selfish genes." Worker bees can actually transmit more of their genetic material to the next generation by assisting the queen to produce sisters than they could by producing their own offspring. Altruism does not improve their own chances of survival, but it does improve the chances that their kin will survive. As offspring of the same queen bee, female workers share three fourths of their genes with other workers (their sisters) and future workers the queen may produce. If female workers were instead able to reproduce, they would pass only one half of their genes to the next generation.

If the same impulse existed in human beings, we would expect altruism to be strong in parents and siblings and weaker in cousins, uncles, aunts, and so on. For nonrelatives, it would not be expected to exist at all (Hamilton 1971). Thus, the parent who perishes while saving her children from a burning building has helped assure the survival of her genes.

As the case of Lennie Skutnick so well illustrates, however, the prosocial behvior of human beings is not limited to close kin. Unlike insects, humans give their time, energy, and sometimes their lives in order to reduce the distress of other members of the species who may be completely unrelated by genetic history. For example, during the summer of 1986, farmers from Moundridge, Kansas, responded to newscasts about a severe drought in the Southeast by loading 64 boxcars with 250 tons of their own hay to feed the starving cattle, and therefore help the drought-stricken farmers in the state of Georgia.... Also in 1986, a New York City fireman, Richard Young, risked serious injury to rescue a total stranger—a truck driver who hung by his arms from the steering wheel of the cab of his truck as it dangled over the edge of a bridge. Arriving on the scene, Young immediately threw himself under the truckdriver's body in order to break his fall. In saving the truckdriver's life, Young received a broken leg, a broken ankle, and severe back injuries.... In 1969, Vietnam soldier Bob Whelan stepped on an 82-millimeter mortar round as he attempted to save the life of his buddy. In the process Whelan lost both of his legs. In 1982, Whelan began his three-year, 4,000 mile journey across the United States, walking on his arms. In 1986, he completed the New York City Marathon in 98 hours and 47 minutes.

Also unlike insects, the behavior of humans is shaped not only by their biology but by what they have learned. Recognizing this complexity of human behavior, several social psychologists have proposed the existence of an *innate altruistic impulse* in human beings which is mediated by *empathic emotion*. More specifically, they suggest that humans are genetically predisposed to respond to the distress of other human beings, especially close kin, with feelings of sympathy and compassion (empathic emotion). This empathic emotion, they contend, can in turn motivate human beings to help reduce the distress of others (Hoffman 1981; Krebs 1975; Batson 1983). For example, a mother is genetically predisposed to feel sympathetic when she witnesses the suffering of her child. She is, in turn, motivated by the arousal of empathic emotion to intervene in order to see that her child's suffering is reduced.

If humans possess a kin-specific altruistic impulse, they should respond with empathic emotion and therefore with altruism *only* to those individuals who are clearly related by kinship (to those who share genes). As we have pointed out, however, this is not the case. According to Batson (1983), one cultural form in human society may extend the range of our "kinship relations" to people we have never met or have little in common with, to people who live thousands of miles away and are genetically independent of us.

Batson points out that religious imagery often involves kinship—religions teach "brotherly love" and preach that we are all God's children. Such imagery may, according to Batson, build "cognitive bridges" between people who are actually from different kinship networks. It may encourage compassion and sympathy within the "family" toward someone whom we are not innately predisposed to respond with altruism—even to the suffering of a total stranger with whom we have little in common.

Looking Back

In this chapter, we have examined prosocial behavior at three different levels: interpersonal attraction, helping, and altruism. Whether or not two individuals like one another is, of course, a function of a wide range of circumstances. Everything else being equal, interpersonal attraction is increased by proximity, physical attractiveness, similarity, and an exchange of rewards.

Although liking also tends to increase helping, it does not assure that someone will come to the rescue. We must also consider the costs of helping, including inconvenience and personal risk, as well as embarrassment. The location of an individual also influences his helpfulness, especially toward strangers. City dwellers may be less helpful because they experience "urban overload."

In order to come to the assistance of a stranger, an individual must notice an event, define it as an emergency, and feel some personal responsibility. Ironically, the presence of other people at any of the above stages reduces the likelihood that any one bystander will intervene. Even if these three conditions are satisfied, witnesses still need to feel competent in order to help. Training to increase competence actually can overcome this reluctance.

Altruism is an extreme form of helpfulness in which there is some personal sacrifice. Altruistic individuals, known as "good samaritans," tend to identify closely with a highly moralistic parent. They may also be high risk takers and play a marginal role in society.

Sociobiologists have attempted to explain apparently altruistic behavior as an effort on the part of an individual to improve the chances that his genes will survive. Even if the sociobiological explanation is accepted, we must still explain why altruistic behavior is frequently aimed at people in distress who are genetically unrelated, even total strangers. Institutions such as religion may be important in this regard, because they extend those regarded as "kin" beyond the family unit.

References

Adorno, T. W., E. Frankel-Brunswick, D. J. Levinson, and N. H. Sanford. 1950. *The Authoritarian Personality*. New York: Harper and Row.

Ajzen, I., and M. Fishbein. 1977. "Attitude-Behavior Relations: A Theoretical Analysis and Review of Empirical Research." *Psychological Bulletin* 84:888–918.

Ajzen, I., and M. Fishbein. 1980. *Understanding Attitudes and Predicting Social Behavior*. Englewood Cliffs, NJ: Prentice-Hall.

Allport, G. W. 1954. *The Nature of Prejudice*. Reading, MA: Addison-Wesley.

Amato, P. R. 1983. "Helping Behavior in Urban and Rural Environments: Field Studies Based on a Taxonomic Organization of Helping Episodes." *Journal of Personality and Social Psychology* 45:571–586.

Anastos, E., with J. Levin. 1983. *Twixt: Teens Yesterday and Today*. New York: Franklin Watts.

Argyle, M. 1975. *Bodily Communication*. New York: International Universities Press.

Argyle, M., and J. Dean. 1965. "Eye Contact, Distance and Affiliation." *Sociometry* 28:289–304.

Arkin, R., H. Cooper, and T. Kolditz. 1980. "A Statistical Review of the Literature Concerning the Self-Serving Attribution Bias in Interpersonal Situations." *Journal of Personality* 48:435–448.

Arms, R. L., G. W. Russell, and M. L. Sandilands. 1979. "Effects of Viewing Aggressive Sports on the Hostility of Spectators." *Social Psychology Quarterly* 42:275–279.

Aronson, E. 1975. "Busing and Racial Tension: The Jigsaw Route to Learning and Liking." *Psychology Today* 8:43–45, 47–50.

Asch, S. 1952. "Effects of Group Pressures Upon the Modification and Distortion of

Judgment." In G. E. Swanson, T. M. Newcomb, and E. L. Hartley (Eds.), *Readings in Social Psychology*. New York: Holt, Rinehart and Winston.

Azrin, N. H., R. R. Hutchinson, and D. F. Hake, 1966. "Attack, Avoidance, and Escape Reactions to Aversive Shock." *Journal of Experimental Analysis of Behavior* 9:191–204.

Bachman, J. G. and P. M. O'Malley. 1986. "Self-Concepts, Self-Esteem, and Educational Experiences: The Frog Pond Revisited (Again)." *Journal of Personality and Social Psychology* 50:35–46.

Baer, R., S. Hinkle, K. Smith, and M. Fenton, 1980. "Reactance as a Function of Actual versus Projected Autonomy." *Journal of Personality and Social Psychology* 38:416–422.

Bandura, A. 1977. *Social Learning Theory*. Englewood Cliffs, NJ: Prentice-Hall.

Bandura, A., D. Ross, and S. Ross. 1963. "Imitation of Film-Mediated Aggressive Models." *Journal of Abnormal and Social Psychology* 66:3–11.

Baratz, J. C. 1972. "Educational Considerations for Teaching Standard English to Negro Children." In B. Spolsky Rowley (Ed.), *The Language Education of Minority Children*. Rowley, MA: Newbury House.

Barnes, J. A. 1972. *Social Networks*. Reading, MA: Addison-Wesley.

Barnett, M. A., J. A. Howard, L. M. King, and G. A. Dino. 1980. "Antecedents of Empathy: Retrospective Accounts of Early Socialization." *Personality and Social Psychology Bulletin* 6:361–365.

Baron, R. A. 1986. "Self-Presentation in Job Interviews: When There Can Be 'Too Much of a Good Thing.'" *Journal of Applied Social Psychology* 16:16–28.

Bar-Tal, D., and L. Saxe. 1976. "Perceptions of Similarly and Dissimilarly Attractive Couples and Individuals." *Journal of Personality and Social Psychology* 33:772–781.

Batson, C. D. 1983. "Sociobiology and the Role of Religion in Promoting Prosocial Behavior: An Alternative View." *Journal of Personality and Social Psychology* 45:1380–1385.

Beck, E. M. 1980. "Discrimination and White Economic Loss: A Time Series Examination of the Radical Model." *Social Forces* 59:148–168.

Becker, H. S. 1963. *Outsiders: Studies in the Sociology of Deviance*. New York: Free Press.

Becker, H. S., and B. Geer. 1957. "Participant Observation versus Interviewing: A Comparison." *Human Organization* 16:28–32.

Becker, H. S., B. Geer, E. C. Hughes, and A. L. Strauss. 1961. *Boys in White*. Chicago: University of Chicago Press.

Becker, J. A., and P. Smenner. 1986. "The Spontaneous Use of 'Thank You' by Preschoolers as a Function of Sex, Socioeconomic Status and Listener Status." *Language in Society* 15:537–546.

Bem, D. J. 1970. *Beliefs, Attitudes and Human Affairs*. Belmont, CA: Brooks/Cole.

Bem, S. L., and D. J. Bem. 1970. "Case Study of a Nonconscious Ideology." In *Beliefs, Attitudes, and Human Affairs*. D. J. Bem (Ed.). Belmont, CA: Brooks/Cole.

Berkowitz, L. 1962. *Aggression: A Social Psychological Analysis*. New York: McGraw-Hill.

Berkowitz, L., and L. R. Daniels. 1963. "Responsibility and Dependency." *Journal of Abnormal and Social Psychology* 66:664–669.

Berkowitz, L. and A. Frodi. 1979. "Reactions to a Child's Mistakes as Affected by His/Her Looks and Speech." *Social Psychology Quarterly* 42:420–425.

Berkowitz, L. and A. LePage. 1967. "Weapons as Aggression-Eliciting Stimuli." *Journal of Personality and Social Psychology* 7:202–207.

Berndt, T. J., and K. A. Heller. 1986. "Gender Stereotypes and Social Inferences: A Developmental Study." *Journal of Personality and Social Psychology* 50:889–898.

Berscheid, E. 1982. "America's Obsession with Beautiful People." *U.S. News & World Report* January 11:59–61.

Biddle, Bruce J., and E. J. Thomas, eds. 1966. *Role Theory: Concepts and Research*. New York: John Wiley.

Birdwhistell, R. L. 1964. "Communication Without Words." In P. Alexandre (Ed.), *L'Aventure Humaine* (pp. 56–71). Paris: Société d'Etudes Litteraires et Artistiques.

Birdwhistell, R. L. 1970. *Kinesics and Context*. Philadelphia: University of Pennsylvania Press.

Blau, P. M. 1964. *Exchange and Power in Social Life*. New York: John Wiley.

Blauner, R. 1972. *Racial Oppression in America*. New York: Harper and Row.

Block, J., and J. Block. 1951. "An Investigation of the Relationship Between Intolerance of Ambiguity and Ethnocentrism." *Journal of Personality* 19:303–311.

Blumer, H. 1939. "Collective Behavior." In R. E. Park (Ed.), *An Outline of the Principles of Sociology*. New York: Barnes and Noble.

Blumer, H. 1953. "Psychological Import of the Group." In M. Sherif and M. D. Wilson (Eds.), *Group Relations at the Crossroads* (pp.185–202). New York: Harper and Row.

Blumer, H. 1962. "Society as Symbolic Interaction." In A. M. Rose (Ed.), *Human Behavior and Social Processes* (pp. 179–192). Boston: Houghton Mifflin.

Blumer, H. 1969. *Symbolic Interactionism: Perspective and Method*. Englewood Cliffs, NJ: Prentice-Hall.

Bobo, L. 1983. "Whites' Opposition to Busing: Symbolic Racism or Realistic Group Conflict?" *Journal of Personality and Social Psychology* 45:1196–1210.

Bock, E. W., L. Beeghley, and A. J. Mixon. 1983. "Religion, Socioeconomic Status, and Sexual Morality." *Sociological Quarterly* 24:545-559.

Bogardus, E. S. 1925. "Measuring Social Distance." *Journal of Applied Sociology* March-April:299–308.

Bohrnstedt, G. W., and R. B. Felson. 1983. "Explaining the Relationships Among

Childrens' Actual and Perceived Performances and Self-Esteem: A Comparison of Several Causal Models." *Journal of Social Psychology* 45:43–56.

Bonacich, E. 1972. "A Theory of Ethnic Antagonism: The Split Labor Market." *American Sociological Review* October:547–559.

Boring, E. G., H. S. Langfeld, and H. P. Weld. 1939. *Introduction to Psychology*. New York: John Wiley.

Boswell, D. A. 1983. *The Construction of Self as a Textual Process*. Paper delivered at the Center for the Humanities, Wesleyan University.

Bourne, R., and J. Levin. 1983. *Social Problems: Causes, Consequences, Interventions*. St. Paul, MN: West Publishing.

Boyanowsky, E. D., and C. T. Griffiths. 1982. "Weapons and Eye Contact as Instigators or Inhibitors of Aggression Arousal in Police-Citizen Interaction." *Journal of Applied Social Psychology* 12:398–407.

Bradley, B. E. 1981. *Fundamentals of Speech Communication: The Credibility of Ideas*. Dubuque, IA: William C. Brown.

Brehm, S. S., and J. W. Brehm. 1981. *Psychological Reactance: A Theory of Freedom and Control*. New York: Academic Press.

Brockner, J., and W. C. Swap. 1976. "Effects of Repeated Exposure and Attitudinal Similarity on Self-Disclosure and Interpersonal Attraction." *Journal of Personality and Social Psychology* 33:531–540.

Brown, R. A. 1973. A First Language. Cambridge, MA: Harvard University Press.

Bull, Peter, 1983. *Body Movement and Interpersonal Communication*. New York: John Wiley.

Burgess, R. L., and R. L. Akers. 1966. "A Differential Association-Reinforcement Theory of Criminal Behavior." *Social Problems* 14:128–147.

Burke, P. J. 1969. "Scapegoating: An Alternative to Role Differentiation." *Sociometry* June:159–168.

Burke, P. J., and J. C. Tully. 1977. "The Measurement of Role Identity." *Social Forces* 55:881–897.

Burkey, R. M. 1971. *Racial Discrimination and Public Policy in the United States*. Lexington, MA: Heath.

Burnstein, E., and P. Worchel. 1962. "Arbitrariness of Frustration and its Consequences for Aggression in a Social Situation." *Journal of Personality* 30:528–541.

Buss, A. H. 1980. *Self-Consciousness and Social Anxiety*. San Francisco: W. H. Freeman.

Byrne, D. 1961. "Anxiety and the Experimental Arousal of Affiliation Need." *Journal of Abnormal and Social Psychology* 63:660–662.

Byrne, D. 1971. *The Attraction Paradigm*. New York: Academic Press.

Callero, P. L. 1985. "Role-Identity Salience." *Social Psychology Quarterly* 48:203–215.

Campbell, D. T. 1975. "On the Conflicts Between Biological and Social Evolution and Between Psychology and Moral Tradition." *American Psychologist* 30:1103–1126.

Carnevale, P. J. D., G. D. Pruitt, and P. I. Carrington. 1981. "Effects of Future Dependents, Liking and Repeated Requests for Help on Helping Behavior." *Social Psychology Quarterly* 45:9–14.

Carver, C. S. 1979. "Cybernetic Model of Self-Attention Processes." *Journal of Personality and Social Psychology* 37:1251–1281.

Carver, C. S., and C. Humphries. 1981. "Havana Daydreaming: A Study of Self-Consciousness and the Negative Reference Group Among Cuban Americans." *Journal of Personality and Social Psychology* 40:545–552.

Cash, T. F., P. J. Begley, P. J. McCown, and B. C. Weise. 1975. "When Counselors are Seen but not Heard: Initial Impact of Physical Attractiveness." *Journal of Counseling Psychology* 22:273–279.

Cash, T. F., J. A. Kehr, J. Polyson, and V. Freeman. 1977. "Role of Physical Attractiveness in Poor Attribution of Psychological Disturbance." *Journal of Consulting and Clinical Psychology* 45:987–993.

Chapko, M., and M. Lewis. 1975. "Authoritarianism and 'All in the Family.'" *Journal of Psychology* 90:245–248.

Chomsky, N. 1957. *Syntactic Structures*. The Hague: Mouton.

Chomsky, N. 1959. "A Review of Skinner's *Verbal Behavior*." *Language* 35:26–58.

Christie, R. and M. Jahoda. 1954. *Studies in the Scope and Method of "The Authoritarian Personality."* New York: Free Press.

Cialdini, R. B., R. J. Borden, A. Thorne, M. R. Walker, and S. Freeman. 1976. "Basking In Reflected Glory." *Journal of Personality and Social Psychology* 34:366–375.

Clark, K. B., and M. P. Clark. 1947. "Racial Identification and Preference in Negro Children." In E. E. Maccoby, T. M. Newcomb, and E. L. Hartley (Eds.), *Readings in Social Psychology*. New York: Holt, Rinehart and Winston.

Clark, M. L. 1986. "Social Stereotypes and Self-Concept in Black and White College Students." *Journal of Social Psychology* 125:753–760.

Clifford, M., and E. Walster. 1973. "The Effects of Physical Attraction on Teacher Expectation." *Sociology of Education* 46:248.

Clore, G. L., and D. A. Byrne. 1974. "Reinforcement-Effect Model of Attraction." In T. Huston (Ed.), *Foundations of Interpersonal Attraction*. New York: Academic Press.

Cohen, A. K. 1955. *Delinquent Boys: The Culture of the Gang*. Chicago: Free Press.

Coleman, J. S. 1963. "Academic Achievement and the Structure of Competition." In N. J. Smelser and W. T. Smelser (Eds.), *Personality and Social Systems*. New York: John Wiley.

Comstock, G., S. Chaffee, N. Katzman, M. McCombs, and D. Roberts. 1978. *Television and Human Behavior*. New York: Columbia University Press.

Condran, J. G. 1979. "Changes in White Attitudes toward Blacks: 1963–1977." *Public Opinion Quarterly* Winter:463–476.

Cook, S. W. 1972. "Motives in a Conceptual Analysis of Attitude-Related Behavior." In J. Brigham and T. Weissbach (Eds.), *Racial Attitudes in America*. New York: Harper and Row.

Cooley, C. H. 1902. *Human Nature and the Social Order*. New York: Scribner.

Cooper, H. M. 1979. "Statistically Combining Independent Studies: A Meta-Analysis of Sex Differences in Conformity Research." *Journal of Personality and Social Psychology* 37:131–146.

Coser, L. A. 1956. *The Functions of Social Conflict*. New York: Free Press.

Cowen, E. L., J. Landes, and D. E. Schaet. 1959. "The Effects of Mild Frustration on the Expression of Prejudiced Attitudes." *Journal of Abnormal and Social Psychology* January:33–38.

Cowgill, D. O., and L. Holmes. 1972. *Aging and Modernization*. New York: Appleton-Century-Crofts.

Crosby, F., and L. Nyquist. 1977. "The Female Register: An Empirical Study of Lakoff's Hypotheses." *Language in Society* 6:313–322.

Cummings, S. 1980. "White Ethnics, Racial Prejudice and Labor Market Segmentation." *American Sociological Review* 85:938–950.

Darley, J. M., and B. Latane. 1968. "When Will People Help in a Crisis?" *Psychology Today* 2:54–57; 70–71.

Darwin, C. 1872. *The Expression of Emotions in Man and Animals*. London: Murray.

Davis, J. A. 1966. "The Campus as a Frog Pond: An Application of the Theory of Relative Deprivation to Career Decisions of College Men." *American Journal of Sociology* 72:17–31.

Davis, L. 1984. "Judgment Ambiguity, Self-Consciousness, and Conformity in Judgments of Fashionability." *Psychological Reports* 54:671–675.

Dawkins, R. 1976. *The Selfish Gene*. Oxford: Oxford University Press.

Deaux, K., and L. L. Lewis. 1984. "Structure of Gender Stereotypes: Interrelationships Among Components and Gender Labels." *Journal of Personality and Social Psychology* 46:991–1004.

Derbyshire, R. L., and E. Brody. 1964. "Social Distance and Identity Conflict in Negro College Students." *Sociology and Social Research* April:301–314.

Dermer, M., and D. Thiel. 1975. "When Beauty May Fail." *Journal of Personality and Social Psychology* 31:1168–1176.

Deutsch, M., and M. E. Collins. 1951. *Interracial Housing*. Minneapolis: University of Minnesota Press.

Deutsch, M., and H. G. Gerard. 1955. "A Study of Normative and Informational

Social Influence Upon Individual Judgments." *Journal of Abnormal and Social Psychology* 51:629–636.

Dicks, H. V. 1972. *Licensed Mass Murder.* New York: Basic Books.

Diener, E., R. Lusk, D. DeFour, and R. Flax. 1980. "Deindividuation: Effects of Group Size, Density, Number of Observers, and Group Member Similarity on Self-Consciousness and Disinhibited Behavior." *Journal of Personality and Social Psychology* 39:449–459.

Dion, K. K., and E. Berscheid. 1974. "Physical Attractiveness and Peer Perception in Children." *Sociometry* 37:1–12.

Dion, K. K., E. Berscheid, and E. Walster. 1972. "What is Beautiful is Good." *Journal of Personality and Social Psychology* 24:285–290.

Dipboye, R. L. 1977. "Alternative Approaches to Deindividuation." *Psychological Bulletin* 84:1057–1075.

Dipboye, R. L., R. D. Arvey, and D. E. Terpstra. 1977. "Sex and Physical Attractiveness of Raters and Applicants as Determinants of Resumé Evaluations." *Journal of Applied Psychology* 62:288–294.

Dollard, J., L. W. Doob, N. E. Miller, O. H. Mowrer, and R. R. Sears. 1939. *Frustration and Aggression.* New Haven, CT: Yale University Press.

Douglas, J. D. 1970. *Deviance and Respectability.* New York: Basic Books.

Drass, K. A. 1986. "The Effect of Gender Identity on Conversation." *Social Psychology Quarterly* 49:294–301.

Duncan, S. 1972. "Some Signals and Rules for Taking Speaking Turns in Conversations." *Journal of Personality and Social Psychology* 23:283–292.

Eagly, A. H. 1978. "Sex Differences in Influenceability." *Psychological Bulletin* 85:86–116.

Eagly, A. H. 1983. "Gender and Social Influence: A Social Psychological Analysis." *American Psychologist* 38:971–981.

Eagly, A. H., and L. L. Carli. 1981. "Sex of Researchers and Sex-Typed Communications as Determinants of Sex Differences and Influenceability: Meta-Analysis of Social Influence Studies." *Psychological Bulletin* 90:1–20.

Eagly, A. H., and S. Himmelfarb. 1978. "Attitudes and Opinions." In M. R. Rosenzweig and L. W. Porter (Eds.), *Annual Review of Psychology* 29:517–554.

Eckman, P., and W. V. Friesen. 1969. "The Repertoire of Non-Verbal Behavior: Categories, Origins, Usage and Coding." *Semiotica* 1:49–98.

Eckman, P., and W. V. Friesen. 1975. *Unmasking the Face.* Englewood Cliffs, NJ: Prentice-Hall.

Edwards, A. I., and A. J. Klockars. 1981. "Significant Others and Self-Evaluation: Relationships between Perceived and Actual Evaluations." *Personality and Social Psychology Bulletin* 7:241–251.

Ehrlich, H. J. 1972. *The Social Psychology of Prejudice.* New York: John Wiley.

Eibl-Eibesfeldt, I. 1974. "Similarities and Differences Between Cultures in Expressive Movements." In S. Weitz (Ed.), *Nonverbal Communication* (pp.20–33). New York: Oxford University Press.

Elliott, G. C. 1986. "Self-Esteem and Self-Consistency: A Theoretical and Empirical Link Between Two Primary Motivations." *Social Psychology Quarterly* 49:207–218.

Elman, M. R., and L. A Gilbert. 1984. "Coping Strategies for Role Conflict in Married Professional Women With Children." *Family Relations* 33:317–327.

Erikson, E. H. 1950. *Childhood and Society.* New York: Norton.

Feagin, J. R., and C. B. Feagin. 1978. *Discrimination American Style.* Englewood Cliffs, NJ: Prentice-Hall.

Fellman, B. 1986. "Do Fish Carry Tales to School?" *Boston Globe* November 17:43.

Felson, R. B. 1985. "Reflected Appraisal and the Development of Self." *Social Psychology Quarterly* 48:71–78.

Felson, R. B., and G. Bohrnstedt. 1979. "Are the Good Beautiful or the Beautiful Good? The Relationship Between Children's Perceptions of Ability and Perceptions of Physical Attractiveness." *Social Psychology Quarterly* 42:386–392.

Felson, R. B., and M. D. Reed. 1986. "Reference Groups and Self-Appraisals of Academic Ability and Performance." *Social Psychology Quarterly* 49:103–109.

Fenigstein, A., M. Scheier and A. Buss. 1975. "Public and Private Self-Consciousness: Assessment and Theory." *Journal of Consulting and Clinical Psychology* 43:522–527.

Festinger, L. 1954. "A Theory of Social Comparison Processes." *Human Relations* 7:117–140.

Festinger, L. 1957. *A Theory of Cognitive Dissonance.* Evanston, IL: Row, Peterson and Company.

Festinger, L., S. Schacter, and K. W. Back. 1950. *Social Pressures in Informal Groups: A Study of Human Factors in Housing.* New York: Harper and Brothers.

Fine, G. A. 1977. "Social Components of Children's Gossip." *Journal of Communication* 27:181–185.

Fine, G. A., J. L. Stitt, and M. Finch. 1984. "Couple Tie-Signs and Interpersonal Threat: A Field Experiment." *Social Psychology Quarterly* 47:282–286.

Fischer, D. H. 1977. *Growing Old in America.* New York: Oxford University Press.

Fishman, J. A. 1972. *The Sociology of Language: An Interdisciplinary Approach to Language in Society.* Rowley, MA: Newbury House.

Folb, E. A. 1980. *Runnin' Down Some Lines: The Language and Culture of Black Teenagers.* Cambridge, MA: Harvard University Press.

Form, W. H., and S. Nosow. 1958. *Community in Disaster.* New York: Harper.

Freud, S. 1930. *Civilization and Its Discontents.* London: Hogarth Press.

Freud, S. 1949. *New Introductory Lectures on Psychoanalysis*. London: Hogarth Press.

Frey, D. L., and S. L. Gaertner. 1986. "Helping and the Avoidance of Inappropriate Interracial Behavior: A Strategy that Perpetuates a Non Prejudiced Self-Image." *Journal of Personality and Social Psychology* 50:1083–1090.

Fromm, E. 1973. *The Anatomy of Human Destructiveness*. New York: Holt, Rinehart and Winston.

Gaertner, S. L., and J. P. McLaughlin. 1983. "Racial Stereotypes: Associations and Ascriptions of Positive and Negative Characteristics." *Social Psychology Quarterly* 46:23–30.

Gambino, R. 1977. *Vendetta*. Garden City, NY: Doubleday.

Gamson, W. A., B. Fireman, and S. Rytina. 1982. *Encounters with Unjust Authority*. Homewood, IL: Dorsey Press.

Gardner, B. T., and R. A. Gardner. 1971. "Two-Way Communication with a Chimpanzee." In A. Schrier and F. Stollnitz (Eds.), *Behavior of Non-Human Primates*. New York: Academic Press.

Garfinkel, H. 1967. *Studies in Ethnomethodology*. Englewood Cliffs, NJ: Prentice-Hall.

Gecas, V., and M. L. Schwalbe. 1983. "Beyond the Looking-Glass Self: Social Structure and Efficacy-Based Self-Esteem." *Social Psychology Quarterly* 46:77–88.

Geen, R. G. 1972. *Aggression*. Morristown, NJ: General Learning Press.

Gelles, R. J. 1985. "Family Violence: What We Know and Can Do." In E. H. Newberger and R. Bourne (Eds.), *Unhappy Families*. Littleton, MA: PSG Publishing Company.

Gerard, H. B., R. A. Wilhelmy, and E. S. Conolley. 1968. "Conformity and Group Size." *Journal of Personality and Social Psychology* 8:79–82.

Gerbner, G., L. Gross, N. Signorielli, and M. Morgan. 1980. "Aging with Television: Images on Television Drama and Conceptions of Social Reality." *Journal of Communication* 30:37–47.

Gergen, K. J. 1972. "Multiple Identity." *Psychology Today* 5:31–35, 64–66.

Gergen, K. J. 1978. "Toward Generative Theory." *Journal of Personality and Social Psychology* 36:1344–1360.

Gergen, K. J. 1982. *Toward Transformation in Social Knowledge*. New York: Springer-Verlag.

Gergen, K. J., and M. M. Gergen. 1983. "Narratives of the Self." In T. R. Sarbin and K. E. Scheibe (Eds.), *Studies in Social Identity*. New York: Praeger.

Gerson, J. M. 1985. "Women Returning to School: The Consequences of Multiple Roles." *Sex Roles* 13:77–92.

Gifford, R., C. Fan Ng, and M. Wilkinson. 1985. "Nonverbal Cues in the Employment Interview: Links Between Applicant Qualities and Interviewer Judgments." *Journal of Applied Psychology* 70:729–736.

Gilligan, C. 1982. *In a Different Voice: Psychological Theory and Women's Development.* Cambridge, MA: Harvard University Press.

Glazer, N. 1976. *Affirmative Discrimination: Ethnic Identity and Public Policy.* New York: Basic Books.

Glenn, N. D. 1963. "Occupational Benefits to Whites from the Subordination of Negroes." *American Sociological Review* June:443–448.

Goethals, G. R., and J. M. Darley. 1977. "Social Comparison Theory: An Attributional Approach." In J. M. Suls and R. L. Miller (Eds.), *Social Comparison Processes: Theoretical and Empirical Perspectives.* Washington, D.C.: Halsted-Wiley.

Goffman, E. 1958. *Asylums.* New York: Anchor Books.

Goffman, E. 1959. *The Presentation of Self in Everyday Life.* Garden City, NY: Doubleday.

Goffman, E. 1961. *Encounters: Two Studies in the Sociology of Interaction.* Indianapolis: Bobbs-Merrill.

Goffman, E. 1963. *Stigma: Notes on the Management of Spoiled Identity.* Englewood Cliffs, NJ: Prentice-Hall.

Goffman, E. 1971. *Relations in Public.* New York: Basic Books.

Goldberg, P. 1968. "Are Women Prejudiced Against Other Women?" *Transaction* 5:28–30.

Goldstein, J. H. 1986. *Aggression and Crimes of Violence.* New York: Oxford University Press.

Goldstein, J. H., and R. L. Arms. 1971. "Effects of Observing Athletic Contests on Hostility." *Sociometry* 34:83–90.

Gonzalez, M. H., J. M. Davis, G. L. Loney, C. K. Kukens, and C. M. Junghans. 1985. "Interactional Approach to Interpersonal Attraction." *Journal of Personality and Social Psychology* 44:1192–1197.

Goode, E. 1984. *Deviant Behavior.* Englewood Cliffs, NJ: Prentice-Hall.

Goode, W. S. 1960. "A Theory of Role Strain." *American Sociological Review* 25:483–496.

Gormly, J. 1974. "A Comparison of Predictions From Consistency and Affect Theories for Arousal During Interpersonal Agreement." *Journal of Personality and Social Psychology* 30:658–663.

Gottlieb, J., and C. S. Carver. 1980. "Anticipation of Future Interaction and the Bystander Effect." *Journal of Experimental Social Psychology* 16:253–260.

Gouldner, A. 1960. "The Norm of Reciprocity." *American Sociological Review* 25:171.

Grabb, E. G. 1980. "Social Class, Authoritarianism, and Racial Contact: Recent Trends." *Sociology and Social Research* 64: 208–220.

Granfield, R. 1986. "Legal Education as Corporate Ideology." *Sociological Forum* 1:514–523.

Grant, P. R., and J. G. Holmes. 1981. "The Integration of Implicit Personality Theory Schemas and Stereotype Images." *Social Psychology Quarterly* 44:107–115.

Griffitt, W., and L. Garcia. 1979. "Reversing Authoritarian Punitiveness: The Impact of Verbal Conditioning." *Social Psychology Quarterly* 42:55–61.

Gross, A. E., and C. Crofton. 1977. "What Is Good Is Beautiful." *Sociometry* 40:80–90.

Gross, E., and G. P. Stone. 1970. "Embarrassment and the Analysis of Role Requirements." In G. P. Stone and H. A. Farberman (Eds.), *Social Psychology Through Symbolic Interaction* (pp. 174–189). Waltham, MA: Ginn-Blaisdell.

Gross, N., W. A. McEachern, and W. A. Mason. 1966. "Role Conflict and Its Resolution." In Bruce Biddle and Edwin J. Thomas (Eds.), *Role Theory: Concepts and Research* (pp. 287–296). New York: John Wiley.

Grossman, J.C., and R. Eisenman. 1971. "Experimental Manipulation of Authoritarianism and its Effect on Creativity." *Journal of Consulting and Clinical Psychology* 34:238–244.

Grubb, H. J. 1986. "The Black Prole and Whitespeak: Black English from an Orwellian Perspective." *Race and Class* 3:67–79.

Gruder, C. L. 1977. "Choice of Comparison Persons in Evaluating Oneself." In J. M. Suls and R. L. Miller (Eds.), *Social Comparison Processes*. Washington, D.C.: Hemisphere.

Grush, J. E., G. Clore, and F. Costin. 1975. "Dissimilarity and Attraction: When Difference Makes a Difference." *Journal of Personality and Social Psychology* 32:783–789.

Grush, J. E., and J. G. Yel. 1979. "Marital Roles, Sex Differences and Interpersonal Attraction." *Journal of Personality and Social Psychology* 37:116–123.

Haimowitz, M. L. and N. R. Haimowitz. 1950. "Reducing Ethnic Hostility Through Psychotherapy." *Journal of Social Psychology* 31:231–241.

Hakmiller, K. L. 1966. "Threat as a Determinant of Downward Comparison." *Journal of Experimental Social Psychology* Supplement 1:32–39.

Hall, E. T. 1966. *The Hidden Dimension*. Garden City, NY: Doubleday.

Halliday, M. A. K. 1972. *Language as Social Semiotic*. Baltimore: University Park Press.

Hallinan, M. T., and S. S. Smith. 1985. "The Effects of Classroom Composition on Students' Inter-racial Friendliness." *Social Psychology Quarterly* 48:3–16.

Hamilton, D. L., L. B. Katz, and V. O. Leirer. 1980. "Organizational Processes in Impression Formation." In R. Hastie et al. (Eds.), *Person Memory*. Hillsdale, NJ: Erlbaum.

Hamilton, W. D. 1971. "Selection of Selfish and Altruistic Behavior in Some Extreme Models." In J. F. Eisenberg and W. S. Dillon (Eds.), *Man and Beast: Comparative Social Behavior*. Washington, D.C.: Smithsonian Institution Press.

Harper, R. G., A. N. Wiens, and J. D. Matarazzo. 1978. *Nonverbal Communication*. New York: John Wiley.

Harrison, R. P., and M. L. Knapp. 1972. "Toward an Understanding of Nonverbal Communication Systems." *Journal of Communication* 22:339–352.

Hartley, E. L. 1946. *Problems in Prejudice*. New York: King's Crown Press.

Harvey, J. H., and G. Weary. 1981. *Perspectives on Attributional Processes*. Dubuque, IA: William C. Brown.

Hays, R. B. 1985. "A Longitudinal Study of Friendship Development." *Journal of Personality and Social Psychology* 48:909–924.

Heiss, Jerold. 1981. "Social Roles." Pp.94–129. In M. Rosenberg and R. H. Turner (Eds.), *Social Psychology: Sociological Perspectives*. New York: Basic Books.

Hepburn, C., and A. Locksley. 1983. "Subjective Awareness of Stereotyping: Do We Know When Our Judgments Are Prejudiced?" *Social Psychology Quarterly* 46:311–318.

Hoffman, M. L. 1970. "Moral Development." In P. H. Mussen (Ed.), *Carmichael's Manual of Child Psychology*. New York: John Wiley.

Hoffman, M. L. 1975. "Altruistic Behavior and the Parent-Child Relationship." *Journal of Personality and Social Psychology* 31:937–943.

Hoffman, M. L. 1981. "Is Altruism Part of Human Nature?" *Journal of Personality and Social Psychology* 40:121–137.

Holmes, D. S. 1972. "Aggression, Displacement, and Guilt." *Journal of Personality and Social Psychology* March:296–301.

Holmes, J. 1986. "Functions of 'You Know' in Women's and Men's Speech." *Language in Society* 15:1–22.

Homans, G. C. 1961, 1974. *Social Behavior: Its Elementary Forms*. New York: Harcourt.

Hong, L. K. 1978. "Risky Shift and Cautious Shift: Some Direct Evidence on the Culture-Value Theory." *Social Psychology* 41:342–345.

Hraba, J., and G. Grant. 1970. "Black is Beautiful: A Reexamination of Racial Preference and Identification." *Journal of Personality and Social Psychology* 16:398–402.

Hudson, L. M., E. A. Forman, and S. Brion-Meisels. 1982. "Role Taking as a Predictor of Prosocial Behavior in Cross-Age Tutors." *Child Development* 53:1320–1329.

Hudson, R. A. 1981. *Sociolinguistics*. Cambridge: Cambridge University Press.

Hughes, M. 1980. "The Fruits of Cultivation Analysis: A Reexamination of Some Effects of Television Watching." *Public Opinion Quarterly* Fall:289–302.

Huston, T. L., M. Ruggiero, R. Conner, and G. Geis. 1981. "Bystander Intervention into Crime: A Study Based on Naturally-Occurring Episodes." *Social Psychology Quarterly* 44:14–23.

Hyman, H. H. 1942. "The Psychology of Status." *Archives of Psychology* 38:No. 269.

Hyman, H. H. 1960. "Reflection on Reference Groups." *Public Opinion Quarterly* 24:383–396.

Hyman, H. H., and E. Singer. 1968. *Readings in Reference Group Theory and Research.* New York: Free Press.

Insko, C. A., and M. Wilson. 1977. "Interpersonal Attraction as a Function of Social Interaction." *Journal of Personality and Social Psychology* 35:903–911.

Jackson, M. R., and M. J. Muha. 1984. "Education and Intergroup Attitudes." *American Sociological Review* 49:751–769.

Jennings, L. B., and S. G. George. 1984. "Group-Induced Distortion of Visually Perceived Linear Extent: The Asch Effect Revisited." *The Psychological Record* 34:133–148.

Jewson, J., J. Sachs, and R. Rohner. 1981. "The Effect of a Narrative Context on the Verbal Style of Middle-Class and Lower-Class Children." *Language in Society* 10:201–215.

Jones, E. 1964. *Ingratiation: Social Psychological Analysis.* New York: Appleton-Century-Crofts.

Jones, E. E., G. C. Wood, and G. A. Quattrone. 1981. "Perceived Variability of Personal Characteristics in In-Groups and Out-Groups: The Role of Knowledge and Evaluation." *Personality and Social Psychology Bulletin* 7:523–528.

Kandel, D. B. 1978. "Similarity in Real-Life Adolescent Friendship Pairs." *Journal of Personality and Social Psychology* 36:306–312.

Kanin, E. 1957. "Value-Conflicts in Catholic Device-Contraceptive Usage." *Social Forces* 35:238–243.

Kanin, E. 1967. "An Examination of Sexual Aggression as a Response to Sexual Frustration." *Journal of Marriage and the Family* 29:428–433.

Kanin, E. 1971. "Sexually Aggressive College Males." *Student Personnel* 112:107–110.

Kanin, E. and S. R. Parcell. 1977. "Sexual Aggression: A Second Look at the Offended Female." *Archives of Sexual Behavior* 6:67–76.

Karlins, M., T. L. Coffman, and G. Walters. 1969. "On the Fading of Social Stereotypes." *Journal of Personality and Social Psychology* September:1–16.

Karp, D. A. and W. C. Yoels. 1979. *Symbols, Selves and Society.* New York: Lippincott.

Karylowski, J. 1976. "Self-Esteem, Similarity, Liking and Helping." *Personality and Social Psychology Bulletin* 2:71–74.

Katz, D. 1960. "The Functional Approach to the Study of Attitudes." *Public Opinion Quarterly* Summer:163–204.

Katz, D., and K. Braly. 1933. "Racial Stereotypes of One Hundred College Students." *Journal of Abnormal and Social Psychology* October–December:280–290.

Katz, I. 1981. *Stigma: A Social Psychological Analysis.* Hillsdale, NJ: Erlbaum.

Keller, H. 1904. *The Story of My Life.* New York: Grosset and Dunlap.

Kelley, H. H. 1968. "Two Functions of Reference Groups." In H. H. Hyman and E. Singer (Eds.), *Readings in Reference Group Theory and Research.* New York: Free Press.

Kenrick, D. T., and S. E. Gutierres. 1980. "Contrast Effects and Judgments of Physical Attractiveness: When Beauty Becomes a Social Problem: *Journal of Personality and Social Psychology* 38:131–140.

Kerckhoff, A. C. 1974. "The Social Context of Interpersonal Attraction." In T. Huston (Ed.), *Foundations of Interpersonal Attraction.* New York: Academic Press.

Key, M. R. 1975. *Paralanguage and Kinesics.* Metuchen, NJ: Scarecrow Press.

Kiesler, C. A., and S. B. Kiesler. 1969. *Conformity.* Reading, MA: Addison-Wesley.

King, W. 1979. "Vengeance for Raid Seen as Motive for 4 Killings at Anti-Clan March." *New York Times* November 5:1.

Knapp, M. L., R. P. Hart, C. W. Friedrich, and G. M. Schulman. 1973. "The Rhetoric of Goodbye: Verbal and Non-Verbal Correlates of Human Leave-Taking." *Speech Monographs* 40:182–198.

Kochman, T. 1983. "The Boundary Between Play and Nonplay in Black Verbal Dueling." *Language in Society* 12:329–337.

Koenig, F. W., and M. B. King, Jr. 1962. "Cognitive Simplicity and Prejudice." *Social Forces* March:220–222.

Kohlberg, L. 1969. *Stages in the Development of Moral Thought and Action.* New York: Holt, Rinehart and Winston.

Korte, C., and N. Kerr. 1975. "Response to Altruistic Opportunities in Urban and Nonurban Settings." *Journal of Social Psychology* 95:183–184.

Kramarae, C., M. Schultz, and W. O'Barr. 1984. *Language and Power.* Beverly Hills, CA: Sage.

Krebs, D. 1975. "Empathy and Altruism." *Journal of Personality and Social Psychology* 32:1134–1146.

Kuhn, M. H. 1960. "Self-Attitudes by Age, Sex, and Professional Training." *Sociological Quarterly* 1:39–55.

Kuhn, T. S. 1970. The Structure of Scientific Revolutions. Chicago: University of Chicago Press.

Labov, W. 1972. *Language in the Inner City: Studies in the Black English Vernacular.* Philadelphia: University of Pennsylvania Press.

Labov, W. 1974. "The Art of Sounding and Signifying." In W. G. Gage (Ed.), *Language in its Social Setting* pp. 84–116. Washington, D.C.: The Anthropological Society of Washington.

Labov, W. 1982. "Objectivity and Commitment in Linguistic Science: The Case of the Black English Trial in Ann Arbor." *Language in Society* 11:165–201.

LaGumina, S. J. 1973. *Wop!* San Francisco: Straight Arrow.

Lakoff, R. 1973. "Language and Woman's Place." *Language in Society* 2:45–79.

Lakoff, R. 1975. *Language and Woman's Place*. New York: Harper and Row.

Lamy, P., and J. Levin. 1986. "Punk and Middle Class Values: A Content Analysis." In S. J. Ball-Rokeach and M. G. Cantor (Eds.), *Media, Audience, and Social Structure*. Newbury Park, CA: Sage.

Landy, D., and H. Sigall. 1974. "Beauty is Talent: Task Evaluation as a Function of the Performers' Physical Attractiveness." *Journal of Personality and Social Psychology* 29:299–304.

Langer, E. J., R. S. Bashner, and B. Chanowitz. 1985. "Decreasing Prejudice by Increasing Discrimination." *Journal of Personality and Social Psychology* 49:113–120.

LaPiere, R. T. 1934. "Attitude and Actions." *Social Forces* 13:230–237.

Larsen, K. 1974. "Conformity in the Asch Experiment." *Journal of Social Psychology* 94:303–304.

Larsen, K. S., and G. Schwendiman. 1970. "Perceived Aggression Training as a Predictor of Two Assessments of Authoritarianism." *Journal of Peace Research* 1:69–71.

Latané, B., and J. M. Darley. 1968. "Group Inhibition of Bystander Intervention in Emergencies." *Journal of Pesonality and Social Psychology* 10:215–221.

Latané, B., and J. M. Darley. 1970. *The Unresponsive Bystander: Why Doesn't He Help?* New York: Appleton-Century-Crofts.

Latané, B., and J. Rodin. 1969. "A Lady in Distress: Inhibiting Effects of Friends and Strangers on Bystander Intervention." *Journal of Experimental Social Psychology* 5:189–202.

Lauer, R. H., and W. Handel. 1977. *Social Psychology: The Theory and Application of Symbolic Interactionism*. Boston: Houghton Mifflin.

Le Bon, G. 1896. *Psychologie des Foules*. Trans. *The Crowd: A Study of the Popular Mind*. London: Ernest Benn, 1896.

Leibowitz, L. 1978. *Anthropology of the Family*. Scituate, MA: Duxbury Press.

Leo, J. 1987. "Exploring the Traits of Twins." *Time* January 12:63.

Lepper, M. R., L. Ross, and R. R. Lau. 1986. "Persistence of Inaccurate Beliefs about the Self: Perseverance Effects in the Classroom." *Journal of Personality and Social Psychology* 50: 482–491.

Levin, J., and A. Arluke. 1982. "Embarrassment and Helping Behavior." *Psychological Reports* 51:999–1002.

Levin, J., and A. Arluke, 1983. "Attitude Similarity and Parent-Child Attractiveness." *Journal of Social Psychology* 120:223–228.

Levin, J., and A. Arluke, 1985. "An Exploratory Analysis of Sex Differences in Gossip." *Sex Roles* 12:281–286.

Levin, J., and A. Arluke. 1987. *Gossip: The Inside Scoop*. New York: Plenum Press.

Levin, J., and J. A. Fox. 1985. *Mass Murder: America's Growing Menace.* New York: Plenum Press.

Levin, J., and W. Leong. 1973. "Reference Group Behavior and Assimilation." *Phylon* 34:289–294.

Levin, J., and W. C. Levin. 1980. *Ageism: Prejudice and Discrimination Against the Elderly.* Belmont, CA: Wadsworth.

Levin, J., and W. C. Levin. 1982. *The Functions of Discrimination and Prejudice.* New York: Harper and Row.

Levin, J., and J. L. Spates. 1970. "Hippie Values: An Analysis of the Underground Press." *Youth and Society* 2:59–73.

Levin, W. C. 1987. "Attitudes Toward Elders in Three Cities." A paper presented at the meeting of the Massachusetts Sociological Association, Worcester, MA.

Levin, W. C., and J. Levin. 1973. "Social Comparison of Grades: The Influence of Mode of Comparison and Machiavellianism." *Journal of Social Psychology* 91:67–72.

Levitt E. A. 1964. "The Relationship Between Abilities to Express Emotional Meanings Vocally and Facially." In J. R. Davitz (Ed.), *The Communication of Emotional Meaning.* New York: McGraw-Hill.

Lewis, J. M. "Crowd Control at English Football Matches." *Sociological Focus* 15:417–424.

Lifton, R. J. 1986. *The Nazi Doctors.* New York: Basic Books.

Linton, R. 1936. *The Study of Man.* New York: Appleton-Century-Crofts.

Lippman, W. 1922. *Public Opinion.* New York: Harcourt.

Liska, A. E. 1981. *Perspectives on Deviance.* Englewood Cliffs, NJ: Prentice-Hall.

Liska, A. E. 1984. "A Critical Examination of the Causal Structure of the Fishbein/Ajzen Attitude-Behavior Model." *Social Psychology Quarterly* 47:61–74.

London, P. 1970. "The Rescuers: Motivational Hypotheses about Christians who Saved Jews from the Nazis." In J. Macaulay and L. Berkowitz (Eds.), *Altruism and Helping Behavior.* New York: Academic Press.

Lorenz, K. 1966. *On Aggression.* New York: Harcourt, Brace and World.

Luckmann, T. 1984. "Language in Society." *International Social Science Journal* 36:5–20.

McHugo, G. J., and J. T. Lanzetta, D. G. Sullivan, R. D. Masters, and B. G. Englis. 1985. "Emotional Reactions to a Political Leader's Expressive Displays." *Journal of Personality and Social Psychology* 49:1513–1529.

McIntyre, J. J., and J. J. Teevan. 1972. "Television Violence and Deviant Behavior." In G. A. Comstock and E. A. Rubenstein (Eds.), *Television and Social Behavior.* Vol. 3. Washington, D.C.: U.S. Government Printing Office.

McWilliams, C. 1948. *A Mask for Privilege.* Boston: Little, Brown.

Mancuso, J. C., and T. R. Sarbin. 1983. *The Self-Narrative in the Enactment of Roles.* In T. R. Sarbin and K. E. Scheibe (Eds.), *Studies in Social Identity.* New York: Praeger.

Mann, L. 1979. "Sports Crowds from the Perspective of Collective Behavior." In J. H. Goldstein (Ed.), *Sports, Games and Play.* Hillsdale, NJ: Erlbaum.

Mann, L., J. W. Newton, and J. M. Innes. 1982. "A Test Between Deindividuation and Emergent Norm Theories of Crowd Aggression." *Journal of Personality and Social Psychology* 42:260–272.

Marsh, H. W., and J. W. Parker. 1984. "Determinants of Student Self-Concept: Is It Better to Be a Relatively Large Fish in a Small Pond Even if You Don't Learn to Swim Well?" *Journal of Personality and Social Psychology* 47:213–231.

Martin, J., and F. Westie. 1959. "The Tolerant Personality." *American Sociological Review* 24:524–531.

Marx, K. 1867. *Capital: A Critique of Political Economy.* Vol. 1. New York: International.

Mathes, E. W. 1974. "The Effects of Physical Attractiveness on Behavior: A Test of the Self-Fulfilling Prophecy Theory." *Dissertation Abstracts International* 34:5226.

Mead, G. H. 1934. *Mind, Self and Society.* Chicago: University of Chicago Press.

Mead, G. H. 1956. *On Social Psychology.* Edited by Anselm Strauss. Chicago: University of Chicago Press.

Mehrabian, A., and S. Ksionsky. 1971. "Anticipated Compatibility as a Function of Attitude or Status Similarity." *Journal of Personality* 39:225–241.

Merry, S. E. 1984. "Rethinking Gossip and Scandal." In D. Black (Ed.), *Toward a General Theory of Social Control.* Orlando, FL: Academic Press.

Merton, R. K. 1957a. *Social Theory and Social Structure.* New York: Free Press.

Merton, R. K. 1957b. "The Role Set." *British Journal of Sociology* 8:560–568.

Middleton, R. 1976. "Regional Differences in Prejudice." *American Sociological Review* 41:94–116.

Milgram, S. 1963. "Behavioral Study of Obedience." *Journal of Abnormal and Social Psychology* 67:371–378.

Milgram, S. 1970. "The Experience of Living in Cities." *Science* 167:1461–1468.

Milgram, S. 1974. *Obedience to Authority: An Experimental View.* New York: Harper and Row.

Miller, D. L. 1985. *Collective Behavior.* Belmont, California: Wadsworth.

Miller, G. A. 1981. *Language and Speech.* San Francisco: W. H. Freeman.

Miller, L. K., and R. L. Hamblin. 1963. "Interdependence, Differential Rewarding and Productivity." *American Sociological Reviews* 28:768–778.

Miller, N. E., and R. Bugelski. 1948. "Minor Studies of Aggression: The Influence of

Frustrations Imposed by the In-Group on Attitudes Expressed Toward Out-Groups." *Journal of Psychology* 25:437–442.

Mitchell, H. 1973. *Authoritarian Punitiveness in Simulated Jury Decision-Making.* Paper presented at the meeting of the Midwestern Psychological Association, Chicago.

Mitchell, H., and D. Byrne. 1972. "The Defendant's Dilemma: Effects of Juror's Attitudes and Authoritarianism on Judicial Decisions." *Journal of Personality and Social Psychology* 25:123–129.

Miyamoto, S. F., and S. Dornbusch. 1956. "A Test of the Symbolic Interactionist Hypothesis of Self-Conception." *American Journal of Sociology* 617:399–423.

Mones, P. 1985. "The Relationship between Child Abuse and Parricide." In E. H. Newberger and R. Bourne (Eds.), *Unhappy Families.* Littleton, MA: PSG Publishing Company.

Montmayor, R. and M. Eisen. 1977. "The Development of Self-Conceptions from Childhood to Adolescence." *Developmental Psychology* 13:314–319.

Morgan, C. S., and A. J. Walker. 1983. "Predicting Sex Role Attitudes." *Social Psychology Quarterly* 46:148–151.

Mosatche, H. S., and P. Bragonier. 1981. "An Observational Study of Social Comparison in Preschoolers." *Child Development* 52:314–322.

Murstein, B. I. 1972. "Physical Attractiveness and Marital Choice." *Journal of Personality and Social Psychology* 22:8–12.

Mussen, P. H., J. J. Conger, and J. Kagan. 1974. *Child Development and Personality.* New York: Harper and Row.

Nadler, A. 1986. "Help Seeking as a Cultural Phenomenon: Differences between City and Kibbutz Dwellers." *Journal of Personality and Social Pscychology* 51:976-982.

Nahemow, L., and M. P. Lawton. 1975. "Similarity and Propinquity in Friendship Formation." *Journal of Personality and Social Psychology* 32:205–213.

National Crime Survey. 1981. U.S. Department of Justice, Bureau of Justice Statistics. Washington, D.C.: U.S. Government Printing Office.

National Institute of Mental Health. 1982. *Television and Behavior: Ten Years of Scientific Progress and Implications for the Eighties.* Washington, D.C.: U.S. Government Printing Office.

Newcomb, T. M. 1943. *Personality and Social Change: Attitude Formation in a Student Community.* New York: Dryden Press.

Newcomb, T. M., K. Koenig, R. Flacks, and D. Warnick. 1967. *Persistence and Change: Bennington College and its Students After 25 Years.* New York: John Wiley.

Nichols, P. C. 1984. "Networks and Hierarchies: Language and Social Stratification." In C. Kramarae, M. Schulz, and W. M. O'Barr (Eds.), *Language and Power* (pp. 23–42). Beverly Hills, CA: Sage.

Nosanchuk. T. A., and B. H. Erickson. 1985. "How High Is Up? Calibrating Social

Comparison in the Real World." *Journal of Personality and Social Psychology* 48:624–634.

Offermann, L. 1986. "Visibility and Evaluation of Female and Male Leaders." *Sex Roles* 14:533–544.

O'Kane, J. M., L. Barenblatt, P. K. Jensen, and L. T. Cochran. 1977. "Anticipatory Socialization and Male Catholic Adolescent Socio-Political Attitudes." *Sociometry* 40:67–77.

Osgood, C. E. 1966. "Dimensionality of the Semantic Space for Communication Via Facial Expression. *Scandanavian Journal of Psychology* 7:1–30.

Owens, G., and J. G. Ford. 1978. "Further Consideration of the 'What is Good is Beautiful' Finding." *Social Psychology* 41:73–75.

Palmer, S. 1960. *The Psychology of Murder.* New York: Crowell.

Pantin, H. M., and C. S. Carver. 1982. "Induced Competence and the Bystander Effect." *Journal of Applied Social Psychology* 12:100–111.

Parker, S., and R. J. Kleiner. 1968. "Reference Group Behavior and Mental Disorder." In H. H. Hyman and E. Singer (Eds.), *Readings in Reference Group Theory and Research.* New York: Free Press.

Parsons, T. 1951. *The Social System.* Glencoe, IL: Free Press.

Parsons, T. 1964. *Social Structure and Personality.* New York: Free Press.

Pearce, P. L. 1980. "Strangers, Travelers, and Greyhound Terminals: A Study of Small-Scale Helping Behaviors." *Journal of Personality and Social Psychology* 38:935–940.

Perrin, A., and R. L. Spencer. 1980. "The Asch Effect—A Child of its Time? *Bulletin of the British Psychology Society* 32:405–406.

Pettigrew, T. F. 1958. "Personality and Sociocultural Factors in Intergroup Attitudes." *Journal of Conflict Resolution* 2:29–42.

Phillips, D. P. 1979. "Suicide, Motor Vehicle Fatalities, and the Mass Media: Evidence toward a Theory of Suggestion." *American Journal of Sociology* 84:1150–1174.

Phillips, D. P. 1980. "Airplane Accidents, Murder, and the Mass Media: Towards a Theory of Imitation and Suggestion." *Social Forces* 58:1001–1024.

Phillips, D. P. 1983. "The Impact of Mass Media Violence on U.S. Homicides." *American Sociological Review* 48:560–568.

Piaget, J. 1948. *The Moral Judgment of the Child.* New York: Free Press.

Piliavin, I. M., J. A. Piliavin, and J. Rodin. 1975. "Costs, Diffusion, and the Stigmatized Victim." *Journal of Personality and Social Psychology* 32:429–438.

Piliavin, I. M., J. Rodin, and J. A. Piliavin. 1969. "Good Samaritanism: An Underground Phenomenon?" *Journal of Personality and Social Psychology* 13:289–299.

Piliavin, J. A., J. F. Dovideo, S. L. Gaertner, and R. D. Clark III. 1981. *Emergency Intervention.* New York: Academic Press.

Porter, N., and F. Geis. 1980. "Women and Nonverbal Leadership Cues: When Seeing is Not Believing." In C. Mayo and N. Henley (Eds.), *Gender and Nonverbal Behavior.* New York: Springer-Verlag.

Powell, G. N. and D. A. Butterfield. 1979. "The 'Good Manager': Masculine or Androgenous?" *Academy of Management Journal* 22:395-403.

Priest, R. F., and J. Sawyer. 1967. "Proximity and Peership: Basis of Balance in Interpersonal Attraction." *American Journal of Sociology* 72:633-649.

Pugh, M. D. and R. Wahrman. 1983. "Neutralizing Sexism in Mixed-Sex Groups." *American Journal of Sociology* 88:746-762.

Quanty, M. B., J. A. Keats, and S. G. Harkins. 1975. "Prejudice and Criteria for Identification of Ethnic Photographs." *Journal of Personality and Social Psychology* 32:449-454.

Quarantelli, E. L., and J. Cooper. 1966. "Self-Conceptions of Others: A Further Test of Meadian Hypotheses." *Sociological Quarterly* 7:281-297.

Raden, D. 1985. "Strength-Related Attitude Dimensions." *Social Psychology Quarterly* 48:312-330.

Raffler-Engel, W. 1983. *Nonverbal Behavior in the Career Interview.* Philadelphia: John Benjamins.

Rees, C. R., and M. W. Segal. 1984. "Intragroup Competition, Equity, and Interpersonal Attraction." *Social Psychology Quarterly* 47:328-336.

Reich, M. 1972. "The Economics of Racism." In R. C. Edwards, M. Reich, and T. E. Weisskopf (Eds.), *The Capitalist System.* Englewood Cliffs, NJ: Prentice-Hall.

Richman, J. 1977. "The Foolishness and Wisdom of Age: Attitudes Toward the Elderly as Reflected in Jokes." *The Gerontologist* 17:210-219.

Ridgeway, C. L., J. Berger, and L. Smith. 1985. "Nonverbal Cues and Status: An Expectation States Approach." *American Journal of Sociology* 90:955-979.

Riesman, D. 1950. *The Lonely Crowd.* New Haven, CT: Yale University Press.

Riskind, J. H. 1984. "They Stoop to Conquer: Guiding and Self-Regulatory Functions of Physical Posture After Success and Failure." *Journal of Personality and Social Psychology* 47:479-493.

Ritzer, G. 1975 *Sociology: A Multiple Paradigm Science.* Boston: Allyn and Bacon.

Rodin, J., and E. Langer. 1980. "Aging Labels: The Decline of Control and the Fall of Self Esteem." *Journal of Social Issues* 36:12-29.

Rokeach, M. 1960. *The Open and Closed Mind.* New York: Basic Books.

Rosa, E., and A. Mazur. 1979. "Incipient Status in Groups." *Social Forces* 58:18-37.

Rose, A. 1962. *Human Behavior and Social Processes.* Boston: Houghton Mifflin.

Rosenberg, M. 1979. *Conceiving the Self.* New York: Basic Books.

Rosenhan, D. L. 1970. "The Natural Socialization of Altruistic Autonomy." In

Altruism and Helping Behavior. J. Macaulay and L. Berkowitz (Eds.). New York: Academic Press.

Rosenhan, D. L. 1973. "On Being Sane in Insane Places." *Science* 179:250–258.

Rosnow, R. L. 1972. "Poultry and Prejudice." *Psychology Today* March: 53–56.

Rubin, I. M. 1967. "Increased Self-Acceptance: A Means of Reducing Prejudice." *Journal of Personality and Social Psychology* 5:233–238.

Rubin, Z. 1970. "Measurement of Romantic Love." *Journal of Personality and Social Psychology* 16:265–273.

Rusbult, C. E. 1983. "A Longitudinal Test of the Investment Model: The Development (and Deterioration) of Satisfaction and Commitment in Heterosexual Involvements." *Journal of Personality and Social Psychology* 45:101–117.

Rushton, J. P. 1982. "Altruism and Society: A Social Learning Perspective." *Ethics* 92:425–446.

Russ, R. C., J. A. Gold, and W. F. Stone. 1979. "Attraction to a Dissimilar Stranger as a Function of Level of Effectance Arousal." *Journal of Experimental Social Psychology* 15:481–492.

Russell, G. W. 1983. "Psychological Issues in Sports Aggression." In J. H. Goldstein (Ed.), *Sports Violence*. New York: Springer-Verlag.

Rysman, A. 1977. "How the 'Gossip' Became a Woman." *Journal of Communication* 27:176–180.

Sachs, P. R. 1982. "Avoidance of Diagnostic Information in Self-Evaluation of Ability." *Personality and Social Psychology Bulletin* 8:242–246.

Sagan, E. 1974. *Cannibalism: Human Aggression and Cultural Form*. New York: Harper Torchbooks.

Sanders, G. S., and T. Schmidt. 1980. "Behavioral Discrimination Against Women." *Personality and Social Psychology Bulletin* 6:484–488.

Sarbin, T. R. 1976. *Contextualism: A World View for Modern Psychology*. Vol. 24 in Nebraska Symposium on Motivation. Lincoln, NE: University of Nebraska Press.

Schafer, R. B., and P. M. Keith. 1985. "A Causal Model Approach to the Symbolic Interactionist View of the Self-Concept." *Journal of Personality and Social Psychology* 48:963–969.

Scheibe, K. E. 1985. Pp. 33–64. In B. R. Schlenker (Ed.), *The Self and Social Life*. New York: McGraw-Hill.

Schlenker, B. R. 1985. *The Self and Social Life*. New York: McGraw-Hill.

Schmitt, R. L. 1972. *The Reference Other Orientation: An Extension of the Reference Group Concept*. Carbondale, IL: Southern Illinois University Press.

Schramm, W. 1972. "How Communication Works." In Alan Wells (Ed.), *Mass Media in Society*, (pp. 182–190). Palo Alto, CA: National Press Books.

Schulz, M. R. 1975. "The Semantic Derogation of Women." In B. Thorne and N. Henley (Eds.), *Language and Sex* (pp. 64–75). Rowley, MA: Newbury House.

Sears, D. O., and H. M. Allen. 1984. "The Trajectory of Local Desegregation Controversies and Whites' Opposition to Busing." In *Groups in Contact*. N. Miller and M. Brewer (Eds.). New York: Academic Press.

Sears, D. O., and D. R. Kinder. 1985. "Whites' Opposition to Busing: On Conceptualizing and Operationalizing Group Conflict." *Journal of Personality and Social Psychology* 48:1141–1147.

Segal, M. W. 1974. "Alphabet and Attraction: An Unobtrusive Measure of the Effect of Propinquity in a Field Setting." *Journal of Personality and Social Psychology* 30:654–657.

Selznick, G. J., and S. Steinberg. 1969. *The Tenacity of Prejudice*. New York: Harper and Row.

Serpe, R. T. 1987. "Stability and Change in Self: A Structural Symbolic Interactionist Explanation." *Social Psychology Quarterly* 50:44–55.

Shaffer, D. R., M. Rogel and C. Hendrick. 1975. "Intervention in the Library." *Journal of Applied Social Psychology* 5:303–319.

Shamir, B. 1986. "Self-Esteem and the Psychological Impact of Unemployment." *Social Psychology Quarterly* 49:61–71.

Shanteau, J., and G. F. Nagy. 1979. "Probability of Acceptance in Dating Choice." *Journal of Personality and Social Psychology* 37:522–533.

Shapiro, E. G. 1980. "Is Seeking Help from a Friend Like Seeking Help from a Stranger?" *Social Psychology Quarterly* 43:259–263.

Shaw, M. E., and P. R. Costanzo. 1982. *Theories of Social Psychology*. New York: McGraw-Hill.

Sherif, M. 1936. *The Psychology of Social Norms*. New York: Harper and Row.

Sherif, M., and C. W. Sherif. 1961. *Intergroup Conflicts and Cooperation: The Robbers Cave Experiment*. Norman, OK: Institute of Intergroup Relations, University of Oklahoma.

Sherif, M., and C. W. Sherif. 1969. *Social Psychology*. New York: Harper and Row.

Sherohman, J. 1977. "Conceptual and Methodological Issues in the Study of Role-Taking Accuracy." *Symbolic Interaction* 1:121–131.

Sherrod, D. R., and R. Downs. 1974. "Environmental Determinants of Altruism: The Effects of Stimulus Overload and Perceived Control on Helping." *Journal of Experimental Social Psychology* 10:468–479.

Shibutani, T. 1972. "Reference Groups as Perspectives." In J. G. Manis and B. Meltzer (Eds.), *Symbolic Interaction: A Reader in Social Psychology*. Boston: Allyn and Bacon.

Shotland, R. L., and L. Goodstein. 1983. "Just Because She Doesn't Want to Doesn't

Mean it's Rape: An Experimentally Based Causal Model of Rape in a Dating Situation." *Social Psychology Quarterly* 46:220–232.

Shrauger, J. S., and T. J. Schoeneman. 1979. "Symbolic Interactionist View of Self-Concept: Through the Looking Glass Darkly." *Psychological Bulletin* 86:549–573.

Sigelman, L., C. K. Sigelman, and C. Fowler. 1987. "A Bird of a Different Feather? An Experimental Investigation of Physical Attractiveness and the Electibility of Female Candidates." *Social Psychology Quarterly* 50:32–43.

Silverstein, B., L. Perdue, B. Peterson, and E. Kelly. 1986. "The Role of the Mass Media in Promoting a Thin Standard of Bodily Attractiveness for Women." *Sex Roles* 14:519–532.

Simpson, G. E., and J. M. Yinger. 1986. *Racial and Cultural Minorities*. New York: Plenum Press.

Singer, E. 1981. "Reference Groups and Social Evaluations." In M. Rosenberg and R. H. Turner (Eds.), *Social Psychology: Sociological Perspectives*. New York: Basic Books.

Sipes, R. G. 1973. "War, Sports, and Aggression: An Empirical Test of Two Rival Theories." *American Anthropologist* 75:64–86.

Sivacek, J., and W. D. Crano. 1982. "Vested Interest as a Moderator of Attitude-Behavior Consistency." *Journal of Personality and Social Psychology* 43:210–21.

Skinner, B. F. 1957. *Verbal Behavior*. New York: Appleton-Century-Crofts.

Skinner, B. F. 1971. *Beyond Freedom and Dignity*. New York: Knopf.

Smith, E. R., and J. R. Kluegel. 1984. "Beliefs and Attitudes About Women's Opportunity: Comparisons with Beliefs About Blacks and a General Perspective." *Social Psychology Quarterly* 47:81–95.

Smith, M. D. 1979. "Social Determinants of Violence in Hockey: A Review. *Canadian Journal of Applied Sport Sciences* 4:76–82.

Snow, D. A., and C. L. Phillips. 1982. "The Changing Self-Orientations of College Students: From Institution to Impulse." *Social Science Quarterly* 63:462–476.

Snyder, C. R., and Fromkin, H. L. 1980. *Uniqueness: The Human Pursuit of Difference*. New York: Plenum Press.

Snyder, M., E. D. Tanke, and E. Berscheid. 1977. "Social Perception and Interpersonal Behavior: On the Self-Fulfilling Nature of Social Stereotypes." *Journal of Personality and Social Psychology* 35:656–666.

Sole, K., J. Marton, and H. A. Hornstein. 1975. "Opinion Similarity and Helping: Three Field Experiments Investigating the Bases of Promotive Tension." *Journal of Experimental Social Psychology* 11:1–13.

Stang, D. J. 1976. "Group Size Effects on Conformity." *Journal of Social Psychology* 98:175–181.

Steiner, I. D., and H. H. Johnson. 1963. "Authoritarianism and Conformity." *Sociometry* March:21–34.

Stember, C. H. 1961. *Education and Attitude Change: The Effect of Schooling on Prejudice Against Minority Groups.* Washington, D. C.: Institute of Human Relations.

Stephan, W. G. 1986. "The Effects of School Desegregation." In R. Kidd, L. Saxe, and M. Saxe (Eds.), *Advances in Applied Social Psychology.* New York: Erlbaum.

Stephan, C. W., and J. H. Langiois. 1984. "Baby Beautiful: Adult Attributions of Infant Competence as a Function of Infant Attractiveness." *Child Development* 55:576–585.

Storr, A. 1968. *Human Aggression.* New York: Atheneum.

Straus, M., R. Gelles, and S. Steinmetz. 1980. *Behind Closed Doors: Violence in the American Family.* Garden City, NY: Anchor/Doubleday.

Strauss, H. M. 1968. "Reference Group and Social Comparison Processes Among the Totally Blind." In H. H. Hyman and E. Singer (Eds.), *Readings in Reference Group Theory and Research.* New York: Free Press.

Strube, M. J., C. L. Lott, G. M. Le-Xuan-Hy, J. Oxenberg, and A. Deichmann. 1986. "Self-Evaluation of Abilities: Accurate Self-Assessment Versus Biased Self-Enhancement." *Journal of Personality and Social Psychology* 51:16–25.

Stryker, S. 1956. "Relationships of Married Offspring and Parent: A Test of Mead's Theory." *American Journal of Sociology* 62:308–319.

Sutherland, E. H. 1924. *Criminology.* Philadelphia: J. B. Lippincott.

Takooshian, H., S. Haber, and D. J. Lucido. 1977. "Who Wouldn't Help a Lost Child? You Maybe." *Psychology Today* 10 (February):67–68.

Tallichet, S. E., and F. K. Willits. 1986. "Gender-Role Attitude Change of Young Women: Influential Factors from a Panel Study." *Social Psychology Quarterly* 49:219–227.

Tan, A. S. 1979. "TV Beauty Ads and Role Expectations of Adolescent Female Viewers." *Journalism Quarterly.* 53:271–279.

Taylor, D. G., P. B. Sheatsley, and A. M. Greeley. 1978. "Attitudes Toward Racial Integration." *Scientific American* 238:42–49.

Taylor, S. E. 1981. "A Categorization Approach to Stereotyping." In D. L. Hamilton (Ed.), *Cognitive Processes in Stereotyping and Intergroup Behavior.* Hillsdale, NJ: Erlbaum.

Taylor, S. E., and H. Falcone. 1982. "Cognitive Bases of Stereotyping: The Relationship between Categorization and Prejudice." *Personality and Social Psychology Bulletin* 8:426–432.

Terrace, H. 1984. *Language in Apes.* New York: Academic Press.

Thibaut, J. W., and H. H. Kelley. 1959. *The Social Psychology of Groups.* New York: John Wiley.

Thomas, W. I., and D. S. Thomas. 1928. *The Child in America*. New York: Knopf.

Thorne, B., and N. Henley. 1975. *Language and Sex*. Rowley, MA: Newbury House.

Triandis, H. C., and L. M. Triandis. 1972. "Some Studies of Social Distance." In J. Brigham and T. Weissbach (Eds.), *Racial Attitudes in America*. New York: Harper and Row.

Turner, R. 1986. *The Structure of Sociological Theory*. Chicago: Dorsey Press.

Turner, R. H. 1956. "Role-Taking, Role Standpoint, and Reference Group Behavior." *American Journal of Sociology* 61:316–328.

Turner, R. H. 1962. "Role-Taking: Process Versus Conformity." In A. Rose (Ed.), *Human Behavior and Social Processes* (pp. 20–40). Boston: Houghton Mifflin.

Turner, R. H. 1976. "The Real Self: From Institution to Impulse." *American Journal of Sociology* 81:989–1016.

Turner, R. H. 1978. "The Role and the Person." *American Journal of Sociology* 84:1–23.

Valenti, A., and L. Downing. 1975. "Differential Effects of Jury Size on Verdicts following Deliberation as a Function of the Apparent Guilt of a Defendant." *Journal of Personality and Social Psychology* 32:655–663.

Van Oudenhoven, J. P., and F. Siero. 1985. "Evaluative Feedback as a Determinant of the Pygmalion Effect." *Psychological Reports* 57:755–761.

Vander Zanden, J. W. 1983. *American Minority Relations*. New York: Knopf.

Vernon, C. and B. S. Stewart. 1957. "Empathy as a Process in the Dating Relationship." *American Sociological Review* 22:48–52.

Verplanck, W. S. 1955. "The Control of the Content of Conversation: Reinforcement of Statements of Opinions." *Journal of Abnormal and Social Psychology* 51:668–676.

Vidmar, N., and M. Rokeach. 1974. "Archie Bunker's Bigotry: A Study in Selective Perception and Exposure." *Journal of Communication* 24:36–47.

Walster, E., E. Aronson, D. Abrahams, and L. Rottman. 1966. "Importance of Physical Attractiveness in Dating Behavior." *Journal of Personality and Social Psychology* 4:508–516.

Walster, E., and G. W. Walster. 1963. "Effect of Expecting to be Liked on Choice Associates." *Journal of Abnormal and Social Psychology* 67:402–404.

Walster, E., and G. W. Walster. 1970. "The Matching Hypothesis." Unpublished Manuscript. University of Wisconsin.

Walster, E., G. W. Walster, and J. Traupmann. 1978. "Equity and Premarital Sex." *Journal of Personality and Social Psychology* 36:82–92.

Weber, M. 1905, 1958. *The Protestant Ethic and the Spirit of Capitalism*. (T. Parsons, trans.) New York: Scribner.

Webster, M. Jr., and J. E. Driskell, Jr. 1983. "Beauty as Status." *American Journal of Sociology* 89:140–165.

Watson, M. W. and T. Amgott-Kwan. 1984. "Development of Family-Role Concepts in School-Age Children." *Developmental Psychology* 20:953–959.

Weitz, S. 1974. *Nonverbal Communication.* New York: Oxford University Press.

Werner, C. and P. Parmalee. 1979. "Similarity of Activity Preferences Among Friends." *Social Psychology Quarterly* 42:62–66.

West, C., and D. H. Zimmerman. 1977. "Women's Place in Everyday Talk: Reflections of Parent-Child Interaction." *Social Problems* 24:521–528.

Westie, F. R. 1964. "Race and Ethnic Relations." In R. E. L. Faris (Ed.), *Handbook of Modern Sociology.* Skokie, IL: Rand McNally.

Wexler, J. G. 1985. "Role Styles of Women Police Officers." *Sex Roles* 12:749–755.

White, G. L. 1980. "Physical Attractiveness and Courtship Progress." *Journal of Personality and Social Psychology* 39:660–668.

Whitehead III, G. I., S. H. Smith, and J. A. Eichorn. 1982. "The Effect of Subject's Race and Other's Race on Judgments of Causality for Success and Failure." *Journal of Personality* 50:193–202.

Whittaker, J. O., and R. D. Meade. 1967. "Sex and Age as Variables in Persuasibility." *Journal of Social Psychology* 73:47–52.

Whorf, B. L. 1956. *Language, Thought and Reality.* Cambridge, MA: MIT Press.

Wicker, A. W. 1969. "Attitudes Versus Actions: The Relationship of Verbal and Overt Behavioral Responses to Attitude Objects." *Journal of Social Issues* 25:41–78.

Williams. R. M., Jr. 1947. *The Reduction of Intergroup Tensions.* Bulletin No. 57. New York: Social Science Research Council.

Wilson, S. R., and L. A. Benner. 1971. "The Effects of Self Esteem and Situation upon Comparison Choices During Ability Evaluation." *Sociometry* 34:381–397.

Witkin, H. A., S. Mednick, F. Schulsinger, E. Bakkestrom, K. Christianson, D. Goodenough, K. Hirschorn, C. Lundsteen, D. Owen, J. Phillip, D. Rubin, and M. Stocking. 1976. "Criminality in XYY and XXY Men." *Science* August:547–555.

Wolfgang, M. E. 1958. *Patterns in Criminal Homicide.* New York: John Wiley.

Wolfgang, M. E., and F. Ferracuti. 1967. *The Subculture of Violence.* London: Tavistock.

Wood, B. 1981. *Children and Communication: Verbal and Nonverbal Language Development.* Englewood Cliffs, NJ: Prentice-Hall.

Wood, J. T. 1986. "Different Voices in Relationship Crises." *American Behavioral Scientist* 29:273–301.

Wrong, D. H. 1961. "The Oversocialized Conception of Man in Modern Sociology." *American Sociological Review* 26:183–193.

Yarkin, K. L., J. P. Town, and B. S. Wallston. 1982. "Blacks and Women Must Try Harder: Stimulus Person's Race and Sex Attributions of Causality." *Personality and Social Psychology Bulletin* 8:21–24.

Yinon, Y., and A. Bizman. 1980. "Noise, Success, and Failure as Determinants of Helping Behavior." *Personality and Social Psychology Bulletin* 6:125–130.

Zander, A., and A. Havelin. 1960. "Social Comparison and Interpersonal Attraction." *Human Relations* 13:21–32.

Zanna, M. P., E. T. Higgins, and C. P. Herman. 1982. *Consistency in Social Behavior*. Hillsdale, NJ: Erlbaum.

Zimbardo, P. C. 1969. "The Human Choice: Individuation, Reason, and Order Versus Deindividuation, Impulse and Chaos." In W. Arnold and D. Levine (Eds.), *Nebraska Symposium on Motivation* 17:237–307.

Zimbardo, P. C., C. Haney, and W. C. Banks. 1973. "A Pirandellian Prison." *New York Times Magazine*, April 8.

Zimmerman, D. H. and C. West. 1975. "Sex Roles, Interruptions and Silences in Conversations." In B. Thorne and N. Henley (Eds.), *Language and Sex* (pp. 105–129). Rowley, MA: Newbury House.

Zurcher, L. A. 1972. "The Mutable Self: An Adaptation to Accelerated Socio-Cultural Change." *Et al.* 3:3–15.

Zurcher, L. A. 1977. *The Mutable Self: A Self-Concept for Social Change*. Beverly Hills, CA: Sage.

Zurcher, L. A. 1983. *Social Roles: Conformity, Conflict and Creativity*. Beverley Hills, CA: Sage.

Zurcher, L. A. 1983a. "Filling a Role Void: Volunteers in a Disaster Work Crew." In Louis A. Zurcher (Ed.), *Social Roles: Conformity, Conflict and Creativity* (pp. 113–134). Beverly Hills, CA: Sage.

Zurcher, L. A. 1983b. "Transforming an Accustomed Role: Priests in a Protest Movement and Felons in a Parole System." In Louis A. Zurcher (Ed.), *Social Roles: Conformity, Conflict and Creativity*. (pp. 211–222) Beverley Hills, CA: Sage.

Zurcher, L. A., D. W. Sonenschein, and E. L. Metzner. 1966. "The Hasher: A Study in Role Conflict." *Social Forces* 44:505–514.

Index

Active self, 18
Adorno, T. W., 238, 243, 244, 246
Aggression, 195-221
  biology and, 203-6
  catharsis of, 213-17
  causes of, 202-13
  definition, 196-99
  displaced, 240-42
  frustration and, 206-12
  in crowds, 200-2
  in family, 217-18
  in sports, 213-17
  murder as, 200, 201-2, 208-10, 211, 212, 213, 214-15
  social learning and, 218-20
  situation and, 197-99
  types of, 199-200
Ajzen, I., 232, 235
Akers, R. L., 87
Allen, H. M., 227
Allport, G. W., 250, 255
Altruism, 282-88 (see Helping)
Amato, P. R., 275
Amgott-Kwan, T., 169
Anastos, E., 83
Anticonformity, 85
Argyle, M., 147, 152, 154
Arkin, R., 21
Arluke, A., 19-20, 35, 68, 228-29, 269-70
Arms, R. L., 215-16
Aronson, E., 254
Arvey, R. D., 265
Asch, S., 76-79, 84
Attitude similarity, 268-70
Attraction, 262-71
  exchange of rewards and, 270-71
  physical attractiveness and, 263-67
  physical closeness and, 262-63
  similarity and, 267-70
Attribution theory, 21-22
Authoritarian personality, 238, 243-44, 245-46, 256-58
Authority, 79-81
Autokinetic phenomenon, 76-77, 87
Azrin, N. H., 207

Bachman, J. G., 109
Back, K.W., 263
Baer, R. S., 85
Bandura, A., 12, 219-20, 281
Banks, W. C., 171
Baratz, J. C., 145
Barenblatt, L., 90
Barnes, J. A., 43
Barnett, M. A., 284
Baron, R. A., 149
Bar-Tal, D., 265
Bashner, R. S., 255
Batson, C. D., 287
Beck, E. M., 248
Becker, H. S., 19, 55-57, 58, 59, 70, 90
Becker, J. A., 137
Beeghley, L., 107
Begley, P. J., 265
Behaviorism, 9-10
Bem, D. J., 234, 249
Bem, S. L., 249
Benner, L. A., 102
Berkowitz, L., 210, 240, 264, 274
Berndt, T. J., 230
Berscheid. E., 264, 265, 266
Birdwhistell, R. L., 127, 146
Bizman, A., 275
Blau, P. M., 270
Blauner, R., 242
Block, J., 239
Blumer, H., 18, 167, 168, 200
Bobo, L., 247
Bock, E. W., 107
Bohrnstedt, G., 34, 267
Bonacich, E., 248
Boring, E. G., 212
Boswell, D. A., 33
Bourne, R., 70, 217, 218, 252
Boyanowsky, E. D., 210
Bragonier, P., 100
Braly, K., 225, 227
Brehm, J. W., 85
Brehm, S. S., 85
Brion-Meisels, S., 284
Brockner, J., 263
Brody, E., 226
Brown, R. A., 125
Bugelski, R., 241
Bull, P., 148
Burgess, R. L., 87
Burke, P. J., 151, 241
Burkey, R. M., 251

Burnstein, E., 240
Buss, A. H., 64, 67, 68, 96
Butterfield, D. A., 229
Byrne, D., 257, 263, 268, 270
Bystander effect, 276-82

Callero, P. L., 191-92
Campbell, D. T., 286
Cannibalism, 203-5
Carli, L. L., 84
Carnevale, P. J., 271
Carrington, P. I., 271
Carver, C. S., 95-96, 280, 281, 282
Cash, T. F., 265
Catharsis, 213-17
Chanowitz, B., 255
Chapko, M., 245
Chomsky, N., 133-35
Christie, R., 246
Cialdini, R. B., 105
Clark, K. B., 43
Clark, M. L., 43
Clark, M. P., 43
Clifford, M., 264
Clore, G., 269, 270
Cochran, L. T., 90
Coffman, T. L., 226, 227
Cognitive dissonance, 233-34
Cognitive theory, 21
Cohen, A. K., 213
Coleman, J. S., 253
Collins, M. E., 252-53
Communication, 115-57
  definition, 116-17
  human vs. nonhuman, 122-25
  language and, 119-46
  meaning and symbols in, 119-30
  nonverbal, 146-56
  significant symbols in, 129
  social order and, 116-19
Comstock, G. S., 219
Conditioning, 10
Condran, J. G., 226
Conformity, 75-88
  and culture, 82-85
  and deviance, 87-88
  as group pressure, 76-79
  as yielding to authority, 79-81
  in disguise, 85-87
  outside the lab, 81-82

Conger, J. J., 264
Cook, S. W., 253
Cooley, C. H., 28, 29
Cooper, H., 21, 84
Cooper, J., 31-32
Coser, L. A., 241
Costanzo, P. R., 21
Costin, F., 269
Counterculture, 87
Cowen, E. L., 241
Cowgill, D. O., 228
Crano, W. D., 235
Crofton, C., 267
Crosby, F., 141, 143
Crowds, 200-2
Culture, 12, 82-85
Cummings, S., 247

Daniels, L. R., 274
Darley, J. M., 100, 274, 276, 278, 279, 280
Darwin, C., 151
Davis, J. A., 100, 109
Davis, L., 83
Dawkins, R., 286
Dean, J., 152
Deaux, K., 265
Definition of the situation, 16-17
Deindividuation, 202
Dependent variable, 2, 8
Derbyshire, R. L., 226
Dermer, M., 265
Deutsch, M., 78, 252-53
Deviance, 69-70, 87-88
  labeling and, 69-70
Dicks, H. V., 82
Diener, E. R., 202
Differential association theory, 87
Diffusion of responsibility, 278-81
Dino, G. A., 284
Dion, K. K., 264, 265
Dipboye, R. L., 265
Discrimination (see Prejudice)
Distributive justice, 11
Dollard, J., 206
Doob, L. W., 206
Dornbusch, S., 31-32
Douglas, J. D., 111
Downing, L., 79
Downs, R., 275
Dramaturgical model, 65-66
Drass, K. A., 150, 151
Driskell, J. E., 265
Duncan, S., 142

Eagly, A. H., 84, 153, 233
Eckman, P., 148
Edwards, A. I., 32
Ehrlich, H. J., 225, 237
Eibl-Eibesfeldt, I., 147
Eichorn, J. A., 250
Eisen, M., 36
Eisenman, R., 256
Elliott, G. C., 62
Elman, M. R., 174-76
Embarrassment, 66-68

Erickson, B. H., 103, 105
Erikson, E. H., 48-51, 55
Ethnomethodology, 20-21
Ethology, 205
Exchange theory, 10-11
Experiment, 8-9

Falcone, H., 237, 238
Feagin, C. B., 233
Feagin, J. R., 233
Fellman, B., 286
Felson, R. B., 34, 35, 91, 105, 267
Fenigstein, A., 96
Ferracuti, F., 213
Festinger, L., 92, 100, 103, 113, 233, 263, 268
Fine, G. A., 35, 153
Fireman, B., 85
Fischer, D. H., 228
Fishbein, M., 232, 235
Fishman, J. A., 129
Folb, E. A., 144
Ford, J. G., 267
Form, W. H., 280
Forman, E. A., 284
Fox, J. A., 87, 200, 208, 213
Freud, S., 43-49, 203-4, 261
Freudian stages of development, 44-47
Frey, D. L., 227
Friedrich, D. W., 148
Friesen, W. V., 148
Frodi, A., 264
Fromkin, H. L., 268
Fromm, E., 206
Frustration-aggression, 206-12, 240

Gaertner, S. L., 227
Gambino, R., 201-2
Game, 41-42
Gamson, W. A., 85
Garcia, L., 256-257
Gardner, B. T., 124-25
Gardner, R. A., 124-25
Garfinkel, H., 20-21
Gecas, V., 34
Geen, R. G., 240
Geer, B., 19
Geis, F., 230
Gelles, R. J., 217, 218
Generalized other, 32, 41, 74
George, S. G., 78
Gerbner, G., 98-99
Gerard, H. B., 78
Gergen, K. J., 33, 62-63
Gergen, M. M. 33
Gerson, J. M., 167
Gifford, R., 149
Gilbert, L. A., 174-76
Gilligan, C., 137
Glazer, N., 252
Glenn, N. D., 248
Goethals, G. R., 100
Goffman, E., 59-60, 65-66, 67-69, 95, 102, 146-47, 152, 155, 192
Gold, J. A., 268
Goldberg, P., 231

Goldstein, J. H., 207, 212, 213, 215
Gonzalez, M. H., 268
Goode, E., 70
Goode, W. S., 173
Goodstein, L., 199
Gormly, J., 268
Gossip, 19-20, 228-29
Gottlieb, J., 280
Gouldner, A., 273-74
Grabb, E. G., 226
Granfield, R., 57-58
Grant, G., 43
Grant, P. R., 227
Greeley, A. M., 226
Griffiths, C. T., 210
Griffitt, W., 256-57
Gross, A. E., 267
Gross, E., 67
Gross, N., 174, 180-83
Grossman, J. C., 256
Group pressure, 75-79
Grubb, H. J., 144
Gruder, C. L., 102
Grush, J. E., 268, 269
Gutierres, S. E., 104

Haber, S., 274-75
Haimowitz, M. L., 255
Haimowitz, N. R., 255
Hakmiller, K. L., 102
Hall, E. T., 154
Hallinan, M. T., 248
Hamblin, R. L., 253
Hamilton, D. L., 237
Hamilton, W. D., 286
Handel, W., 129, 169
Haney, C., 171
Harkins, S. G., 239
Harper, R. G., 151, 152
Harrison, R. P., 130
Hart, R. P., 148
Harvey, J. H., 21
Havelin, A., 267
Hays, R. B., 263, 270
Heiss, J., 160
Heller, K. A., 230
Helping, 271-88
  biology and, 285-88
  bystander effect and, 276-82
  costs of, 271-73
  Good Samaritan and, 283-84
  in cities, 274-75
  norms for, 273-74
  personal competence and, 281-82
  role taking and, 284-85
Hendrick, C., 280
Henley, N., 139
Hepburn, C., 249
Himmelfarb, S., 233
Hoffman, M. L., 219, 284, 287
Holmes, D. S., 241
Holmes, J., 137, 227
Holmes, L., 228
Homans, G., 11, 270
Hong, L., 25
Hornstein, H. A., 273

Howard, J. A., 284
Hraba, J., 43
Hudson, L. M., 284
Hudson, R. A., 139
Hughes, M., 99
Humphries, C., 95-96
Huston, T. L., 281-82
Hyman, H. H., 88, 92, 101

"I," 29-30, 36, 47
Immediate situation, 7-12
Imitation, 40-41
Impression management, 64
Independent variable, 2, 8
Innes, J. M., 204
Insko, C. A., 263

Jackson, M. R., 258
Jahoda, M., 246
James, W., 62
Jennings, L. B., 78
Jensen, P. K., 90
Jewson, J., 145
Johnson, H. H., 238
Jones, E., 271
Jones, E. E., 237

Kagan, J., 264
Kandel, D. B., 268
Kanin, E., 198
Karlins, M., 226, 227
Karp, D. A., 42
Karylowski, J., 268
Katz, D., 225, 227, 236, 237
Keats, J. A., 239
Keith, P. M., 33
Keller, H., 125
Kelley, H. H., 91, 270
Kelly, E., 104
Kenrick, D. T., 104
Kerckhoff, A. C., 268
Kerr, N., 275
Key, M. R., 129, 140
Kiesler, C. A., 75
Kiesler, S. B., 75
Kinder, D. R., 247
King, L. M., 284
King, M. B., 239
King, W., 240
Kleiner, R. J., 104
Klockars, A. J., 32
Kluegel, J. R., 250, 251
Knapp, M. L., 130
Kochman, T., 144
Koenig, F. W., 239
Kohlberg, L., 51, 53-54
Kolditz, T., 21
Korte, C., 275
Kramarae, C., 139
Krebs, D., 287
Ksionsky, S., 267
Kuhn, M. H., 35-36, 55
Kuhn, T., 21

Labeling theory, 69-70
Laboff, W., 143, 144, 145
LaGumina, S. J., 247

Lakoff, R., 137, 140, 141, 142
Lamy, P., 88
Landes, J., 241
Landy, D., 265
Langer, E. J., 70, 255
Langfeld, H. S., 212
Langiois, J. H., 265
Language, 119-46
 acquisition of, 129-38
 in everyday use, 138-46
 meaning, symbols and, 119-30
LaPiere, R. T., 232
Larsen, K., 83
Latane, B., 274, 276, 278, 279, 280
Lau, R. R., 63
Lauer, R. H., 129, 169
Lawton, M. P., 263
LeBon, G., 202
Leibowitz, L., 205
Leo, J., 2
Leong, W., 112
LePage, A., 211-12
Lepper, M. R., 63
Levin, J., 19-20, 35, 68, 70, 87, 88, 100, 109, 112, 200, 208, 213, 217, 218, 228, 229, 235, 246, 250, 252, 269-70
Levin, W. C., 100, 109, 228, 235, 246, 250
Levitt, E. A., 153
Lewis, J. M., 215
Lewis, L. L., 265
Lewis, M., 245
Lifton, R. J., 61-62
Linton, R., 163
Lippman, W., 225
Liska, A. E., 70, 235
Locksley, A., 249
London, P., 283
Looking-glass self, 28, 34, 71
Lorenz, K., 205-6, 261
Lucido, D. J., 274-75
Luckmann, T., 117

Mancuso, J. C., 33
Mann, L., 204, 215
Marsh, H. W., 100
Martin, J., 238
Marton, J., 273
Marx, K., 16
Mason, W. A., 174, 180-83
Mathes, E. W., 264
Mazur, A., 153
McCown, P. J., 265
McEachern, W. A., 174, 180-83
McHugo, G. J., 152
McIntyre, J. J., 220
McLaughlin, J. P., 227
McWilliams, C., 242
"Me," 29-32, 36, 47
Mead, G. H., 18-19, 28-33, 36, 39-42, 43, 47-48, 52, 62, 64, 74, 110, 120, 121, 123, 129, 167, 168
Meade, R. D., 83
Mehrabian, A., 267
Merry, S. E., 109

Merton, R. K., 92, 101, 106-7, 165, 232, 236
Middleton, R., 246
Milgram, S., 79-82, 84, 275
Miller, D. L., 200
Miller, G. A., 123
Miller, L. K., 253
Miller, N. E., 206, 241
Mitchell, H., 257
Miyamoto, S. F., 31-32
Mixon, A. J., 107
Montmayor, R., 36
Morgan, C. S., 232
Mosatche, H. S., 100
Mowrer, O. H., 206
Muha, M. J., 258
Murstein, B. I., 268
Mussen, P. H., 264

Nadler, A., 273
Nagy, F., 268
Nahemowa, L., 263
National crime survey, 198
National Institute of Mental Health, 219
Newcomb, T. M., 92-95, 268
Newton, J. W., 202
Nichols, P. C., 146
Nonverbal communication, 146-56
Nonverbal language, 130
Norm of reciprocity, 273-74
Nosanchuk, T. A., 103, 105
Nosow, S., 280
Nyquist, L., 141, 143

O'Barr, W., 139
Offerman, L., 229, 230
O'Kane, J. M., 90
O'Malley, P. M., 109
Owens, G., 267

Palmer, S., 207-8
Pantin, H. M., 282
Paradigm, 22
Paralanguage, 129
Parcell, S. R., 198
Parker, J. W., 100
Parker, S., 104
Parmalee, P., 267
Parsons, T., 14-16
Participant observation, 19
Pearce, P. L., 280
Perdue, L., 104
Perrin, A., 83
Personality, 43-48
Peterson, B., 104
Pettigrew, T. F., 246
Phillips, C. L., 38
Phillips, D. P., 197, 214-15
Piaget, J., 51-53, 54
Piliavin, I. M., 272, 273, 274
Piliavin, J. A., 272, 273
Play, 41
Porter, N., 230
Powell, G. N., 229
Prejudice and discrimination, 223-59
 as attitude, 225-28, 232-35

definition, 224-25
education and, 258-59
elements of, 224-35
functions of, 235-49
intergroup contact and, 252-54
law and, 250-52
persistence of, 226-28
reduction of, 249-59
social distance and, 226
stereotypes and, 225-26
Priest, R. F., 263
Prosocial behavior, 261-88
altruism as, 282-88
attraction as, 262-71
definition, 262
helping as, 271-82
Protestant ethic, 14-15
Pruitt, G. D., 271
Pugh, M. D., 84

Quanty, M. B., 239
Quarantelli, E. L., 31-32
Quattrone, G. A., 237

Race and racism, 42-43, 143-45, 223-24, 225, 226-27, 232-35, 237-39, 240-41, 242-43, 244-45, 246, 247-49, 250, 251-54, 258-59
Raden, D., 235
Raffler-Engel, W., 149
Reactance theory, 85
Reed, M. D., 91, 105
Rees, C. R., 253
Reference group (see Reference others)
Reference others, 73-113
absent, 88-90
and American competition, 111-12
definition, 74
functions of, 90-106
groups vs. categories as, 105-9
in immediate situation, 75-88
negative, 94
oversocialized conception and, 109-11
social comparison and, 100-6
Reich, M., 248
Relative deprivation, 106-8, 210
Research methods, 24
Richman, J., 228
Ridgeway, C. L., 153
Riesman, D., 91, 169
Riskind, J. H., 150
Risky shift, 25
Ritzer, G., 7, 16
Rodin, J., 70, 272-73, 280
Rogel, M., 280
Rokeach, M., 244, 250
Role ambiguity, 188-89
Role conflict, 173-85
Role making, 167, 189-91
Roles, 159-93
definition, 160
qualities of, 161-67
role making and, 167, 189-91
role strain and, 172-89
role taking and, 167-72

self and, 191-92
Role sets, 165-67, 174-83
Role strain, 172-89
Role taking, 167-72, 284-85
Rosa, E., 153
Rose, A., 92
Rosenberg, M., 62
Rosenhan, D. L., 60-62, 284
Rosnow, R. L., 225
Ross, L., 63
Rubin, I. M., 255
Rubin, Z., 152
Rusbult, C. E., 270
Rushton, J. P., 282
Russ, R. C., 268
Russell, G. W., 215, 216
Rysman, A., 228
Rytina, S., 85

Sachs, P. R., 102
Sagan, E., 203-5
Sample, 14
Sanders, G. S., 230-31
Sandilands, M. L., 215-216
Sarbin, T. R., 33
Sawyer, J., 263
Saxe, L., 265
Schacter, S., 263
Schaet, D. E., 241
Schafer, R. B., 33
Scheibe, K. E., 33
Scheier, M., 96
Schlenker, B. R., 48
Schmidt, T., 230-31
Schmitt, R. L., 92
Schoeneman, T. J., 32
Schramm, W., 118
Schulman, G. M., 148
Schulz, M., 139, 140
Schwalbe, M. L., 34
Sears, D. O., 227, 247
Sears, R. R., 206
Segal, M. W., 253, 263
Self, 27-71
active, 18, 33-35
conflict with society, 43-47
consistency in, 61-63
definition, 28-29
development of, 39-54
divided, 61-63
evidence for, 30-33
in adult life, 54-63
in social interaction, 28-38
institutional vs. impulsive, 36-38
labeling the, 69-70
phases of, 29-30, 36, 47
presentation of, 62-70
specific aspects of, 51-54
stages of, 39-42
throughout the life cycle, 48-51
vs. personality, 47-48
Self-concept, 35-38
Self-consciousness, 66-68, 96
Self-fulfilling prophecy, 266
Self-perception theory, 234
Selznick, G. J., 258

Serpe, R. T., 62
Sex roles and sexism, 45-46, 84-85, 105, 108, 137-38, 139-43, 150-51, 152-53, 177-80, 228-29, 230-32, 238, 244-45, 250-51
Shaffer, D. R., 280
Shamir, B., 63
Shanteau, G., 268
Shapiro, E. G., 273
Shaw, M. E., 21
Sheatsley, P. B., 226
Sherif, C. W., 92
Sherif, M., 75, 86, 92, 246, 253, 254
Sherohman, J., 167, 169
Sherrod, D. R., 275
Shibutani, T., 91, 92, 97
Shotland, R. L., 199
Shrauger, J. S., 32
Siero, F., 128
Sigall, H., 265
Silverstein, B., 104
Simpson, G. E., 226, 235
Singer, E., 92
Sipes, R. G., 217-18
Situated identities, 64
Sivacek, J., 235
Skinner, B. F., 10, 129-32
Smenner, P., 137
Smith, E. R., 250, 251
Smith, M. D., 215
Smith, S. H., 250
Smith, S. S., 248
Snow, D. A., 38
Snyder, C. R., 268
Snyder, M., 266
Social and cultural forces, 12-16
Social behaviorism, 18-19
Social construction of reality, 16
Social definition, 16-20
Socialization, 12, 39-63
anticipatory, 89-90
early, 39-48
retrospective, 89-90
throughout the life cycle, 48-51
to careers, 55-58
to total institutions, 58-61
Social learning theory, 11-12
Social order, 116-17
Social psychology, 2-25
and common sense, 5-7
definition, 2
perspectives, 7-25
Social structural theory, 14-16
Society, 12
Sole, K., 273
Spates, J. L., 88
Spencer, R. L., 83
Stang, D. J., 79
Stember, C. H., 258
Steinberg, S., 258
Steiner, I. D., 238
Steinmentz, S., 219
Stephan, C. W., 265
Stephan, W. G., 253
Stewart, B. S., 169

Stigma, 69
Stone, G. P., 67
Stone, W. F., 268
Storr, A., 216
Straus, M., 217-19
Strauss, H. M., 103-4, 110
Strube, M. J., 101
Stryker, S., 85, 166
Subculture of violence, 213
Survey, 13
Sutherland, E. H., 87
Swap, W. C., 263
Symbolic interactionism, 18-20

Takooshian, H., 274-75
Tallichet, S. E., 178, 183, 231
Tan, A. S., 104
Tanke, E. D., 266
Taylor, D. G., 226
Taylor, S. E., 237, 238
Teevan, J. J., 220
Terpstra, D. E., 265
Terrace, H., 125
Thibaut, J. W., 270
Thiel, D., 265
Thomas, W. I., 115
Thorne, B., 139
Total institutions, 58-61
Town, J. P., 244
Traupmann, J., 12

Triandis, H. C., 238
Triandis, L. M., 238
Tully, J. C., 151
Turner, R., 160
Turner, R. H., 36-37, 167, 189, 191
Twenty statements test, 35-38

Urban overload, 275

Valenti, A., 79
Vander Zanden, J. W., 225, 250
Van Oudenhoven, J. P., 128
Vernon, C., 170
Verplanck, W. S., 10
Vidmar, N., 250
Violence, 195, 196, 213, 217-19 (*also see* Aggression)

Wahrman, R., 84
Walker, A. J., 232
Wallston, B. S., 244
Walster, E., 12, 263, 264, 265, 268
Walster, G. W., 12, 268
Walters, G., 226, 227
Watson, M. W., 169
Weary, G., 21
Weber, M., 14
Webster, M., 265
Weise, B. C., 265
Weitz, S., 147
Weld, H. P., 212

Werner, C., 267
West, C., 142, 143
Westie, F., 238, 246
Wexler, J. G., 184
White, G. L., 268
Whitehead, G. I., 250
Whittaker, J. O., 83
Whorf, B. L., 135-37
Wicker, A. W., 233, 234
Williams, R. M., 240
Willits, F. K., 178, 183, 231
Wilson, M., 263
Wilson, S. R., 102
Witkin, H. A., 2
Wolfgang, M. E., 213, 218
Wood, G. C., 237
Wood, J. T., 131, 137-38
Worchel, P., 240
Wrong, D. H., 109

Yarkin, K. L., 244
Yel, J. G., 268
Yinger, J. M., 226, 235
Yinon, Y., 275
Yoels, W. C., 42

Zander, A., 267
Zanna, M. P., 232
Zero-sum game, 111
Zimbardo, P. C., 171, 202
Zimmerman, D. H., 142, 143
Zurcher, L. A., 37-38, 160, 184-85, 186-88, 189-90